Black Empire

# New Americanists

A SERIES EDITED BY DONALD E. PEASE

# Black Empire

THE MASCULINE GLOBAL IMAGINARY

OF CARIBBEAN INTELLECTUALS

IN THE UNITED STATES,

1914–1962

Michelle Ann Stephens

DUKE UNIVERSITY PRESS · DURHAM AND LONDON · 2005

© 2005 Duke University Press   ALL RIGHTS RESERVED
Printed in the United States of America
on acid-free paper ∞
*Designed by* Andrew Shurtz
*Typeset in* Adobe Caslon *by* Keystone Typesetting, Inc.
Library of Congress Cataloging-in-Publication Data
appear on the last printed page of this book.

2nd printing, 2006

To my parents,
CAROLE AUDREY and GEORGE STEPHENS,
and in memoriam to MICHAEL SPRINKER,
for their intelligence and care

There will be a turning point in the history of the West Indies . . . [T]he people who inhabit that portion of the Western hemisphere will be the *instruments of uniting a scattered race* who, before the close of many centuries, will found an Empire on which the sun shall shine as ceaselessly as it shines on the Europe of the North today.

—MARCUS GARVEY


It is at the heart of national consciousness that international consciousness lives and grows. And this two-fold emerging is ultimately only the source of all culture.

—FRANTZ FANON

# CONTENTS

# ACKNOWLEDGMENTS

THIS PROJECT BEGAN under the thoughtful steerage of Hazel Carby, my dissertation advisor at Yale University, and Michael Denning, my advisor in American Studies. My first thanks goes to them both for, among so many other things, pushing me to engage fully the multiple fields within which this work can be situated. To my other readers and advisers at Yale, Paul Gilroy and Vera Kutzinski for their engaged readings through to the end, and the scholar-teachers who so shaped my graduate career, including Jean-Christophe Agnew, David Montgomery and Robert Stepto, I also owe my thanks. Two special life-friends and mentors whose attentiveness I continue to cherish: Michael Sprinker, who started me on this intellectual path and whose voice I still hear at every step along the way; and Amy Kaplan who continues to believe in this work and always offers her encouragement and support.

I owe an equally powerful debt to the members, organizers, coordinators, staff, and team leaders of GESO, the Graduate Employees and Students Organization, who shared with me so many of the tensions of being in both the academy and in the union. My thanks to those who now continue the struggle, and a special thanks to those friends who also served as personal anchors along the way—Emily Bernard, Kathleen Clark, Prudence Cumberbatch, Greg Grandin, Alethia Jones, Corey Robin, Sandhya Shukla, Wendi Walsh, and Cynthia Young.

It is a real blessing to find in one's lifetime not one but two supportive intellectual communities. This book has been buoyed by the warmth and friendship of the remarkable group of faculty who teach at Mount Holyoke College. I am so happy to have this opportunity to thank my colleagues in English, American studies, African American and African studies and throughout South Hadley for their continued support. Also, the book could not have been finished without generous institutional support, including leaves, fellowships, and grants, for which I have the dean of the faculty and the president of the college to thank. An NEH summer stipend played a crucial role in my path toward completion during the summer of 2002, and the fellowship and support of CISA and Five College Inc. deserve a word of appreciation.

At the crucial stage of moving the manuscript from a dissertation to a book, a very special group of readers kept me on my interdisciplinary toes: my thanks to Sandhya Shukla, for always pushing me to transcend enumeration; Martha Guild, for helping me to hone the metaphoric; Lucas Wilson, for challenging me to sharpen the analytic; and Amy Martin, my co-conspirator across the ocean in British Empire studies. Also, my gratitude to my editor Reynolds Smith, my anonymous readers, and all at Duke University Press who helped to make this book more than it could have been in my hands alone.

To my immediate family and the rest of the gang from Jamaica—Enet, Gabrielle, Marjan, Mimi, Paul and Sonya—one love. Bless my parents for the good humor and examples they set; my sister Sandra for her creative inspiration and, of course, Alexandria, the love of our lives. Finally, my deepest debt is owed to Louis Prisock, co-parent and intellectual partner. Who, in addition to sharing childcare and housework and creating culinary masterpieces while finishing a dissertation, partnered me through important stages of writing, conferencing, presenting, and even just brainstorming; for this, after it all, you have my most profound love and gratitude.

Black Empire

Black Star Line stock certificate.

Source: The Marcus Garvey and UNIA Papers Project, UCLA.

# INTRODUCTION: THE ISLES AND EMPIRE

IN OCTOBER 1921, an article appeared in the black American magazine *The Crusader* stating the following: "A Race without a program is like a ship at sea without a rudder. It is absolutely at the mercy of the elements. It is buffeted hither and thither and in a storm is bound to flounder. It is in such a plight as this that the Negro race has drifted for the past fifty years and more."[1]

This statement, sponsored by Caribbean radical Cyril V. Briggs, the editor of the *Crusader*, on behalf of his militant revolutionary organization the African Blood Brotherhood (ABB), proceeded to lay out a program to "supply a rudder for the Negro Ship of State." As Robert Hill has further described, this "Program of the ABB" called upon fellow organizational leaders, such as Marcus Garvey of the Universal Negro Improvement Association (UNIA), to create "a federation of all existent Negro organizations, molding all Negro factions into one mighty and irresistible factor."[2]

This call for a world "Negro federation" emblematizes one of the central concerns of this book—namely, how certain black leaders and intellectuals of Caribbean descent chose to imagine African Americans as part of a global political community during the early years of the twentieth century. The image of the black ship of state also serves as a powerful organizing metaphor. *Black Empire: The Masculine Global Imaginary of Caribbean Intellectuals in the United States, 1914–1962*, tells a story of the first half of the twentieth century in which black male subjects from the English-speaking Caribbean attempted to chart a course for the race somewhere in the interstices between empire, nation, and state. The Negro ship of state at sea without a rudder images the black peoples of the African diaspora in America in a state of political limbo, as a floating colony perpetually drifting somewhere between slavery and freedom, yet bound together, sharing a common transatlantic history and destiny.

The image of the Negro ship of state also reveals one of the primary preoccupations of early-twentieth-century political discourse.[3] In the years during and immediately following World War I, nationalism and the model of the nation-state rapidly became *the* international political norms of the early twentieth century.[4] Caribbean male intellectuals living in the United States during these years experienced the politics of self-determination through a very particular set of concerns. As Caribbean immigrants they had no easily identifiable national homelands, arriving in America from diverse island colonies whose only bond was, at best, their shared history of colonialism and European exploitation.

In his autobiography *North of Jamaica*, Jamaican poet Louis Simpson described the subsequent difficulties in constructing a Caribbean national or even ethnic identity in the United States: "As Jamaicans did not govern themselves they felt inferior in other respects. . . . They were only a remote branch of England. They were not self-sufficient, and had created no important works. The history of Jamaica was the history of the Europeans who had ruled it."[5] For Simpson, political questions of self-governance and cultural questions of self-construction had a mutual and reciprocal effect on each other. The lack of political self-determination in the Caribbean produced a "colonial mentality" in Caribbean subjects, preventing their cultural self-determination and self-representation—a sense of Jamaicanness, Caribbeanness, or nationality. The colonial experience did not match that of European nationals migrating to the United States who could conceive of themselves as sharing a particular linguistic and cultural heritage that had grown and developed over time, within a single geographic territory. Instead, the Caribbeans's experience was one of two acts of displacement, the middle passage from Africa and the journey from the colony to America. Hence, early-twentieth-century Caribbean immigrants to the United States had uncertain ethnic identities, unimaginable in solely national terms.

The challenge for certain Caribbean intellectuals, then, was precisely how to represent some form of black nationality. Political leaders, writers, and intellectuals such as Marcus Garvey, Claude McKay, and C. L. R. James searched for models of black self-determination—black nationalisms—that they could use to locate and ground their political identities. Garvey, McKay, and James also attempted to imagine black nationality in terms that stood outside of the colonial and Western imperial order. Their writings during their years in the United States immediately after World War I must be read through the lens of a particular set of questions: Were black colonial subjects in the West included in the new European nationalisms? If not, could they turn to Africa as an originary homeland? Or should they locate home and nationalism in American citizenship?

These questions lay at the heart of their engagement with transnational frameworks of identity during this period, as they attempted to construct an oppositional form of black nationalism and political representation in an international imperial world that did not yet recognize black colonial subjects as national peoples. Within this context, as Robin D. G. Kelley has pointed out, for many black intellectuals "ethnic nationalism and internationalism were not mutually exclusive" categories.[6] If national status for locally situated black subjects was the goal and the European global imperialists were the obstacle, the black struggle for self-determination would have to occur as a transnational one. Here the Russian revolution would serve as a partial model, for if the Bolsheviks could ground revolutionary identity not in the nation but in international proletarian solidarity, black subjects could strengthen their individual nationalist struggles and aspirations through international racial formations, transnational race-based networks conceived in terms of communism, diaspora, or even imperialism.

Recently in scholarship in contemporary black studies we have seen an upsurge in interest in the "internationalism" of the New Negro of the 1920s and 1930s. The pioneering work on black Communists by Robin Kelley in the 1990s and work by other scholars of black radicalism and Pan-Africanism before him see their most recent theoretical elaboration in Brent Hayes Edwards's *The Practice of Diaspora*.[7] Edwards describes the contemporary political unconscious that shapes his own account when he says:

[*The Practice of Diaspora*] is written with "something of the fever and the fret" of a moment when discourses of internationalism and globalization are resurgent. . . . In the time when the notion of an efficacious black internationalism seems but the pipe dream of a few haggard lobbyists and scattered radicals, this book attempts to hear the border of another future of black internationalism in the archive of its past.[8]

*Black Empire* shares a similar political unconscious, but where Edwards is interested in how the diasporic movements of the twenties worked to disarticulate notions of blackness, this work is interested in how male intellectuals from the Anglophone Caribbean attempted to imagine a transnational form of black nationality that could both transcend nationalism and reimagine the state itself.

As in his previous work, Edwards deploys terms such as "diaspora" and "translation" to reveal the discursive heterogeneity and disjunctures within literatures of black internationalism during this period.[9] As he states in his prologue, diaspora is the space for the activity of disarticulating blackness as much as for the creation of new racial solidarities.[10] Edwards uses the French word "décalage," which "can be translated as 'gap,' 'discrepancy,'" to argue for a theory of international blackness in which:

> *Décalage* indicates the reestablishment of a prior unevenness or diversity; it alludes to the taking away of something that was added in the first place, something artificial. . . . *Décalage* is the kernel of precisely that which cannot be transferred or exchanged, the received biases that refuse to pass over when one crosses the water. . . . *Décalage* . . . provid[es] a model for what resists or escapes translation through the African diaspora.[11]

Edwards sees in certain political ideologies of black internationalism from the early twentieth century, a desire on the part of those who found difference disabling for a global vision of blackness, to prop up blackness with some kind of prosthetic call for an artificial racial unity.

While stimulating as a method for imagining new ways of theorizing global blackness, Edwards's discussion of décalage also foregrounds, without articulating as such, the *political* stakes of difference in the black internationalisms of the period. For while difference for its own sake provides a haunting indicator of more complicated ways of thinking about blackness, much of the differences in blackness Edwards is interested in, such as differences in language, also reveal the much larger structure that not only haunted but effectively created differentiated and heterogeneous understandings of blackness in the period under consideration, that is, the nation-state. In other words, as we seek to translate the cultures of black internationalism from the early decades of the twentieth century to the present time, we realize how much these different languages of blackness carry the traces of discussions of nationality that were so prevalent in the discourse of modern political identity in the immediate period after World War I. Blackness, then, as much as any other racialized consciousness during this period, was an imaginary burdened by the national. To say that the black internationalism of the New Negro was structured by difference and the tensions of the national is to some degree our very starting point. It was certainly the starting point for black internationalists eager to imagine the race as a single global community in the early years of the twentieth century. The challenge for many of the black West Indian radicals discussed here was to understand and express what exactly was at stake in articulating a black internationalist politics in the first place, that is, what such a politics might make visible about black identity that would otherwise be occluded by the politics and cultures of metropolitan nationalism.

*Black Empire* offers a more materialist theory of black internationalism, one that would also locate it in relationship to and at the intersection of multiple discussions about the nature of both internationalism and nationalism in the immediate period after World War I. These were discussions in which the New World Negro was placed right at the core. The usefulness of taking a notion of diasporic blackness apart occurs only with some awareness of what was at stake in putting those prostheses together in the first place. During and immediately after World War I, various forms and expressions of black internationalism were linked by a profound investment in the ideal of racial sovereignty. Black notions of sovereignty—the political self-determination of the race as a worldwide community; black freedom grounded in and embodied by a vision of the independent black state—emerged very much in the face of and in opposition to new formations of empire following from World War I and manifested in the nation-state structures of the League of Nations.

Empire, then, provided the material conditions for black solidarities to emerge across nation, language, gender, and even class. If, as Edwards argues, "*diaspora* . . . makes possible an analysis of the institutional formations of black internationalism that attends to their constitutive differences," black internationalism as a real political philosophy, radical epistemology, and institutional practice did not function only to create linkages between different black populations.[12] Rather, the desire for racial freedom and unity stemmed from a prior radicalization; black subjects found themselves asking deeper structural questions of capital and the political world around them that would then lead them to an analysis of the forces that produced the differences that divided them in the first place. Black internationalisms asked not only how we can create linkages within the race, but also what are the forces that create many of the differences that make up a heterogeneous blackness? They also asked how might we eradicate those specifically national differences by articulating them to broader transnational histories and structures?

These questions bring us to another way in which the image of a Negro ship of state serves as such a crucial starting point for this account. *Black Empire* argues that in the service of creating a global vision of the race that superseded and transcended black nationalist discourses in both the United States and the Caribbean, Caribbean male intellectuals drew from a less visible transatlantic maritime history of the black world, one that shadows histories of empire and colonization in the Americas in ways fundamental to the creation of discourses of black masculinity. Here both the figures of the Negro ship and the black seaman serve as key sites in which a blended Caribbean and African American vision of a global black masculinity could emerge—one might say, the vision of a more *worldly* New Negro. To understand that discourse, both its traces and the source of its power in constructions of twentieth-century black globality at the beginning of the twentieth century, we must travel back into colonial and imperial histories that precede and shape twentieth-century geopolitics and black international politics. In this sense, *Black Empire* brings to contemporary discussions of black nationalism and black diaspora a necessary regrounding of questions of black subject and gender formation in imperial discourses and colonial frameworks of consciousness.

MARCUS GARVEY, CLAUDE MCKAY, AND C. L. R. JAMES

*Black Empire* foregrounds three male intellectuals of Caribbean descent as central in this project of crafting a specifically black and masculine global imaginary to meet changing political needs and terms of debate in the early years of the twentieth century. Marcus Garvey, Claude McKay, and C. L. R.

James are seen here as offering original imaginings and representations of black subjectivity within the context of the new world order taking shape after World War I. There is already a substantial body of scholarly literature on these three figures—one could argue that each already fits within well-defined subfields within the broader fields of African American and Caribbean studies.

Marcus Garvey's years in the United States, 1916 to 1927, are most often explored in terms of the history of black nationalist movements and leaders in the United States and the Caribbean, from the earlier scholarship of Tony Martin and Robert Hill to the more recent work of Judith Stein and Irma Watkins-Owens.[13] Scholars such as Stein, Watkins-Owens, and, most explicitly, Ula Taylor in her recent biography of Amy Jacques Garvey have highlighted the specifically gendered politics of Garveyism as a philosophy and movement. Analyses of Claude McKay's work appear more often in discussions of Harlem Renaissance literature and Caribbean literature, reflecting his own status in both worlds. While earlier biographical studies of McKay situated him more in an African American context and read his work explicitly in terms of the Harlem Renaissance, scholars such as Winston James have argued for the determinative shaping influence of the Caribbean on McKay's radicalism and cultural work.[14] Here gender also appears as a concern, as scholars such as Heather Hathaway, Belinda Edmondson, and Brent Edwards read McKay's work critically in terms of his constructions of black female sexuality and mobility.[15] C. L. R. James appears in studies of the history of black radicalism by scholars such as Paul Buhle[16] and in scholarship placing that history within and in dialogue with postcolonial and Caribbean studies.[17] More recently, there has been a new focus on James's work in American studies[18] and a more serious engagement with constructions of black masculinity in James's work by Hazel Carby and Belinda Edmondson.[19]

This previous scholarship is important to the argument of *Black Empire* in establishing primary terrains of influence in which these figures held sway while living and working in the United States. The more recent analyses also begin to point out how their own positions as male Caribbean intellectuals shaped the gendered nature of their politics, their narratives, and their discursive constructs. However, the questions being asked of these three men and their intellectual work while in the United States have so far precluded a way of analyzing and viewing their work textually and syncretically. By this I mean, first, that while there is a tendency to assume connections between them based simply on their race politics and the fact that they are Caribbean, because they span such different fields and disciplines no one has yet done a study that links the work of these three figures as somehow engaged together in a common enterprise. Few scholars have been able to approach these figures in a way that integrates their Caribbean and American intellectual identities and projects.[20] And while individual analyses of their writings exist, no one has identified the ways in which these three men contributed to a particular kind of discourse on black masculinity and political subjectivity as part of a construction of the race as a *global* formation and political unit and consciousness. My focus in *Black Empire* is to highlight a more discursive and philosophical level of consistency and shared themes specific to the American work and thought of these three Anglophone-Caribbean figures, a discourse in which "the race" is gendered and global or *gendered as global* in particular ways. *Black Empire's* analysis, then, operates in a discursive space that attempts to cross and move beyond the disciplinary and methodological boundaries of the above-mentioned fields and approaches.

More specifically, what I argue to be consistent in their writing provides the justification for thinking of the work of these three male figures together. Taking as our starting point this powerful metaphor of a black ship of state, *Black Empire* argues that these three Caribbean intellectuals created a global vision of the race that drew on transatlantic histories of movement, the movements of fugitive slaves and imperial civilizations, the colonized and colonizers, and black colonial subjects and the agents of empire to gender notions of black masculinity in ways different from those recently identified in current feminist discussions of masculinity, nationalism, and the gendered nature of diaspora discourse. In *Black Empire* the argument is twofold: First, we have missed identifying a black global political consciousness that develops in tandem with the discourses of both imperial civilization and the modern nation-state, an archive of black reflections on political modernity that is a hybrid discourse representing multiple political forms and hybrid political bodies as they have emerged over centuries in colonial space. Second, the inescapable hybridity of imperial history is revealed in black global stories and world histories that embody black political desires in specifically gendered and sexualized constructions of the race.

Hence, this work contextualizes current discussions of black mobility specifically within the framework of empire, bringing the study of empire and its relevant discourses front and center into African American and Caribbean studies, and bringing African American and Caribbean analyses of empire more centrally and frontally into American studies. The work of Garvey, McKay, and James forces us to place notions of diaspora, nationhood, transnationalism, and even the status of the modern state back within the context of empire and coloniality. We need to add back to our discussions of nationalism the work of black intellectuals who specifically theorize and engage with colonial space. In so doing we also broaden our discussion to thinking of empire not simply as a political formation that passed at the beginning of the twentieth century and now reemerges as a form most explicitly in the United States at the beginning of the twenty-first century, and not simply as a discourse primarily engaged with constructing notions of whiteness or supporting white racial and sexual formations. Rather, as recent scholarship in postcolonial studies and American studies has shown, empire has been a discourse rife with multiplicity and hybridity, shaping and directing international politics in multiple ways since the beginning of the twentieth century.

THE STATE OF EMPIRE

There has been a resurgent interest in notions of empire sparked by Michael Hardt's and Antonio Negri's influential work of the same name.[21] Early in their study Hardt and Negri make a distinction between "imperialism" and "Empire," using "imperialism" to represent the history of four centuries of European conquest and colonization of most of the rest of the world.[22] This history plays a key, if not always articulated, role in contemporary discussions of nationalism and the development of the modern state. While there is certainly a substantial body of historical scholarship on European imperialism,[23] the more specific interest here is in a brand of scholarship focused on the more discursive cultural features of imperialism and colonization, the scholarship on colonial discourse arising out of the broader field of postcolonial studies and Edward Said's influential work, *Orientalism*.[24] As Robert J. C. Young describes, orientalism represented "the introduction of the idea that colonialism operated not only as a form of military rule but also simultaneously as a *discourse* of domination."[25] This notion of imperialism as a discursive and cultural formation shapes the current interest in new forms of imperialism represented by and manifested in United States foreign policy and operations across the globe throughout the century.[26]

The study of empire and its languages took a new turn with the publication of Hardt's and Negri's *Empire* in 2000, and their return to political theory and philosophy. Arguing that "Empire" with a capital E represented "something altogether different from 'imperialism,'" Hardt and Negri also shifted attention away from Europe, arguing that in the geopolitical landscape of the twentieth century the United States played a key role in defining and modeling languages and structures of empire. While acknowledging that "if the nineteenth century was a British century, then the twentieth century has been an American century," Hardt and Negri asserted that, "Imperialism is over. No nation will be world leader in the way modern European nations were. . . . The United States does indeed occupy a privileged position in Empire, but this privilege derives not from its similarities to the old European imperialist powers, but from its differences." In essence, for Hardt and Negri the United States plays a central role in discussions of Empire because it provides very different languages of statehood and sovereignty that have come to define the new global political order.[27]

In *The Modern State*, Christopher Pierson describes sovereignty as an essential characteristic of the modern nation-state, the "idea that, within the limits of its jurisdiction . . . no other actor may gainsay the will of the sovereign state."[28] Territoriality and sovereignty in particular are seen as characteristics that distinguish the modern state from the premodern empires of the classical era.[29] As Pierson argues, drawing from scholars such as Tilly and Giddens:

> traditional states (especially the expansive traditional empires) were delimited not by clear borders but by much more indeterminate frontiers. . . . They might exercise a sort of *rule* over a particular territory, but generally they lacked the administrative or military capacity to *govern*. . . . These traditional state forms generally lacked conceptions of sovereignty.[30]

Hardt's and Negri's innovation was to argue that politically, in relation to questions of sovereignty, new forms of Empire bear more of a resemblance to the structures of premodern empires than to the modern states created in and emerging from imperialism. In their words, "Our basic hypothesis is that sovereignty has taken on a new form, composed of a series of national and supranational organisms united under a single logic of rule. This new global form of sovereignty is what we call Empire," and in contrast to imperialism, "Empire establishes no territorial center of power and does not rely on fixed boundaries or barriers. It is a *decentered* and *deterritorializing* apparatus of rule that progressively incorporates the entire global realm within its open, expanding frontiers. Empire manages hybrid identities, flexible hierarchies, and plural exchanges."[31] It is in this sense that the United States serves as a particular model and source for these new languages of Empire. In the introduction to her most recent work, *The Anarchy of Empire in the Making of U.S. Culture*, Amy Kaplan describes her own interest in "the way anarchy becomes an integral and constitutive part of empire, central to the representation of U.S. imperialism . . . as a network of power relations . . . riddled with instability, ambiguity, and disorder, rather than as a monolithic system of domination that the very word 'empire' implies."[32]

The irony is that this experience of Empire is not at all new to the inhabitants of colonial space. It is this book's contention that Caribbean intellectuals have been living and therefore wrestling with these particular imperial languages of hybridity and sovereignty as well as their transformations and mutations in world politics over the course of the twentieth century. Within the context of all of these varying discussions of empire—as the history of imperialism; as imperial cultures, languages, and discourses; as agent for the development of modern statehood and sovereignty; as the enactment of new languages and practices of sovereignty—the colony itself needs to reemerge as a privileged site for the analysis of empire and as a space of critical resistance, generating alternative forms and formulations of a global imaginary.

*Black Empire* asserts that understanding empire[33] as a discourse with multiple forms has been the Caribbean intellectual's special experience of and contribution to the twentieth-century global imaginary. As colonial subjects sitting at the intersection of the decline of the European empires after World War I and the rise of the United States as an empire in the same moment, they are both the figures for and the voices of a colonial world subject to the multiple and evolving languages of exclusion and inclusion of various imperial formations. They also understand intimately the conceptual division that has been used to territorialize those languages in particular geographic spaces, such as the nation versus the colony.[34] These "worlds of color," as Du Bois would describe them in 1925, represent colonial spaces and subjects excluded from discussions of the meaning of nationhood and nationality for the twentieth century. But they also constitute the very terrain of hybridity which empire's discourses outside the nation are created to manage. Empire, then, is the context shaping all black travels, displacements, and even engagements with various forms of internationalist discourse throughout the twentieth century, those attempting to both counter empire (such as Bolshevism) but also to reinvent it (such as American internationalisms throughout the century).

The form of internationalist thought that has been most often and explicitly associated with Caribbean intellectuals in the United States during the first half of the twentieth century is of course Pan-Africanism. My focus here is not on Pan-Africanism as a political movement to liberate Africa, but rather as itself offering a unique theoretical approach to the geopolitics of the century, offering new insights, observations, and analyses of both empire and coloniality. It was Pan-Africanists who would understand that the colony was the very site of empire's hybridity, while the nation was being constructed as the site of imagining community through national homogeneity. This hybridity was a hybridity of races, and a hybridity of political forms, overlapping with, drawing from, and at times mutating or complicating the ideals of pure sovereignty.[35]

As new political forms, codes, languages, and symbols of the developing modern European state traveled from Europe to the New World, so too did a discourse of race and nationality that linked both together symbolically through the color of a people's skin. In asking what happens if we think of modernity as a "region" rather than as a "period," Paul Gilroy points out that enlightenment aspirations toward universality were immediately distorted upon entering colonial space.[36] For Gilroy, "modernity's new political codes must be acknowledged as having been compromised by the raciological drives that partly formed them," and the colony represents the space in which those drives were most brutally enacted, despite European civilizations' desire for modernity and aversion to barbarism.[37]

Walter Mignolo has since taken this logic of "barbarism" and reapplied it to the form of thinking and subjectivity he defines as integral to "coloniality," the very site of an "other thinking."[38] He identifies moments of imperial epistemological vulnerability, "instances where the civilizing mission began to crack and the oppositions civilization/barbarism, first world/third world, and developed/underdeveloped are superseded by the self-relocation and restitution of thinking and theorizing within and by barbarians, third-world people, the underdeveloped, women, and people of color." Colonial space becomes "the location where a new consciousness, a border gnosis, emerges from the repression subjected by the civilizing mission." This form of border-thinking does not, however, simply reside on the margins. What is important to Mignolo is precisely our understanding that the worldviews of colonial subjects and intellectuals also migrate and then have a shaping and transformative impact on the broader geopolitical world around them: "Third-world theorizing is also *for* the first world."[39] In theorizing both colonial space *and* empire, colonial subjects create their own worldly discourse that re-creates the full global imaginary from a subaltern perspective. Mignolo states: "'Worldly culture' could be translated to my vocabulary as the rearticulation and appropriation of global designs by and from the perspective of local histories."[40]

In the discussions by Gilroy and Mignolo, the colony emerges as the central site that must be reengaged in our contemporary discussions of empire. To say that empire is a space of hybridity is to point to its multinationality—the multiplicity of ways of imagining (national, local) communities and the multiplicity of political forms and languages created out of the encounter between imperialism and colonial space. Empire, then, can be seen as a space of multinational "blackness," with multiple national and local communities defined in the British empire as native or black, stretching across Asia, Africa, America, and the islands of the sea. Diaspora too, then, must be the sign for a multinational blackness, but not one that is free-floating.[41] Rather, here diaspora is precisely that space of blackness that has been shaped by empire's international reach and global designs. The diasporic condition then also becomes one of profound desire, what David Lloyd has described (in the context of discussions of Ireland as a colony) as "the desire of nationalism for the state" which occurs precisely in those colonial contexts in which the state seems furthest out of reach.[42]

To understand diaspora as such is to understand it as a space of multiple racial cultures and political forms, drawing from discourses of empire in its desire for a state, reflecting the hybridity of empire in its multinationality.[43] *Black Empire* argues that for the male Caribbean intellectuals discussed here, these desires and longings for the state were captured in and embodied by powerfully gendered and sexualized metaphors—the vision of the sovereign state figured in the black male sovereign; the desire for home at a more affective level figured in the woman of color. *Black Empire* also identifies and interprets a third, less acknowledged strand: through an understanding of colonial space as a transatlantic or circumatlantic geography that included both the colony and its surrounding seas, we discover the subsequent imaging of a black transnational community as black men traveling in colonial space in a common state of desiring, desiring freedom, language, community—and each other. *Black Empire* asks why—in important moments, in the irresistible charisma of the black male sovereign as performed by Garvey, in the homosocial bonding created in Claude McKay's "crew" of black mariners and drifters, and in the forms of social intimacy reimagined by James on the American ship of state, essentially when the diaspora is imaged as a fugitive, multinational colony floating in the tempestuous transatlantic seas of modernity—does the colony become primarily a space of men desiring?

As this digression into the worlds of imperial discourse and colonial theory has, I hope, made clear, in *Black Empire* the focus is not on a figure such as Marcus Garvey as a black nationalist or even as a Pan-Africanist per se.[44] Rather, my goal in *Black Empire* is to pursue how one might analyze Garvey as a "black transnationalist," based on a starting premise that transnationalism here represents more than our contemporary historical moment (globalization) and more than new forms of migration and immigration, but also an actual political and cultural black discourse that has throughout the twentieth century theorized issues of black nationalism and statehood by placing them within a global geopolitical context. This discourse, in the hands of these three figures in particular, drew from broader transatlantic histories of both (black) travel and (white) settlement within the confines of colonial space. In so doing, they also used particular elements of imperial ideology to make their own political and representational claims.

Black transnationalist discourse in the early years of the twentieth century was troubled by the power of race as a category for destabilizing and limiting the ability of modern black subjects to participate in the forms of political freedom emerging at the beginning of the century. Each of the three figures studied here developed a discourse that explored key features of black transnationality, reimagining black mobility, black nationality and cultural belonging, and the geography of new black economies. However, in so doing, these figures drew first on a key element of imperial and national discourse—the belief in the *sovereignty* of both the self and of the state. That investment in sovereignty created the space for highly masculine definitions of racial freedom, embodied in varying male figures and tropes for the black, revolutionary hero.

*Black Empire*, then, offers a particularly gendered analysis of black transnationalism and internationalism, informed by a feminist critique of imperial formations and nationalist constructions.[45] The black global imaginary described here was also inherently masculine, created to fit the needs of a new and modern black male subject entering onto the stage of world politics. In this focus on the male sovereign it must be understood that these figures were working with the most powerful symbols and definitions of modern political identity available during this period. As they sought to imagine a form of racial sovereignty for a disenfranchised and still colonial world population, they drew key elements of imperial discourse along in their wake, racialized and gendered elements of empire and nation that would shape their own visions of the black state in the twentieth century.

As we enter into this realm of longing and belonging, it is important to understand one key set of parallel differences between discourses of "nation" and "diaspora" on one hand and discourses of the "state" and "empire" on the other, as I am using them here. While discourses of nation and diaspora are often seen in opposition to each other, involving bounded versus unbounded notions of both geography and the self,[46] both can still mobilize imaginings of the self that operate on an affective and sentimental level, a level most commonly seen to operate outside of the direct jurisdiction of the state in the realm of culture. Notions of both the state and empire, on the other hand, directly involve ideas of structures of government and governance, that is, the very consolidation and integration of nationally, colonially, and even diasporically imagined communities into the actual governmental structures of colonial empires and nation-states (think of the relationships here between Pan-Africanism as a diasporic movement and the subsequent consolidation of both Pan-Africanist sentiment and various liberation movements on the continent into independent nation-states during the era of decolonization). One purpose of these governmental structures is to ensure and protect the state's sovereignty. In another sense, then, one could think of empire as the extension of a state's sovereignty across national borders.[47]

Coloniality, then, the island-colony, remains a highly liminal space, attached to state structures and discourses of empire but rife with both new national desires and hybrid, diasporic, affective senses of belonging, longings for both integration and mobility within the world-system.[48] It is this longing for integration—the integration of the black subject within the modern nation-state and of the black state within the modern world-system—and a desire on the part of the colonized for the consolidation of national sentiment and diasporic affiliations into the ideal of the sovereign state that also often entail the mobilization of gendered discourses. As both the new national state and the older imperial governments get figured as masculine "fatherlands," women remain, seemingly contradictorily, the figures for more open-ended, sentimental, affective, and relational dimensions of both imagined national and diasporic communities—the imaginary homeland as a motherland.[49]

Hence, *Black Empire* argues, the woman of color often becomes in black transnational discourse a figure for the more affective and hybrid dimensions of nation and diaspora, while male heroic figures function as types for an image of the consolidated, racially unified, sovereign black nation. This imagined black nation-state, in imagining the extension of its own sovereignty across national and imperially drawn borders to represent the entire race, also then finds itself drawing from transnational rhetorics of sovereignty created by the once imperial nations.

In *Black Women, Writing and Identity: Migrations of the Subject*, Carole Boyce Davies first took on the task of both identifying and then theorizing the place of black women in discourses of migration and histories of black travel as they shape questions of female subjectivity.[50] As Boyce Davies describes, home and nation often become contested spaces in the hands of Caribbean women writers, specifically those living and working in the United States like their male counterparts described here. To quote Boyce Davies: "Home, conflated here as a move toward a 'myth of unitary origin' as is nationalism, becomes radically disrupted. . . . The woman as writer then doubly disrupts the seamless narrative of home and so of nation." For Boyce Davies, the black woman writer abroad becomes the most resistant figure in a global imperial context, redefining herself "against Empire constructs," in essence capturing "the most poignant, tragic representation of the transnational, capitalist, postmodern condition" in her representations of herself as the "figure of the displaced, homeless person." Reviewing and interpreting a comprehensive range of Afro-diasporic female narratives, Boyce Davies's work has been central for demonstrating that while the woman of color may at first appear invisible in narratives of both nationalism and postcolonialism, it is because she is "somewhere else, doing something else" in less territorial transnational spaces. In Boyce Davies's account, the woman of color becomes the figure for a less triumphalist vision of home, nation, and empire and an often vulnerable mobile subjectivity.[51]

In the United States context, Farah Jasmine Griffin's work has also been central in defining both the genre of the "African-American migration narrative" and the place of the black female subject and writer within that genre.[52] The migration narrative is certainly in dialogue with both the black empire narratives and sea stories that will be described here, as black American subjects throughout the twentieth century negotiated both the possibilities for movement within the national landscape and beyond it. Particularly inspiring is Griffin's identification of the black female migrant as "stranger" and "streetwise reporter," who uses her mobility and homelessness to record both national events and "the daily lives of ordinary black urbanites."[53] Both Griffin's identification of the black female traveler as reporter and recorder and Boyce Davies's discussions of the central role of the Caribbean female migrant in recording and critiquing the movements of Empire are crucial to my own concluding observations on when and where the Caribbean American woman writer enters the black male transnational narrative.

Hazel Carby's and Belinda Edmondson's works are also key to the analysis of gender formation described here: Carby for showing how masculinity and nationalism get projected onto the body of the New Negro in an early twentieth-century United States context and Edmondson for demonstrating the gendered discourses shaping constructions of the New World Negro, the figure for the Caribbean male subject in the region's nationalist literary and political traditions.[54] In her discussion of Caribbean manhood and constructions of Caribbean nationality, Edmondson focuses on Victorian debates concerning whether or not the Caribbean region was deserving of independence, as these debates also entailed questions of the nature of West Indian masculinity. Arguing that West Indian nationalism mobilizes a specific discourse of manhood with its origins in Victorian England—a notion of "gentlemanliness"—Edmondson then uses that trope to trace the masculinist origins of West Indian literary nationalism itself.

While *Black Empire* does not address black women writers specifically or address questions central to discussions of discourses of masculinity within Caribbean and African American *national* frameworks, this work does address the gendering of masculine constructs of *diaspora*, linking the writings of Caribbean male intellectuals to feminist concerns. First I demonstrate how the race's hybridity gets mapped onto the body of the woman of color. The second discussion, which takes place at more length, is one that seeks to demonstrate how a masculine vision of the race's *transnationalism* has also been projected onto the black male body, through both the more recognizable figure of the black male sovereign and the much less visible figure of the black seaman. This latter figure of the black mariner is only identifiable and risible as a trope in black writing across the diaspora, through an analysis that takes seriously the presence in black discourse of a developing worldly consciousness, creating global frameworks for imagining racial freedom that operate alongside national ones. In this account, in domestic spaces it is the figure of the black male sovereign who takes center stage, leaving the tropological woman of color with no access to the transformative narrative resolution of finding a home for the female diasporic body politic in the vision of a multiracial state. However, when we leave the terrain of the nation-state for the deterritorialized spaces of ships on the seas, while we still leave behind the woman of color, a new figure emerges for a global black masculine subjectivity, that of the seafaring black mariner.

The absence of women in both narratives of and scholarship on a black diaspora has been a central concern in the field, prompted by the important research and critiques of scholars such as Carole Boyce Davies and Hazel Carby.[55] However, in the specifics of how I choose to address this gap, my work also benefits from the insights of anthropologist Jacqueline Nassy Brown, herself focused on theorizing gender in her analyses of and approaches to the black diaspora. Noting the invisibility of women in diaspora studies, Nassy Brown asserts:

> These well-intentioned critiques notwithstanding, I would urge diaspora studies to attend more directly to the politics of gender rather than to "women's experiences." . . . Hence, rather than reifying women's experi-

ences and practices in the name of gender balance in diaspora studies, we should interrogate how particular practises (such as travel) and processes (such as diasporic community formation) come to be infused with gender ideologies (or become "gendered"), and how such gendering effectively determines the different positionalities men and women can occupy.[56]

This is the focus of the gendered analysis provided here. *Black Empire* contributes to the feminist critique of black diaspora studies by suggesting that the gendering of black transnational discourses, particularly in the hands of male Caribbean writers and intellectuals, can be traced directly to structural questions and political frameworks embedded in the discourse of empire more broadly. The overriding masculinity of the black global imaginary can be located specifically in twentieth-century black intellectuals' investments in consolidating the transnational political desires of the race, their forms of imagined community, in state forms. It is in this sense that Garvey, McKay, and James were, initially, proponents of a black empire. As black intellectuals shaped by the political contexts, exigencies, and discourses of the era after World War I, they too were attached to certain languages of empire through their belief in the necessary sovereignty of the black state in a global arena. They embraced the rhetoric of empire not simply as a metaphor for or as a way of envisioning the diaspora. Rather, empire's language of sovereignty specifically became a way for black intellectuals to imagine the future freedom of the race, in sovereignty and statehood.

However, as we trace the travels of these three figures through the actual landscapes of this imaginary black empire, we discover in their writings alternative visions of black community that transform or move beyond imperial, gendered visions of sovereignty. Garvey, McKay, and James recognized the hidden truth of sovereignty as an imperial discourse. The sovereignty of some often limits the free movement of others, and in the geopolitical context of the post–World War I era, the movements being limited were often those of colonial black subjects. While these three intellectuals lived and worked in the United States, their disinvestments from the languages of empire were paired with their concomitant ability to identify *free movement* specifically as a political value far more important for black subjects in the context of twentieth-century race war. This race war, one W. E. B. Du Bois would image geographically as a "color line" that encompassed "the relation of the darker to the lighter races of men in Asia and Africa, in America and the islands of the sea," was the world conflict hidden between the new national boundary lines and maps being drawn by the imperialists at Versailles after World War I.[57]

Black transnationalism, then, references both the construction of a global imaginary that drew from the masculinist rhetoric of sovereignty essential to both imperial and national visions of the state and an alternative set of tropes and symbols representing clues to alternative ways of imagining black freedom, alternatives that deviated from the paradigms of empire. In the works of these three intellectuals we see a shift away from visions of sovereignty for the race embodied in the figure of the revolutionary male sovereign who leads the racial community in its struggle and claiming of particular state forms toward the crafting of more mobile insurgent forms of black resistance politics emphasizing primarily black subjects' right to (free) movement versus independent statehood. As George Lamming, Caribbean contemporary of C. L. R. James, would conceptualize human freedom, "Free is how you is from the start, an' when it look different you got to move, just move, an' when you movin' say that is a natural freedom make you move."[58] The result would be a global imaginary that still primarily constituted black transnationality through masculine tropes, but ones focused on the facilitating of black movement rather than on nation building. In short, the black captains and fellow mariners of the Negro ship of state took center stage, if not displacing at least troubling the role of the black sovereign, in the race's quest for and narrative of freedom.

Part I, "Blackness and Empire: The World War I Moment," begins by firmly historicizing the intellectual and political processes of Garvey, McKay, and James with specific reference to the political and cultural conjuncture represented by World War I. Building from previous historical work by scholars such as Benedict Anderson and Eric Hobsbawm, I provide a context for fleshing out the significance of the immediate postwar moment in shaping what we might call a geopolitics of *black* nationalisms. If critics often argue that notions of the "black (trans)atlantic" or "black transnational," especially when used by scholars in cultural studies, are used ahistorically, my point in focusing so fixedly on World War I, going so far as to mark it in the periodization of the book's title, is precisely to situate the black and Caribbean New World discourse I am describing as being specifically located in certain global events and contexts. These contexts shape the subjects of chapters 1 and 2, the formation of a more worldly New Negro in the United States by the 1920s and the presence of a branch of African American literature neglected in discussions of the literary world both immediately prior to and during the Harlem Renaissance. The emergence of a New Worldly Negro and the black empire literature of late nineteenth and early twentieth century African Americans form the context for defining the contours of a Black Internationale world at the beginning of the twentieth century.

As these opening chapters demonstrate, the contours of that worldview are gendered and masculinized in particular ways as they both inherit and transform tropes of black masculinity from mid- to late nineteenth-century racial and sexual discourses. Chapter 3 then demonstrates how the gendered discourses and geopolitics of the moment shaped Marcus Garvey's gendered performances of New Negro masculinity in the figure of the black sovereign. Chapter 4 rereads the politics of travel in Garveyism, interpreting the Black Star Line as the very embodiment of the metaphoric Negro ship of state and the UNIA as a particular organizational attempt to embody and legitimize the politics of black travel and the dreams for Negro federation.

Marcus Garvey and Claude McKay formed the core of a specifically transnational formation of black intellectuals during the New Negro movement in Harlem of the 1910s through the 1920s. In part II, "Mapping New Geographies of History," I turn to Claude McKay's and C. L. R. James's work, exploring the alternative ways of imagining black identity and belonging made possible for each as they became disillusioned with the promise of freedom offered by the nation-state. In chapters 5 and 6 I offer a reading of McKay's novels informed specifically by questions of gender and sexuality. I argue that a queer reading of McKay's work informed by feminist critique reveals both the romance of heterosexuality that undergirds narratives of home and nationality and the necessary homosociality and even homoeroticism of an alternative space where black men renounce nationality and domesticity by leaving behind the woman of color.[59] In chapter 6 "nationality doubtful" also becomes "sexuality doubtful," a figure for both the uncertainties of citizenship and the ambivalences of home defined through prescribed heterosexual gender roles.

C. L. R. James's work serves as a coda, a transition between a modern colonial world and a postmodern transnational world, in the sense we have come to understand transnationalism after globalization and decolonization.[60] Chapters 7 and 8 demonstrate how James would take one of the central features of contemporary transnationalism—the erosion of the independence of the national state—and of (a belief in the effectiveness of) certain kinds of sovereignty and argue for a Caribbean nationalism based on the migratory histories of both Caribbean islanders and urban black American subjects. James serves as a useful conclusion precisely because he took the central metaphors and debates of black transnationalism during the 1920s, such as the figure of the black emperor himself, and revised them for the new world he saw emerging in the 1940s and the 1950s. Throughout my discussions of all three figures I trace their movements both physically and figuratively away from home, statehood, nation, and empire and their relevant discourses, toward the privileging of alternative discourses emphasizing free movement.

James's work also helps to bring us most clearly into the present, into the contemporary debates about empire sparked by Hardt's and Negri's recent work. *Black Empire* closes by suggesting how the work of these three figures can be crucial in contextualizing our current global and geopolitical context. Specifically, the work of Caribbean intellectuals is crucial to the project of approaching American studies from a transnational perspective. Like other intellectuals from the Third World, their analyses help us to broaden our geographic sense of the object of study, revealing what we can learn about the United States as an entity abroad as much as a nation at home.

THE CARIBBEAN ARCHIPELAGO:
A CONCLUSION AND A BEGINNING

What becomes clear as we pursue the work of these three Caribbean intellectuals is that the discussions of nationalism and statehood that they engaged in anticipated and highlighted new forms, discourses, and cultures of imperialism that would emerge in the twentieth century and continue to shape our world today. If a figure such as Marcus Garvey offered a counterdiscourse to the oppressive impact of European imperialism on black subjects and laborers, *Black Empire* also argues that an enterprise such as Garvey's fleet of ships, the Black Star Line, focused as much on securing the free movement of black workers as on taking them back to Africa. In this sense the work of all three figures provides a counterdiscourse to contemporary forms of imperialism and oppression now captured under the rubric of globalization and also termed transnationalism.

*Black Empire* very directly engages the work of Hardt and Negri and others before them, who also identify the immediate years after World War I as a key conjuncture in constructing a new world order based on new forms of sovereignty and statehood.[61] In our current climate of embracing "American Empire,"[62] scholars and political pundits on both the left and the right find themselves returning to this era to uncover the seeds of our current geopolitical crises.[63] *Black Empire* suggests that in the images, tropes, and discourses of the Caribbean isles, black intellectuals found ways both to sharpen their understanding of these new tropes and meanings of empire but also to engage them on their own terms. Neither their critique nor their creativity has been a central part of current revisionary takes on the immediate post–World War I moment. In this sense the color line continues to operate, shaping our very limited sense of the range of intellectual visions of a modern political world operating at the beginning of the twentieth century.

This book aims to remedy that by offering the image and discourse of the isles as both a construct and a territory that resists empire both imaginatively and geohistorically. The Caribbean islands have not been without their own discourses of interpretation, as early as 1960 when George Lamming first asserted, "The entire Caribbean is our horizon; for Caliban himself like the island he inherited is at once a landscape and a human situation. We can switch from island to island without changing the meaning."[64] For a figure such as Lamming the isles were the space to contemplate exile, both its pleasures and its displeasures. Caliban's centrality as the masculine trope for this enraged and deprived sense of Caribbeanness has been well explored in scholarship that ranges across the language barriers that leave their own marks on the Caribbean landscape.[65] In the late 1980s and early 1990s the Caribbean became a postmodern text. In the work of Edouard Glissant and Antonio Benítez-Rojo we see a space shaped by the very disruptions of meaning and history that so characterize the postmodern sensibility.[66] In this same period and moving into contemporary discussions, for anthropologists such as James Clifford, Linda Basch, Nina Glick Schiller, and Cristina Szanton Blanc, the Caribbean also became the site of heterogeneity and mobility; the "Caribbean world" is a world "hybrid and heteroglot," Clifford asserted,[67] and the Caribbean subject's experience of transnationality and migration, Basch, Glick Schiller, and Szanton Blanc argued, was not "a special case [but] rather . . . a growing global pattern."[68]

In the more recent turn to recovering an active, revolutionary black Atlantic tradition that encompasses both land and sea, the Caribbean island colony emerges as a liminal space in transatlantic history. In Peter Linebaugh's and Marcus Rediker's account of a revolutionary Atlantic spanning the seventeenth century, the isle of Bermuda is recovered as the space of mutiny, when a shipwrecked group of castaways originally intended for the newly founded British New World colony of Virginia choose instead to abandon the colonizing mission and create a utopia for themselves on an alternative isle.[69] This historical event, catalyzed by the wreck of the British ship the *Sea Venture* in 1609, allows the authors to offer a subversive reading of the Shakespearean play based on the same event, *The Tempest*, and of the figure of Caliban as more than simply the native deprived and left behind on the shores of empire. Caliban also becomes a space for imagining alternative meanings of the Caribbean and alternative imaginings of "rebellious masculinity" made possible in the metaphoric New World space of the island.[70] Bermuda, as a tropic figure for the Caribbean, also becomes a counter space to Virginia, the figure for the United States, offering a parallel moment in the history of New World discovery and colonization and a parallel way of telling a founding story of the Americas.[71]

In a transatlantic history as old as the history of imperialism, spaces resistant to empire and occupied by the movements of traveling colonial subjects have appeared among the islands of the Caribbean Sea. When contemporary scholars theorize the Caribbean's postmodern hybridity and position the Caribbean migrant as a model for newly transnational senses of national belonging, they miss the historical significance of the region, in its *geo*historical materiality, as simultaneously a hybrid and resistant, desiring and integrating, space in the encounter with imperial sovereignty over the course of four centuries of modernity.[72]

Moving forward from the world of the transatlantic history of the Americas, or at least linking that world to early-twentieth-century geopolitics, in 1925 W. E. B. Du Bois also saw the Caribbean as a space that posed a particular kind of challenge to empire. This is a challenge it has yet to resolve, even now at the beginning of a new millennium when empire wears the American face of United States troops installing democracy in Iraq and throughout the Middle East. The challenge can be described as a crisis in imperial sovereignty.

In an essay entitled "Worlds of Color" republished in Alain Locke's anthology of *The New Negro* in 1925, but originally written for the journal *Foreign Affairs*,[73] Du Bois returned to his formulation of the "the problem of the twentieth century is the problem of the color line" from the beginning of the century, now saying: "To-day . . . let us examine the matter again, especially in the memory of that great event of these great years, the World War. Fruit of the bitter rivalries of economic imperialism, the roots of that catastrophe were in Africa, deeply entwined at bottom with the problems of the color line."[74]

Using the islands of the sea as merely one striking instance of both the possibilities and the challenges posed by colonial space to the once imperial governments immediately following World War I, Du Bois noted "the characteristic of all color-line fights," the inability of the "official" European nations and the United States to extend their own ideals across and into the colonial world: "With a democratic face at home, modern imperialism turns a visage of stern and unyielding autocracy toward its darker colonies." But the significance of this contradiction for Du Bois was the real challenge it posed to the former empires domestically, as they attempted to justify back home their own behavior abroad: "This double-faced attitude is difficult to maintain and puts hard strain on the national soul that tries it." Traveling throughout the colonial world on his way to and from various Pan-African Congresses in the early decades of the century, Du Bois identified repeatedly Europe's "problem of democratic rule in her colonies. . . . the question of the practicality of ruling a world nation with one law-making body." In Africa specifically, Du Bois argued:

> Insurgent Morocco, independent Abyssinia and Liberia are, as it were, shadows of Europe on Africa unattached, and as such they curiously threaten the whole imperial program. On the one hand, they arouse democratic sympathy in the homeland which makes it difficult to submerge them; and again, they are temptations to agitation for freedom and autonomy on the part of other black and subject populations. What prophet can tell what world-tempest lurks in these cloud-like shadows?[75]

Du Bois then described the British West Indies's special relationship to the conjuncture represented by World War I:

> Never before has black Britain spoken so clearly or so cogently. . . . Since the war not only has West Africa thus spoken but the colored West Indies have complained. They want Home Rule and they are demanding it. They asked after the war: Why was it that no black man sat in the Imperial Conference? Why is it that one of the oldest parts of the empire lingers in political serfdom to England and industrial bondage to America? Why is there not a great British West Indian federation, stretching from Bermuda to Honduras and Guiana, and ranking with the free dominions?[76]

Here in the specific context of the British West Indies, Du Bois mirrored the radical call of Caribbean compatriot Cyril Briggs and the other members of the African Blood Brotherhood for "A Great Negro Federation" for African Americans that would unite "all Negro organizations . . . on a Federation basis, thus creating a united, centralized Movement."[77] Throughout the first half of the twentieth century, Caribbean intellectuals would continue to use this idea and trope of Federation as an attempt to organize their scattered and oppressed kinsmen into an autonomous and transnational political unit.

World War I was a war of empire that incorporated troops from around the world, including black subjects in the United States and the colonial dependencies.[78] The place of the English-speaking colonial soldier in this European war was justified by the centuries-long history of the British empire's efforts to Anglicize the colonial native, by "stretching the short, tight, skin of the nation over the gigantic body of the empire."[79] This was precisely the imperial task challenged by world war: "The strains of twentieth-century total war on the states and peoples involved in it were so overwhelming and unprecedented that they were almost bound to stretch both to their limits."[80] It was to manage those limits and stresses that the League of Nations was created after the war. United States President Woodrow Wilson proposed to set up the "all-embracing 'League of Nations,'" a worldwide political institution meant to manage the tense postwar merging of national interests with international geopolitics.[81]

The League of Nations thus represented the first step in establishing a new international hegemony of the nation-state. Benedict Anderson's image of the first session of the league points to the symbolic power of this new imperialist national order:

> The First World War brought the age of high dynasticism to an end. By 1922, Habsburgs, Hohenzollerns, Romanovs and Ottomans were gone. In place of the Congress of Berlin came the League of *Nations*, from which non-Europeans were not excluded. From this time on, the legitimate international norm was the nation-state, so that in the League even the surviving imperial powers came dressed in national costume rather than imperial uniform.[82]

Eric Hobsbawm also describes: "The map of Europe had to be redivided and redrawn [and] the basic principle of re-ordering the map was to create ethnic-linguistic nation-states, according to the belief that nations had the 'right to self-determination.'"[83] While this map of the imperial world was being redrawn, by the close of the deliberations at Versailles it was clear to black and colonial intellectuals that the map of the colonial world, Du Bois's worlds of color, seemed to be staying the same.

For Du Bois, the reason for the failure of the idea of West Indian federation in the 1920s "was clear and concise—Color. . . . The dominating thing in that [British Imperial Conference] was the fear of the colored world."[84] Black intellectuals saw a league which, though maybe not excluding non-Europeans in theory, certainly still did in praxis. As Marcus Garvey would assert:

> England, France, Italy, Spain, Belgium, Portugal, have assumed within the last fifty years the right politically to parcel out the land of our fathers. . . . At the Versailles Conference, at the League of Nations, the representatives of those governments created certain mandates without asking us. . . . We are here in Europe to say something about it. We are here to let not only Europe but the world know that the new Negro is not going to be railroaded into slavery, into becoming a peon, into becoming a serf, as was so easily done in the centuries gone by.[85]

The idea of nationhood brought with it the revolutionary notion that populations, colonial populations at that, could level the playing field of world politics. Nationhood, self-determination, internationalist revolution—they all offered the possibility that the multitudes of the colonial world could change the global relations of the races. For the black New World intellectuals studied here, Marcus Garvey, Claude McKay, and C. L. R. James, 1919 stands as the pivotal year when the politics and discourse of nationhood proved unable to go beyond the boundaries of race. When neither Woodrow Wilson nor V. I. Lenin could find a viable way to include black and colonial subjects within their global political imaginations, the utopian possibilities of nationhood shrunk for many intellectuals from the Caribbean living and working in the United States.

Here the isle is seen as that part of the world that empire has had to stretch the hardest to contain, figuratively imaged in Benítez-Rojo's sense of the Caribbean as the space of chaos, resisting the order seeking to be imposed by state structures such as empires with territorial interests: "The character of an archipelago . . . [is that of] a discontinuous conjunction [of] unstable condensations, turbulences, whirlpools, clumps of bubbles, . . . sunken galleons . . . , uncertain voyages of signification; in short . . . Chaos."[86] The Caribbean isle functions here as the outpost of empire and nation, attached but never fully containable, continually being pulled away by the currents of different racialized political needs, motives, and goals.

In 1962, during the latter years of decolonization processes Du Bois anticipated in his 1925 essay, and at the end of the time frame that spans this book, C. L. R. James wrote an appendix entitled "From Toussaint L'Ouverture to Fidel Castro" for a new edition of his revolutionary classic *The Black Jacobins*.[87] The timing was interesting not only because of the recent revolution in Cuba in 1959, but also because 1962 was the year Jamaica and Trinidad became the first two West Indian colonies to gain national independence. That national triumph also marked an accompanying failure, for with the withdrawal of Jamaica and Trinidad as the two largest English-speaking islands in the West Indian federation, this particular movement for "Negro federation" in the Caribbean reached its political end. The failure of West Indian federation and the rise of the Caribbean nation-state mark the end of a period in black transnational discourse, and the end of the story *Black Empire* seeks to tell.

Yet as he reflected back on the politics of the region C. L. R. James provided an image of the Caribbean archipelago that links it to our starting metaphor of the drifting Negro ship of state, always potentially floating out of the reach and hands of empire. In 1962 James described national independence as still only one stage in what had been and would continue to be "a Caribbean quest for national identity." James too used a language of chaos and turbulence to characterize revolutionary movement in the Caribbean as "the Caribbean territories drifted along." For James this was also a metaphor for the inherently revolutionary nature of Caribbean history, imaged as a wave rolling turbulently and persistently through the Caribbean sea, throughout the twentieth century: "In a scattered series of disparate islands the process consists of a series of uncoordinated periods of drift, punctuated by spurts, leaps, and catastrophes."[88] James's image of the tempestuous movement of the islands in the Caribbean sea was different from the hope of Cyril Briggs and the African Blood Brotherhood, at the beginning of the twentieth century, that federation would provide the Negro ship of state with a united, centralized movement with clear leadership, direction, and purpose.[89] James's account of Caribbean movement resembles more closely that of scholar Franklin W. Knight, who has said of the region: "The Caribbean is caught up in the movement of political consciousness, but it is not at all certain that all the units are moving simultaneously in one direction or the other."[90]

For James, movement in the Caribbean in the twentieth century was given focus and direction by the many male leaders who have shaped nationalism in the region: his essay's title names two of them—Toussaint L'Ouverture and Fidel Castro. If the Caribbean as a space has always had a story to tell in relationship to the discourses of European empire, then this has often been a definitively male space and a definitively male story, in which women are represented in certain ways but do not act as agents in those particular constructions. As Belinda Edmondson has also argued: "The desire of the novel of revolution to liberate the Caribbean space by remaking it, literally and figuratively, in the image of Caribbean man, is tied to its corresponding impulse to 'erase' the symbolic body of the black woman," who becomes both "a symbol of the slave past" and representative of the "subjugated status of [black] Caribbean men to white European men."[91] Part of Edmondson's project in *Making Men* is to show how the writing of immigrant West Indian women "is literally 'making' the West Indian nation from another direction."[92] This book is primarily engaged with showing the masculinist origins of a Caribbean American notion of black globality, one that constructs sovereignty, hybridity, and the politics of both black travel and desire in gendered ways. It remains the task of a second project to explore more fully what it means to say that women of color in the Caribbean represent hybridity and diaspora in a way that is new from the ways they represent the nation.[93]

While there is more and more theoretical work available asserting that Caribbean women have also been involved in migrations of the subject throughout the twentieth century, to use Carole Boyce Davies's term, unfortunately the question of black female agency through mobility is not a clearly articulated part of the masculinist framework of a political black transnationalist imaginary that this work identifies. This discourse, specifically engaging with war and revolution and sitting at the onset of the twentieth century at the intersection of multiple internationalisms—Bolshevism, Americanism, and Pan-Africanism to name the most dominant in the period—would not place as its central focus the liberation in mobility, of the female black colonial subject.[94]

In the shadows of empire, to use Du Bois's bold term for multiple colonial spaces, the hybridity of colonial history and politics were mapped onto the bodies of the people, constituting the multiracial body politic of the nations they would go on to create and the multiracial world that shapes the Caribbean landscape. Du Bois, looking at this same colonial and Caribbean world in 1925, described "the shadow of two international groups" rising above the contemporary world of postwar politics.[95] Comparing "the Jews and the modern Negroes," Du Bois likened modern colonial subjects to Jewish peoples "who are, in blood, Spanish, German, French, Arabian, and American."[96] Du Bois's world community of black peoples, including "the modern black American, the black West Indian, the black Frenchman, the black Portuguese, the black Spaniard and the black African,"[97] is the not-so-micro cosmos of the Caribbean archipelago itself, a world of "nearly thirty million inhabitants scattered across hundreds of islands and the mainland enclaves of Belize, Guyana, Suriname, and French Guinea represent[ing] an eclectic blend of almost all the peoples and cultures of the world."[98] As black nations drifting in a sea of color, the Caribbean has the potential to enact multiple identifications among colonial populations of different races and to create societies that could model the types of multinational and multiracial democratic formations that were beyond the limits of Europe's and America's global political imaginations in the world crafted after 1919. These are empire's multitudes, and given the Caribbean region's own fragmented and scattered history, it makes sense that a small group of island intellectuals would be some of the first to dare to tell a story of the race with global significance and implications.[99]

No landscape better reflects the movements of the Negro ship of state than that first described by the European traveler Père Labat in 1743 when he said, "You are all together, in the same boat, sailing on the same uncertain sea . . . the position and predicament which History has imposed upon you."[100] Caribbean intellectuals have always been able, throughout the twentieth century, to use their knowledge and experience of the older European empires to inform even in contrast their more current experience of the United States as global hegemon. Black male intellectuals offer an alternative story of empire precisely because they did not cede the space of the isle to the global narrative of colonization or the trope of the ship of state to the new forms, discourses, and cultures of imperialism and globalization that would emerge in the twentieth century and continue to shape our world today. Instead, they attempted to reclaim these tropes and discourses to imagine the tragic, mournful journey of a drifting race and their own vision of a future utopia. They have a special vantage point in our contemporary moment. Both resisting empire and carrying its tropes along in their wake, they charted a course through dark waters that this book now seeks to retrace.

# PART I

# Blackness and Empire: The World War I Moment

With nearly every great European empire to-day walks its dark colonial shadow, while over all Europe there stretches the yellow shadow of Asia that lies across the world. One might indeed read the riddle of Europe by making its present plight a matter of colonial shadows, speculating on what might happen if Europe became suddenly shadowless—if Asia and Africa and the islands were cut permanently away. At any rate, here is a field of inquiry, of likening and contrasting each land and its far-off shadow.

—W. E. B. DU BOIS

CHAPTER I

# The New Worldly Negro: Sovereignty, Revolutionary Masculinity, and American Internationalism

The New Negro is here . . . no more courageous than the Old Negro who dropped his shackles in 1863 . . . but better informed. . . . He is aware that the balance of power is shifting in the world and so are his cousins in Africa, in India, in Malaysia, the Caribbean and China.

—GEORGE SCHUYLER[1]

IN THE FEBRUARY 1920 issue of *The Crusader*, a little more than a year before the African Blood Brotherhood's manifesto, the first installment of a serialized story entitled "The Ray of Fear: A Thrilling Story of Love, War, Race Patriotism, Revolutionary Inventions and the Liberation of Africa" appeared with the byline "C. Valentine." Comparing the language, style, and argumentative approach of entries by C. Valentine throughout *The Crusader* with those of the magazine's editor Cyril Valentine Briggs, it is clear that the one was a loosely veiled pseudonym for the other.[2] The story was a romance of black revolution, an internationalist tale involving the revolt of the black world against worldwide imperial and colonial powers and the resulting establishment of independent black states.[3]

In "The Ray of Fear's" opening conversation between Princess Nazima,[4] the main female protagonist, and her beloved, the black revolutionary Paul Kilmanjaro, blackness reveals itself as a term with shifting cultural and political meanings. Announcing the Black Republic's declaration of a war "for the glory of the Republic, the redemption of the fatherland and the liberation of our oppressed and scattered kinsmen," Kilmanjaro's comments reveal that various ideas of nationhood—nation as fatherland, homeland, black republic—and the notion of a diaspora—our oppressed and scattered kinsmen—occupy here the same imaginary world. While in contemporary discourse the terms nation and diaspora are often posed in opposition to each other,[5] in certain forms of black discourse from the early decades of the twentieth century they constituted two equally determinative and linked notions of blackness. Both allowed for the expression of a certain *affective* dimension in black literature, the race's longing for some form of self-determination and sovereignty.

Notably, as we shall see in chapter 2, this level of affect, the "desire for the state," was often signaled in black narratives in gendered terms through the figure of the woman of color. But this chapter focuses first on her historical male counterpart, the New Negro male as he was being imagined in both politics and literature in the first two decades of the twentieth century. Why did some Caribbean intellectuals such as Briggs, living and working in the United States in the early years of the twentieth century, feel compelled to tell these global, revolutionary stories of the race? What were the conditions that made these types of narratives possible, and what were the political hopes and fears these narratives were meant to address? The historical answer lies in political world events that immediately followed World War I and the Russian Revolution and their convergence with the specific African American cultural and intellectual formation of the first two decades of the twentieth century, captured in the trope of the New Negro as the particular figure for a new modern masculine construction of black subjectivity.

*Black Empire* begins with the argument that Pan-African politics during the 1920s were based on a collective historical reality. Black colonials were not included in any imagination of world citizenship occurring during the postwar discussions of peace at Versailles. Instead, in the shift from world empires to an international League of Nations, Europe sharpened the distinctions between empire and republic by drawing a firm racial line between the nations and the colonies, a color line that would then become the defining mode for distinguishing a modern First World from an underdeveloped Third World.[6] The modern twentieth-century world after World War I was understood by black intellectuals to be a *white* world of European nation-states, a world that could not imagine black Africa, for example, as part of the global body politic. Both the war and these immediate postwar events compelled many black intellectuals to view domestic racial relations and race politics in the United States from a more global perspective. Their lens tended to be much wider than that of the imperial powers, as seen in the starting premise of Du Bois's 1925 essay that the war had left behind more than simply a new Europe of nation-states.

However, at the same time that modern black subjects were keenly observing events in the European metropoles, they were also witnesses to the drama of social revolution. The Russian Revolution produced a different internationalist vision than that of the League of Nations, one that provided alternative class-based rather than nation-based models for modern political identity. The Bolshevik alternative to the politics of nation and nationality made a deep and lasting impression on early-twentieth-century black intellectuals. The Russian Revolution became a motivating force for shaping an alternative vision of racial revolution. It gave black intellectuals from the New World, already armed with centuries of critical engagement with and resistance to empire and colonization, a way to envision racial revolution in the modern terms of early-twentieth-century capitalist world society.

The Russian Revolution's impact can be seen in a specific way in stories such as "The Ray of Fear." In the revolutionary male Paul Kilmanjaro's description of impending war, international conflict is understood very much according to the logic of the *Communist Manifesto*, the logic of two opposing camps facing each other on the battlefields of history.[7] Yet though the story is set against the backdrop of the 1917 Bolshevik revolution, in "The Ray of Fear" class warfare is understood from a black, colonial perspective as a *race war* between "the Negro race" and "the white oppressors and murderers." This understanding of *race* war, as opposed to *class* war, as the motor of history, is a key feature of strands of revolutionary black internationalism during this period. In studies of black radicalism scholars have consistently failed to see that black and Caribbean intellectuals borrowed selectively from Marxist and Russian models of internationalism. They chose the *logic* of class relations as a global narrative of modern world history and capitalist relations, but located the origins of that story even further in the past in the racial epistemologies of colonialism. With the notion of *race war*, they substituted race instead of class as the grounding term for their analyses of both world history and the future potential of world revolution.

Paul Kilmanjaro's later repetition of his opening announcement raises a further illustrative point about race war in "The Ray of Fear." Heralding the beginnings of a black revolution that is itself conceived in internationalist and multinational terms, Kilmanjaro reports back to the Black Republic's president, "It is war, sir! The war of the races. The war for the liberation of the Negro race and its holy fatherland. The war against the white oppressors and murderers."[8] Here, Kilmanjaro's description of world events moves the story's readers away from nation and diaspora as the two frames for understanding black identity in the early twentieth century; instead, race is invoked, but take note—this notion of "the race" crystallizes in the context of war. Nazima's and Paul's oppressed and scattered kinsmen become a race when faced with a "war against the white oppressors and murders."[9] Race here, then, shadows empire as the global category broad enough to narrate the race's war with the empires on a world stage. For certain black intellectuals that race war had a centuries-long genealogy, one that utilized notions of race and culture to create a European imperial discourse of competing African and colonial barbarisms against European and imperial civilizations.

"The Ray of Fear" was only one of innumerable fables, stories, plays, and longer fictional narratives written during the first third of the twentieth century that attempted to imagine some version of an internationalist revolutionary black state. These black empire narratives were tales created by black New World intellectuals from the Caribbean and the United States, primarily male. They were part of a broader discourse on international black self-determination during this period that I have termed here "black transnationalism." They are evidence of a black, masculine, transnational, political, narrative imaginary during this period, which runs from the 1914 declaration of war that led to international political formations such as the League of Nations to the granting of national independence in 1962 to the first two island-colonies of the British West Indies.[10] I use the image of a black empire to capture this imaginary because it describes a formation that is immediately racial and global. By pairing blackness and empire I seek to recapture the tension of a cultural politics constituted by both radical and reactionary impulses—impulses toward racial revolution, movement, and freedom and impulses toward militarism, statehood, and empire. In the late nineteenth century certain African American writers merged discourses of blackness and empire, reaching back into transatlantic history to mobilize often problematic aspects of the racialized discourses of empire and civilization they were seeking to contest. The trope of a black empire, then, becomes another way of portraying the early-twentieth-century black imaginary I represented in the metaphor of a

Negro ship of state. The icon of the black empire captures the contradiction between specific notions of racial nationalism—based in ideals of national sovereignty and imperial civilization, the ship of state itself—and the openness of the alternative routes that ship has taken in its quest for racial freedom.

The black internationalism of the New Negro during this period takes place within the specific domestic cultural context of a new expression of black subjectivity shaping arts and letters within the United States. W. E. B. Du Bois is an apt African American figure to open with, since he straddles nicely the fence usually separating these two worlds of the political and the aesthetic. He participated and helped to shape the movement of the New Negro within the realm of domestic cultural politics, and he traveled to Versailles during the immediate postwar period in an effort to help shape the global discourse and decisions of the moment to better benefit the New Negro in the world at large. A broader discussion of the New Negro movement within the black internationalist framework that is the focus here also reveals why certain literary expressions of this black global imaginary took the particular forms they did during this period, particularly in relationship to the construction of gender.

BLACK INTERNATIONALE:

CARIBBEAN RADICALS AND THE TROPE OF THE NEW NEGRO

During the early twentieth century, "the new Manhood Movement among American Negroes" represented its own series of breaks with black and white American racial ideologies of the nineteenth century.[11] As the twentieth-century world was experiencing the upheaval and the aftermath of world war and revolution, black migrants from both the American South and the English-speaking Caribbean were traveling to northern cities such as Harlem in unprecedented numbers.[12] They came to escape poverty and racial discrimination in the South and in the colonies and to benefit from wartime economic prosperity in the North. They also joined the war effort in significant numbers, with some 380,000 black soldiers serving in World War I, "11 percent of whom were actually assigned to combat units."[13] As I have argued elsewhere, they represented the proletarianization of black peasantry from the rural Caribbean and the American South into the modern industrial economies of the northern United States.[14]

The confluence of world war, revolutionary internationalism, and mass black migration was felt on the ideological and intellectual level in the evolution of the trope of the New Negro. The New Negro was the ideological figure for a new black cultural and political identity for the twentieth century. New Negro ideology originated, post-Reconstruction, in the desire for the fair representation of the race. Henry Louis Gates Jr. has pointed out that this desire for representation was fundamentally a cultural politics: "Black Americans sought to re-present their public selves in order to reconstruct their public, reproducible images."[15]

The image of the New Negro was that of the "spontaneously generated black and sufficient self," one who had turned away from the Old Negro of slavery.[16] The New Negro was also undeniably male, the symbol for a new racial manhood as John Henry Adams would describe him visually in 1904: "Here is the real new Negro man. Tall, erect, commanding, with a face as strong as Angelo's Moses and yet every whit as pleasing and handsome as Reuben's favorite model. There is that penetrative eye . . . that broad forehead and firm chin. . . . Such is the new Negro man."[17] Gates argues that black masculinity was at stake in early-twentieth-century African American conceptions of the New Negro partly due to contemporary debates surrounding the military capabilities of black soldiers and officers. In 1899 Theodore Roosevelt had argued that inherent racial weaknesses prevented black officers from commanding successfully. Part of the project of re-presenting blacks, then, included histories of black involvement in American wars. As Gates points out: "To have fought nobly, clearly, was held to be a legitimate argument for full citizenship rights."[18]

By linking the formation of New Negro masculinity and subjectivity to Roosevelt's particularly racialized discourses on citizenship and manhood, Gates's reconstruction of the history of the trope also intersects directly with a broader discourse on American masculinity during this period, identified by Gail Bederman in *Manliness and Civilization*.[19] Arguing that "During the decades around the turn of the century, Americans were obsessed with the connection between manhood and racial dominance," Bederman identifies Theodore Roosevelt in particular as the primary architect of a version of white supremacy with masculinity at its center.[20] Her analysis of Roosevelt takes place within the broader context of identifying a broader shift in American discourses of manhood during this period, from Victorian notions of "manliness" which emphasized strong character, a certain moral "uprightness," and sexual self-restraint to a desire for a more aggressive and virile form of American manhood captured in the increased use and developing meanings of the term "masculinity" between 1890 and 1917. Tellingly, as Bederman observes, black American men were placed centrally in this discussion, revealing the importance of black masculinity to domestic discourses of American manhood that would continue well into the twenty-first century.[21]

Bederman's text opens by recounting the important boxing match between white heavyweight Jim Jeffries and his black opponent Jack Johnson. This 1910 bout became the staging ground for articulating whether white men could have access to a certain primitive or savage masculinity seen as the specific attribute of black men without white men thereby losing their own "manliness" and civilized virtues, seen as distinctly and hereditarily not available to their black counterparts. Bederman's point is further proven by the fact that, as evidenced in Gates's account, the trope of the New Negro male represented a striving on the part of certain African American male intellectuals to emulate the manly virtues of the Victorian gentleman in order to prove their own claims to military prowess and the national entitlements of citizenship.[22]

Yet the New Negro also functioned as a new trope for blackness for West Indian intellectuals living and working in Harlem during the early years of the twentieth century. For black colonials from the Caribbean, the Old Negro represented continuing colonial exploitation while the trope of a New Negro offered an alternative and empowering vision of self-determined blackness, seemingly free from certain imperial connotations not as available in the Caribbean. Belinda Edmondson's work on early-twentieth-century Caribbean masculinity helps to frame the gendered discursive context in which the New World Negro's Caribbean masculinity was being constructed simultaneous with the period Gates is describing in the United States.

If the New Negro male represented modern and self-determined black subjectivity in the United States, Belinda Edmondson has argued that in the Caribbean the image of the politically freed, national black subject was also gendered as male. In the Caribbean, however, the blackness of the free male subject was intimately in dialogue with his Englishness.[23] Specifically, "For nonwhite, non-English men to make a case for self-government, they [had to] state their case as *gentlemen*, which means they [had to], in essence be 'made' into Englishmen."[24] Edmondson argues persuasively that the notion of the gentleman intellectual functioned as the central trope in "a Victorian 'master' text to Caribbean national identity."[25] In creating their own national identities from this gentlemanly discourse, Caribbean male intellectuals were essentially working with similar Victorian features of manliness as their American and African American counterparts.[26] This could lead one to argue, as Judith Stein does in relationship to Pan-Africanist discourse specifically, that across the diaspora even in different national contexts, all the attributes of citizenship and self-government—independence, self-reliance, self-determination, enfranchisement—would be linked, for a transatlantic grouping of black males from a certain class, to empire's Victorian notions of the manly, educated gentleman intellectual.[27]

However, in the American context, as the trope of the New Negro male moved further into the twentieth century, he also benefited from new internationalist discourses emerging to shape discussions of modern political subjectivity during this era. The international discussions of self-determination following World War I would privilege nationality as a global universal and citizenship as the right of the modern political subject in the nation-state. The Russian revolution of 1917 would ground a revolutionary conception of political identity in an internationalist class consciousness not bound by national borders. The unique situation afforded by World War I was that both native and immigrant blacks in the United States were provided with two suitable models of free and self-determined political and cultural identity—a national grounding of identity in the political model of the nation-state and a radical grounding of identity in revolutionary internationalism. As black soldiers returned home from World War I, they observed the mismatch between the needs and hopes of black subjects and the political forms of representation then being made available to them. While self-determination offered an empowering vision of freedom, the realization of its inaccessibility for black subjects had a radicalizing effect. Revolutionary internationalism then provided new ways of imagining and articulating black identity and ethnicity outside the bounds of the national. Bolshevik revolutionary ideology allowed Caribbean American intellectuals to recognize the potential in founding racial freedom in internationalism, as they marked the discrepancy between colonized black identities across the diaspora and the new political entity of the European imperial nation-state being envisioned to protect and represent them.

Black soldiers' and black male intellectuals' relationships to the various conceptions of empire, nation, and revolution emerging from World War I helped shape black masculine identity formation in these early years of the twentieth century. The impact of war and revolution on questions of black identity produced formulations of the black transnational as intellectuals engaged with the question of how to guarantee the political and artistic representation of black subjects in modernity. This transnational cultural force played a crucial role in the formation of New Negro masculinity during the postwar period.

As black transnational intellectuals constructed their own sense of black masculinity in the literature and politics of the period, they were distinguished in one key respect from Caribbean colonial intelligentsia, Caribbean exiled writers from the middle class, and an African American middle class male looking to define his own relationship to the United States domestically.[28] Without a clearly defined national community to represent or territory to belong to, geopolitical and cultural discourses merged to open the field for alternative articulations of black political subjectivity and, concomitantly, black masculinity. Untied to a specific national framework, black transnational intellectuals could draw from new languages of internationalism gaining currency in the period in the context of both the war and the revolution. Unlike Louis Simpson and a generation of Caribbean writers and scholars in exile, the most famous being V. S. Naipaul,[29] transnational Caribbean colonial intellectuals mediated their sense of exile in the United States by forging a new set of identifications with the American New Negro. In so doing, they also broadened the trope to reflect their own experiences and concerns as New World intellectuals.

One element of the modern appeal of the trope of the New Negro for Caribbean intellectuals lay in his Americanness, not so much as a figure for their desire to be American, but representative of their desire to claim for black subjects the entitlements of nationality and citizenship being framed in the period. While black migrants from the South and Caribbean immigrants to the United States represented a black peasantry slowly transitioning from old colonial plantation economies into the new modern economies of the industrial nations, unlike colonial migrants the American New Negro already had an existing claim on citizenship in the United States.[30] This was an important point of stability for his international migrations. American citizenship both grounded the traveling black American subject and protected him. As limited or disfranchised as he may have felt, the black American male held a modern citizenship that no black colonial had yet experienced. Even as gentlemen, Caribbean men in the early decades of the twentieth century still experienced the world as colonial subjects, but not (yet) as national citizens.

As the trope developed over time, the other modern feature of the New Negro that made him attractive to black transnational colonial intellectuals was his working-class politics. The New Negro of the Harlem Renaissance, unlike his earlier incarnation at the beginning of the twentieth century, started to move away from the more bourgeois features of nineteenth-century Victorian narratives, in both their British imperial and early African American incarnations.[31] For men with a radical politics aiming to represent movements of the black masses rather than the elites, he seemed able to represent a whole new brand of modern, revolutionary, black male leadership.[32] The New Negro male could lead a worldwide community of black laboring subjects newly incorporated within industrial modernity.

For the three male intellectuals studied here, the New Negro movement was important precisely as a movement of and for the black masses. Marcus Garvey would explicitly distance himself from the bourgeois nationalism and elite politics of his West Indian gentleman compatriots on the islands. His unwillingness to accommodate himself to the elite politics of his fellow nationalist leaders in the West Indies led directly to his immigration to the United States. Once in the United States, Garvey would position his Universal Negro Improvement Association as an organization specifically for the masses rather than the elites of American race politics.

C. L. R. James's subsequent interest in Garvey's movement and in the "Negro movement for freedom" was also part of his broader interest in the history of Pan-African revolt developed through the lens of his Marxist belief in the worldwide movement of the proletarian masses. As Robin D. G. Kelley has described, in his historical narratives James "revised African and diasporic history by focusing on the masses. . . . there are leaders, but like Toussaint L'Ouverture in San Domingo, leaders are made by the masses and the times in which they live."[33] Claude McKay was also a believer in proletarian internationalism during the 1910s and 1920s. His literary project in the novel for which he is most famous, *Home to Harlem*, was specifically an attempt to imagine the black American world in Harlem through the eyes of its common men rather than its black bourgeois leaders.[34]

The Harlem Renaissance figure who often best represented both the working-class internationalism and the modern mobility of the New Negro was the Pullman porter, a prominent player in both the fiction and the politics of the period. In socialist A. Philip Randolph's organizing efforts among black Pullman porters during this period lay an internationalist consciousness of the black working-class as a social and political force in United States history. The New Negro represented elements of proletarianism as a member of the industrial working class in the North. This made the trope of a New Negro male valuable for a black transnational politics eager to step away from the elite nationalism of both Caribbean and African American political discourse.

One could say that, as a trope, the New Negro was a cousin to the Caribbean New World Negro, to borrow the language of black American intellectual George Schuyler who described a Black Internationale composed of American New Negros with a broader global consciousness connecting them to black populations in the colonial world.[35] A leader of the black male working-class, grounded in American nationality and citizenship as either a point of origin with stable meanings or a form of naturalization with a high degree of security, this more "worldly" New Negro encountered in his travels throughout the modern colonial world alternative forms and processes of identification.

Henry Gates identifies the period from 1895 to 1925 "as the era of the myth of a New Negro, a New Negro in search of a Renaissance suitable to contain this culturally willed myth."[36] Another way of thinking about this is to imagine the masculine figure of the New Negro as a utopian construction of a free black selfhood, seeking a movement in which to find its truest and fullest expression. Gates argues that this quest had two distinct phases. Early uses of the trope of a New Negro at the turn and during the first decade of the twentieth century had a more political focus, characterized for example by a militant attitude toward the issue of black self-defense. With the publication of Alain Locke's 1925 anthology *The New Negro*, the representative text of the Harlem Renaissance, Gates argues that the trope and the movement for a New Negro adopted a more cultural focus. In Gates's words, "Locke's New

Negro . . . transformed the militancy associated with the trope and translated this into an apolitical movement of the arts."[37]

Tracing the trajectory from an Old Negro of slavery to a politicized New Negro at the beginning of the twentieth century to an artistic use of the trope during the Harlem Renaissance, Gates's periodization leaves out the black and Caribbean radicalism of the 1910s and 1920s. This radical period of the New Negro movement, identified and researched by historians such as Ernest Allen Jr., Robin D. G. Kelley, Mark Naison, and Winston James, was the moment when the radical beliefs and activities of Caribbean radicals such as Cyril V. Briggs would intersect with the cultural politics and hopes for the African American New Negro.[38] The cultural politics of this period that runs roughly from 1915 to the mid-1920s was fundamentally shaped by geopolitical events following the war. As Allen has also described, while there existed "an African American tradition [of nationalism] extending back to the free black population of the late eighteenth century . . . this trend to nationalism was given greater impetus during the war by demands for self-determination oc-curring within Europe."[39] In Allen's account, the radical aspects of the New Negro movement included "African American and African Caribbean nation-alists—who should really be called Pan-Nationalists since what they sought was the political liberation of both Africa and her dispersed descendants of the New World."[40] The radical intellectual formation Allen first identifies as nationalism and then broadens to "Pan-Nationalism" to include movements for independence throughout the diaspora is precisely what is captured here by the term "black transnationalism." Allen uses these multiple names to cap-ture the paradoxical mixture of nationalism and internationalism that seemed to so characterize the radical black discourse and politics of this period.

*Black Empire* builds on historical and literary accounts of this new Man-hood Movement among American Negroes by addressing the difference the Caribbean makes in our studies of the political movement and the cultural front that accompanied it: the Harlem Renaissance.[41] First, neither historians nor literary scholars have fully explored the strands of internationalist thought that ran throughout black discourse and culture in the United States during the late 1920s and the 1930s. Defining the Harlem Renaissance period as that of the cultural New Negro, the consensus has been that the cultural was also the apolitical. Since few discuss the internationalist ideologies interwoven throughout main streams of black political and literary discourse during this period, their significance as an alternative way of thinking about black subjectivity remains to be fully appreciated.[42] Unlike other manifestations of the New Negro, among this group of intellectuals the trope was used to introduce fundamentally internationalist notions of black masculine subjectivity.

The black internationalism of the period was profoundly shaped by the experiences of coloniality provided by West Indian intellectuals in Harlem. The 1920s were the era of Marcus Garvey, of increased activity among Caribbean radicals in Harlem.[43] To call these years nonpolitical is to discount both the presence and the colonial politics of West Indian radicals in Harlem during this period. During the 1910s and 1920s, African American political and cultural discourse expanded from the uplift narratives of the early decades of the century to include an anticolonialist perspective emerging out of the critique of the postwar world order. That black internationalist politics, in which Caribbean radicals played a key role, provided the background for the black anticolonial activism of the 1940s described, for example, by Penny Von Eschen in *Race Against Empire*.[44]

The internationalism of the New Negro movement was shaped by key institutional mechanisms which helped to sustain the movement and give it its international character: a constellation of black and radical journals; mass political movements and organizing efforts in the postwar era, just prior to the Depression; a host of international conferences and conventions, such as Du Bois's Pan-African Congresses; and novels and literary productions during the Harlem Renaissance. Cyril Briggs, Marcus Garvey, and Claude McKay all had some connection to these forms and institutions during their careers in the United States. Briggs worked as a journalist at the *Amsterdam News* before he founded his own journal, *The Crusader*; McKay wrote for and edited the *Liberator* (and the *Worker's Dreadnought* in England); and Garvey both sponsored and wrote for the *Negro World*.[45]

The merger of internationalism and black nationalism was also fostered and developed in the transnational spaces of a variety of international conferences. Briggs attended the second congress of the Comintern in 1921, McKay the third in 1922. Briggs also attended Marcus Garvey's influential and spectacular Universal Negro Improvement Association's International Conference of the Negro in 1920, reputedly the largest international gathering of blacks ever witnessed in the Western world. Du Bois's Pan-African conferences and the League of Nations Convention itself in 1919 also reflected this encouragement of a more transnational way of thinking in the space of the international convention. While clearly attached to the national, the significance of these international conventions was their ability to function as networks that could then be used to organize collective identity in spaces outside of the national.

The internationalism of the Harlem Renaissance, however, has perhaps been less evident because scholars have defined the literary texts in which the politics of black internationalism appeared as some of the period's lesser works. Key early twentieth-century political fictions, black empire narratives such as W. E. B. Du Bois's *Dark Princess* and George Schuyler's *Black Empire*, have been marginalized even within these authors' own corpuses. In chapter 2 I argue that it is precisely in these narratives that we see a masculine transnational politics of the New Negro being articulated during the Harlem Renaissance.

If what scholars define as nationalist in the black radical discourse of the New Negro movement is the focus on black political representation and statehood, my interest is in those intellectuals who used black nationalist movements for citizenship and statehood as a gateway to imagining and then representing a more diasporic sense of black identity. More than just anticolonialism, in the black internationalism of the New Negro movement we find an interest in framing a new political entity that could represent the African diaspora and a new, more worldly sense of black collectivity and subjectivity, specifically gendered in masculinist terms. This went beyond a nationalist politics confined to communities of blacks in individual states in the United States and in the Caribbean and beyond a Pan-Africanist politics fighting for African national independence. Fundamentally this meant constructing the impossibly utopian ideal of a black "internationalist nation," a global vision which also required multiple identifications of blackness and more global definitions of black nationality and citizenship. Their narratives reflect African American articulations of a black transnationality beginning in the latter half of the nineteenth century. Black empire narratives, as I term them here, serve as examples of an alternative black internationalist literary tradition, also present during the New Negro movement of the Harlem Renaissance. They also offer alternative internationalist constructions of black masculinity during this period, differentiated from more nationally oriented tropes such as that of the Victorian Caribbean gentleman or the manly, educated Victorian New Negro. In their envisioning of a black masculine globality, authors of black empire narratives would express both the race's desire for nationhood—envisioning sovereignty as a universal global concept actualized in performances of black stateliness—and the race's right to the essential freedoms associated with modernity and nationality, such as their freedom of movement both within the nation and without.

The participation of Caribbean intellectuals in the politics and culture of Harlem during the 1910s and the 1920s helped to shape the internationalist black imaginary that was as much a part of the literary output of the New Negro movement as the more recognizable literary and cultural products of the Harlem Renaissance. Their contribution to that masculine imaginary can be seen most directly in the radical anticolonial discourse of Caribbean and African-American Pan-Africanists during the period. The broader sense of the race as a multinational diaspora *within* the nation was also partly produced by the actual multiethnic nature of the black community in Harlem at the beginning of the twentieth century. Even the Caribbean itself functioned as a landscape in which alternative visions of black freedom could be imagined. We have reached a point in our study of the New Negro where we can synthesize and broaden the trope to include at its center, in a more integrated manner, black Caribbean intellectuals living in the United States. Men such as Marcus Garvey, Claude McKay, and C. L. R. James not only participated in African American cultural, literary, and political movements, they also engaged in a black transnational cultural politics that came specifically out of their own experience of modernity as black colonial subjects. The coloniality of this black transnational cultural politics went much further than a critique of colonialism. Variously termed "nationalist," "Pan-Nationalist," "Pan-Africanist," and "internationalist," what made this black intellectual formation transnational was its vision of a modern black political identity constituted by multiple black nationalities, the belief in black subjects' inherent right to free movement, and the recognition of their perennial desire for a state. More than an anticolonial politics, and more than the organizing of an international black working class, black transnational intellectuals were fundamentally engaged in finding ways to represent a multiply national global black community. What distinguishes their transnational cultural politics from the accounts of black masculinity, radicalism, and the arts that have so far defined this period is that their work inhabits a black *transatlantic* space between and moving back and forth across the national landscapes of Caribbean and African American Studies.

Black transnationalism, both as a narrative imaginary and as an intellectual formation, emerged from the political events that ushered in the twentieth century—World War I and the Russian Revolution. The debate between nationalism and internationalism that shaped discussions about the nature of modern political freedom also created in black subjects the compulsion to tell their own global stories. However, if early-twentieth-century political events provide the conjunctural and historical answer to this chapter's opening questions—what were the conditions that made black empire narratives and stories of black international revolution possible; what were the political hopes and fears these narratives were meant to address—a second discourse of internationalism specific to the United States during this period also helped to empower a figure such as Caribbean radical Cyril V. Briggs to imagine a role for the New World Negro in the discussions taking place in Versailles after World War I. No story of the Black Internationale would be complete without an account of Brigg's own initial engagements with and ultimate critique of brands of American internationalism also current during this period, as he gave them voice in the words of United States President Woodrow Wilson. The story of the United States's special role in radical black intellectuals' engagement with imperial international politics during the early twentieth century can be seen in the pages of Briggs's *Crusader* as international events unfolded between 1917 and 1919. This story properly begins on 2 April 1917 when Woodrow Wilson made his address to the joint session of Congress calling upon the United States to join the war against Germany.

THE UNITED STATES OF AMERICA:
EMPIRE OR TRANSNATIONAL FEDERATION

As with the recommendations of the fictional president and congress in the story "The Ray of Fear," Woodrow Wilson's call to war was "international in scope and representation."[46] Wilson's assertion that the world must be made safe for democracy served as the catalyst for intense expressions of patriotism and internationalism, some of which the president himself had not anticipated. We see this reflected in the career of Cyril Valentine Briggs, the Carib-

bean radical intellectual who founded the revolutionary black organization the
African Blood Brotherhood and whose short story began our discussion. As a
compatriot of Garvey and McKay, yet one who was directly engaged in print
with Woodrow Wilson's internationalist rhetoric, a brief look at Briggs's career helps to bring the United States's geopolitical role during this period into
sharper focus.

The sentiments of "The Ray of Fear" parallel and reflect Briggs's fundamental disillusionment with the promise of the imperially imagined nation-
state, as the racial and colonial politics of the League of Nations revealed
themselves between 1919 and 1920. On 8 January 1918, when President Wilson
first gave his fourteen points speech asserting the principle of national self-
determination, Briggs was only one of many black intellectuals who believed
this to be the real end to empire and the beginning of freedom and world
peace. These hopes coincided with the emerging Pan-Africanist movement,
as black intellectuals turned their attention to the global struggle for realizing
an autonomous black Africa.[47] As historian Ernest Allen Jr. has also recounted:

> If the League of Nations found self-determination for eastern European
> nations an appropriate course of action, then self-determination for peo-
> ple of African descent was equally valid. Variations upon this common
> theme were to be found among African American and African Caribbean
> nationalists, communists, and socialists.[48]

Invoking the flags of the Allies, the banners of the new national states in
Europe, Briggs argued that the modern black colonial's participation in an
international struggle for African national independence was the only effective direction in the race war against imperialism. Yet the reality that the
league's international agenda still suffered from the legacy of colonial politics
became more and more apparent as the peace conference wore on. In his
editorial "The League of Nations," Briggs critically identified the league's
model of the self-determined national state as an imperial fiction working
against the interests of the black and colonial world. Beginning with the
assertion, "Evidently the proposed League of Nations is designed not only to
prevent wars between one nation and another, but to suppress all revolutions
upon the part of the oppressed and dissatisfied," Briggs argued that the peace
secured in a world order of nation-states was at the expense of revolutionary

movements for freedom in the colonial world.[49] It was precisely this colonial world that Du Bois took his readers on a journey through in "Worlds of Color." Du Bois drew a map of the world on the dark side of the color line, a world of shadows that threw the boundary lines of global politics into stark relief as they were being drawn by the United States and other world leaders in the League of Nations.

By 1919 Cyril Briggs was thoroughly disillusioned with the promises of the League of Nations. In a March editorial attacking the league he focused specifically on the role of the United States. Reminding his readers of the hopes peace was supposed to fulfill—"new nations are to be formed. . . . Subject races are to be freed. Geography is to be no more merely the expression of imperialistic greed and plunder"—Briggs asked, "But how can these things be compassed with imperialistic England, greedy France . . . and the hypocritical murderer of Haitian freedom [the United States, one of] the leading spirits of the League?"[50] Here Briggs exposed the shadow of empire underlying American internationalist rhetoric: "Is America ready to step out of Haiti and San Domingo and return their country to the Hawaiians? Is she ready to recognize the demands of the Filipinos for independence or to apply self-determination to Mississippi and South Carolina and democracy to the South in general?" Briggs then underscored his critique of the United States by constructing his own narrative of American internationalism.

In a June 1919 editorial entitled, "What Does Democratic America in Haiti? [*sic*]," Briggs created an imaginary conversation between "the President" of the United States, the German "Kaiser," and "a Dominican revolutionist" named Venizelos.[51] The Kaiser makes the following address to the American President:

> You set yourself up, as [you] yourself have said, to be the world's supreme internationalists . . . But what did you do? [In] July 1914 you prepared to attack Haiti. . . . You denied that peace in Haiti was an international concern. You maintained that it was a concern for the United States alone.

The Kaiser then pays Wilson's America the supreme ironic compliment: "[They] spend their spare time shouting internationalism and international courts across the Atlantic to us in Europe, and [meanwhile] they are absolutely successful in getting an empire of vassal states for themselves." The Caribbean revolutionary, Venizelos, caps the discussion by pointing out, "The

American people profess a pure anti-imperialism. But they have an empire. And they are increasing it surreptitiously. Will the republic of the United States soon become openly and in name, as it has already become to all purposes and intents, an Empire?"

The Caribbean revolutionary's vision of the American republic as "an Empire" stands in striking contrast to the more progressive vision of the United States's international significance constructed during the same period by Briggs's contemporary, American left intellectual Randolph Bourne. Also writing within the context of World War I, Bourne first used the term "transnational" to describe an American state that could travel beyond the imaginative borders and ideological limits of European nationalism. As Bourne stated, "In a world which has dreamed of internationalism, we find that we have all unawares been building up the first international nation."[52] Bourne's essay on a "trans-national America" proved the most progressive vision of United States internationalism during this period, borrowing the language and metaphors of federation to imagine America as a more inclusive model of multiracial political democracy:

> Do we not begin to see a new and more adventurous ideal? Do we not see how the *national colonies in America*, deriving power from the deep cultural heart of Europe and yet living here in mutual toleration . . . may work out a federated ideal? *America is transplanted Europe, but a Europe that has not been disintegrated and scattered in the transplanting as in some Dispersion.*[53]

Bourne's account of the transnational American nation was limited precisely by what he chose to leave out: the two terms I have made central to this discussion, blackness and empire. Despite his hopes that "Whatever American nationalism turns out to be, we see already that it will have a color richer and more exciting than our ideal has hitherto encompassed," his discussion of America's multiple nationalities ignored the tricky question of the nature of African American citizenship.[54] Bourne also ignored the worlds of color directly outside the United States's borders. In this essay he remained mute on the question of the impact of United States imperialism in the Caribbean and Latin America and in the greater colonial world. Finally, in his sense of America as a transplanted Europe but one "that has not been disintegrated and scattered in the transplanting," he revealed his own bias toward seeing the United States as the new territorial homeland of a *European* diaspora. Bourne used the metaphors of a scattered colonial world to imagine a new home for empire's populations in the American nation.[55]

Even progressive constructions of United States internationalism such as Bourne's were unable to detach themselves from a racialized global imaginary, limited primarily to populations in and from Europe and inextricably linked with the ideal of the territorial and sovereign American state. Placed beside Briggs's critique of an American empire and Du Bois's mapping of adjacent worlds of color, Bourne's essay on an American transnation reveals in miniature what the broader field of American studies has lost by avoiding the shadow of empire in United States history. It also reveals what American studies has to gain from a dialogue with Pan-Africanism and black transnationalism. Both would allow for a clearer understanding of the imperial character of the U.S. state, both the source of its expansiveness and the nature of its limits.

In 1932, political theorist Carl Schmitt identified the League of Nations as an "interstate" system rather than a true "universal [or] even an international organization," and defined "true" internationalism as "international movements which transcend the borders of states and ignore the territorial integrity, impenetrability, and impermeability of existing states as, for example, the [Communist] Third International."[56] Here Schmitt highlighted the still imperial legacy of the league, the conversion of empire into an international system of states that while shedding its imperial skin, still maintained certain state structures in the colonial worlds that prevented the expression of black self-government and free movement. For black intellectuals such as Garvey, McKay, and James, the African diasporic population scattered by the slave trade and colonial settlement was a world population that could and did "transcend the borders of states and ignore the territorial integrity, impenetrability, and impermeability of existing states." Colonial history and the slave trade had created its own diaspora in the transplanting of Africans to multiple territories throughout the New World, creating a colonial condition in which statelessness and the lack of an official nationality would be the defining political experience for modern black subjects.[57] This lack, resulting from original forced dispersions such as the Middle Passage, was only reinforced for a new century in the politics of the League of Nations. But for the early-twentieth-century intellectuals discussed in *Black Empire*, the benefit of not having a Caribbean national identity was the ability to imagine a transnational black identity uniting black subjectivities across the Americas and beyond. In place of nations and nationality, the race would represent itself as and through global movement.

What Caribbean colonial intellectuals knew in the early years of the twentieth century was that, despite the rhetoric, race was precisely the principle which limited how far ideas of democracy—free governments—and economic expansion—free markets—could travel in the modern world and into the colonial world. If political sovereignty threatened to limit economic expansion in the First World, economic dependence limited political democracy in the Third World. And throughout the twentieth century, the ideal of state sovereignty has worked to exclude populations who were not originally imagined to be a part of the imagined community of the European or American nation-states.

In his 1920 collection of essays on postwar geopolitics, *Darkwater: Voices From Within the Veil*, W. E. B. Du Bois asserted the following in reference to the League of Nations: "No federation of the world, no true inter-nation— can exclude the black and brown and yellow races from its counsels."[58] The shadow of race in contemporary global politics is revealed in the continued inability of the United States as the dominant world power to accord once-colonial subjects and racial others an equal place as nations in the new economic arrangements of our current global order.

Paul Robeson and Princess Kouka in *Jericho* (1937). Courtesy of the Douris Corporation (www.classicmovies.com).

CHAPTER 2

# The Woman of Color and the Literature
# of a New Black World

Of West Indian and American parentage—her mother was from Washington, D.C.,
and her father from the island of Barbadoes, B.W.I.—and of African birth, she
represented in her person the fatherland group and two of the most important of
the scattered groups of her race. And add to this the fact that she had relations, on
her father's side, in the Republic of Brazil and Mazima's broad and international
outlook is partly explained.[1]

STORIES SUCH AS "The Ray of Fear" can most obviously be read as black
nationalist tales in which racial freedom rests on the separatism of an autonomous black state. However, that would also mean ignoring the hybrid, multinational, and even multiracial nature of blackness as it is represented in these
tales of international black revolution. In "The Ray of Fear," the symbol
for the hybridity and multinationality of the race is the "intensely patriotic"
daughter of the president of the Black Republic, Princess Nazima (Nazima
and Mazima are both used throughout the story). In black internationalist
narratives, female protagonists often come to represent a multinational and
multiracial black world, one that could be seen as mirroring the hybridity of
the world of empire, more so than representing separate and separatist racial
ideologies.

This chapter seeks to historicize and interpret the gendered features of
certain early-twentieth-century black transnational narratives, as they were
shaped and influenced by late-nineteenth-century and early-twentieth discourses on black subjectivity and agency. As the many links between masculinity and nationality continue to be explored in studies of nationalism,
*Black Empire* argues that particular visions of black masculinity and femininity

were put in the service of tales narrating the race's quest for a black state. The early years of the twentieth century saw a cross-cultural exchange of gendered tropes of black subjectivity between Caribbean and African American intellectuals. In their attempts to create a transnational discourse of blackness, early African American narratives split the race into gendered tropes in order to reflect the differences between a more open-ended vision of the diaspora as a virtual, global nation, linked culturally, historically, and emotionally, and a more territorial sense of the race as a transnational political community consolidated through the power of a sovereign state. Since these narratives provide an important literary context for the gendering of discourses of black transnationality by Caribbean intellectuals during the first half of the twentieth century, this chapter analyzes a few specific examples of such narratives from the late nineteenth century and the early twentieth.

The goal here is twofold: first, to establish a literary genealogy of black transnational discourse in the Americas stretching back to the nineteenth century, with literature and narrative functioning here as black transatlantic cultural forms in much the same way Gilroy established oral forms as central to the cultures of a black Atlantic.[2] Second, literature specifically reveals the gendered constructions inherent in and endemic to both the black quest for national statehood and the narratives of international revolution that have shaped twentieth-century black discourse. If Caribbean intellectuals living and working in the United States drew from African American discourses of a New Negro that dated from the post-Reconstruction era, they also took with them the gender roles endemic to those particular constructions of black identity.

However, many black empire narratives by African Americans in the late nineteenth century also held within them a vision of black freedom that centered less on the race's right to statehood in Africa, and more on the New Negro's right to travel freely the colonial spaces of an emerging modern world. We find in these nineteenth-century black empire narratives and their early twentieth-century descendants a journey through the diaspora that is hard to categorize strictly in terms of the themes inherent to the canon of African American literature. They can only be understood as existing in a black transatlantic space between the Caribbean and America, a space that extends back into the history of colonialism itself.[3] The traces of this black transnational imaginary lie in internationalist narratives from the late nineteenth century that put the New Negro in motion across a much wider world than that of the nation. These journeys would be the precursor to an alternative vision of black internationalism focused less on the consolidation of statehood and the securities of home and more on the inherently insurgent and oppositional nature of free black movement within a racialized global context.

The movements of this traveling black subject, a more worldly New Negro, were not circumscribed within the boundaries of the United States.[4] As a result of their transnational travels, worldly black subjects developed a much broader, more global sense of their own blackness and their relationship to other colonial subjects. They imagined and moved through a black, colonial, and diasporic world, one that existed in the shadows of empire both geographically and imaginatively. The white, modernist, and nationalist formations dominant during the 1910s and 1920s were not then the only sources for the twentieth-century New Negro's primary identifications. Rather we see in the traveling New Negro the traces of alternative forms of identification that developed among hybrid, multinational, and multiracial populations traveling in the spaces between the New and the Old Worlds, throughout the centuries of colonial settlement and imperial development.

Black empire narratives constitute an important feature of a modern black transnational imaginary. They represent a desire on the part of marginalized modern black subjects to tell global stories of the race in the context of empire and conquest. Black empire narratives also represent the survival of alternative ways of imagining political community and multiracial global democracy. Hence, in addition to providing textual examples for a closer gendered analysis of black transnationalism, these tales also elucidate some of the broader themes in black transnational discourse from the late nineteenth century and early twentieth.

This chapter begins by examining three key texts in a canon of black empire narratives in late-nineteenth-century African American discourse, Martin R. Delany's *Blake; or, The Huts of America* (1859), Sutton E. Griggs's *Imperium in Imperio* (1899), and Pauline Hopkins's *Of One Blood* (1902–3).[5] Like the later romance "The Ray of Fear," these narratives placed marginal black and colonial populations at the center of a new narrative that imagined their self-determination in the form of an empire in the Caribbean, Africa, or the United States. Besides their formal elements these three nineteenth-century black empire narratives also shared one key feature that would remain a constant well into the twentieth century. All three addressed issues of black self-determination within the context of world imperialism. Each narrative presented a political strategy—emigrationism in *Blake*; separatism in *Imperium in Imperio*; and Pan-Africanism in *Of One Blood*—that could provide the answer to the central question that would persist into twentieth-century black transnationalist discourse.[6] Is the route to black freedom one of mobility or stasis—the constant, growing movement in search of a black state or the determined location of that state in a particular territory?

Nineteenth-century black empire narratives tended to stay within the framework of identifying some organizational form of the black state as the main resolution of the narrative. These narratives abounded throughout popular African American culture in the late nineteenth century and early twentieth, appearing in numerous fictions and dramatic spectacles during this period and constituting a literary prehistory to early-twentieth-century black transnationalism. However, in the early twentieth century, black authors began to frame their revolutionary politics in new languages of internationalism specific to the period. This chapter then ends with a comparison of two central African American black empire narratives from the 1920s and 1930s, George Schuyler's *Black Empire* and W. E. B. Du Bois's *Dark Princess*.

## ETHIOPIANIST UTOPIAS: THE TROPE OF A BLACK EMPIRE IN NINETEENTH-CENTURY AFRICAN AMERICAN NARRATIVES

The trope of a black empire appears throughout late-nineteenth-century popular African American fiction, representing the attempt by black authors to imagine the ideal political entity that could represent a worldwide, African diasporic community. The trope drew from languages of Ethiopianism, a Pan-Africanist discourse of African liberation and redemption based on the following Biblical passage from Psalms 68:31: "Princes shall come forth out of Egypt; Ethiopia shall soon stretch forth her hands unto God."[7] With an already built-in focus on the masculine sovereign as Ethiopia's heroic, princely sons, Ethiopianist discourses included accounts of majestic Old World African kingdoms.[8]

Martin Delany's narrative *Blake*, the ur-text of the genre, focuses on Blake, (Henricus Blacus/Henry Holland), a West Indian falsely enslaved in Louisiana.[9] Blake is the pure black revolutionary hero who, racially, is of unmistakable African origin.[10] He is also strong, focused, intelligent, and educated—both a manly and masculine leader of his people. Blake fits within what Robert A. Hill and R. Kent Rasmussen have called the "paradigm of the black liberator" in an "Afro-American literary tradition of conspirational novels in which blacks quest for sovereign states in order to protect their freedom."[11] He also prefigures a discussion on black masculinity and its role in uplifting the race that began after Reconstruction and found its real-life representative figures in leaders such as Frederick Douglass and later Booker T. Washington and W. E. B. Du Bois.[12] As a diasporic hero created by an African American yet described as a West Indian, the character Blake provides early evidence of the type of cross-cultural exchange that was occurring between and among black diasporic and colonial communities as they tried to imagine a New World Negro for the twentieth century. The notion of a mobile transnational black masculinity was prefigured in the character Blake himself in his epic transatlantic journey throughout the course of Delany's novel.

Blake is paired with a female character Maggie, whose domesticity re-appears in female characters in later black empire romances. Heroines of twentieth-century black empire narratives also tended to fit within a certain paradigm of female subjectivity, the paradigm of home. As black and feminist scholars across the diaspora have long identified, in male-authored, nationalist revolutionary narratives black female subjectivity is often constructed as domestic, in multiple senses of the word. Female subjectivity is often imagined as immobile and bound to region, island, nation, or any other conception of home.[13] In the late nineteenth century and early twentieth, the internationalism of the black female working class was also less evident since black women were seen as domestic rather than proletarian labor.[14] At the beginning of the twentieth century women were also seen to exist primarily in the private versus the public sphere—hence the difficulty seeing them as race leaders.[15] And finally, as postcolonial feminists among others have attested, in political discourse women have more often been used as nationalist versus internationalist symbols.[16]

In both Delany's *Blake* and Briggs's later story, "The Ray of Fear," the female characters are represented as passive figures for domestic safety and home. However, while rarely mobile themselves, women of color did come increasingly to embody the worlds of color black male protagonists were traveling to and through on their political quests for the race. Female characters in black empire narratives did represent home, but a home understood as encompassing the heterogeneity and hybridity of the diaspora. Like stories of passing from the post-Reconstruction era, black empire narratives also focused on issues of miscegenation, but they took the narrative of race and purity of blood in a slightly different direction. While in passing narratives the main story is about crossing the color line, tales of a black empire attempted to move beyond double consciousness to the multiple identifications made possible in a world of color.

In "The Ray of Fear," for example, the idea of a Black Republic expresses a form of internationalism that occurs neither on the level of politics nor on the level of history, but in the imagination. This Ethiopianist utopianism seeks to imagine a new geopolitical reality—the coming together of the Asian, African, communist, and colonial worlds into a new multiracial democratic political order, beyond blackness yet united against whiteness and empire. This metaphoric, diasporic, and ultimately worldly Black Republic is embodied in the story of Princess Nazima's hybrid black heritage. Yet while Princess Nazima's international personhood and outlook encompass the Black Republic and by extension the colonial diaspora, she is unable to effect her own political freedom. Princess Nazima of Briggs's story plays the role of passive catalyst; she represents the home the black revolutionary liberator, Paul Kilmanjaro, is fighting for. Here, home is figured as a feminized, deterritorialized, diasporic space, as opposed to the masculine national principle of the African fatherland described by Paul Gilroy[17] or even the older trope of the mythic motherland in Ethiopianist myth. In the discourse of black transnationalism the female principle of home is inert, open ended, and undefined—generally a passive figure of multiplicity and hybridity. For the male writers and intellectuals discussed here, it was the male principle that was more actively being constructed in the project of defining a modern black subjectivity.

The element that makes *Blake* a precursor to twentieth-century black transnational novels is the mobility of the novel's male protagonist and the global geography traced in the plot's structure. As the story progresses Delany traces a number of the possible routes envisioned throughout the nineteenth century for African American freedom. Each section of the plot places Blake in a different location in the diaspora employing a different revolutionary strategy.[18]

Ultimately, Delany's narrative ends on the brink of a black slave revolution in Cuba, and since the story's ending has never been found, the novel leaves a legacy of perpetual revolutionary possibility for black empire narratives to come.[19] I define *Blake* as an ur-text in the genre because it traces the geography of the black Atlantic—from the South to the North, from the New World to Africa and back—in its attempts to imagine a revolutionary solution to black freedom. As in "The Ray of Fear," the Black Republic ends up both everywhere and nowhere at one and the same time.

However, I also define *Blake* as an ur-text in the genre because of its own political context as the fictional expression of an ideology on the part of its author that has all the elements of early black transnationalism. As Floyd J. Miller describes in his introduction to the text, the narrative was written in 1859 while Delany was attempting to raise funds for a proposed African exploring venture. Delany's hopes for that venture were laid out clearly in his 1852 publication, *The Condition, Elevation, Emigration, and Destiny of the Colored People of the United States*. In this polemical work, Delaney laid out a history of the Negro condition in America that had some key components of a transnational and transatlantic discourse on black freedom. First, Delaney described the black slave and colored populations as *men* intensely desirous of a place in America:

> In our own country, the United States, there are *three million five hundred thousand slaves;* and we, the nominally free colored people, are *six hundred thousand* in number; estimating one-sixth to be men, we have *one hundred thousand* able bodied freemen, which will make a powerful auxiliary in any country to which we may become adopted. . . . We love our country, dearly love her, but she don't love us—she despises us, and bids us begone, driving us from her embraces.[20]

Delany cast the American nation as a woman necessarily left behind in the search to construct another motherland: "We shall not go where she desires us; but when we do go, whatever love we have for her, we shall love the country none the less that receives us as her adopted children." He also placed the Negro's history in the United States within a colonial history that begins with Christopher Columbus and the landing of the first Portuguese slave traders in Africa. By so doing, Delany tells the history of the development of American civilization from the colonial subject's point of view and situates the African American as himself being in a disenfranchised position similar to that of a colonial subject.[21]

*The Condition, Elevation, Emigration, and Destiny of the Colored People of the United States* was prompted by the specific context of the fugitive slave laws which, for Delaney in 1862, were essentially acts of the state preventing the free black American's desire for and movement toward citizenship. Hence, as Delany argued in the book's first chapter, African Americans represented "a nation within a nation," whose only recourse was emigration. In *The Condition, Elevation, Emigration, and Destiny of the Colored People of the United States* then, Delaney articulated a vision in which black subjects' lack of movement and the status of their citizenship within the nation were linked. Delany also believed that the immobility of the slave was connected to the futility of his desires: "Every [people] other than we, have at various periods of necessity, been a migratory people; and all when oppressed, shown a greater abhorrence of oppression, if not a greater love of liberty, than we. We cling to our oppressors as the objects of our love." Pitting emigration as an alternative to domestic racial uplift, Delany advocated that the free could do more for their enslaved brethren by leaving them behind to create a model of free black nationhood abroad: "It is true that our enslaved brethren are here, and we have been led to believe that it is necessary for us to remain, on that account. . . . We believe no such thing. We believe it to be the duty of the Free, to elevate themselves in the most speedy and effective manner possible."[22]

Delany then turned to imagining black movement and access to statehood beyond American borders, exploring the possibilities for nationhood in a variety of territories of color ranging from Liberia, "the Canadas," Central and South America and the West Indies, Nicaragua and "New Grenada," and ending finally with the vision of an African empire. This mental journey through the diaspora expressed Delany's interest in black statehood in the universal rather than the search for origins in the specific African motherland. In the early twentieth century, as black intellectuals were seeking to dress themselves in the Victorian attire of New Negro manliness, texts such as Delany's revealed the ideological traces of alternative conceptions of black manhood as a masculinity set in motion by a global rather than a national vision of the race's political future.

*Blake* shares a similar publication history with two other black empire narratives of the post-Reconstruction period, Sutton E. Griggs's *Imperium in Imperio* and Pauline Hopkins's *Of One Blood*. All three were popular black fictions meaning they were written specifically for a black audience and often appeared serially in popular black magazines. The fact that these narratives were part of a *popular* tradition in black literature is a crucial one for demonstrating that black internationalism, with its critique of existing world societies and imagining of future racial utopias, has been an indigenous part of the cultures of the black Atlantic throughout the course of modernity.[23]

*Imperium in Imperio* has a simpler storyline than *Blake*. It follows the lives of two main characters, the first again a "pure black" named Belton Piedmont, the second a "mulatto" named Bernard Belgrave, through the educational systems of the South and the North and finally into a black revolutionary organization, the Imperium in Imperio stationed in Texas. In this empire within an empire, an imaginary black government within the United States, we see the explicit attempt to define a New Negro subjectivity for the turn of a new century. As the narrator describes, "The cringing, fawning, sniffling, cowardly Negro which slavery had left, had disappeared, and a new Negro, self-respecting, fearless, and determined in the assertion of his rights, was at hand."[24] *Imperium in Imperio* repeats the gendered terms of black empire narratives both before and after it. Bernard and Belton can only claim their roles as black leaders after they have extricated themselves from their domestic relationships with black women.[25] Ultimately the friends split on the question of how to envision the relationship of their organization—this empire within an empire, a black government internal to the United States—to the greater United States.[26]

Blood, race, and the black family are the central metaphors in Hopkins's *Of One Blood; or, The Hidden Self.* The most Ethiopianist of the three narratives, Hopkins's story traces the male character Reuel Briggs's quest for identity. On an archeological expedition the hero discovers the descendants of a long-lost tribe of Ethiopians, who then identify Briggs as their long-awaited king, Ergamenes. After a series of twists and turns, Briggs accepts his destiny and marries the tribe's virgin queen, Candace. Throughout the narrative, the hint of Briggs's ancestry is revealed in the mystical powers he seems to possess. In *Of One Blood* this mysticism functions as a vehicle for transnational communication among the race. As Ai, one of the tribe's ruling council of sages, tells Briggs, "we can hold communion with the living though seas divide and distance is infinite."[27]

In *Of One Blood* we see some of the main elements of the Ethiopianist myth, the narrative of Ethiopia's redemption by her princely sons. The story's Ethiopianism is also reflected in Hopkins's creation of an alternative world history—one in which Africa, as Ethiopia, holds an esteemed place as a great ancient civilization among the many that made up a multiracial premodern world, a world before European imperialism. In addition, however, as Hazel Carby argues in her introduction, the search for the race's political freedom is metaphorically represented as a search for family, and the search for family becomes a metaphor for the search for diaspora.[28] Carby also argues that the establishment of an African genealogy represents a reaching out by African Americans to contemporary Africa, providing the basis for Hopkins's early Pan-Africanism.

Delany's, Griggs's, and Hopkins's stories provide examples of some of the main formal elements of narratives in the black empire genre. All three stories focus on black male leaders of the race who, in their quests and travels, trace a geography of the black world, both colonial and diasporic. These educated leaders, either as individuals or as the heads of black and internationalist organizations, negotiate a dialogic relationship with Euro-American imperial organizations and nation-states. These black heroes also become the vehicles for nineteenth-century black authors to articulate an Ethiopianist utopian romance of the race. Finally, in their domestic relationships with black women and women of color, these male heroes create the gendered terms of a black internationalist politics in each narrative.

But Delany's *Blake* stands out because in this text we also see the traces of a new type of black masculine hero. In the different roles he imagined for Blake throughout the story, Delany provided the seeds for a different vision of transnational black freedom. As the representative figure of black leadership, the character Blake maps out different political strategies and routes for the race. Mostly he seems to fit within the paradigm of the black liberator as Hill and Rasmussen have defined him, as he moves from being a rebel leader of slaves, much like a maroon, to a fugitive slave, and to the leader of the grand Council of the race. But as a Negro seaman on the African slaver *Vulture*, Blake shifts temporarily out of the paradigm of black leadership and toward a new paradigm of a mobile black male subjectivity, one which gains more prominence in the black transnational discourse on masculinity in the twentieth century. If the home of the race, represented most often by female characters,[29] is imagined as a deterritorialized imaginary and utopian space, how did some black intellectuals in the early twentieth century imagine a revolutionary black masculinity moving through that space?

In the figure of the Negro seaman, a mobile New Negro detached from territory, Delany described features of a new trope for a revolutionary black masculinity. As Delany himself described in *Blake*, not only was the modern black seaman essential to the imperialists' navigation of the colonial world, but he also had the means to seize control of the vehicles that moved through that world and use them for his own revolutionary ends. Like the Negro seamen in Briggs's imaginary black revolution, loyal not to a single national principle but to a larger, internationalist and racial ideal, this figure was both a mobile and easily mobilized representation of black male subjectivity. Negro seamen led the more nomadic lifestyle modeled by their pre-twentieth-century revolutionary predecessors on land, maroons and fugitive slaves. Existing between the mobility of the fugitive slave and the territorial stability of the national and working-class race leader, black seamen would play a central role in the twentieth-century fictions of black transnationalism. They seemed to offer an alternative to the type of black masculinity represented in earlier black empire narratives.

The trope of a black empire was an important literary phenomenon in black popular literature in the United States during the nineteenth century. Narratives such as Delany's, Griggs's, and Hopkins's established key features of the genre; they were immersed in historical debates about black self-governance that were specific to the United States but also shaped by a larger imperial context. They form part of a nineteenth-century tradition of Pan-Africanism that includes historical figures such as Henry Sylvester Williams and the founders of Liberia. They also mark the nineteenth-century transition from the world of the Old Negro in slavery to the world of the freed New Negro of the Reconstruction and post-Reconstruction periods.

The trope would carry these resonances into the twentieth century but with a significant difference. The vision of a black empire would be reshaped by a host of new internationalist ideologies emerging out of World War I and the social revolution in Russia. These ideologies would, in turn, create room for a black internationalism of the era, marked by the blending of discourses of a New Negro from the Harlem Renaissance with the transnational sensibilities of Caribbean colonial intellectuals. This shift was best expressed in narratives by two leading figures of the Harlem Renaissance, Du Bois and the journalist George Schuyler.

THE NEW WORLDLY NEGRO: TWO TALES OF BLACK EMPIRE
FROM THE EARLY TWENTIETH CENTURY

The black internationalism of the 1920s and 1930s consisted of both an anticolonial politics and an assertion of the rights of an international black population, seen in colonial terms as both multiracial and multinational, to secure their modern freedom in territory, self-determination, and statehood. These are the political ideals we see developed in Du Bois's and Schuyler's black empire narratives from the period.[30] Both *Dark Princess* and *Black Empire* embody key aspects of the black internationalist vision of the New Negro movement along with features of older nineteenth-century black empire narratives.[31] Like their nineteenth-century antecedents, each narrative follows the movements of a black male hero who traces a colonial and diasporic geography between the New World and the Old. In both narratives this hero also comes from the educated classes: Du Bois's hero Matthew Towns begins the narrative as a young medical student, and Carl Slater from Schuyler's *Black Empire* is an educated Columbia University graduate now working as a journalist for the *Harlem Blade*.

However, unlike Belton Piedmont, Bernard Belgrave, and Reuel Briggs, within the first few pages of the book, Matthew Towns is expelled from medical school because of his race, and Slater is forced to abandon his literary profession when he is kidnapped to become the secretary of Dr. Henry Belsidus's race organization. This exile of the black hero from the conventional nineteenth-century narrative of the educated male protagonist signals that in the early twentieth century the New Negro's political freedom was not as easily imagined through the avenue of education as was the case for his earlier post-Reconstruction counterpart. Thrust immediately out of this particular mode of black male subjectivity, the international travels of these two male heroes become the source of a different kind of education in globality and masculinity. In Du Bois's narrative, as in *Blake*, the story's different sections map different diasporic spaces. The politics of the main character, Matthew Towns, evolves with each shift in geography. This is made explicit in the titles for each section of the narrative, which reflect the different roles the black protagonist assumes throughout the story: "The Exile"; "The Pullman Porter"; "The Chicago Politician"; and "The Maharajah of Bwodpur."

Towns travels first as an exile to Berlin. The introduction of Europe, the imperial metropole, as a new site for the construction of a worldly black male subjectivity is one of the first signs of the features of a new internationalism, an internationalism grounded in the events of World War I and the Russian Revolution. In Europe Towns meets Princess Kautilya of India and her "international team of people of color who are forming an organization to resist Western imperialism."[32] Unlike Blake's Grand Council of slaves in Cuba and Bernard and Belton's Imperium in Imperio for black Americans in Texas, this Great Council of the Darker Peoples is now multinational and multiracial, a fact embodied by Kautilya herself.

The second sign of black internationalism appears in part II, the narrative of the Pullman porter. Here the black male hero is now situated in modern urban space among an urban proletariat, as Towns returns to the United States to secretly work for the Princess's organization as a Pullman porter. In this role Towns becomes the classic Harlem Renaissance figure for a modern New Negro subjectivity, the Pullman porter representing a new and revolutionary black mobility for modernity.

George Schuyler's hero Carl Slater follows a similar trajectory as that of Matthew Towns. Within the first few pages of *Black Empire* the protagonist, whom we are told also "worked as a Pullman porter every summer,"[33] meets and becomes fascinated with Dr. Henry Belsidus, "the ruthless, elegant genius who runs a vast, deadly, and secretive organization known to its members as the Black Internationale."[34] Here the utopian elements of the black empire narrative are taken to their most deadly extreme, as the race war imagined by Cyril V. Briggs eighteen years before is given its most elaborate articulation. In *Black Empire* the rhetoric of revolution, race freedom, and liberation is paired with militarism, violence, and the language of race supremacy—in Schuyler's words, "black genius."

As part I, "Black Internationale," progresses, Slater observes the development of Belsidus's plans to destroy "white world supremacy."[35] Like the mysticism of Hopkins's magical Ethiopians or the ray of fear possessed by Briggs's

Black Republic, Belsidus's Black Internationale has "science of which the white man has not dreamed in our possession."[36] The Black Internationale also has numerous maps, tracing a new geography of Black Internationale cells across the United States and the globe. Belsidus takes Slater on a journey back to the South that takes Blake's nineteenth-century organizer's tour of the United States to new organizational heights:

> Down through Maryland, Virginia, the Carolinas and the lower South we sped, visiting truck farms, poultry farms, plantations and other enterprises until we were well into central Texas. Each establishment was equipped with its well-appointed private airfield and usually located some distance from a city. Each was headed by some bright young colored man or woman.[37]

Slater describes this week of travel as "a dream, like traveling in some strange world." This is the new world of freedom and black self-determination available to the black imagination after World War I and the maps of Versailles. It encompasses a modern black organizational vision that incorporates more of the world than was possible in nineteenth-century black empire narratives. As plans for Belsidus's revolutionary war increase in intensity, the map of the Black Internationale broadens to include "two hundred other cells . . . in as many cities, and . . . our half hundred national cells in Europe, Asia, Africa, South America and the West Indies."[38]

Both *Dark Princess* and *Black Empire* are Ethiopianist, utopianist, racial romances. Both narratives include elements of early fantasy and science fiction and features of the older, nineteenth-century, Ethiopianist myth.[39] This fantasy element can be seen in Du Bois's opening epigram, a reference to the mythic Queen of Faerie that likens her to Princess Kautilya, the main heroine of *Dark Princess*. The futuristic elements of early science fiction are also present in the imaginative agricultural programs and technological gadgets of Schuyler's Black Internationale. Together these scientific elements introduce modern features into Schuyler's racial romance of a black empire.

But the racial romance also occurs in the more conventional form of the love story, as we saw in the contemporaneous piece, "The Ray of Fear." In the final part of *Dark Princess*, "The Maharajah of Bwodpur," fantasy, Ethiopianism, and racial romance come together as Du Bois charts the movements of the couple, Towns and Princess Kautilya, and their love story between the northern United States and India. Their romance plays out the tensions between domesticity and mobility that are embedded in the race's political movement between statehood and diaspora. Their journey culminates in Virginia in the birth of their multiracial son, the Maharajah of Bwodpur, who is then proclaimed the "Messenger and Messiah to all the Darker Worlds."[40] As with Hopkins's narrative, family and genealogy become metaphors through which to imagine the future diasporic state of the race. However, as embodied in this multiracial boy, in Du Bois's black international narrative that future imagines a multinational world order that goes beyond blackness.

The same is true in Schuyler's *Black Empire*, where the culmination of Dr. Belsidus's plans to found a black nation in Africa is mirrored in the consummation of a love affair between the hero Carl Slater and the main heroine, Patricia Givens. Givens is also described in terms evoking a multiracial, Afro-Asian hybridity, in Slater's words: "Facing me . . . sat the prettiest colored girl I've ever seen. She had the color of a pale Indian with the softness of feature of the Negro."[41] However, in this narrative Givens is unique in that, as head of the Black Internationale's air force, she has much more revolutionary agency than her female counterparts in other black empire tales. She has that key facility usually reserved for the male heroes of black empire narratives, as Hill and Rasmussen describe in their afterword: "As a pilot, she has mobility—the freedom to transport Slater and the story almost anywhere."[42]

As examples of black empire narratives of the early twentieth century, both *Dark Princess* and *Black Empire* more explicitly imagine the black international nation as multinational and multiracial—a representative of the broader colonial world, pitted against the world of empire. Their political geographies include both the colonies and the colonial populations in the metropoles, both the Old World and the New. Also, in each narrative, the international mobility of the New Negro hero is framed as an essential component of his modern masculinity. The New Negro's leadership of the race is more explicitly based on his ability to travel the spaces of the modern postwar world, those in Europe and the United States and those in "Africa, India, China, and the islands of the sea."[43] He provides a model of freedom through international movement rather than through education or literacy,[44] which becomes one of the defining characteristics of a black transnational discourse on masculinity.

Both of these modern internationalist racial romances represented the merging, in African American literature, of a black form of internationalism, combining anticolonialism and transnationalism with the discourse of a New Negro. Schuyler joined these two discourses explicitly in his 1938 essay, "The Rise of the Black Internationale."[45] The essay provides us with a fitting point of closure, for here Schuyler described a New Negro masculinity forged in the multiracial, multinational, and colonial spaces of the Black Internationale. This more worldly New Negro lived and worked in the international context of race war:

> The New Negro is here. . . . He is aware that the balance of power is shifting in the world and so are his cousins in Africa, in India, in Malaysia, the Caribbean and China. . . . He believes that to combat [the] White Internationale of oppression a Black Internationale of liberation is necessary. He sees and welcomes a community of interest of all colored peoples.[46]

Schuyler, like Du Bois, pits the worlds of color against the world of empire. What is also striking about these narratives of black internationalism when read together is the degree of similarity they share to each other and to their nineteenth-century antecedents. This is one reason why I argue that they, and other revolutionary racial romances like them, constitute their own canon in black American literature with its own defined and consistent formal features. In the case of Du Bois and Schuyler, this similarity is all the more striking since during this period these two authors occupied such opposite ends of the political spectrum.[47] While Du Bois's fairy-tale romance expressed his progressive utopian vision of a future world order,[48] Schuyler intended his stories to be parodies of that vision and its nationalist elements.[49] Their narratives demonstrate the ways in which the trope of a black empire was put to different political uses throughout the late nineteenth century and early twentieth.

Despite the multiracialism of their romances, however, both Schuyler and Du Bois ultimately turned to Africa for the resolution of their narrative quests for black freedom. Schuyler's *Black Empire* ends on the African continent where Belsidus leads the effort to build "an empire of black men and women working toward a cooperative civilization unexcelled in this world."[50] While *Dark Princess* itself ends ambiguously in the American South with the birth of an Indian prince who will represent "the darker world," Du Bois's own life journey would end in Ghana, a culmination prefigured in the end to his 1925 essay, "Worlds of Color":

My ship seeks Africa. Ten days we crept across the Atlantic; five days we sail to the Canaries. . . . slowly we creep down the coast. . . . Yonder behind the horizon is Cape Bojador whence in 1441 came the brown Moors and black Moors who through the slave trade built America and modern commerce. . . . And now we stand before Liberia; Liberia that is a little thing set upon a Hill; . . . but it represents to me the world. . . . [If] Liberia lives it will be because the World is reborn.[51]

Here Du Bois envisioned the African nation-state at the center of a new world order that could include black statehood, mobility, and political freedom for the New Negro. However, if in the prehistory of the modern New Negro Pan-Africanists from the late nineteenth century and the early twentieth were turning to Africa as the grounding continental metaphor for a modern Black Internationale, in the New World history I am telling the real life drama of black empire would be staged not in continental Africa but in the circum-atlantic Americas. Leaving behind the language of Africa as motherland, that black imperial politics would also leave little place for the symbolic woman of color.

Paul Robeson in *The Emperor Jones*. Courtesy George Eastman House.
Reprinted with permission of Joanna T. Steichen.

# CHAPTER 3

# Marcus Garvey, Black Emperor

The paradox of imperial official nationalism was that it inevitably brought what were increasingly thought of and written about as European "national histories" into the consciousness of the colonized.

—BENEDICT ANDERSON[1]

THERE IS A popular image of Paul Robeson in full costume as the Emperor Jones, the main character in the 1920 Eugene O'Neill play of the same name. The image is striking in its portrayal of black masculinity: Robeson turns a grim, brooding face, half in shadow, toward the camera, the shimmering gold brocade of his shoulder epaulet shining in stark contrast to the dark, rich, velvety tones of his imperial jacket.[2] Though visually stunning on its own merits, the image also resonates in its resemblance to another iconic image and figure of the period, that of the charismatic popular leader Marcus Garvey, parading through Harlem dressed in his own imperial robes.[3] The suggestion here that Garvey's movement was the object of dramatic parody in O'Neill's play is not so far-fetched, for the visual spectacle of Garveyism was legendary and particularly well suited for dramatic reinterpretation. As Du Bois, Garvey's contemporary, wryly described:

> When Mr. Garvey brought his cohorts to Madison Square Garden, clad in fancy costumes and with new songs and ceremonies, and when, ducking his dark head at the audience, he yelled, "We are going to Africa to tell England, France, and Belgium to get out of there," America sat up, listened, laughed, and said here at least is something new.[4]

In August 1920, the year of the first Universal Negro Improvement Association (UNIA) convention and just three months before the first production of *The Emperor Jones*, the black colonial "nations" that were excluded from the discussions at Versailles and the 1919 League of Nations sent their delegates to Garvey's convention in New York dressed in their own national costumes. These costumes got increasingly more militaristic as each year's congress occurred. As one *Negro World* reporter described, everyone "wore the same brilliant variegated color uniforms, indicative of their respective offices, with gold trimmings and gold sashes, and with swords, helmets and plumed hats . . . giving them a striking military appearance."[5] The image of Garvey himself, "clad in a field marshal's uniform of World War I vintage, plumed and gold-braided," is a popular one even today, bearing an iconographic status in both American and Caribbean popular culture. As Robert Hill has described, "Garvey dresse[d] the part of commander-in chief of his visionary African empire."[6] Another description from the *Negro World* in 1921 is especially stunning:

> The Provisional President of Africa wore a military hat, very pointed, tipped with white feathers, broadcloth trousers with gold stripe down the side, a Sam Browne belt crossing the shoulder and around the waist, gold epaulets, gold and red trimmings on the sleeves, gold sword and white gloves.[7]

The majesty of Garvey's first conference in 1920 and the symbolic ideal of empire it spectacularized was precisely what impressed members of his American audience, such as the playwright Eugene O'Neill. In O'Neill's description of Emperor Jones's imperial costume we see the real specter of Garvey as the popular black emperor:

> A light blue uniform coat, sprayed with brass buttons, heavy gold chevrons on his shoulders, gold braid on the collar, cuffs, etc. [The Emperor Jones's] pants are bright red with a light blue stripe down the side. Patent leather laced boots with brass spurs, and a belt with a long-barreled, pearl-handled revolver in a holster complete his make-up.[8]

"Yet," even O'Neill had to add, "there is something not altogether ridiculous about his grandeur. He has a way of carrying it off." Here O'Neill captured in a sentence the mysterious charismatic appeal of Garvey and his mass movement for an American national audience, as he organized black subjects not only in the United States and the Caribbean but across the diaspora.

The connections that can be made between *The Emperor Jones* and Marcus Garvey continue. Marcus Garvey's emergence as a national cultural figure and political leader in the United States occurred in the same year of the play's first production.[9] The play, set on "an island in the West Indies,"[10] would have provoked audience awareness of the rise of the self-fashioned Caribbean black imperial ruler, whose movement was at the peak of its American prominence and strength in 1920. However, in O'Neill's comic tragedy of an African American male assuming the mantle of emperor, the playwright also pointed to the postwar decline of the European empires, both symbolically and politically, in his description of the island's "form of native government" as temporary: "for the time being, an Empire." Additionally, while indicating the end of European imperialism he pointed to the potential for a new form of empire in his description of the island "as yet not self-determined by White Marines."[11] Here O'Neill referenced the United States's own imperial presence in the Caribbean, with her recent invasion of Haiti in 1915.[12]

In addition to these various meanings, there is a fourth layer of significance to be found in the figure of the main protagonist himself. In the incongruous figure of the black emperor, O'Neill's play also effectively made fun of the idea of black self-determination.[13] O'Neill's initial description of the main character Brutus Jones, whose failure at sovereignty and self-government is ultimately a fitting punishment for his "'igh an' mighty airs,"[14] was a striking combination of discourses of manliness and masculinity, with similarities to descriptions of the New Negro male also being propounded by black intellectuals at the time: "Jones. . . . is a tall, powerfully built, full-blooded negro of middle age. His features are typically negroid, yet there is something decidedly distinctive about his face—an underlying strength of will, a hardy, self-reliant confidence in himself that inspires respect."[15] While in black empire narratives the journeys of the revolutionary male protagonists allowed them to develop and even fulfill these and other liberated features of a modern black masculinity—the freedom to move and the fulfillment of their desire for statehood—in O'Neill's play each stage in Jones's journey through the island signifies his return to a more primitive and savage state of nature. As Jones devolves from railway porter, to runaway convict, to transatlantic African slave, his migrations of the subject entail diminishing forms of black masculine freedom and mobility. Instead of culminating in a vision of the sovereign black self with a new diasporic consciousness, Emperor Jones's movements produce an image of the modern black subject as divided in a choice between civilization or savagery.

In her account of gender formation in the United States at the turn of the century, Gail Bederman argues that there is a history to the association of certain forms of masculinity with civilization on one hand and savagery on the other. Civilized manly virtues were specifically connected to imperialism through Theodore Roosevelt's sense of himself as being able, as a white man, to adopt a form of masculine savagery abroad in confrontation with the inherent savagery of men of other races and retain the essential characteristics of civilized manliness necessary for government at home. For black men, while they could be masculine they could never be manly, as Bederman demonstrates in her reading of the boxing match between Jim Jeffries and Jack Johnson in 1910. Hazel Carby also shows how their attempts to be manly, to demonstrate a civilized form of manhood, required a focus on gender construction and invention, particularly through dress.

As Bederman also describes, by the time of the Jeffries-Johnson match, American popular culture had begun to absorb some of the racialized terms that constituted an imperialist discourse of American masculinity. The match was seen as one in which "manly white civilization" battled "unmanly swarthy barbarism," or as she says elsewhere, "the manly civilized heir to Shakespeare" encountered "a masculine modern-day savage."[16] Despite the anxiety produced by Jeffries getting trounced, or maybe because of it, Bederman's account ends in 1917 with the celebration of white masculine savagery domestically in popular cultural forms, such as Edgar Rice Burroughs's *Tarzan of the Apes*, a story with the classic narrative formula of the white man "gone native," followed in 1920 by Rudolph Valentino's portrayal of "primitive Arab" masculinity in *The Sheik*.[17] Carby takes Bederman's account one step further to argue that even the image of the black masculine savage was being contained culturally by the mid-1920s. In Nickolas Muray's nude photographs of Paul Robeson in 1925, the black male body represented a tamed Americanism and a homoerotic modernist fascination with the primitive black masculine.[18] In Carby's account, the narrative of white civilization becomes by the 1920s a narrative of American national belonging and nationhood, and it is in this modern context that the black masculine savage must be assimilated to modernity.[19]

In *The Emperor Jones* Eugene O'Neill, the modern American heir to Shakespeare, created his own celebration of masculine savagery through the character of Brutus Jones. In the figure of the black emperor we see, on one hand, the white playwright giving voice to Caliban, the black colonial subject and savage slave. But as a burlesque of black attempts at self-government, the character Emperor Jones also represented the black male subject in the trappings and costumes of civilization, the black and colonial savage aspiring to a civilized imperialism.

The figure Robeson cut in his portrayal of the black emperor inspired just the type of fear of masculine savagery and regression that civilization hopefully tamed and ensured against. Walter White dramatically described a particular performance of the play in New York in an essay included in Locke's 1925 *New Negro* anthology:

> For years I had nourished the conceit that nothing in or of the theatre could thrill me. . . . But the chills that chased each other up and down my spine . . . [at] the sympathetic terror evoked by Paul Robeson as he fled blindly through the impenetrable forest of the 'West Indian island not yet self-determined by white marines.'
>
> Nor was I alone. When, after remaining in darkness from the second through the eighth and final scene, the house was flooded with light, a concerted sigh of relief welled up from all over the theater. With real joy we heard the reassuring roar of taxicabs and muffled street noises of Greenwich Village and knew we were safe in New York. Wave after wave of applause, almost hysterical with relief, brought Paul Robeson time and time again before the curtain to receive the acclaim his art had merited.[20]

Not surprisingly, in *The Emperor Jones* black masculinity ultimately fails to contain its innate savagery, and the particular feature that serves as the visual marker for the black emperor's cultural reversion is his costume. By the end of the play Brutus Jones's impressive imperial uniform has been replaced by a prehistoric loincloth: "His pants have been so torn away that what is left of them is no better than a breech cloth."[21]

I begin the story of Garvey's years in the United States by referring to O'Neill's drama of black empire for a number of reasons. One could argue that in the context of both the geopolitics and the cultural discourses of masculinity shaping the period, Garvey put the black emperor back in his robes and used the language of civilization to assert not just the Negro's manliness but his stateliness—his deserving of the rights and privileges of modern nationalism, world civilization in all its new and modern political forms. Garvey drew on a racialized civilizational rhetoric in his constructions of an African past, but he did so more self-consciously than critics gave him credit for. He also did so *not* in the service of creating a black nationalist narrative but rather in the service of performing a *global* sense of the race, a task that had never been performed before for a mass and diasporic audience. It is in this sense that Garvey plays such a unique and special role as a starting point for this book.

By literally putting the spectacle of black statehood *in motion* across the diaspora, Garvey contributed in material ways to the development of a modern black global consciousness. In this sense he drew on a transatlantic legacy that has rarely been seen as a context in which to place both his domestic spectacles and his maritime adventures.[22] Like O'Neill's *The Emperor Jones*, Garvey used techniques of dramatic spectacle to reach a popular audience both in the United States and throughout the Caribbean. His were specifically gendered performances, related to the special needs of his transnational audience.

While the discourse of civilization establishes a dichotomy in humanity between the culturally developed and the primitive, it also strives to tell a global story, a "master" narrative that makes claims to encompass the history of the entire planet and its peoples. Marcus Garvey dared to ask if the black savage could also make claims to a globalizing, civilizational story. As he drew on a civilizational race rhetoric as a way of capturing the global condition of the race, he also mirrored for the imperial world the racial and masculinist features of their own imperial and state ideologies.

Here I rely on the discussions of cultural nationalism in the work of Benedict Anderson and Anne McClintock and then deviate from their analyses in one key respect. Anderson, in his arguments concerning the development of nationalism, makes specific claims about the formation of colonial nationalisms and intelligentsia that provide an interesting backdrop for tracing Garvey's trajectory from the island colony of his birth, Jamaica, to the United States. Anne McClintock has provided an important feminist revision of Anderson's argument by asserting that "all nationalisms are gendered," a concession rarely found in the work of male scholars of nationalism.[23] McClintock also argues that gender is most evident in nationalism in the forms of popular spectacles that mobilize mass audiences. These are the popular audiences who, unlike Anderson's literate European masses or the colonial intelligentsia, may not be involved in everyday print culture.

As McClintock further describes, forms of visual spectacle lay at the heart of modern expressions of nationalism. Her focus on the ways nationalisms have been not just imagined but performed lead her to an important modification of Anderson's construction of print as the medium through which nationalism spread throughout both the Americas and Europe. In her discussion of nationalism as fetish spectacle McClintock argues instead that

> national collectivity is experienced preeminently through spectacle. Here I depart from Anderson. . . . Indeed, the singular power of nationalism since the late nineteenth century, I suggest, has been its capacity to organize a sense of popular, collective unity through the management of mass national *commodity spectacle*.[24]

By "commodity spectacle" McClintock means to invoke the myriad fetish objects of modern nationalism such as flags and uniforms, organized in various events of collective display such as military displays and mass rallies. In his play O'Neill took these symbols of black self-determination—flags, anthems, uniforms and costumes—and mimicked them in his construction of the black imperial majesty of the Emperor Jones. But Garvey's parades and conventions used similar techniques to create a new and "theatrical performance of invented community" for a distinctively shaped transnational black audience.[25]

McClintock's focus not so much on the intellectuals but on the popular audience allows her to access those modern subjects whose nationalistic desires and sentiments are focused through a specific gendered performance of the state in spectacle. However, both Anderson and McClintock still take as their starting premise that these popular nationalistic spectacles are attempts to imagine *national* communities, communities that can then be absorbed within future territorial nation-states. This chapter argues, in contradistinction to those who focus on Marcus Garvey's nationalism, that even though his politics have conventionally been defined as black nationalist, the utopianism of his vision of a future black state is not merely a failure in his political vision or evidence of his naiveté. Rather, the feature that distinguishes his mass movement from national movements also changes its shape and character. In Garveyism we see a *global* rather than a *national* imaginary. The power of the imaginary black emperor of a West Indian isle was precisely that he had the potential to step outside of the national terms in which black racial identity could be understood in the United States. O'Neill's Emperor Jones captured the imagination of black actors and audiences during the Harlem Renaissance because his was a character that strayed beyond the limits of stock Negro types, beyond the locale of the regional stock character.[26]

The true tragedy of the black emperor was precisely that he had the power to evoke urges and desires for black self-determination that originated outside of and stepped beyond the nation, diasporic desires that cut across an American nationalist consciousness. Even more dangerously, his transnationalism spoke most powerfully to a specific segment of the black American population, the group least likely to find social acceptance and the rights of full citizenship in America and, therefore, the group least interested in their cultural Americanization, the black working poor.[27]

Garvey would take the black masculinity of the New Negro to new heights in the figure he cut as the real-life black emperor, parading throughout the streets of Harlem and on the docks of port cities throughout the black New World. Garveyism, as a mass movement, had a fundamentally global imaginary, shaped by Garvey's understanding of the race as a global entity. Through him we may even go so far as to say that blackness itself, in its multiplicity, multinationality, and hybridity, was never strictly national. Garvey's performances of a black nationality were always diasporic, constituted out of the race's desire for a future black nation. Those performances would then require both the invention of a cohesive race and a vision of that imagined community's potential for future statehood.

It is in this narrative and global vision of the race that the desire for the state can be seen as fetishistic, with the state itself becoming a fetish, symbolized in the image of the masculine, phallocentric male sovereign. Elsewhere in her essay McClintock confirms the argument that women are usually represented as the bearers of nationalism without agency. McClintock, referencing Homi Bhabha's dismissal of the woman of color in his discussion of the specific context of black nationalist movements, observes that in such movements the woman of color often becomes the figure for an excess that cannot be contained in the political trajectory of a liberation movement that ultimately leads to statehood. This latter form of "anticipatory nationalism," premised on a "premature utopianism" that "grabs instinctively for a future,

82   THE WORLD WAR I MOMENT

projecting itself by an act of will or imagination beyond the compromised political structures of the present," is also still a territorial politics in which colonial nationalists can imagine reclaiming actual territory from the colonizer for a future colonial nation-state. McClintock argues that only one form of nationalist agency is operative: "the privileged national agents are urban, male, vanguardist . . . violent . . . progressive."[28]

What happens when there is no territory in which to ground one's vision of an imagined community? When, without the consolidating end goal and focus provided by a territorially grounded national politics, one is left with "an altogether more open-ended and strategically difficult view of national agency [where] agency is multiple rather than unitary, unpredictable rather than immanent. . . . There is no preordained rendezvous with victory; no single, undivided national subject . . . agency is heterogenous."[29] This was the diasporic terrain from which Garvey attempted to draw his mass of followers. Aware of geopolitical realities and the fact that the Treaty of Versailles was leaving the modern black subject without territory in a no-man's-land after the war, Garvey's attempts to create an imagined community drew on the multiplicity of the diaspora to create a global consciousness of the race. Instead of nationality Garvey imagined a different sense of political community, a race united not by territory but by its own history making, its movement as a hybrid diasporic civilization crisscrossing multiple territories, with the special qualities of the peoples of continental Africa as its point of origin.

In Garvey's black transnational versus national imaginary, where not just the community but the state itself is still only virtual and imagined, the black state becomes a fetish, the object of desire. As the black emperor Garvey constructed himself as the embodiment of state fetishism, and blackness, the special racial features that tied the future imagined state to a historical civilization, took on its own special, magical qualities. In Garveyism the suppressed woman of color becomes the repressed figure for the excess, the multiplicity, hybridity, and multinationality inherent in transnational blackness that Garvey displayed in his UNIA parades. These were the qualities he then subordinated to a fetishistic performance of blackness as the black emperor, his goal to maintain a singular vision of the heterogeneous race, representable in the lone figure of the black sovereign. It is this quality—what some have called nationalistic and what Paul Gilroy has more recently called fascistic, the fetishization of an imaginary black state and its historically derived racial features—

that Garvey performed in the figure of the black sovereign. In Garvey's transnational discourse the black state became a fetish that was never realizable but always metonymically available in the figure of the black emperor.

Marcus Garvey was the product of a century and a half history of nationalism, revolution, and empire spreading from Europe across the globe to the colonial world. Hence, his model of the self-determined black state was a complex articulation of multiple and contradictory internationalisms. It was revolutionary and democratic in its imagination of a free, self-governing black proletariat, one that included the masses of the entire worldwide colonial community. It was imperial in its attachment to the gendered hierarchies and patriarchal logic of racial nationalism and limited in its fetishistic use of race thinking as the philosophy undergirding a masculine vision of multinational and multiracial self-government. To the degree that he was invested in the ideal of state sovereignty, the black emperor adopted and mimicked the visual politics of imperialism and its racial languages, embodying the search for black freedom in statehood in a masculine, militaristic, and majestic vision of representative black leadership.

Just before Garvey arrived in the United States in 1916, he reflected on the movement for black freedom in the English-speaking Caribbean. His essays, including one entitled "The British West Indies in the Mirror of Civilization: History Making by Colonial Negroes," set the stage for his political activities in the United States. On the eve of his departure it was clear that Garvey had imbibed, as much as anyone else, the new nationalist languages of freedom sweeping over the European empires in the context of World War I. As he began that piece: "In these days when democracy is spreading itself over the British Empire, and the peoples under the rule of the Union Jack are freeing themselves from hereditary lordship . . . it should not be amiss to recount the condition of affairs in the British West Indies."[30] Here Garvey confronted imperial authority with a demand for reform of colonial rule. This prenationalist consciousness would later blossom across the Caribbean into the movement for national independence and self-governance.

In the essays Garvey revealed his own formation as a young colonial intellectual, coming to political consciousness precisely at the moment of the transition in Europe from empires to nation-states. This liminal period is reflected in Garvey's own language, in a letter he wrote to the secretary of state for the colonies in 1914:

> We the members of the Universal Negro Improvement and Conservation Association and African Communities League . . . being mindful of the *great protecting and civilizing influence of the English nation and people*, of whom we are subjects, and their justice to all . . . their Negro Subjects scattered all over the world, hereby beg to express our loyalty and devotion to His Majesty the King, and Empire and our sympathy with those of the people who are in any way grieved and in difficulty in this time of National trouble.[31]

Garvey's tone here reveals a discursive uncertainty as to the status of both the empire and the colony in this the first year of the war. While he invokes the "protecting and civilizing influence" of empire, he also addresses the metropolitan state as that of the "English nation and people." Black colonials are clearly not citizens of this burgeoning European nation-state, nor even "English people," but imperial Subjects, "scattered all over the world" as opposed to being bound in any defined national territory. While Garvey's appeal is here made to the King of the Empire, he also recognizes the war as ushering in a period of "National trouble" for the European metropolitan state.

By the time Garvey was ready to migrate to the United States, his political language and perspective were clearer. He saw himself less as speaking to the empires on the behalf of colonials who were merely their Negro Subjects and turned his attentions to those colonials themselves, reminding them of the "*national* interest of the downtrodden race of which you are a member."[32] Garvey's shift in language and orientation can be attributed to his discovery, through travel, of the denationalized and therefore disfranchised status of black subjects as a global population. The impact of his travels must be understood as placing him, as a young intellectual representing the colonial world, within the politics of nationalism shaping global discussions of modern political identity during this period.

Marcus Garvey was a product of imperial official nationalism in the West Indies. As a printer, he was one of the young colonial intelligentsia positioned right at the intersection of print culture, vernacular nationalism, and official nationalism that Benedict Anderson has described.[33] As Amy Jacques Garvey recounted: "At fifteen young Marcus was sent to learn printing at his god-father Burrows' shop. There was a back room at the shop containing books, magazines, and old newspapers, where he could read and think deeply."[34] Here in this printing shop Garvey was privy to two types of education. In the "back room" he would read about the cultures of the Western empires, while up front he would listen to "Mr. Burrows' old cronies and friends . . . exchange news and reminisce about the old slave days, plantation stories and slave rebellions" of black Atlantic history.[35]

Through print culture Garvey discovered the writings of Dr. Robert Love, a black man from Nassau who published the Jamaican *Advocate*. This Carib-bean print journalist "was a landed proprietor who qualified for the 'better class' category" of Jamaicans, the class of articulate, traditional, colonial gen-tleman intellectuals whom Belinda Edmondson has described as so central to Caribbean nationalist politics. Love saw as his mission the voicing of the vernacular nationalist sentiments of the "submerged 'lower class.'" It was one of Love's editorials that first hinted at the burgeoning presence of a popular nationalism in the West Indies.[36]

Print continued to play a central role in Garvey's early politicization. In 1907, at age eighteen, Garvey went to Kingston, the capital, and got a job at Benjamin's printery. There he got involved in a failed Printer's Union strike that left him disturbed by the working conditions of blacks in the colonies. In 1909 he traveled to Costa Rica and once again observed the exploitative conditions and discriminatory treatment of black workers:

> In all these Spanish-speaking republics were West Indian workers who had left their overpopulated islands because of unemployment and pov-erty to work on the fruit farms of Guatemala, Costa Rica, and Bocas-del-Toro and in the mines of South America. They had built the Panama Canal, but in the canal zone they were classified as 'silver employees' and given less pay than white men who were called 'gold employees.'[37]

In all these republics Garvey attempted to organize the workers and called on the British consul to protect them. But, "his protest to the British consul was answered with bureaucratic indifference. He was learning his first lesson about the arrogant stubbornness of a European colonial power."[38] As Amy Jacques Garvey also described, "Invariably he was told that the Consul was there to see after the interests of His Majesty's government and did not intend to disrupt friendly relations with these republics because of West Indian migrants."[39] Garvey's only means of further communication was to reach the local community and officials through print: "Whenever he could Garvey published a little paper to voice the migrants' feelings and views. In Costa Rica it was called *La Nacionale*, in Panama *La Prensa*."[40]

When he returned to Jamaica in 1910 Garvey joined the National Club, a nationalist organization that published a fortnightly called *Our Own* and took part in local elections. This club provided him with his first experience of both newspaper publishing and political campaigning. In these years Garvey resembled nothing less than the young colonial intellectual coming to political and nationalist consciousness through print-culture and language. As a fellow club member would describe him, "He was fiercely proud of being black. He carried a pocket dictionary with him and said he studied three or four words daily, and in his room he would write a paragraph or two using these words."[41]

However, in Anderson's analysis of the transformation of the colonial state into the nation-state, anticolonial rebellion was generated from the fact that imperial official nationalism "circumscribed the ascent of creole functionaries" to the geographical and caste borders of the colony.[42] As Anderson describes, though "a young brown or black Englishman came to receive some education or training in the metropole . . . that was typically the last time he made this bureaucratic pilgrimage."[43] Colonial nationalism developed both from the colonial intellectual's sense of his own limited movement and also from his encounters with other, similarly situated, bicultural traveling companions within the nation, with whom he came to feel a growing sense of commonality and community.

The crucial difference between Marcus Garvey's trajectory and that of the typical colonial intelligentsia was precisely that Garvey's colonial travels were *not* circumscribed to his own island only. He traveled also throughout Central America, and he made this trip throughout another part of the colonial world *before* he went to the metropole. By the time of his trip to London, Garvey had already begun the process of forming multiple identifications with other colonial subjects beyond his own island's burgeoning sense of nationality. He had already begun to identify with the trials of a *globally* imagined black community. This transnational community of black, migrant, proletarianized colonials would later serve as his primary political constituency. As Amy Jacques

Garvey attested: "West Indians working in foreign lands . . . These people were an asset. . . . They formed the nucleus of the soon-to-be organized Universal Negro Improvement Association."[44]

In England Garvey would then make an additional crucial connection that would place him even further on the path to a black transnational politics. While in the metropole Garvey "worked around the docks of London, Cardiff and Liverpool and gained a wealth of information from African and West Indian seamen. As he told them, they told him, and all concluded that suffering was indeed the common lot of the race, no matter where they lived."[45] Given these experiences of migration Garvey, the "energetic-minded young colonial" returned to Jamaica with a somewhat different and more ambitious vision than when he had left home.[46]

In July 1914, three months before the breakout of World War I, Garvey organized the UNIA within five days. His motivation was directly related to his travels abroad, as he described in his autobiographical writings years later. When Garvey first left Jamaica in 1907 to travel through the Spanish-speaking republics, migration was merely his individual response to racial discrimination and colonialism in Jamaica. As he described, "At the age of 18 I started to take interest in public affairs. The politics of my country so disgusted me that I started to travel, in which course I visited several countries in South and Central America and in Europe."[47] Garvey's encounters with West Indian workers suffering under exploitative conditions soon gave him a more collective and global understanding of the racial politics of colonialism. It was his awareness of worldwide prejudice against blacks, an awareness created through travel, that then inspired him to organize the UNIA upon his return to Jamaica: "From early youth I discovered that there was prejudice against me because of my colour, a prejudice that was extended to other members of my race. This annoyed me and helped to inspire me to create sentiment that would act favorably to the black man."[48]

The UNIA was an organization with both a nationalist and a transnationalist conception of itself, evident at the outset in its founding goals—to unite "all the Negro peoples of the world into one great body and to establish a country and government absolutely their own." This dual politics—the creation of one, territorially bound, "country and government" to unite a worldwide, stateless and mobile, community of "Negro peoples"—was also evidenced by Garvey's own appointment as both the organization's "President" and its "Traveling Commissioner."[49]

Had things developed differently, Marcus Garvey could have had a different influence on the history of black nationalism once he returned to Jamaica in 1914. His activities in the island of his birth after his time in England fit neatly into the paths which led many a colony into the movement for national independence. However, Garvey deviated from the path taken by his cohorts in the colonial intelligentsia and began to draw on the experiences of other diasporic communities in constructing his own politics for the race. Upon his return to Jamaica Garvey called for the replacement of the colonial system of education with "African American style" colleges inspired by Booker T. Washington's Tuskegee Institute. Garvey was sharply criticized by his peers for this idea, "the more articulate circles" of Jamaican intellectual and political society whom Garvey would also describe as "Men and women as black as I and even more so, [who] had believed themselves white under the West Indian order of society."[50] Armed with the knowledge of international black working conditions gained from his travels throughout Central America and England and drawn to the developing racial ideologies of the New Negro in the United States, Garvey returned to Jamaica only to find that his racialized and politicized sense of the world gained from his travels abroad was unpopular: "I was simply an impossible man to use openly the term 'negro.'" It was at this point that Garvey made a historical decision: "I had to decide whether to please my friends and be one of the 'black-whites' of Jamaica, and be reasonably prosperous, or come out openly, and help improve and protect the integrity of the black millions, and suffer. I decided to do the latter."[51] That decision would ultimately lead to his migration to the United States.

As he would describe in a pamphlet distributed shortly before he embarked for America, *A Talk with Afro-West Indians: The Negro Race and Its Problems*: "For the last ten years I have given my time to the study of the condition of the Negro, here, there, and everywhere, and I have come to realize that he is still the object of degradation and pity the world over, in the sense that he has no status socially, nationally or commercially."[52] Unlike other colonial intellectuals, Garvey moved away from understanding black subjectivity and the possibilities for black freedom and representation in the West Indies in purely nationalist terms. In "The British West Indies in the Mirror of Civilization," he would take this diasporic political consciousness even further, reimagining a potential Caribbean state. There he went beyond the question of Island government to envision a future Caribbean federation: "There have been several movements to federate the British West Indian Islands, but owing to parochial feelings nothing definite has been achieved. Ere long this change is sure to come about because the people of these islands are all one."[53] Of course the seed of the metaphor of empire, as Garvey's chosen way of enacting the transnational spirit of that particular vision of black political community, was also present in these pre-American essays, as Robert Hill has also observed:

> Such, at that time, was Garvey's vision of the future—"unmolested liberty" for the British West Indies, the uniting of a scattered and subjected race through a federal grouping of the various Islands on the foundation of which would in time be established a Black West Indian "Empire." The vision was in all respects a West Indian vision. It would still have some considerable distance to travel before it transformed itself into a vision of a free and sovereign "African Empire."[54]

Garvey's vision had two components that would reappear in the discourse of Caribbean transnationals over the course of the twentieth century, first the notion that Caribbean people would play a crucial role in uniting the black diaspora, and second that the end result of their work would be a black empire, "a civilized imperialism that would meet with the approval of established ideals."[55]

Garvey's movement away from that specific Caribbean vision of federation led him to his fascination with a form of territorial nationalism located in Africa that developed during and as the partial result of his travels and stay in the United States. The geopolitical struggle over colonial Africa after World War I gave Garveyism and other movements for black freedom such as Cyril Briggs's a real-life focus and a worldly enemy against whom to wage their battle in the race war against imperialism, the imperialists at Versailles. The fight for Africa's independence during the immediate postwar years and during Garvey's first years in the United States gave his worldwide movement a territorial focus. By the time of his historic first UNIA International Convention of the Negro Peoples of the World at Madison Square Garden in 1920, the cry "Africa for the Africans, those at home and those abroad," would rally both West Indian immigrants and displaced African American migrants from the South.

An image from the essay Garvey wrote on the eve of his departure for the United States in 1913, the mirror of civilization, serves as a useful metaphor for capturing his and other black subjects' desires to see the race's agency and sovereignty reflected in world history. This would require an act of history making, constructing history on one's own terms. What Garvey saw in the mirror of civilization was a mobile and free black masculine subject, dressed in the military robes of black conquest and endowed with a highly masculinized sense of leadership. At a grander level, he saw in premodern African civilization a way to represent the mobility and glory of the race over a broad historical period. That narrative used languages fundamental to an understanding of empire as constitutively hybrid, as interacting and incorporating, through cultural and military conquest and domination, other cultures, races, and worldviews. In imagining the movements of an African imperial civilization along these lines, Garvey then also reflected back to the European empires a vision of themselves as also a hybrid racial formation.

In his philosophy of African fundamentalism Garvey made the racial languages of empire the focus; he then made these languages visible and manifest by embodying them in his performances. Those spectacles included gendered and patriarchal hierarchies that are often referenced and are now beginning to be explored in more historical depth in Garvey scholarship. My focus is on demonstrating the particularly gendered and fetishistic power of the male sovereign that Garvey physically embodied and displayed. His representation of black masculinity is itself a crucial indicator of the masculine politics of statehood that would also require the subordination of black women both within the Garvey leadership and within the broader visual culture of the movement at large.

Garvey's own metaphor of the mirror of civilization is useful for capturing the reflective nature of his imperial ideology. Although his performances were more self-reflective and ironic caricatures of empire than he is sometimes given credit for, in African fundamentalism, Garvey's philosophy of blackness and empire, we see his fetishization of racial ideologies of white supremacy. If Garvey's philosophy of African fundamentalism was a more straightforward and less self-conscious reflection of the racial ideologies of modern imperial discourses of nationhood, what they reflected was the fetishism of race in European imperial discourse.

With African fundamentalism Garvey constructed a prehistory to black statecraft that reflected his imperial desires and his own seduction by European raciology. Unlike Cyril Briggs's Black Republic in "The Ray of Fear," Garvey's model of the free black state originated not in social revolution but in imperial and political conquest. In essays with titles such as, "Nothing Must Kill the Empire Urge," Garvey asserted the dominance of empire as a model and ideal for black self-determined identity. African fundamentalism was essentially a philosophy of black empire that looked consciously to a past imperial paradise, rather than a future socialist utopia, for its model of a diasporic blackness.

Its reversal of imperial discourse involved envisioning a premodern and preimperial past in which the black diaspora itself, usually seen as scattered by imperialism and slavery, was now the product of a coherent, *black* imperial urge for conquest.

Garvey's formulation of the worldly New Negro and his turn away from the Old Negro of slavery required the construction of a new history of the imperial African homeland:

> So while Europe and Asia lagged behind . . . Africa steadily took her growth upwards . . . The black man started to build, and succeeded in building the first civilization the world ever saw, and by contact and by natural prowess and conquest he came in contact with the peoples of the other countries, and imposed their morality upon them, so that they found it a grand and glorious opportunity to be in companionship with the Ethiopians.[56]

In Garvey's imperial fiction the black diaspora was created out of the imposition of Ethiopian "morality" and color on the rest of the world. In Garvey's version of the self-determined New World Negro, the racial legacy and the imperial legacy were one and the same: "Look to the colours of the Race; look to the colours of the Negro for your inspiration; look to the colours of that great Empire of Ethiopia that is now scattered all over the world."[57] African fundamentalism erased the disempowering history of European imperialism and its role in the formation of black subjectivity. It promoted instead a historical black empire that once possessed political structure and self-determination. Also, Garvey's romantic fictions of the Ethiopian past gave black mobility a new source and meaning. Again, instead of the narrative of the race scattered by slavery and forced movement, in Garvey's black empire narrative the black diaspora was created from the self-conscious movement, upward and outward, of premodern black migrations and black civilization. That narrative, emphasizing the creation of multiple colors of Ethiopia, also emphasized the processes of hybridization that also constitute imperial histories.

In *Against Race*, Paul Gilroy strenuously argues that we see Marcus Garvey's movement, this dictatorship of the black proletariat, as part of a tradition of "black fascism."[58] Gilroy quotes C. L. R. James who, in 1938, compared Garvey to Hitler, saying "all the things that Hitler was to do so well later, Marcus Garvey was doing in 1920 and 1921." These included the fetishistic elements of nationalist spectacle identified by McClintock, as James continued to describe: "[Garvey] organized storm troopers, who marched, uniformed, in his parades, and gave colour to his meetings."[59] As further described by Gilroy, Garveyism also included a belief in "land: a sovereign territory, a national homeland to legitimate their aspirations" and a form of race-thinking exacerbated by class tensions within the imagined black community. Fleshing out this last feature of black fascism Gilroy explains, "In the urban centers where diasporic populations often live. . . . [w]ith the advent of upward and outward mobility, rich and poor no longer live in the same communities. . . . Paradoxically, this divergence in black experience and history has been accompanied by a new emphasis on race."[60] With global and domestic forms of capitalist integration providing social and physical mobility for some members of the Caribbean and African American middle classes, for the black working poor race can become a language in which to articulate their desire for freedom and movement. With their awareness of their lack of access to certain privileges of nationality and full economic citizenship, such as social mobility and integration, comes an increased color or race consciousness. This fetishism of race compensates for the lack of full access to nationality and its concomitant privileges.

However, despite its militancy and race politics, Garvey's movement is not only comprehensible through the lens of black racial nationalisms. Rather, there are further insights to be gained from thinking about Garvey as creating a transnational imaginary. Specifically, Garvey's movement forces us to think about how some modern forms of black nationalism, those without any real hope of political realization in the territorial form of a national state, spring from and then generate further fetishistic desires for statehood and nationality, spurred by colonial subjects' sense of their lack of access to precisely those institutions.

In the immediate postwar era, black subjects were as eager to benefit from the securities and promises of nationhood as any other modern subjects.[61] Garvey's vision of the black empire was itself a product of imperial official nationalism, the result of his access to "models of nation, nation-ness, and nationalism distilled from the turbulent, chaotic experiences of more than a century of American and European history."[62] This access often came from his colonial education, as he described it: "He [the white man] will have a hard time bluffing this Marcus Garvey who has been through the same schools he has been through, who has shouldered with him in college and university, who has met him on the same campus, and imbibed every idea from Socrates and Plato, to Lloyd George and Woodrow Wilson."[63] One of these ideas he copied was the racial ideology of European imperialism: "The white race has a system, a method, a code of ethics laid down for the white child to go by, a philosophy, a set Creed to guide its life."[64] Garvey had a great deal of respect for this "system," race as a systematic ideology facilitating world conquest: "It was complimentary to the white man to have done what he did, exercising prowess in the law of monopoly . . . I do hope that this will be an inspiration to some black man or woman to some black boy or girl to go through the world accomplishing something grand and great as the white man is now doing."[65] The creed of African fundamentalism as the philosophy of blackness meant, similarly, "to serve as a guide to the Negro Peoples of the World."[66]

For Gilroy this racial logic finds its origins in the Enlightenment.[67] Using Frantz Fanon's notion of "epidermalization," Gilroy describes this specifically as a visual politics, a modern inability to see human subjectivity "beyond the skin." "Epidermalization," he continues, "refers to a historically specific system for making bodies meaningful by endowing them with quantities of 'color.' It suggests a perceptual regime in which the racialized body is bounded and protected by its enclosing skin."[68] Race thinking, or color consciousness, inevitably tainted how we think about modern subjectivity by imposing an inability to see beyond the skin in our modern self-conceptions. Modern white subjects suffered deeply from this process; unable to see their own exposure to racial nationalism, "their self-consciousness was, as Fanon would have put it, amputated."[69]

Gilroy's purpose in *Against Race* is precisely to identify and then argue against a vision of race, blackness, and cultural identity as a form of property, using Fanon.[70] However, one can also find in Fanon a slightly different notion of blackness, one that supports the idea of race as a fetish. It can be equally useful to think about the history of race through the lens of the commodity form, not so much as a form of property to be owned but as having the materiality of an object circulating within a transatlantic market of cultural meanings. Marx described the special fetishistic qualities displayed by the commodity form in the following evocative terms:

> The form of wood, for instance, is altered if a table is made out of it. Nevertheless the table continues to be wood, an ordinary, sensuous thing. But as soon as it emerges as a commodity, it changes into a thing which transcends sensuousness. It not only stands with its feet on the ground, but, in relation to all other commodities, it stands on its head, and evolves out of its wooden brain grotesque ideas, far more wonderful than if it were to be dancing of its own free will.[71]

Marx's insights about the commodity form can be applied in a materialist analysis to race, if we think of skin color as a natural, sensuous thing, transformed by humans into various ways of defining cultural meaning and identity. When the first Portuguese traders interacted with darker skinned peoples on the West coast of Africa, skin color became elevated to the status of a thing—to that of a fetish commodity. Quoting Marx once again:

> The products of the human brain appear as autonomous figures endowed with a life of their own, which enter into relations both with each other and with the human race. So it is in the world of commodities with the products of men's hands. I call this the fetishism which attaches itself to the products of labor as soon as they are produced as commodities, and is therefore inseparable from the production of commodities.[72]

In *Things of Darkness: Economies of Race and Gender in Early Modern England*, Kim Hall quotes the opening of Fanon's chapter in *Black Skin, White*

*Masks* as evidence for her argument that blackness in early modern England had the status of a "thing." As she states: "Fanon's haunting articulation of colonized black male subjectivity . . . has a disturbing resonance when one thinks of the status of blacks in early modern England."[73] Fanon's opening is striking for its invocation of Marx's language of the commodity fetish, now used in the context of describing the colonized male subject's experience of himself as raced, his experience of his own epidermalization:

> I came into the world imbued with the will to find a meaning in things, my spirit filled with the desire to attain to the source of the world, and then I found that I was an object in the midst of other objects. . . . Sealed into that crushing objecthood, I turned beseechingly to others. Their attention was a liberation, running over my body suddenly abraded into nonbeing, endowing me once more with an agility that I had thought lost.[74]

In this essay Fanon goes on to describe his discovery of his blackness not so much as a form of property but as having the special properties of the fetish commodity: "I subjected myself to an objective examination, I discovered my blackness, my ethnic characteristics; and I was battered down by tom-toms, cannibalism, intellectual deficiency, fetishism, racial defects, slave ships . . . I took myself far off from my own presence, far indeed, and made myself an object."[75]

The evasion of the constructed nature of racial nationalisms has also been an evasion of the ways in which those racial meanings of identity have been exchanged back and forth between imperial and colonial geographies, haunting the European world histories and political philosophies of modernity with the black faces of cultural nationalists such as Garvey. While for Gilroy Garvey represents the epitome of the black fascist, it was also the black emperor who, in his mimicry of empire's racial ideologies, exposed the modern state newly clad in the uniform of nationhood for what it still was, a form of racial nationalism and fetishism without its imperial robes. In Garvey's performance of the role of the black emperor, it was the proud European empires, not the black Brutus Jones, whose nakedness was ultimately revealed, rather like the emperor in Hans Christian Andersen's eighteenth-century fairy tale, who "marched in the procession under the beautiful canopy, and all who saw him in the street and out of the windows exclaimed: 'Indeed, the emperor's new suit is incomparable!" Empire's political unconscious is revealed by the colonial subject who sees beneath the robes and masks of statehood to the fetishes of racial nationalism that still lie beneath the skin: " 'But he has nothing on at all,' said a little child at last. . . . 'But he has nothing on at all,' cried at last the whole people."[76]

In the 1920s the black emperor Marcus Garvey attempted to strip the emperors at Versailles of their national costumes. In 1923, when Robert Morse-Lovett labeled Garvey "a caricaturist of the great White Race," the critique was also an apt characterization of the political sources and impact of Garvey's dramatic political theater.[77] As Garvey himself lectured his followers, "If others laugh at you, return the laughter to them; if they mimic you, return the compliment with equal force."[78] The colonized was simply reflecting and expressing the colonizer's reality, the true paradox and parody of imperial official nationalism. As Garvey also said, "They say Mr. Garvey is spectacular. Now what does that mean, anyway? There is no such word in the African dictionary as spectacular. Therefore, if Mr. Garvey is spectacular he has copied it from them."[79]

Robert Hill has persuasively argued for the cohesive intention and form present in Garvey's performances, that Garvey's politics of representation "rested on something more substantial than mere fascination with gaudy pageantry. His histrionics and constant role-playing possessed a definite coherence." Hill then draws from a variety of sources to demonstrate, first, that Garvey's visual spectacles and parades had Caribbean and American antecedents and were specifically forms meant to poke fun at imperial authority in a carnivalesque fashion. Second, Hill argues that Garvey was keenly aware of his effect: "A man given to enigmatic twists, dazzling histrionics mixed with constant role-playing, Garvey was a master manipulator of the visual image. He was certainly one of the pioneers in the political use of the visual arts to communicate his political message."[80] For Hill, Garvey's spectacular ideology was an intentional burlesque of the rituals of European imperialism and statecraft.

Garvey's mimicry, however, reflected more than simply the desire to poke fun at empire. Rather, when he wryly observed, "there is no such word in the African dictionary as spectacular," he was also pointing to the necessary trappings of modern nationalism, invoked, for example, by Benedict

Anderson in his image of the imperial superpowers arriving at Versailles "dressed in national costume rather than imperial uniform."[81] As Garvey would also observe:

> Can you tell me where you can find more titles and robes than in Europe? . . . If you watch the picture from Buckingham Palace to the House of Commons in Westminster you will see hundreds of men with all kinds of uniform, all kinds of turbans, all kinds of breeches, all kinds of uniform—the whole thing looking like one big human show and everybody going to the circus to see.[82]

Garvey saw the connections between empire's fetish spectacles and a new focus on investing modern political subjects as citizens in the nation-state. He was not unaware of the politics of imperial official nationalisms as they developed around him in the early decades of the twentieth century. As he would also say, "The question of the age is that of political freedom, political liberty and political emancipation for all people."[83] Garvey also understood that models for state-construction and political self-governance required dramatic and spectacular imaginations: "This thing of governments is a big idea, very, very big, is the biggest thing of the age, is the thing men are seeking everywhere."[84] For Garvey the New Negro was not only going to join that discussion by "going to Africa to tell England, France, and Belgium to get out of there."[85] He was also going to don the robes, the fetishes, the political style and the visual language of imperial official nationalism: "We say, therefore, that since they have found some virtue in being spectacular we will try out the virtues there are in being spectacular."[86]

When Garvey wryly observed that "if Mr. Garvey is spectacular he has copied it from them," he pointed to the necessary trappings and racialized imperial legacies of modern European nationalism. In the act of imagining a black empire he was taking the dramatic and oppositional leap of investing black subjects with the imagination to create their own forms of self-government. Essentially, he used the symbols and fetishes of an imperial order already in decline—"Frankly in the manner of the governments which have gone out of style in Europe," as another contemporary quoted by Hill would observe—to perform the unimaginably modern notion of the sovereign black state: "It was a ceremonial that may correctly be regarded as a revival of the ancient glory . . . of Ethiopia in the days of the Queen of Sheba . . . [yet also] comparable to similar state functions held in the ceremonial courts of England, Germany, Italy, France, and the United States."[87] Garvey's ultimate brazenness and impudence was that in his racialized vision of a hybrid, conquering African civilization, he also claimed to own the *original* of the copy: "What the white man has done are but copies, replicas, are but duplicates, facsimiles of what the black man originated and endowed civilization with."[88]

## THE SPECTACLE OF STATE FETISHISM
## AND BLACK TRANSNATIONALITY

In his popular performances during the 1920s, Garvey's self-conscious goal was to capture the hearts and minds of his worldwide popular black audience. As another of his contemporaries would describe in 1925, "All the gorgeous periphery in dress, court display, fantastic titles were very relevant to his aim—the capture of the heart (if not the head) and the imagination of the masses of his people."[89] Another contemporary would attest in 1927 that no other Negro organization had the same power to "reach the common people or stir their imagination" as Garvey's UNIA.[90] Marcus Garvey's historical significance lay in his ability to imagine and then mobilize the black masses around a spectacular vision of black transnationality. This was at the precise moment when the major European and American architects of modern nationalism seemed unable to incorporate black and colonial populations within their imagination of modern democracy and self-government.

Garvey's spectacles of black statehood allowed his black and colonial spectators to envision the impossible—the virtual or imagined fulfillment of their desires for inclusion within the world order of nation-states in construction after World War I. As historian John Henrik Clarke described, "Marcus Garvey would instill in a people the gift of dreaming that would make them *visualize* again being a whole people ruling nations."[91] And as Worth Tuttle commented in his reportage of the UNIA's 1921 mass meeting, Garvey "thrilled" black subjects "with the joys of a nationality without, as yet, any of its responsibilities."[92]

When Garvey paraded throughout the streets of Harlem, he displayed a dream of the diaspora with the state majesty of empire. Garvey's black empire was a vision of the race as a transnation. He offered a way of imagining racial empowerment and representation in statehood that cut across the power of other geopolitical formations. Hence, while Gilroy is certainly accurate in casting Garvey as the black fascist on the stage of world politics, there is much to learn about the languages and desires mobilized by empire if we also recast Garvey's race movement within the framework of his performance of a global vision of the black state. This was a performance he circulated throughout the diaspora on his own black ships of state, the utopian fleet of the Black Star Line as it traveled throughout the black New World. His sea story moves us beyond the history of racial nationalism, imperialism, and state fetishism that Gilroy's account of Garvey elaborates to take us on a journey through the terrain of a transatlantic conception of blackness that Garvey was the first to articulate in mass movement terms. Garvey's cultural politics can then be seen not simply as an expression of black nationalism or even black fascism but rather as a spectacular traveling portrayal of the race's right to statehood; to use Joseph Roach's term, as a circumatlantic performance of black transnationality.

Alongside the more fascistic elements of Garvey's imperial model of diaspora also lay a political hope: "not only the inspiration of the Empire: but its solidarity," as he described it.[93] Ultimately, Garvey hoped that his sovereign black empire could provide the race with political protection from the divide and conquer strategy embedded within the European model of nationhood:

> Everybody is looking towards Empire to insure protection—a protection for their own. "African Fundamentalism" points to Imperialism. Imperialism means that whether we are in Africa or abroad, we are united with one tie of life blood, with one tie of race, and as Four Hundred Million we must stand together, willing to fall together or die together. That is the thought we are echoing throughout the world.[94]

Garvey's black nationalism held within it a necessary disrespect for the boundaries established in Western imperialism's definition of modern nationalities: "The Negro, as I have always pointed out, owes his nationality in the Western world to accident, so whether he be an American or West Indian should not count when we have before us the big idea of rescuing ourselves from the common enemy."[95] Instead, Garvey tried to demonstrate an alternative conception of black political subjectivity, one in which blackness rested solely on the racial diaspora and not on European definitions of nationality: "The Negro must be united in one *grand racial hierarchy. Our union must know no clime, boundary, or nationality* . . . let us hold together under all climes and in every country, making among ourselves a Racial Empire upon which 'the sun shall never set.' "[96] To understand Garvey's imperial fictions as protective strategies that relied on the combined strength of all the members of the racial diaspora is to shift to assessing the historical strength and imaginative power of the transnational network Garvey envisioned beyond the reach of the imperial nation-states. Through that network Garvey hoped to shape a modern discourse of black identity that, while relying on imperial fictions and gendered hierarchies in its imagination of the diaspora, also rejected European nationalism and nationality as a source of identity for blacks in the Western world. Marcus Garvey's vision of the black empire was a self-conscious act of mimesis, an imaginative yet highly political fiction similar, in many ways, to the modular nationalisms developed elsewhere. But precisely because Garvey's community of listeners, the scattered race, was not an easily imagined national territorial community, Garveyism required both broader definitions of nationality, and a spectacular means of communicating this to a wider, transnational, black audience.

One similarity Garvey shared with O'Neill's black emperor was that in parodying empire, he also mirrored and displayed the tragedy of empire as it struggled to survive across the globe. If World War I saw the decline of certain forms of imperial ideology and state structures, the blackface of the decline of empire would be the rise of new racial nationalisms and colonial liberation movements in Africa, Asia, and the West Indies, movements that Garveyism both predicted and prefigured. The ability of future black intellectuals and radicals to see their struggles as bearing any connections to each other beyond a territorial nationalist politics was partly made possible by transnational political and cultural networks and new ways of envisioning black nationality, created by Garvey's spectacular ideologies. For it was largely due to Garvey's comic opera, as A. F. Elmes said in 1925, that "Negroes all over the world have come to think of themselves as a Race—one in hope and destiny, as never before."[97]

Crew of the S.S. *Yarmouth*.

# CHAPTER 4

# The Black Star Line and the Negro Ship of State

I have settled on the image of ships in motion across the spaces between Europe, America, Africa, and the Caribbean as a central organizing symbol for this enterprise. . . . The image of the ship—a living, micro-cultural, micro-political system in motion.

—PAUL GILROY[1]

IMAGINING SHIPS as the vehicles to facilitate circumatlantic performance and circumcaribbean movement, Marcus Garvey literally attempted to place ownership of the means of production in the hands of working black subject populations. This observation departs from previous interpretations by arguing that in so doing, Garvey was not just mirroring the geopolitics of his own imperial moment. He was also drawing on a previous black transatlantic legacy which has yet to be fully elaborated as a maritime context for Garvey's own movements throughout the Atlantic.

As W. Jeffrey Bolster has pointed out, during the period Gail Bederman describes within the United States there were different notions of masculinity circulating in the waters of the black Atlantic and in its Caribbean seaports. In constructing their senses of manhood some black men had seafaring traditions to draw from, with a genealogy stretching back into the late eighteenth century. In her work on black Liverpool, Jacqueline Nassy Brown has described the role black seafaring played in creating forms of black community throughout the diaspora. She observes, "Black Liverpudlian narratives credit seamen for giving birth to the black community itself."[2] However, attentive to the gendered politics of travel and the status of seafaring as a "domain . . . too uniformly male to foster an understanding of women's agency in producing the black Atlantic," Nassy Brown also asserts, "it is *precisely* because seafaring is so staunchly male that it forms such a fertile object of inquiry [providing] a window on the centrality of gender ideologies to the production of diasporic space."[3] In her work on the seaport town of Black Liverpool, Nassy Brown demonstrates how exploring the history of black seafaring can help us to better understand both the gendered politics of black travel and the gendering of diasporic spaces and processes of community building.

Between 1740 and 1820, there was a sharp increase in the number of black sailors traveling and employed on the Atlantic.[4] Linebaugh and Rediker have described this maritime world of labor and community building on ships as a world of "hydrarchy" that, reaching back into the late seventeenth century, specifically countered imperial power and the laws of the maritime state.[5] Pirate ships in particular were highly uncontrollable, motley spaces, "multinational, multicultural, and multiracial." According to Linebaugh and Rediker, "Indeed, pirate ships themselves might be considered multiracial maroon communities, in which rebels used the high seas as others used the mountains and the jungles."[6]

Beginning in the late seventeenth century but continuing into the eighteenth, the world of hydrarchy contrasted with the domestic world of the nation and the world of empire, creating different meanings and constructions of masculinity. As W. Jeffrey Bolster further describes: "For a black man, then, ships provided a workplace where his color might be less a determinant of his daily life and duties than elsewhere . . . whether asserting themselves in the spaces allocated to them aboard ship or fleeing oppression, African American men found considerable maneuvering within maritime society."[7] Voyaging in the late eighteenth century and throughout the first half of the nineteenth had a psychological impact that Bolster argues "persisted, and was considerably more profound than that associated with other unskilled and semi-skilled work, affirming blacks' capacity for masculine bravado and transcendence of the ordinary."[8] In a historical narrative that spans the entire geography of the Atlantic, linking the journeys and labors of African, Caribbean, and American black sailors between 1740 and 1820, Bolster argues that "Seafaring was central to the community life and masculinity."[9]

The autobiographical narrative of Captain Harry Dean, a black sea captain from the late nineteenth century and early twentieth, falls squarely within this tradition of a revolutionary, black maritime Atlantic described by Linebaugh, Rediker, Nassy Brown, and Bolster.[10] *Umbala* is another early-twentieth-century black empire narrative, but one whose genealogy can also be traced to the significant and often invisible maritime tradition that exists within African American culture and the broader cultural and political history of the black Atlantic. That history has produced its own narratives, sea stories that trace different routes than either the slave narratives written up to and throughout the eighteenth century or the black empire narratives of the late nineteenth century and early twentieth.[11]

As Bolster confirms, in addition to a confidence gained from work and increased workplace freedom afforded on board ships, storytelling was a key component of the empowerment black seamen both felt and provided to others: "By setting blacks in motion, maritime slavery . . . provided black seamen with perspectives denied to island-bound slaves." In the 1850s, around the time Samuel Delany was writing of the travels of his fictional character Blake through the American South, seafaring "Free dark young men from the North stood out in the lower South. . . . Embodying black freedom of movement and black-white equality in the work-place, northern sailors subverted local racial mores with their very presence. . . . They subverted slavery more actively with travel stories and news of free life." Most compellingly, "Seamen spoke passionately on the conditions of black people elsewhere—a topic of constant interest throughout the African diaspora," Bolster tells us.[12]

In *Black Jacks* Bolster provides us with a crucial social and labor history of the black transatlantic, offering a material foundation for black literary and cultural studies interested in exploring the consciousness and formation of modern black subjectivity beyond the domestic borders of plantations and urban cityscapes. Even as fugitive slave laws were limiting the movements of blacks within the United States, "Like waves on a beach, black sailors kept coming," bringing with them a larger consciousness of themselves as part of a global racial community. Some sailors who then crossed back over into the nation became important figures in the antislavery movement, including Paul Cuffee, Denmark Vesey, and the sailors who first helped David Walker spread his appeal. Bolster's account ends with a series of Negro seamen's acts throughout the 1830s that, like the fugitive slave laws, ultimately stemmed the tide of black involvement in the maritime industry.[13]

Despite Bolster's conclusion of the story of black seafaring in the 1830s, the power of this history for shaping constructions of black masculinity can still be seen in later periods, traveling forward in time to shape sea voyage narratives such as the one of Captain Harry Dean. Captain Dean's narrative offers one of many interesting starting points for rethinking Garvey's own maritime enterprise, his fleet of black-owned steamships, the Black Star Line.[14] *Umbala* provides a nice bridge for thinking through the relationships between Garvey's desires for racial statehood, his attempts to fulfill them in motion and performance, and his relationship to a previous black transatlantic maritime history.

Captain Harry Dean, a descendant of Paul Cuffee (famous in diasporic history for outfitting a brig named *The Traveller* with a crew of fugitive slaves and escaping the United States to ultimately found Liberia), was a world traveler by the time he was fifteen. Between 1876 and 1879, he joined his uncle Silas Cuffee on *The Traveller II* for a three-year voyage circumnavigating the globe. This journey provided Dean with important lessons in world geography, political economy, anthropology, and imperial geopolitics, lessons that he could not have learned by staying at home in the United States. While on this journey Dean decided to "instigate a movement to rehabilitate Africa and found such an Ethiopian Empire as the world had never seen," as he related in his autobiographical writings.[15] As he described his own imperial and territorial dreams:

> It would be greater than the empire in Haiti, for while that island kingdom, with its Toussaint L'Ouvertures and Christophes, produced great palaces, and forts, and armies—battalions strong enough to beat the best soldiery of France—yet the island itself is a mere pin-point on the earth's surface compared with the great continent of Africa, where I planned to build my empire.[16]

While Captain Dean never met Garvey, his account does link a twentieth-century focus on the territorial possibilities of an African empire with an older black maritime tradition within Atlantic history.[17] In Dean's narrative his ship, the *Pedro Gorino*, plays its own central role as a character in the story's plot, facilitating Dean's quest at a number of key points in the narrative.[18] The black sea voyage narrative introduces not just the black seaman as a new character in black Atlantic history, but the space of the ship itself as running alongside that of the plantation, the colony, or the revolutionary nation.

As Maggie Montesinos Sale has also argued, ships provided both physical and metaphorical spaces for imagining and producing alternative notions of black "rebellious masculinity" in discourses of the United States as a revolutionary nation during the nineteenth century.[19] As white men used the trope of revolutionary struggle to define a liberal theory of the nation, African American men such as Frederick Douglass in his 1853 novella *The Heroic Slave* used the notion of a slave ship revolt to offer competing narratives and used the trope of revolutionary struggle precisely to pose black rebellious masculinity as that which the national discourse could still not encompass.[20] Sale argues that "Ships by their very nature are liminal spaces that move between state and national boundaries."[21] Hence, she continues, in the nineteenth-century slave ship revolts specifically brought competing images of the United States as a nation into conflict with each other: "In international relations, the United States was conceived of as a nation among a community of nations . . . But in relation to matters such as slavery, the United States was thought of as a confederation of sovereign states. . . . slave rebellions brought into conflict these two versions of U.S. national identity."[22] Sale confirms that what was at stake in both of these discussions was the association of revolutionary struggle solely with masculinity. Ships, she argues, were "masculine spaces, despite the occasional presence of women, historically always 'manned' by men, who played the gender counterpart to the vessel they commanded, always referred to as 'she.'"[23]

Black sea stories such as *Umbala* differed from slave narratives in their representations of the black seaman and his counterpart, the seafaring fugitive or slave in revolt, as the image of a mobile, free, black masculine subjectivity, one that existed alongside the dominant image of black subjectivity during the period, that of the plantation slave.[24] The figure of the black mariner as he evolved in narratives such as Dean's in the late nineteenth century and early twentieth moved increasingly away from those Victorian definitions of manliness and gentlemanliness shaping black domestic constructions of the masculinity of both the New Negro and the New World Negro.[25] In sea voyage stories the black seaman becomes less and less a national or domestic figure. Like Captain Dean and unlike Anderson's national hero and Garvey's sovereign black emperor, his masculine adventures take place not on territory within national boundaries, but more often than not in the watery worlds and deterritorialized spaces of the oceans and the seas. Dean's narrative is unique precisely as a text that links the black search for territory and empire with the black sea voyage narrative. Its ultimate definition here as more a narrative than a tale of black empire rests on the way Dean's tale ends, with a classic image of the black mariner as a drifter, bereft of both his visions of statehood and the vehicle that could have gotten him there.

Forced to abandon his ship "in dry dock," Captain Dean also leaves behind his black imperial mission and ends his narrative with a description of his own free-floating movement in unstable waters. Arriving in the island colony from which his ancestors first departed, a Scottish pirate and an African native, Dean laments:

> Driven from my motherland by foreigners and usurpers. . . . I slipped ashore at Funchal, Madeira, a fugitive from justice. And I thought how like I was to Said Kafu and McKinnon Paige, who had come to Funchal a century and a half before. And, like those two, I haunted the resorts of seamen that lie along that dirty, lively, wild crescent bay, seeking passage aboard any ship for any country whatsoever.[26]

Dean's ending to his black empire narrative is not Du Bois's nor Schuyler's. His ship does not seek Africa or Liberia but sails away from both the reality and the idea of the motherland, a fugitive in the quest for black autonomy and statehood. Ashore on the island of Funchal, Dean becomes part of a motley crew of pirates, fugitives, and seamen, without nationality yet still working together to imagine and create communities.

In 1963 Captain Hugh Mulzac, once a captain of the first ship Garvey bought for the Black Star Line, the *Yarmouth*, also wrote his autobiography, another black mariner's narrative.[27] Mulzac's *A Star to Steer By* connects a broader history of black travel within a now modern maritime commercial context to Garvey's ambitious dream to own and operate a fleet of black steamships that could place subjects from across the diaspora in trading relationships with each other and the wider modern world. Unfortunately, these goals were not so admirable to Captain Hugh Mulzac, who was a vocal critic of Garvey's leadership of the Black Star Line as a financial enterprise. As the captain described, one of the most striking aspects of Garvey's ships on their travels throughout the diaspora was their symbolic power as fetish spectacles that enabled black subjects to visualize Garvey's imperial dreams and their own potential stateliness. In an excerpt from his autobiography, "Memoirs of a Captain of the Black Star Line," Mulzac described the reception of Garvey's ships in ports across the diaspora:

> The *Yarmouth's* arrival [in Cuba] had been heralded . . . and sympathizers flocked from all parts of the island toward the docks to greet the first ship they had ever seen entirely owned and operated by colored men. . . . Finally, [we] . . . left for Jamaica. Again hundreds greeted us at the docks. . . . Then we left for Colon, the Panama Canal Zone, and the biggest reception of all. Literally thousands of Panamanians swarmed over the docks with baskets of fruits, vegetables, and other gifts. I was amazed that the *Yarmouth* had become such a symbol for the colored citizens of every land.[28]

Mulzac's praise was given grudgingly; his overall comments were critical of Garvey precisely because, in his view, "The use to which the worthless Black Star ships were put represented the triumph of propaganda over business." Garvey used the steamship plan to build momentum for the movement: "The UNIA celebrations in both ports [in which the ship landed] were spectacular affairs, with thousands joining the parades. Garvey made impassioned speeches, whipping the people into frenzied support of the association." This strategy confused the captain, intent as he was on the commercial as opposed to the symbolic value of Garvey's steamship operation: "The *Yarmouth* was simply being used as a propaganda device for recruiting new members to the Universal Negro Improvement Association. It was a helluva way to run a steamship."[29]

Garvey's steamships had a function greater than commerce, not comprehensible to Captain Mulzac and many Garvey critics at the time, but also not comprehensible within a language of the Black Star Line as simply a failed business enterprise or hoax, as it has essentially been understood throughout years of Garvey scholarship. As a mode of cultural production and political organizing, Garvey's ships helped him to realize, imaginatively, his vision of a politically united black diaspora, one in which free movement was also the imagined racial community's central political goal. Here I argue Garvey's shipping enterprise must be explored in terms of its cultural politics, for what it offered as an alternative route to transnational conceptions of black identity within the overarching narrative of his vision of empire. If Garvey's back to

Africa movement represented a larger belief in a worldly New Negro's right to travel freely throughout the modern world, much in the manner of Captain Harry Dean and other black seamen like him, then Garvey's boldness lay in his attempt to materialize that right to mobility by placing ownership of its means of production, ships, in the hands of black subjects themselves.

Garvey's own deportation from the United States in 1927 would confirm one of his strongest initial instincts in creating the Black Star Line as part of the Universal Negro Improvement Association (UNIA). In Garvey's case, control over the means of mobility proved to be as important a political priority in his race war against imperialism as control over the means of production was in the class war against world capitalism. To the degree that Garvey's story takes on a new meaning in the context of a revolutionary maritime tradition of black mobility from the sixteenth century on, this chapter identifies a different way of thinking about the Black Star Line, not as significant in the nationalist search for a territorial homeland—back to Africa—but as the vehicles to facilitate a black transnational dream of free movement in modernity, taking the black male away from the nation and toward other conceptions of his own freedom and masculinity. Garvey understood those latter rights precisely because travel had so shaped his own identity and insights into the modern black condition. This chapter rereads the organizational goals of the UNIA in this light and ends by exploring the convergence of Garvey's politics of the Black Star Line with Cyril V. Briggs's dreams for a Negro ship of state. Unfortunately, the gendered hierarchies endemic to Garvey's masculine and imperial imaginary—the politics of the black sovereign—would be the source of that Negro federation's ultimate failure.

## THE UNIVERSAL NEGRO IMPROVEMENT ASSOCIATION AND
## THE NEW WORLD NEGRO'S RIGHT TO TRAVEL

Like his contemporaries Randolph Bourne and Cyril Briggs, Marcus Garvey's thinking on questions of racial, ethnic, and national identity was fundamentally shaped by the developments of World War I and "by the perfervid debate surrounding the settlement of the nationalities question and the issue of national self-determination, matters that were important parts of the protracted peace negotiations" at Versailles.[30] As Garvey would describe his observations when he first arrived in the United States: "Just at that time . . . other races were engaged in seeing their cause through—the Jews through their Zionist movement and the Irish through their Irish movement—and I decided that, cost what it might, I would make this a favorable time to see the Negro's interest through."[31]

But Garvey's subsequent political practice was also shaped by his further travels within the United States. When Garvey's New Negro sentiments found little popularity in colonial Jamaica, forcing him to emigrate, upon his arrival he expanded his own knowledge of discrimination against blacks gained during his earlier travels by undertaking a series of intranational migrations throughout the United States:

> I arrived in America in the spring of 1916, after which I started to study the sociological, economical and political status of the Negroes of America. This took me through 38 states. It was after my return from these trips to New York that I founded in New York the New York division of the Universal Negro Improvement Association.[32]

Garvey incorporated the UNIA and started building branches throughout 1919. However, his own experiences as a black migrant were so uppermost in his mind that his first venture after incorporation was to secure black ownership of the means of travel:

> The Black Star Line Steamship Corporation that I organized in 1919, under charter from the State of Delaware, was the great attraction that brought to the Universal Negro Improvement Association millions of supporters from Central America, South America, Africa and the West Indies. . . . The idea became immediately popular—that of having ships.[33]

When scholars and contemporaries discuss Garvey's steamship ventures, they are usually framed as part of his nationalist desire to return to Africa. But in his descriptions of his motives, it is precisely the creation of diaspora, rather than nation or even empire, he ultimately wished to facilitate:

> [There was a] great need for steamship communication among the different branches of the Negro race scattered in Africa, the Americas and the West Indies. It was in keeping with this need that I founded the Black Star Line in 1919.
> Having traveled extensively throughout the world and seriously study-

ing the economical, commercial and industrial needs of our people, I found out that the quickest and easiest way to reach them was by steamship communication. So immediately after I succeeded in forming the Universal Negro Improvement Association in America, I launched the idea of floating ships under the direction of Negroes. Growing up as I did in my own island, and traveling out to the outside world with open eyes, I saw that the merchant marines of all countries were in the hands of white men.[34]

Garvey's steamship ventures, then, were not solely nation-building enterprises in the traditional sense. As he traveled throughout the modern and colonial worlds, the most pressing problem he saw was the restriction of the mobility of the black subject throughout the national states and colonial territories of modernity. Garvey facilitated the creation of a modern black diaspora by sponsoring transnational movement and communication; black freedom represented primarily as the unrestricted migration of the black subject. Garveyism and the UNIA were not just other names for the back to Africa nationalist desire to return to one fixed, essential racial home. Rather, with the project of building steamship communication across the black diaspora, Garvey's nationalist movement was fundamentally transnationalist from the outset: "The moment the first ship of the Black Star Line was launched the whole movement of the Universal Negro Improvement Association was referred to as The Black Star Line Movement."[35]

Garvey's ships never made it to Africa, and that failure has blinded us from focusing more intently on the success of the journeys his fleet did undertake in mobilizing the black world's sense of itself as a global racial community. Some ships were used for trade and "passenger service between Central America and the West Indies."[36] They were necessary for the distribution of Garvey's *Negro World* throughout the diaspora and metropolitan and colonial worlds, and when the paper itself was banned from the colonies, black Garveyite seamen became the sources of information about the movement. As Captain Mulzac grudgingly observed, they helped to visually spread Garvey's message, all of which had an even greater effect: the creation of a vision of worldwide blackness as a heterogeneous, multiracial, and multinational world community, united in a global politics against empire. This was the vision of black transnationality, created in diaspora and put in circulation throughout the black world, that was then also put on display in Harlem in the spectacle of Garvey's first national UNIA convention and parade.

Garvey organized the political energy of the diaspora, an energy multiple, inchoate, created partly through the spectacle of his own steamships, and harnessed it in his 1920 International Convention: "The state of world enthusiasm having reached to such a height, I thought the best thing to do was to call a world convention of the Negro race."[37] The historical impossibility of Garvey's dream of black empire did not diminish the cultural politics of diaspora that dream enabled and attempted to concretely facilitate. His imperial fictions produced a transnational political reality that, at the time, explicitly countered the national order being constructed during World War I and exemplified in the League of Nations. Hence, Garvey was perceived by those forces and institutions as a clear, potential geopolitical threat. Garvey revealed the real and potentially explosive power of the black, transnational, desire for forms of statehood: "Notice was therefore served throughout the world that on the first of August, 1920, an international convention of the Negro peoples of the world was to be called to assemble at New York, to which each Negro community was to send delegates."[38] The reality of the lack of black nation-states across the imperial world meant that these delegates could only represent nations symbolically. But in reality, as they physically marched down the streets of Harlem in their own stately processions, they demonstrated the potential of international black mobilization, a reality whose threatening nature was reflected in the extreme interest of both the American and colonial authorities in Garvey's movement. The delegation met, appropriately enough, in "Liberty Hall, 120–140 W. 138th street." Garvey continued, "August 1st, 1920, was the red letter day for the Negro peoples of the world."[39]

Garvey's international convention was not a popular nationalism easily converted into American official ideologies of self-determination. This was the empire in revolt, a popular, hybrid black internationalism that reached beyond the boundaries of European nationality:

> Representatives of the race from every known part of the world . . . came in groups of one hundred, in scores, dozens, tens and in units. We had them from Nigeria, the Gold Coast, Sierra Leone, Liberia, West Africa, from Cape Town and Johannesburg, South Africa, and from East and Central

Africa, from every known island in the West Indies, including Cuba, Haiti, Jamaica, Barbados, Trinidad, Grenada, and all the groups of the Leeward and Windward islands. They came from South and Central America: from Europe and from Asia. Contingents of thousands [c]ame from Philadelphia, Detroit, Chicago, Cincinnati, in the United States, and from every other nook and corner of the republic.[40]

This was a dream of diaspora that had both the fetishistic majesty and the hybridity of empire: "It reminded one of the great ceremonies at the courts of Europe, or one of the coronation celebrations at Westminster Abbey, London. The people were greatly impressed—the thousands inside of Liberty Hall, and numerous thousands peeping through the windows on the outside."[41]

Regardless of what we ultimately think of the historical accuracy and political significance of Garvey's account of his convention, its cultural significance lay in its ability to imaginatively represent for blacks in the United States the multinational racial diaspora as a new conception of home. Garvey's convention was impressive for the imaginative leap it represented in providing an empowering international narrative of black freedom that could step far outside of the terms of racial being to which blacks were subjected in the United States and in the colonies. The spectacle of the parade that followed the convention demonstrated a broader understanding of racial freedom and movement than was possible within the bounds of the American nation-state: "After the morning display at Liberty Hall there was the parade and review throughout the streets of Harlem. . . . Fully 30,000 people saw the parade from the streets and homes in Harlem. The demonstration was of such as never seen in Harlem before and probably not to be seen again."[42]

Garvey's speech at the end of this march made explicit the racial politics of the event: as a public demonstration of new militant black subjectivities, intent on enacting and fulfilling their own desires for political freedom at this moment of early-twentieth-century imperial restructuring and race war. As Garvey described it:

It was at the Madison Square Garden that I made the famous speech that brought me into the limelight of the political world. At 11:00 this night I made the official speech in opening the convention, in which I declared in the height of my enthusiasm that: "Four hundred million Negroes were sharpening their swords for the next world war."[43]

Not surprisingly, Garvey's comments sparked intense official surveillance of the Garvey movement by the Federal Bureau of Investigation and other colonial authorities. Their counterstrategy was to restrict the spread of Garveyism by restricting Garvey's own migratory freedom:

> Among all the things I said these words were taken out and cabled to every capital in Europe and throughout the world. The next morning every first class newspaper proclaimed me as the new leader of the Negro race and featured the unfortunate words I used. Words which have been making trouble for me ever since 1920. . . . France closed her doors against me in Africa; and Italy and Portugal also and England became so scared and America watched me at every move.[44]

The International Convention of the Negro made their own war demands by sponsoring a bill of rights with a number of resolutions. Interestingly, despite Garvey's rhetoric, nowhere was it mentioned initially that blacks had the right to form their own nation-state.[45] Rather, the bill asked for civil rights according to the laws of the various Western nations in which blacks had taken up residence: "We do declare that Negroes, wheresoever they found a community amongst themselves, should be given the right to elect their own representatives to represent them in legislatures, courts of law, or such institutions as may exercise control over that particular community."[46] The right of black subjects to Africa was not so much essentialist as anti-imperialist, framed in direct reference to the international context of imperial warfare and the mandates of the Treaty of Versailles:

> 14. We believe in the inherent right of the Negro to possess himself of Africa, and that his possession of same shall not be regarded as an infringement of any claim or purchase made by any race or nation.
>
> 15. We strongly condemn the cupidity of those nations of the world who, by open aggression, or secret schemes, have seized the territories and inexhaustible natural wealth of Africa, and we place on record our most solemn determination to reclaim the treasures and possession of the vast continent of our forefathers.
>
> 16. We believe all men should live in peace one with the other, but when races and nations provoke the ire of other races and nations by attempting to infringe upon their rights . . . war becomes inevitable. . . .

45. Be it further resolved, that we as a race of people declare the League of Nations null and void as far as the Negro is concerned, in that it seeks to deprive Negroes of their liberty.[47]

While the bill of rights put little focus on black nationalism for its own sake, the protection of the rights of the black transnational migrant received extensive treatment, underscoring its importance in Garvey's racial philosophy and cultural politics:

33. We vigorously protest against the increasingly unfair and unjust treatment accorded Negro travelers on land and sea by the agents and employees of railroad and steamship companies . . . and insist that for equal fare we receive equal privileges with travelers of other races.

34. We declare it unjust for any country, state or nation to enact laws tending to hinder and obstruct the free immigration of Negroes on account of their race and color.

35. That the right of the Negro to travel unmolested throughout the world be not abridged by any person or persons, and all Negroes are called upon to give aid to a fellow Negro when thus molested.

36. We declare that all Negroes are entitled to the same right to travel over the world as other men. . . .

50. We demand a free and unfettered commercial intercourse with all the Negro people of the world.

51. We declare for the absolute freedom of the seas for all peoples.[48]

The Declaration of 1920 demonstrated Garvey's goal to build a transnational movement of blacks across the diaspora. Other black intellectuals of the period, such as his Caribbean contemporary Cyril V. Briggs, were able to recognize during the early stages of his career in the United States the radical potential of such a movement, concretely facilitated in the organizational forms of both the UNIA and the steamship enterprise. This chapter ends with an account of the failed attempt to merge Briggs's militant African Blood Brotherhood (ABB) and the UNIA in a great Negro federation, representing a brief moment when Briggs's radical critique of empire could have enhanced the liberatory potential of Garvey's politics of mobility without his imperialist pretensions.

Unlike Garvey's UNIA, Cyril V. Briggs's ABB was not well known beyond an immediate circle of black radical organizers and intellectuals in Harlem during the late 1910s. Since many of these figures would soon become members of the Communist Party, the organization's primary interest for historians and scholars has been its role as a precursor to black Communism.[49] The ABB has garnered little historical attention on its own merits precisely because it never had the reach and impact of Garvey's more well-known mass organization, the UNIA. At its peak, the UNIA had hundreds of members in branches scattered all over the world.[50]

The failure of the merger of the ABB and the UNIA reveals the limits of the masculine and hierarchical politics of the black emperor, an internationalist politics that focused on the single representative sovereign as a masculine race leader. Garvey's investments in this particularly gendered vision of masculinity and leadership hampered the abilities of a joint ABB/UNIA to truly organize for multiracial, multinational democracy. If the union had succeeded, the two organizations together might have embodied the utopian internationalist black organizations so pervasive in black empire fictions.

Early issues of *The Crusader* reveal Briggs's initial respect for Marcus Garvey as a race leader. Certainly at the level of political imagination, both of these Caribbean colonial intellectuals were animated by a vision of a free and autonomous black state, be it Briggs's black republic in "The Ray of Fear" or Garvey's black empire, and hence their cooperation in print against the League of Nations in 1919. In the December 1918 issue of *The Crusader*, the first piece in a "Digest of Views" with no byline called on the European powers to recognize a free Africa and to include black delegates in the peace conference. Here Briggs's competitor, Garvey's magazine the *Negro World*, was identified as one of "the more enlightened Negro publications" and the author quoted "its editor Marcus Garvey" as saying, "[The German colonies in Africa] neither belong to England nor to Germany. They are the property of the blacks, and . . . we are going to have them now or some time later, even if all the world is to waste itself in blood." As the piece continued, "Over 2,000 Negroes joined with the Universal Negro Improvement Association and African Communities League at Palace Casino, New York, in framing demands for a free Africa."[51]

Garvey was dogged, however, by repeated attempts on the part of the United States government to curb his influence by investigating the financial operations of the UNIA and the collection of funds from the members of his steamship company. In August 1919, one of Briggs's editorials revealed caution in its position on Garvey's financial and legal misfortunes, pointing to "Mr. Garvey's own indiscretion" as the chief cause of his recent legal tangle. The article ended, however, on a positive note:

> Mr. Garvey has already taken steps to rectify his [mistake]. . . . So far, so good. His friends are satisfied. . . . Because of his splendid work in the past, and the greater promise of the future, we would be extremely sorry to have aught happen that would destroy or in any way affect for the worst the wide influence of Mr. Garvey.[52]

In this article Briggs endorsed Garvey's Black Star Line in particular to *The Crusader's* readership:

> The *Crusader* has received many inquiries relative to the Black Star Steamship Corporation; as to the feasibility of the project of launching a fleet of steamships to be manned and operated by Negroes for the purpose of carrying on trade and establishing closer relations between the Negro peoples of the world, and as to the honesty and ability of the officials and employees of the corporation.[53]

The editor spoke in favor of the project's "feasibility," pointing to its existing successes: "It has its first steamship and an efficient Negro crew to man it"— and further challenged readers to take note of the difficulties still to come: "The white banks assuredly will not help the Black Star Steamship Corporation. . . . Therefore the Black Star Steamship Corporation must have its own banks."[54] For the editor of *The Crusader*, the back to Africa aspect of Garvey's shipping enterprise was not the focus and was not even mentioned. Garvey's character also got the most ringing endorsement:

> As to the honesty and ability of the officials and employees of the corporation . . . the former can be inferred by an outstanding quality in the characters of Mr. Garvey and most of his colleagues. When men

are willing to *die* for a cause they are not likely to be dishonest to that cause.[55]

Yet by September 1920, Marcus Garvey had come to represent to Briggs all that was dangerous in the black movement in the United States. When Garvey was formally accused and later imprisoned for mail fraud, this was taken as banner evidence of his treason in the fight for genuine race representation. Briggs would describe his movement as "at times wobbling under the sway of narrow-minded autocracy and unintelligent fanaticism."[56] By 1924, Briggs would play a leading role in the U.S. government's deportation case against Garvey.

It is important to understand this split between two of the leading Caribbean activists of this period not merely as a fight between personalities but also as itself a part of the historical dynamic of this political moment. Briggs's early comments in *The Crusader* do reveal a sense on his part that Garvey's real purpose was to activate the diaspora around a particular global story of racial freedom. As time would tell however, Briggs disagreed with the representative politics of Garvey's vision of himself as a race leader. Though Briggs never articulated the gender dimensions of his critique, the notion of representativeness that he chose to focus on has always, as both Robert Levine and Kevin Gaines have argued, had clear gendered components and masculinist connotations in African American political discourse.[57]

In March 1920 Briggs wrote a full-length feature essay on Garvey entitled "A Paramount Chief of the Negro Race." He began by describing the UNIA's announcement of its first "International Convention of Deputies for August 1st, 1920, for the purpose of electing 'his Supreme Highness, the Potentate, His Highness, the Supreme Deputy, and other high officials, who will preside over the destiny of the Negro peoples of the world until an African Empire is founded.'" As Briggs remarked, "To many this announcement may seem high-flung and even comical." But, he added, that response comes from "those 'leaders' whose only followers now are their shadows, and who have long since lost touch with the masses of their people." These "jackal leaders" would "undoubtedly miss the vast importance attached to the quoted announcement . . . they have kept themselves as ignorant as possible of the meaning, the strength and the possibilities of the movement engineered by the U.N.I.A.A.C.L."[58]

For Briggs, Garvey's convention was important for three main reasons.

First, the race actually did need "a paramount chief or supreme leader of the race, deriving his powers and authority from the race and thus enjoying its confidence." Here Briggs was calling for a representative leader who could win the hearts and minds of the people through democratic, persuasive leadership, as opposed to monarchical right and fiat, "great enough for his opinions to command universal respect and making it possible for wholesale and whole-hearted support for his policies." Such a leader, a "pilot at the helm," was needed if the race was to achieve direction and focus.[59] However, Briggs was naive in his own belief that any singular form of black leadership, conceived of as resting in one individual, could unite the scattered and chaotic movements of the Negro ship of state. Precisely the inchoate nature of black transnational desires and forms of mass nationalist agency, the very energy Garvey was trying to harness, represented here by Briggs in the form of multiple black organizations, would make the politics of the black sovereign ineffective and also insufficient.

Second, Briggs recognized that the UNIA's strength was such that it "is sufficiently great to command obedience from a very large number of Negroes throughout the United States, Africa and the West Indies." It was precisely this potential that he felt could not get diverted by "internal struggle and divided authority." Hence, the third important and necessary feature of the convention, more Briggs's recommendation than a planned part of the event, which was that "to make such acceptance [of a race leader] possible and probable all purely Negro bodies outside of the U.N.I.A.A.C.L. should be invited to send delegates to the convention." Here Briggs was calling on Garvey to create a space large enough within the UNIA to reflect the hetero-geneity of the black community, embodied in and expressed through its multi-ple organizations.[60]

Briggs's call was significant enough to prompt a response from Garvey, which Briggs printed in *The Crusader's* next issue as part of his own editorial entitled "A Letter from Marcus Garvey." Garvey wrote directly to Briggs as editor saying, "A copy of your March number of *The Crusader* has just reached my hands . . . [your article] has struck me forcibly. It is the most intelligent explanation of the real purpose of our Convention that I have read from the pen of a contemporary journalist who is not himself a member of the Execu-tive Body." Garvey then issued a personal invitation to Briggs to attend the Convention.[61]

This pivotal exchange marked both the first real public dialogue between these two significant forces in the cultural formation of a transnational New Negro and the first appearance of real conflict between Briggs and Garvey. For while Briggs thanked Garvey for responding graciously to what was meant as "friendly and constructive criticism," he added:

> However, to be frank, Mr. Garvey's letter misses the most important point in the article to which he refers, viz.: the necessity of extending to all Negro bodies throughout the world the invitation to attend and take part in the proposed Convention. . . . In our opinion this proposal to elect a Potentate or Paramount Chief is fraught with danger to the unity of the race.[62]

In Briggs's mind the issue was not whether the race needed such an elected official, but the process by which the race would achieve one: "The need is supreme, but the task for such an election calls for immense and careful preparation." At issue here was the UNIA's ability, as an international black organization, to represent the multinationalism of the black diasporic community.

The following month, in a related piece on the UNIA, Briggs's critique began to extend from the politics of the convention to the politics of the organization as a whole:

> The Universal Negro Improvement Association is the biggest thing in modern Negro organizations. It has ramifications in every part of the globe. (On a genuine cooperative basis it could be made a wonderful factor for Negro improvement.) Collapse of the movement or failure of any of its important enterprises would be nothing less than a racial calamity. Yet such collapse may occur (and failure already threatens one of its enterprises), unless the vast membership body is willing to take a larger personal interest in the control of the organization.[63]

Two months before the convention Briggs did another full length piece that was followed two pages later with a piece on the ABB.[64] By the time of these two pieces *The Crusader* had adopted a much harsher tone toward Garvey and the UNIA. The central question in the first article was "whether the August gathering will be a real race convention or a sorry farce."[65] What becomes clear in this piece is that issues surrounding the forms that black representation should and could take in the modern world order were being encapsulated in the debate over the representative nature of the race leader. Was the race leader's purpose to model the multiple forms of identification possible in a world of blackness? Or was it his role to provide a single vision, one clear direction around which the scattered race could be consolidated? Was the worldwide Negro ship of state drifting across multiple routes toward freedom, or as Briggs would describe later, seeking only a "united, centralised movement"?[66]

Briggs raised the same issues in the following comment: "Some monarchies are quite as democratic in spirit as some republics. What governments are depends chiefly upon what peoples are. . . . What is of the deepest concern is that this individual should receive his appointment direct from the Negro peoples."[67] Briggs captured here the tension that structured Garvey's movement. The UNIA's mass reach indicated its potential as an organization that could represent the multinational and heterogeneous nature of its worldwide black audience and membership. However, the challenge was precisely how to imagine a form of black government, essentially, a form of the state, that could organically capture and represent such a diverse community. Briggs's hopeful feeling was that "it is exactly on this point that the U.N.I.A. may score a great strategical victory for the race" against the imperialists.[68] Briggs was pushing for real as opposed to symbolic representation, guaranteed in principle by firm democratic links between elected leadership and their constituents and in practice by clear chains of accountability between the UNIA and the other organizations involved in the global movement for black freedom.

In September 1920, the month after the convention, Briggs gave a mixed evaluation of the movement's future. On one hand, he admitted that Garveyism could be that Renaissance suitable enough to realize the myth of the new Negro: "The U.N.I.A. Convention in New York City is by far the most important event in the history of the Negro . . . occupying the stage with the Asiatic and Arab renascences."[69] His involvement in the fight for a more representative convention had also produced some positive results: "Up to the time of our going to press . . . [t]here has been a noticeable infiltration of liberal ideas as evidenced by the scrapping of the potentate proposition and the open nomination for the election of the various leaders."[70] Instead, Garvey was elected by all as "Provisional President of Africa," making the convention's struggle for actual political freedom and representative power in world affairs "well within the realm of the serious." What remained to be seen was whether "Mr. Garvey can broaden out to fit his high position . . . by being less narrow in his dealings with others of his race."[71]

The decisive turning point and break in the ABB's relationship with the UNIA came with a historic meeting of the ABB somewhere between May and June of 1921.[72] The meeting included Claude McKay, recently returned to America from England and now editing the white radical journal *The Liberator*.[73] Earlier, in January 1921, Robert Hill describes, Briggs had been attempting to imagine what a "radical revision of the concept of black self-determination combining the preexisting ideal of racial sovereignty with a revolutionary vision of a communist society" could look like.[74] By the time of the ABB meeting Briggs had found his answer in the idea of a federation of international black organizations.

The ABB met prior to the UNIA convention, with Claude McKay as their intermediary, precisely to decide how to use Garvey's UNIA to communicate this particular revolutionary vision of federation. The federation plan involved the joining of all black organizations into one governing body that could serve the needs of the racial diaspora as a whole and be powerful enough to challenge the imperial states. In the view of the ABB members, the federation would be a modern political entity that could center and direct the black transnational community. As such it was a political idea and a new conception of the race as a global political unit within an international framework. In October 1921, the article on the "Program of the ABB" appeared in *The Crusader* imagining the race as drifting and further stating the following: "It is to meet this unfortunate condition and to supply a rudder for the Negro Ship of State—a definite directive force—that the following program adopted by the African Blood Brotherhood is herewith offered."[75]

Richard B. Moore, one of Garvey's West Indian contemporaries who was also a founding member of the ABB and later a West Indian federationist, attended the convention as one of the ABB's delegates. In an article written in 1974 Moore gave his account of the ABB's impact on the UNIA convention:

> The program of the African Blood Brotherhood was never officially brought before the UNIA Convention, though the call for this Convention had urged attendance of delegates from "Negro organizations." Briggs afterward declared that Garvey "felt it necessary to prevent them from officially presenting for the consideration of the delegates the program

formulated by the ABB" . . . because he saw the program gaining favor in the eyes of most of the delegates who had given cheerful consideration to the printed forms distributed by the ABB.[76]

Theodore G. Vincent, in his study *Black Power and the Garvey Movement*, had a slightly different reading: "The Garveyites broke with the ABB . . . because of the Brotherhood's extremism . . . the Brotherhood left Garvey no choice; it wanted revolution now."[77] Ultimately, Garvey's assessment of the ABB's plan as an attempt to co-opt his organization with the idea of federation led to the expulsion of the ABB delegates from the 1921 convention. This action marked the final split between Briggs and Garvey and the failure of an alliance between the underground ABB and the popular mass UNIA.

*The Crusader* and Briggs then played a central role in providing the information of fraud and financial mismanagement that the United States government used to imprison and deport Garvey. The magazine's last years of existence were primarily focused on discrediting Garvey. Even McKay would complain in later years that both *The Crusader* and the ABB had become "strictly a paper organization run by Cyril Briggs, in opposition to the Marcus Garvey 'Back to Africa' movement."[78] As Robert Hill has also described, Briggs's attempt to imagine international political representation for blacks faltered as he became "preoccupied with very little else besides exposure of what [he] saw as Garvey's 'fraudulent representations.' "[79]

The federation plan is one that reappears for later generations of Caribbean American intellectuals wrestling with similar questions.[80] In some respects, the desire that lies behind the idea of black federation is the same as the desire that animated Garvey's vision of a black empire—uniting a stateless, heterogeneous, geographically dispersed black world in the face of the oppression of world imperialism. In Garvey's actual politics narrow and fetishistic ideas of blackness were fixed onto the image of the imperial state and onto the male body of the representative leader. However, as a performance of the idea of black nationality and self-determination, a performance that Garvey was able to put in motion across the diaspora in the moment that the race was in need of a global story, Garvey's movement did ultimately enable precisely the kinds of multiple identifications Briggs was hoping for.[81] Although Briggs and Garvey represented somewhat different creative responses to the situation produced from imperial war and social revolution, they were both fundamentally shaped by the general international realities and imperialist national projects emerging from World War I.[82]

By 1923 the Black Star Line became the source of Garvey's downfall in the United States. Garvey was imprisoned in Atlanta State Penitentiary for mail fraud by the United States government. Historians have shown that not only did the magnitude of his punishment, imprisonment, and ultimate deportation in 1927, not fit the scale of his crime, but that United States government authorities had been trying to build a criminal case against him for years prior to his actual arrest and conviction. The state's response to Garvey, deportation as opposed to mere detention, only further emphasized Garvey's point. By curtailing his freedom of movement into and across American state lines, the United States government effectively tried to prevent the Black Emperor, and his show of smoke and mirrors, from eroding the coherence of the state's racial and ideological borders from within. Garvey's symbolic ships and imperial visions foregrounded the more disruptive elements in the story of American nationalism, that is, slavery, imperialism, revolution, and race war.

# PART II

# Mapping New Geographies of History

Times would pass, old empires would fall and new ones take their place, the relations of countries and the relations of classes had to change, before I discovered that it is not quality of goods and utility which matter, but movement; not where you are or what you have, but where you have come from, where you are going and the rate at which you are getting there.

—C. L. R. JAMES

CHAPTER 5

# Claude McKay and Harlem,
# Black Belt of the Metropolis

As the setting sun sets its last crimson light from the heights that hold the Hudson from
the Harlem, it floods 138th Street and lights three blocks. One is a block of homes built by
the Equitable Life Insurance Society, but now sold to negroes, some crowded, some carelessly kept, but most of them beautiful, even luxurious, perhaps as handsome a block as
middle-class America, white or black, affords.

—W. E. B. DU BOIS[1]

IN HIS ESSAY "The Storyteller," Walter Benjamin describes two different
tellers of stories: "someone who has come from afar" and "the man who has
stayed at home." He continues: "If one wants to picture these two groups
through their archaic representatives, one is embodied in the resident tiller of
the soil."[2] This storyteller is a common figure for the African American writer
during the years leading up to and during the Harlem Renaissance. In Charles
Chesnutt's classic *The Conjure Woman* or Jean Toomer's *Cane*, these storytellers reconstructed for new black migrants to the North local tales and
traditions from their Southern past.[3] They created stories that, in nurturing
the memory, history, and tradition of community, remedied the dislocation
experienced by black subjects upon their great migration north.

While Claude McKay has always been seen as one of the leading literary
forerunners of the Harlem Renaissance, he also stands in a peculiar relationship to this African American tradition. McKay was someone come from afar
in more than one sense of the word. Born in Jamaica, McKay migrated to the
United States in 1912 at age twenty-two, spent seven years in America, and
then traveled to London where he settled for over a year and a half. He
returned to New York in the winter of 1921, but in less than a year he signed on

129

as a stoker on a merchant ship bound again for England, working his way across the Atlantic and finally landing in Russia in time to attend the Fourth Congress of the Communist International. In May 1923, McKay began his most sustained period as an expatriate in Europe. After leaving Petrograd he ultimately landed in Paris, where he would encounter white expatriates and students and fellow travelers from Africa, the French West Indies, and North Africa. Like Garvey, McKay met black dockworkers on his journeys through Europe and "exchanged with them ideas and life histories."[4] Never one to tarry in one place for too long, by January 1924 McKay left Paris to journey up and down the French coast, making friends with the sailors and seamen he met in small towns along the way. It was in Marseilles that McKay would meet the "black dockers, beached seamen, and other black residents . . . who composed a small, transient international community of black men from Senegal, South Africa, Dahomey, Morocco, the West Indies, and the United States."[5] Here, as Wayne Cooper has described, "McKay found . . . a community of interests and a sense of kinship he had found nowhere else in Europe."[6] It was also during this time that McKay would write his first two novels, *Home to Harlem* and *Banjo*, the latter itself a fictional account of the picaresque international black community he encountered in Marseilles.[7]

McKay finally left Marseilles in the summer of 1928, the year *Home to Harlem* appeared in the United States amid a storm of controversy from the leaders of the Harlem Renaissance. He journeyed to Morocco, traveling between 1929 and 1931 in Tangier, Madrid, and Paris before settling in an Arab village in Tangier, where he went on to write *Banana Bottom* and several short stories. Finally, in October 1933, short of funds and depressed by the lack of success of his later work, McKay applied to the U.S. consul in Tangier for a visa to return to the United States. He returned to the United States in late January 1934 after an absence of twelve years. His experiences abroad would be preserved in the work that would become his autobiography, *A Long Way From Home*.

If the resident tiller of the soil provides us with one image of the writer, his alter ego, according to Benjamin, is the traveling and trading seaman, who adds to the richness of national culture "the lore of faraway places."[8] In his autobiography and in his novels McKay attempted to be just such a storyteller, whose "tracks are frequently evident in his narratives."[9] In his autobiography

McKay tells the story of his own subject formation as a narrative of travel and exile, each chapter and stage of his life organized and titled according to his geographic location. The self he describes is merely the sum of "an impressionistic record of my observations" yet, as with any good storyteller, his record from afar had implications for the larger racial community.[10] McKay hoped that his memoir, the written exchange of his experiences, could teach African Americans how to use travel abroad "to see and understand more clearly and broadly the social and cultural position of the American Negro."[11]

McKay's primary contribution to a black transnational imaginary during this period was to write the world's story from the perspective of a traveling black subject. With all the various internationalist and nationalist narratives organizing world history and culture in the 1910s and 1920s, McKay provided an account of global events informed by his unique position as a colonial subject assigned to the margins of these new narratives. If Garvey circulated a triumphalist vision of the race at the center of a new global world order, McKay's *Home to Harlem* was a story of the race's failure at and ultimate incompatibility with the romance of nation and statehood.

But McKay's search for an alternative to the nation led not, as was the case for his traveling white American compatriots of the period, to a state of simple exile in Europe. Rather, as McKay's travels took him away from Harlem to haunt the resorts of seamen throughout France and Northern Africa, so too in his hands does the black modernist narrative stretch to accommodate a vision of a globalized, black, and male community of travelers, whose movements around the world are shaped by the changing geopolitical terrain of empire in the early decades of the twentieth century. In McKay's hands, visions of black social mobility and domestic content captured in the national romance are reinterpreted, as *Home to Harlem* explores how heterosexuality fundamentally shapes both the global drama of race war and the story of the black search for home. McKay's novels must be read not only through the lens of a gender analysis but also through the lens of a queer reading that explores how constructions and discourses of sexuality shape McKay's ultimate turn away from stories of home.

McKay was not fully a member of the literary formation known as the Harlem Renaissance in the sense that his views on black identity, politics, and culture were generated out of his experiences of the world and the African diaspora throughout his travels in the 1920s and early 1930s. McKay's autobiography and his earlier novels were works whose implications went beyond the consolidation of a national African American culture. If anything they represent his attempts to effect a reconciliation between his internationalism and his desire for cultural belonging. This chapter begins by examining McKay's relationship to the Harlem Renaissance and his search for the proper narrative form in which to tell the story of black modernity.

A LONG WAY FROM HOME:
MCKAY AND THE HARLEM RENAISSANCE

As white American expatriates were criticized for their self-imposed exiles in Europe during the 1920s, McKay was often remembered by his contemporaries for his own relationship of exile to the Harlem Renaissance and the New Negro movement. When Garvey was deported to Jamaica in the late 1920s, his contemporary and countryman McKay had already left the United States for what would become his extended sojourn in Europe and Africa.[12] While in exile McKay wrestled with the question of whether the United States could provide the worldly New Negro with any kind of home.[13]

In the early 1930s, as both *Home to Harlem* and *Banjo* were selling well throughout both North America and Europe, friends such as James Weldon Johnson implored McKay "to return to America to participate in the Negro renaissance movement."[14] McKay was not unmoved by this call, as he described in the chapter of his autobiography entitled "The New Negro in Paris":

> The Johnson letter set me thinking hard about returning to Harlem. All the reports stressed the great changes that had occurred there since my exile, pictured a Harlem spreading west and south, with splendid new blocks of houses opened up for the colored people . . . many successful colored shows on Broadway, the florescence of Negro literature and art.[15]

Harlem's growth represented a real sense of opportunity for black migrants, both literally and figuratively. Harlem, the capital of the Negro world, was establishing itself as a significant presence on North American soil, creating a cultural environment in which African Americans and other black immigrants could put down roots and imagine a home.

But the storytellers and black intellectuals at home were not happy with McKay's literary perspective from afar. As McKay recounted, "The resentment of the Negro intelligentsia against *Home to Harlem* was so general, bitter and violent that I was hesitant about returning to the great Black Belt."[16] Du Bois in particular had an especially strong reaction to *Home to Harlem*, as he described in his review of the novel: "For the most part [it] nauseates me, and after the dirtier parts of its filth I feel distinctly like taking a bath."[17] McKay specifically identified his trip to Russia and his engagement with Communist internationalism as one reason for his lack of critical popularity. By McKay's definition, African Americans were themselves black colonial subjects in search of a national home, in ways similar to the plight of other black colonials in Africa and the Caribbean. In Russia McKay argued for a definition of nationalism that could see "the great Black Belt" of the American South as a nation in its own right, deserving of self-determination. He also saw the natives of that Black Belt in terms similar to that of the Communists, as he said of *Home to Harlem*: "I consider *Home to Harlem* a real proletarian novel . . . about proletarian life . . . truthfully, realistically and artistically portrayed."[18]

But the newly formed Harlem community—"a Harlem spreading west and south, with splendid new blocks of houses opened up for the colored people"—was not at all the Southern Black Belt.[19] In Harlem, cultural advancement and class mobility within the United States were seen as more effective steps toward national recognition than the self-determination of the Black Belt. McKay's solution to the sense of displacement felt by African Americans seemed out of step with the aspirations of the growing northern black middle class. This was the perspective Du Bois articulated in an essay strongly denouncing McKay's contemporary, Garvey.

In a 1923 piece entitled "Back to Africa," Du Bois evaluated the merits and weaknesses of Garvey's movement, offering Harlem itself as a more compelling American alternative to the quest for an African homeland. He used images of domesticity as a way of representing the positive benefits of American citizenship for the African American. Du Bois's hope was that the United States could provide a home for that vision of a democratic, multiracial, and multinational society that so animated black and white progressive internationalist politics during this period. While he described the Black Star

Line's attempt to connect the diaspora as an "original and alluring program," Du Bois was wary of Garvey's potential success precisely because he had the possibility of creating "a new, autonomous, and hostile black world in league with the brown and yellow peoples."[20] His critique of Garveyism stemmed from his own internationalist vision of racial cooperation. Garvey was dangerous precisely because he came too close to success in his efforts to mobilize black subjects in a race war.

Equally interesting was Du Bois's representation of Harlem as a block of black homes, "some crowded, some carelessly kept, but most of them beautiful, even luxurious, perhaps as handsome a block as middle-class America white or black, affords."[21] With this view of Harlem Du Bois reminded African Americans that they had both a history and a future in the modern American nation. In Du Bois's construction Harlem was the home of social mobility rather than revolutionary struggle, a mobility represented in the following image of the black church:

> Down beyond, on 138th Street, the sun burns the raising spire of Abyssinian Church, a vast and striking structure built by negroes who for a hundred years have supported one organization and are now moving to their newest and luxurious home of soft carpets, stained windows, and swelling organ.[22]

Here Du Bois's images reflected the pride African Americans experienced as Harlem physically expanded and established itself around them. The impact of this urban growth on important black figures during the period is telling; both Du Bois and James Weldon Johnson, in his letter to McKay, represent Harlem's potential in the image of more and more black-owned homes appearing on more and more black-populated streets—African Americans gaining ground and territory on American soil, both literally and figuratively.

However, Du Bois's images also represent the domestic antithesis to black transnationalism and Garvey's race movement—a rootedness in Harlem, a belief in the steady advance of black life in America through class mobility, racial integration, and national citizenship. This American home of the New Negro had no room for a Garvey:

> Finally the dying rays hit a low, rambling basement of brick and stone. . . . Marcus Garvey roofed it over, and out of this squat and dirty old "Liberty

Hall" he screams his propaganda. As compared with the homes, the business, the church, Garvey's basement represents nothing in accomplishment and only waste in attempt.[23]

Ultimately for Du Bois, Garvey's call for an international black movement in struggle for an African homeland was simply a dangerous counternarrative to white supremacy: "Here is Garvey yelling to life, from the black side, a race consciousness which leaps to meet . . . [the] worshipers of the great white race. . . . [If this] sometime blazes to real flame, it means world war." Instead, Du Bois's essay ended on this note:

> On the other hand, back of all this lurks the quieter, more successful, more insistent, and hopeful fact. Races are living together. They are buying and selling, marrying and rearing children. . . . Their faith in their ultimate and complete triumph are these homes, this business block, this church, duplicated a hundred thousand times in a nation of twelve million. Here, then, are the two future paths, outlined with a certain sullen dimness in the world's blood-crimson twilight. . . . Which path will America choose?[24]

Du Bois's closing image of Harlem offered African Americans class mobility as one path toward achieving home in America. It also replaced the global vision of his essay "Worlds of Color" with a more optimistic map of the domestic world of the American New Negro, in which Harlem represented not so much a colony as the promise of multiracial national community: "Races are living together." This was the dream that also initially inspired McKay's exploration of the United States as a site for black love and home in *Home to Harlem*.

However, McKay's response to critics of *Home to Harlem* in 1932 revealed the slightly different ways in which he was thinking about Harlem as a home for the New Negro.[25] McKay's approach drew on a proletarian internationalism emanating from the Russian revolution. For McKay the issue was not whether to portray a black cultural community at home in America but rather, which aspects of that community and culture? Was the resident tiller of the soil searching for the high or the low in African American culture and society? Du Bois and other critics called for writing that reflected the best elements and highest sentiments of the national black community. Du Bois's dismissal of McKay's novel was as complete as his dismissal of Garvey and along similar lines. Both represented, as spectacles for public consumption, all that seemed sordid and unclean in Harlem life: "Whole chapters here and there . . . are on the same dirty subject. As a picture of Harlem life or of Negro life anywhere, it is, of course, nonsense. Untrue, not so much as on account of its facts, but on account of its emphasis and glaring colors."[26] McKay, however, sought to represent in his world of colors "all the lowly things that go to the formation of the Aframerican soil in which the best, the most pretentious of Aframerican society still has its roots."[27] As McKay described it, because of his focus on the lowest classes of Harlem society he had become in the minds of critics such as Du Bois "a hog rooting in Harlem, a buzzard hovering over the Black Belt scouting for carcasses."[28]

McKay portrayed those marginal figures in Harlem who had no access to Du Bois's narrative of upward mobility—the unemployed, the drifters, the criminal. But McKay not only represented a class that other writers chose to ignore. In addition, he felt that the Harlem underworld reflected a certain cosmopolitanism that made the notion of a purer, high-class African American identity unreal:

> The time when a writer will stick only to the safe old ground of his own class of people is undoubtedly passing [especially] in America, where all the peoples of the world are scrambling side by side and modern machines and the ramifications of international commerce are steadily breaking down the ethnological barriers that separate the peoples of the world.[29]

For McKay class distinctions and racial classifications were being subsumed under and organized by a general globalization of culture, one generated by modern capitalism and active within the nation's boundaries. At the beginning of the twentieth century McKay pointed to tensions that reemerged less than a century later, the difficulties in trying to maintain and preserve national cultures and identities in an increasingly internationalized world. He questioned the usefulness of staying at home, writing only on the local tales and traditions of one's group or class, when Harlem itself looked more colorful, more like the colonial worlds beyond United States borders, than the simple black and white dichotomies of American national culture.

With this brief comment McKay demonstrated a perspective on Harlem's place within the American empire much more in line with Du Bois's black transnationalism than is evident in the latter's attack on the back to Africa movement.[30] McKay's internationalism, his attempt in his fiction to engage with and imagine alternatives to nationalism and American nationality, also came with his realization of the exclusion of black Americans from the nation-building processes of the United States. McKay did not share Du Bois's optimism in the American state as the site for experiments in true multiracial democracy. McKay traced his pessimism back to his experiences as a new immigrant during the race riots of the summer of 1919. As he would describe in response to his critics:

> Before I published *Home to Harlem* I was known to the Negro public as the writer of the hortatory poem "If We Must Die." This poem was written during the time of the Chicago race riots. I was then a train waiter in the service of the Pennsylvania Railroad. Our dining car was running between New York, Philadelphia and Pittsburgh, Harrisburg and Washington and I remember we waiters and cooks carried revolvers in secret and always kept together going from our quarters to the railroad yards, as a precaution against sudden attack.[31]

McKay and his fellow black working-class migrants, far from being able to participate freely in a vibrant national community, were fugitives on the run from their fellow citizens, refugees within the urban centers of the nation-state. Here, McKay called into question the vision of happy domestic integration that Du Bois's images of Harlem strived to project. He revealed the "dirty" details of emerging black urban conditions in America and the subsequent "revelation of bitterness in Negro life."[32] As a black colonial subject McKay saw himself as a displaced fugitive from the nation rather than as an exile, and his enduring question was, what was the basis of community among a people perpetually in flight?

In *Home to Harlem* McKay wrestled with these tensions between free mobility and the New Negro's desire to feel at home in both the city and in the state. These were the tensions that also divided Du Bois's vision of African American domestic refuge and class mobility in Harlem, from Garvey's vision of the black diaspora's political freedom and mobility outside of the United States's physical and imaginative borders. While Du Bois pictured Harlem as a new home for African Americans, McKay saw in Harlem the new world for the twentieth century, a world that included an internationalized black working class. The two questions that animated his own literary quest then were, what kind of imagined community was the American nation, and was there room for the New Negro within it? If not, what forms of cultural belonging were made possible for the New World Negro in the global context of empire and colonization, war and revolution?

IN THE SHADOW OF RACE WAR:
MCKAY'S SEARCH FOR NARRATIVE FORM

World War I had an amazing impact on black writers in the United States during the early decades of the twentieth century. As McKay would describe it soon after he migrated to the United States in 1912: "The world was then a vast theater full of dramatic events. The capital of the Empire was full of British and Allied officers and soldiers. And they and the newspapers impressed upon one the fact that the world was passing through a universal upheaval."[33] McKay saw the world as a theater in which a particularly European drama was being staged, a drama whose features he would see even more clearly during a brief visit to England from 1919 to 1920. In conversations with intellectuals such as George Bernard Shaw, McKay got a sense of the effects of the war on intellectual and creative life in Europe. He observed that the "slaughter and carnage" of World War I had "had a shattering effect" on his generation of European intellectuals.[34] It was also George Bernard Shaw who first made a passing comment on the formal consequences of the war for the profession of writing. Upon hearing that McKay was a poet Shaw warned, "Poets remain poor, unless they have an empire to glorify and popularize like Kipling."[35]

In a sense, Shaw was pointing to the fact that as world events were promising to make certain notions of empire obsolete, they would also erase the need for the traditional forms and intellectuals of empire, poets such as Rudyard Kipling. Other intellectuals such as Frank Harris impressed upon McKay the idea that the political and historical events that defined the early twentieth century also required new forms of writing. Specifically, Harris would argue that the twentieth century was the "age of prose":

This is an age of prose and not of poetry. Poetry was the unique literary expression of the feudal and semi-feudal age, the romantic periods. But this is the great machine age, inventions upon inventions bringing a thou-

138 MAPPING NEW GEOGRAPHIES OF HISTORY

sand new forces and objectives into life. Language is loosening and breaking up under the pressure of new ideas and words. It requires the flexibility
of prose to express this age.[36]

McKay would later add, "Frank Harris again. . . . inspired me toward a new
achievement—the writing of prose."[37]

However, McKay was also aware that World War I had different meanings and effects for colonial subjects. For many colonial blacks participation in
the war had involved little patriotic sentiment and more imperial force. World
War I had serious implications for colonial peoples who, though themselves in
an ambiguous political status somewhere between Negro subjects of the empires and loyal citizens of the new European national states, found themselves
often on the front lines of the imperial conflicts. McKay remembered a moment during his childhood in Jamaica when "the local militia was disbanded
[because] the people of the West Indies could not be concerned in any imaginary war of the future. . . . Seven years later conscription was declared in
Jamaica . . . before it became effective in England."[38] In the United States
black involvement in the war would lead many a New Negro to develop
heightened expectations of equal treatment upon his return to the home front.
As Cyril V. Briggs would put it, "Loyalty between citizen and country does
not begin with the citizen, but with the country, which must of necessity
nurse, nourish and protect the citizen . . . in times of peace before it gets the
right to call upon that citizen to defend it in times of war."[39]

During his travels throughout Europe in the immediate postwar years,
McKay developed his own sense of the conflicts that would emerge from the
Russian Revolution. In his autobiography he described the impact of the
revolution on his own political formation: "Millions of ordinary human beings
and thousands of writers were stirred by the Russian thunder rolling round the
world. And as a social-minded being and poet, I too was moved."[40] But
McKay had another reason to look to Russia for models of revolution, self-
determination, and freedom. As he would describe the immediate postwar
period at the time of his visit to England in 1919: "The World War had ended.
But its end was a signal for the outbreak of little wars between labor and
capital and, like a plague breaking out in sore places, between colored folk and
white."[41] As the class war was breaking out McKay also observed a developing
race war, erupting in local outbursts in urban centers throughout both the

New and the Old Worlds. In his further elaboration of his experience of the race riots during the Red Summer of 1919, he presented this picture of modernity, one of black men imprisoned and immobilized by racial fear:

> Our Negro newspapers were morbid, full of details of clashes between colored and white, murderous shootings and hangings. Traveling from city to city and unable to gauge the attitude and temper of each one, we Negro railroad men were nervous. . . . We stuck together, some of us armed, going from the railroad station to our quarters. We stayed in our quarters all through the dreary ominous nights, for we never knew what was going to happen.[42]

This experience of race conflict and the ever-present threat of violence shaped the forms of community New Negro men in particular could create and imagine in Harlem during the early twentieth century. For the returning soldiers, conscripted from either the colonies or America to fight for the empire's democracy, urban life at home resembled nothing other than the desperate life of the fugitive. As Houston Baker Jr. has also described, "The world of *The New Negro* represents . . . a marooned society or nation existing on the frontiers or margins of *all* American promise."[43] This marooned society lived in the shadows of empire Du Bois described, colonial shadows that existed within the United States as much as without.

McKay's poetry during this period reflected the development of his own outsider mentality, but one that was less that of the exile than that of a racialized colonial mentality, shaped by his own initial Caribbean experiences of and formation within the context of empire. In his poem "White House," a title McKay intended to evoke the United States capital and metonym for the state, he voiced the New Negro's savage and bitter realization that he was not a part of the imagined domestic community: "Your door is shut against my tightened face, / And I am sharp as steel with discontent / . . . Oh I must search for wisdom every hour,/ . . . To hold me to the letter of your law!"[44] In the sonnet he is most famous for, "If We Must Die," McKay expressed his own rage at the violence against blacks perpetrated during Red Summer. If, according to Shaw, the poet was the literary agent of empire, here McKay used the sonnet, the most traditional of poetic forms, to call on the black subjects of empire to "face the murderous cowardly pack, / Pressed to the wall, dying, but fighting back!"[45] In McKay's mind, this was his one and only successful poetic attempt to represent the collective: "For I am so intensely subjective as a poet, that I was not aware, at the moment of writing, that I was transformed into a medium to express a mass sentiment."[46]

McKay envisioned his own migration to the United States as part of a process of transcending his bitter colonial mentality. As he would describe in his autobiography years later, "I had no desire to return home. . . . I desired to achieve something new, something in the spirit and accent of America." This spirit of America was modern, urban, and national. This was the revolutionary New World of the nation-state, not the world of empire and not the world of the colony: "Jamaica was too small for high achievement. There, one was isolated, cut off from the great currents of life." Instead, McKay would bring his uniquely colonial experience to bear on the life of the American nation: "Against its mighty throbbing force, its grand energy and power and bigness, its bitterness burning in my black body, I would raise my voice to make a canticle of my reaction."[47] In his language he expressed a masculine identification with America, the territory most representative of a new global modernity.

The question of the form of writing appropriate to express the unique circumstances of modernity would remain a major preoccupation of McKay's life and hence a major theme in his autobiography. The challenge for the black writer was how to use the novel's narrative form to represent a scattered, colonial, and fugitive black male population, constantly on the run like the Pullman porters McKay became acquainted with during Red Summer. McKay's search for the proper words and narrative can be seen as a groping for forms in which to express both the travels and the desires for refuge among this community. As a Pullman porter himself, writing in the intervals between station stops, he captured in a passing sentence the physical challenges imposed on the constantly moving Negro writer as he attempted to write his own romance of the nation: "It was much easier to create and scribble a stanza of poetry in the interval between trains than to write a paragraph of prose."[48]

Few scholars have interrogated the significance of McKay's shift in the early twenties away from poetry and toward fiction in the form of novels and short stories.[49] But this shift was an important and decisive one; in the years between 1928 and 1933, McKay produced four published volumes of fiction, including *Home to Harlem* (1928), *Banjo* (1929), *Banana Bottom* (1932), and *Gingertown* (1932), and an unpublished piece ultimately titled "Romance in Marseilles" (1930). These books came out of short stories and concepts McKay was developing as early as 1923, while he was in Europe and Africa. His autobiographical comments show that he was thinking about turning to prose as early as 1919 while he was still in the United States.

McKay's turn to the novel can be interpreted as his attempt to write the New World Negro into the nation in a romance set within a modern urban context. This attempt was inspired by discussions on the nature of statehood and political community that defined the age. His experiments with a novel of black nationhood that could represent the special, fractured, and mobile nature of the black diasporic male community required the merging of black national and transnational impulses, a merging evident in *Home to Harlem* and *Banjo: The Story Without A Plot*. In these two novels McKay tried to manage the contradictions of this twofold emerging, in black male "couplings" that embody different visions of home, movement, and ultimately black masculinity and sexuality.

Also present in both narratives is a gendered assumption. In order for transnational male protagonists to remain mobile, either within the nation or throughout the diaspora, they must forfeit a vision of home represented by women of color, domesticity, and heterosexuality. In McKay's later novel *Banana Bottom*, the writer returns to the Caribbean island as the original site of home through the narrative of a female protagonist's return to the home island and the Caribbean national romance.[50] In *Home to Harlem* and *Banjo*, however, the black male heroes are left to move freely throughout the diaspora, unattached and undomesticated.

In *Home to Harlem* McKay would turn ideas of black home and upward mobility on their heads by imagining the New Negro literally gaining ground in America through his freedom of movement in America's urban centers. In this domestic narrative, the New Negro male's movement within the nation is also envisioned as a form of trench warfare. As black American subjects (and their neighborhoods) advanced steadily throughout Harlem, they laid claim to territory within the nation as they tried to lay claim to their own equal rights as citizens.[51] *Home to Harlem* therefore represented McKay's attempt to write a national romance of the race, using here the term Doris Sommer has coined within the context of Latin American literature.[52]

Questions of domestic loyalty and national sentiment are central ones in McKay's exploration of the meanings of home, Harlem, and America for the African American citizen after World War I. These issues are raised immediately in the novel with the introduction of the lead character Jake Brown, an African American soldier who, disillusioned with the role he was given to play in the "great crusade against democracy," returns to Harlem after bouncing around Europe AWOL through the latter end of the teens.

In "Irresistible Romance: The Foundational Fictions of Latin America," Doris Sommer argues that, structurally, if one is attempting to write a national romance of a community fractured by race and gender distinctions and class stratifications, the plot must at some point find a mechanism to reconcile multiple points of identification and "bring the hero home."[53] Sommer argues that in Latin American novels of nationhood that mechanism has typically tended to be the "romance" or the "love story."[54] The story of "starcrossed lovers who represent particular regions, races, parties, or economic interests which should naturally come together" would serve as the form for a fractured political community to imagine nationhood. As Sommer continues to describe, "historical romances" would marry the sentimental novel and the heroic romance in an "idealizing 'new-comic' plot . . . (boy gets, loses, and regains girl)." In these new "patriotic romances," love stories "helped to domesticate romance, to bring the adventurous hero back to earth and back home." Sommer resolves the generic distinction between the novel and the romance in the Latin American context by arguing that, "Whether we fix on a notion of romance as an erotic quest for stable love or on romance as the quest for freedom that apparently gives up stability, the North American examples finally bring their heroes home." Wild romance and adventure get contained within the Latin American romance novel by the hero's return home, as "manly independence gave way to domesticity" and heterosexuality.[55]

If manliness gives way to feminized domesticity in Sommer's account, then gender identity and mobility can also be linked in Benedict Anderson's discussion of the relationship between the novel as a literary form and the imagined community of the nation. Anderson also describes the route of the hero in the national novel in the following terms: "This picaresque *tour d'horizon* . . . is nonetheless not a *tour du monde*. The horizon is clearly bounded."[56] This is the horizon of the nation-state, mirrored at the domestic level in the boundaries placed on the heterosexual male subject by the marriage contract. For McKay, this combination of limits to both sexual freedom and freedom of movement within the nation was also the bounded horizon facing the black soldier returning home to Harlem. When McKay imagined the worldly black soldier hero returning to the nation from war, his challenge was to reconcile this hero's desire for both home and freedom of movement, with his real domestic confinement within and by the American state.[57] In the first chapter of *Home to Harlem*, "Going Back Home," layers of irony and ambivalence are embedded in the word home as it represents America for the black male subject. The intertwined convergence of boundaries shaping both black male sexuality and mobility during this period are quickly made apparent by Jake's recounting of his experiences as a black soldier and citizen during the war.

After enlisting in 1917 Jake is sent to Brest, Germany, full of anti-German sentiment informed by United States war propaganda: "Jake thought he would like to have a crack at the Germans . . . [so] he enlisted." Jake is quickly disappointed, however, at his lack of involvement in actual front-line trench warfare: "In the winter he sailed for Brest with a happy chocolate company. Jake had his own daydreams of going over the top. But his company was held at Brest. Jake toted lumber—boards, planks, posts, rafters—for the hundreds of huts that were built around the walls of Brest . . . to house the United States soldiers."[58] While it is clear to the reader that Jake's circumscribed role in the war has everything to do with his being in a black company, his disillusionment with the racist underpinnings of national prowar sentiment actually comes two years later after he has deserted the army and is working on the docks in London during the Armistice of 1919. There he sees mirrored the Red Summer in the United States, a summer of dramatic racial tension and race riots throughout America's cities and Europe's capitals. Jake's intense alienation during this period produces his very different understanding of twentieth century war as race war:

> And that summer Jake saw a big battle staged between the colored and white men of London's East End. Fisticuffs, razor and knife and gun play. For three days his woman would not let him out-of-doors. And when it was all over he was seized with the awful fever of lonesomeness. He felt all

alone in the world. He wanted to run away from the kind-heartedness of his lady of the East End.[59]

Unlike European modernists or the American expatriates of the Lost Generation, Jake's modern sense of alienation is not produced directly by the horrors of the war being staged between the European empires, or even from his disillusionment with his own country's treatment of black soldiers. Rather, he is responding to the racial war between "colored and white" provoked by the decline of the imperial order. A clear distinction develops for Jake at this point as he, reminiscent of Garvey and Briggs, draws the lines of war differently: "Why did I ever enlist and come over here? . . . Why did I want to mix mahself up in a white folks' war? It ain't ever was any of black folks' affair."[60]

In *Home to Harlem* World War I produces in the black male subject a sense of alienation and loss from the refuge that is represented by home, women, and domestic love. Jake's realization immediately turns him cold to the affections of his white British lover: "Jake's woman could do nothing to please him now. She tried hard to get down into his thoughts and share them with him. But for Jake this woman was now only a creature of another race—of another world."[61] As the racial distinction becomes clearer to this modern black soldier in the context of urban class warfare, the race war begins to organize his own sexuality and romantic choices.

Jake's realization then produces an image of home that is not America and whiteness but specifically Harlem and blackness and, ultimately, a Harlem blackness that is embodied by black women:

It was two years since he had left Harlem. Fifth Avenue, Lenox Avenue, and One Hundred and Thirty-fifth Street, with their chocolate-brown and walnut-brown girls, were calling him. . . . Brown girls rouged and painted like dark pansies. Brown flesh draped in soft colorful clothes. Brown lips full and pouted for sweet kissing. Brown breasts throbbing with love.

"Harlem for mine!" cried Jake. . . ."Oh, boy! Harlem for mine! Take me home to Harlem, Mister Ship! Take me home to the brown gals waiting for the brown boys that done show their mettle over there. Take me home, Mister Ship."[62]

Here, the cohesiveness of a black masculine identity—made evident on the international and geopolitical stage in acts of courage, bravery, and valor in war—is secured as the black male hero imagines refuge in the arms and "brown flesh" of the woman of color. In the 1933 film *The Emperor Jones*, Brutus Jones articulates a black male experience of women during this period as tethers to their masculine mobility.[63] Jones's sentiment while in Harlem—"you's got to keep changing them [women] if you want to keep travelling light"—becomes even more firm on the island when he announces, as part of his imperial rise, "women is women, and Brutus Jones is through." However, at the outset of *Home to Harlem*, "brown women" seem to represent everything good about "black home" and its attendant values, domesticity and heterosexuality.

The novel then seems to resolve quickly the question of the location of home. Within moments of his arrival in Harlem in chapter 2, Jake meets and spends the night with Felice, "a little brown girl" whose "shaft hit home."[64] The next morning Jake wakes up "in a state of perfect [domestic] peace":

> She brought him hot coffee and cream and doughnuts. He yawned. He sighed. He was satisfied. He breakfasted. He washed. He dressed. The sun was shining. He sniffed the fine dry air. Happy, familiar Harlem.
>
> "I ain't got a cent to my name," mused Jake, "but ahm as happy as a prince, all the same. Yes, I is."[65]

The shift in and the catalyst for the novel's narrative plot occurs when Jake realizes that he has no way to get in touch with Felice after they part. The real plot of the novel begins as we follow Jake's journey through Harlem, to Philadelphia and back, into the fortuitous arms of his Harlem beloved. *Home to Harlem* does not begin as a search for an undefined home, but as a quest for a home lost and recovered within the pages of the novel itself. However, this plot is thicker than simply the search for Felice or happiness—the love story of the nation described by Sommer as "the idealizing 'new-comic' plot of the historical romance (boy gets, loses, and regains girl)."[66] Rather, the whole novel's structure is based on the premise that through Jake's intranational travels he will discover something about the meaning of the nation as home that he may not have understood before.

Harlem represents home for Jake because it provides refuge from official punishment for his desertion of the American nation-state by leaving the army. Harlem, then, is a home for black fugitives, a fugitive nation or colony existing in the shadows and "on the margins of *all* American promise," as

Houston Baker described.[67] When Jake describes where he has been during the war to his friend Zeddy Plummer he is warned:

> But you must keep it dark, buddy. . . . Don't go shooting off your mouth too free. Gov'mant still smoking out deserters and draft dodgers. . . . But I'll tell you this for your perticular information. Niggers am awful close-mouthed in some things. There is fellows here in Harlem that just telled the draft to mount upstairs. Pohlice and soldiers were hunting ev'where foh them. Ant they was right here in Harlem. Fifty dollars apiece foh them. All their friends knowed it and not a one gived them in.[68]

From the beginning of the novel then Harlem is set up as an internal space within the American nation that hides and therefore protects black male subjects from larger state structures of law and order. Home in Harlem, draft dodgers become internal refugees from the nation-state. By entering Harlem Jake has crossed a racial and a national divide; he has gone underground, entered a criminal space that renders him invisible to the state. He has entered an *internal* fugitive colony.

This understanding of Harlem is reflected further in the language Mc-Kay uses to describe one of the main Harlem cabarets, the Congo: "In spite of formidable opposition and foreign exploitation . . . the Congo was a real throbbing little Africa in New York. It was an amusement place entirely for the unwashed of the Black Belt."[69] By describing white ownership of Harlem's night life as foreign exploitation, McKay reinforces the reader's sense that external America, white America, is a separate nation. The language of this description also reflects the emerging discourse on the self-determination of the Black Belt prevalent during this period.[70] However the question raised by the novel is precisely, to which nation does the African American citizen belong? Where can he place his loyalty? What happens to the conjugal national romance when the lovers find that their enemy is the state itself?

If Harlem is the figurative image of a self-determined Black Belt, then the ideal of self-determination also appears more symbolically as a personal ideal black men and women are searching for in their relationships with each other. Black love more generally is under threat in the novel, marked and constituted by the racial tensions between the "colored and the white" in a state of national warfare. United States imperialism and internal colonialism disrupt the romantic national narrative of benevolent domesticity. As Sommer describes for the soldier citizen under these conditions, "The geopolitical reality of United States domination makes a new homecoming seem remote."[71]

In America, however, Jake's loss of home is not as straightforward as his withdrawal from his white English lover. In America national warfare is precisely about the invasion and defense of ideas of home and territory that are figured in the body of the female:

> [Women] were the real controlling force of life. Jake remembered the bal-musette fights between colored and white soldiers in France. Blacks, browns, yellows, whites. . . . He remembered the interracial sex skirmishes in England. Men fought, hurt, wounded, killed each other. Women, like blazing torches, egged them on or denounced them. Victims of sex, the men seemed foolish, ape-like blunderers in their pools of blood. Didn't know what they were fighting for, except it was to gratify some vague feeling about women.[72]

Here a certain sexualized, and to McKay's mind dangerous, notion of black masculinity is tied up with the national imaginary, one invested in heterosexual constructs. As racial and (hetero) sexual identity become linked in *Home to Harlem*, women become the embodiments of the black male citizen's right to happy domesticity in the nation. They are both the battleground and the prize for the hero against his enemies in the nation-state.

In these struggles over women, Jake's brown girl and others like her represent something different and racially authentic. The Congo is an important Black Belt cabaret precisely because it is a place where Jake and his black male compatriots can find refuge from war in authentically homegrown black women who embody the romanticized home of the black South. As Zeddy describes it, the Congo is "always packed with the best pickings. When the chippies come up from down home, that's where they hangs out first. You kain always find something that New York ain't done made a fool of yet."[73] It is this domesticated vision of sexual home that Jake begins to lose as he becomes immersed in the Harlem lifestyle. The warring relations between black men and women, and between men in general over women, begin to dominate as Jake slowly loses sight of the vision afforded him in his initial encounter with Felice. Hence, Jake leaves Harlem: "Well, I'd better pull outa that there mudhole. . . . It wan't what I came back to Gawd's own country foh. No, sirree! You bet it wasn't."[74]

In part I of *Home to Harlem* McKay, through the character Jake, sets out the various benefits and losses of Harlem as a site for homemaking for the modern African American male, an alienated fugitive from official American nationalism and the state. On one hand, Harlem serves as an internal colony where Jake can find refuge in the protective security of his racial identity and culture, somewhat immune to the whiter influences of the larger nation as a whole. However, in locating home in the arms and body of the black woman, Jake finds himself falling subject to the traps that come with the contestations over home, the war between men of all races fought over the bodies of black women. This struggle, the battle for territory that is epitomized by World War I and translated in the black colonial's terms as a war for Harlem and the black woman, is precisely what Jake attempts to escape through intranational migration. Jake's job with the Pennsylvania railroad and his ventures in Philadelphia are figures for the internal migration of southern blacks throughout this part of the century and, in a more metaphorical sense, the migrations and escape of the black male subject from notions of masculinity intertwined with the racial battle and the heterosexual, national romance.

In part II of the novel the character Ray is introduced, a Haitian intellectual whom Jake meets while working as a Pullman porter on the railroad. Ray provides Jake and the reader with another romance of home, nation, and masculinity that offers the African American male a transnational model for his quest. Upon first meeting Ray, Jake makes clear his homeless, nationless, fugitive status: "I was way, way ovah there after Democracy and them boches, and when I could'nt find one or the other, I jest turned mah black moon from the A.E.F."[75] However Jake is thrown into confusion by Ray's ability to speak French: it disrupts his sense of who the "we" are in the subaltern war between imperial European whiteness and colonized blackness.[76] As Ray states:

> "French is my native language. I—"
> "Don't crap me," Jake interrupted.
> "Ain'tchu—ain'tchu one of us, too?"
> "Of course I'm Negro," the waiter said, "but I was born in Hayti and the language down there is French."

"Hayti . . . Hayti," repeated Jake. "Tha's where now? Tha's—"

"An island in the Caribbean—near the Panama Canal."[77]

This introduction of the Caribbean island of Haiti, one that will become explicitly transnational in a second, takes Jake and the reader firmly away from the more provincial and ethnically stereotypical constructions of West Indians we find in part I. There, West Indian and African American relations are bound by immigrant and ethnic racial and cultural tensions produced by the boundaries of the nation as a whole.[78] Ray provides a wholly new context for Jake to understand West Indians as compatriots in an international search for black nationhood that keeps the diaspora at the center. As the character Ray develops over the course of the novel, it also becomes clear that his romance of the race is primarily a romance between black men; in *Home to Harlem* Ray is the figure who offers the most explicit critique of heterosexuality as a formation serving to domesticate the black male subject within the nation-state. Not surprisingly, Ray leaves the novel a fugitive from domesticity, only to reappear among the black male community in Marseilles in *Home to Harlem*'s sequel, *Banjo*.

However, when Ray first appears in *Home to Harlem* his initial function is to frame the questions of black masculine freedom and mobility within the specific context of empire. Ray's story of his origin and background in Haiti serves as his own shadow narrative of United States imperialism. His narrative brings to light the dark side of American nationality with a specific critique of America's own imperial ventures. Ray's story of his own migration to and presence in America explicitly implicates the nation in the act of imposing imperial military force against Third World black revolutions:

> "Uncle Sam put me here."
>
> "Whadye mean Uncle Sam?" cried Jake. "Don't hand me that bull."
>
> "Let me tell you about it," the waiter said. "Maybe you don't know that during the World War Uncle Sam grabbed Hayti. My father was an official down there. He didn't want Uncle Sam in Hayti and he said so and said it out loud. They told him to shut up and he wouldn't, so they shut him up in jail. My brother also made a noise and American marines[79] killed him in the street. I had nobody to pay for me at the university, so I had to get out and work. *Voilà!*"[80]

This narrative is one that Jake, the American Negro, is unaware of. But Ray provides much more than an anti-imperialist exposé, adding to his critique of empire an invocation of the spirit of black revolution as the necessary foundation to his narrative of Haiti's national independence:

> Jake sat like a big eager boy and learned many facts about Hayti before the train reached Pittsburgh. He learned that the universal spirit of the French Revolution had reached and lifted up the slaves far away in that remote island; that Black Hayti's independence was more dramatic and picturesque than the United States' independence and that it was a strange, almost unimaginable eruption of the beautiful ideas of the "Liberté, Egalité, Fraternité" of Mankind, that shook the foundations of that romantic era.[81]

Unlike Garvey, the story of nationhood and independence that Ray tells starts from the perspective of black revolution rather than empire. Ray's story then enables Jake to see the unimaginable: black revolution as a self-determining counterforce to imperial race war, one that can overthrow official nationalisms and the colonial mentality.

Ray's story of black nationhood is also a story of racial manhood, as Jake's immediate reaction makes clear. Upon hearing about Toussaint L'Ouverture he exclaims, "A black man! A black man! Oh, I wish I'd been a soldier under sich a man!"[82] Jake, the black soldier citizen, recognizes his true national loyalties in the race war between colonizer and colonized, and the figure of the black male sovereign once again becomes central to this dream, the metonymic embodiment of this masculine global imaginary Ray is helping Jake to envision. The narrator adds, "It was incredible to Jake that a little island of freed slaves had withstood the three leading European powers."

While Ray begins his tale with the story of black revolution, with blacks seizing freedom and self-determination for themselves, the second half of his narrative provides the postcolonial vision of nation-building. As he relates the story of Dessalines he emphasizes the struggle to maintain black nationhood in the context of Western imperialism: "Dessalines, who carried on the fight begun by Toussaint L'Ouverture and kept Hayti independent."[83] Ray's description of Haiti that follows for the next few pages is a crucial one in understanding the function of his transnational discourse at this stage of the novel. Ray is here weaving a romance of self-determined blackness that, unlike the Harlem vision, explicitly counters the imperial wars with a vision of black revolution that relies on black racial solidarity. His story of racial solidarity is a transnational one because it pulls Jake out of his own nationality, both as an American and as a Harlemite, and into a more internationalist imagining both of racial home and his own black masculinity.

> Jake felt like one passing through a dream, vivid in rich, varied colors. It was a revelation beautiful in his mind. That brief account of an island of savage black people, who fought for collective liberty and was struggling to create a culture of their own. *A romance of his race*, just down there by Panama. How strange!
>
> Jake was American in spirit and shared a little of that comfortable Yankee contempt for poor foreigners. And as an American Negro he looked askew at foreign niggers. Africa, was jungle, and Africans bush niggers, cannibals. And West Indians were monkey-chasers. *But now he felt like a boy who stands with the map of the world in colors before him, and feels the wonder of the world.*[84]

In this romance of his race Jake experiences an epistemological rebirth and an identity transformation simultaneously, as he stands like a boy facing a new map of the worlds of color. Jake's epiphany at this point in the novel represents his transition from the national romance to the transnational one. As he imagines "the map of the world in colors before him," he sees a vision of a multiracial blackness, a world that enables multiple identifications across national lines, in the name of blackness. He sees Garvey's Negro world, Du Bois's colonial worlds of color, and the romance of Ray's narrative is precisely that it escapes the boundaries of the American nation: "A romance of his race, just down there by Panama."

The "map of the world in colors before him" is an image of the race that is also similar to Garvey's notion of "the colors of that great Empire of Ethiopia that is now scattered all over the world."[85] At first the shift in language, from empire to maps, seems to represent an ideological shift in the definition of the race from imperial racial hierarchies to equally dangerous, naturalized, and nationalist myths of racial authenticity. For McKay, black self-determination is rooted in an authentic blackness that serves as the foundation of any sort of organized imagined community. In Harlem home also represents a solid rootedness in racial identity, an essentialism that serves as the fundamental ground for the shifting colors and classes of blacks within the internal colony itself. As the narrator describes Harlem:

> Ancient black life rooted upon its base with all its fascinating new layers of brown, low-brown, high-brown, nut-brown, lemon, maroon, olive, mauve, gold. Yellow balancing between black and white. Black reaching out beyond yellow. Almost-white on the brink of a change. Sucked back down into the current of black by the terribly sweet rhythm of black blood.[86]

However, while discussions of McKay's work and *Home to Harlem* in particular have tended to foreground these aspects of McKay's racial philosophy as a form of racial primitivism, the one place where he locates authentic blackness and home, I would also suggest that within this vision of "ancient black life rooted" are multiple racial significations that, like mercury, flow both toward and away from ideas of blackness as an essentialist physiological basis to racial identity. The passage quoted above images race as a viscous and mobile fluid, constantly "balancing," "reaching out beyond," "on the brink," then "sucked back down into the current." The stickiness of this image, flowing neither smoothly nor straightforwardly in a particular direction, though some essential notion of blackness remains its final destination, makes it a perfect metaphor in McKay's account for the hybridity of black subjectivity and the geographic black world.

The discourse of race has always been central to the political language of nationalism and home, a discourse of attachment that describes national loyalty as "something to which one is naturally tied . . . nation-ness is assimilated to skin-color, gender," all compulsive attractions and affinities—"all those things one can not help."[87] The transnational perspective and story offered by the Caribbean intellectual Ray does not so much replace as complicate that reading. For like Garvey, while Ray's story is a black nationalist one, its import as a heroic narrative of a hybrid racial diaspora is much more wide-ranging. Ray's *telling* of the story is also important for his ability to enable a transnational epiphany or revelation. The story the West Indian character brings to the American Negro internationalizes the latter's own racial and masculine identity.

As Ray continues to spin narratives of the black nation their import is not individual but collective and accumulative, providing a global vision of black transnational revolution that can serve as an alternative ground for constructing black nationalities to the framework of sexually bounded domesticity in the nation:

> He told Jake of the old destroyed cultures of West Africa and of their vestiges, of black kings who struggled stoutly for the independence of their kingdoms: Prempreh of Ashanti, Tofa of Dahomey, Gbehanzin of Benin, Cetawayo of Zulu-Land, Menelik of Abyssinia. . . . Had Jake ever heard of the little Republic of Liberia, founded by American Negroes? And Abyssinia, deep-set in the shoulder of Africa, besieged by the hungry wolves of Europe? The only nation that has existed free and independent from the earliest records of history until today! Abyssinia, oldest unconquered nation, ancient-strange as Egypt, persistent as Palestine, legendary as Greece, magical as Persia.[88]

These Ethiopianist narratives of African nationhood are important as global examples of unconquered and undomesticated black masculinity and struggles for liberation that include American blacks. They resonate with Garvey's discourse precisely because they provide the image not so much of individuals and families acquiring black citizenship in a steadily upward social climb within the nation, but rather, the image of armies of black male leaders and soldiers seizing black nationhood for the race around the globe. They also provide an image of ancient African and classical European worlds as overlapping historical spaces of cultural exchange, creating a geohistorical space from which many races can find a useable past, beyond the simple narrative of the superiority of Western civilization.

Ray's story lies at the heart of McKay's romance of blackness in *Home To Harlem*. It is an imagination of home as racial diaspora that troubles the domestic romantic boundaries of the novel's narrative of the nation. In a sense it mirrors the older form and function of the romance as Sommer has described, less the modern historical and national novel than the romance of old, "a tale of wild adventures in love and chivalry," a form "more boldly allegorical" than the bourgeois love story.[89] But Ray's story functions less as an allegory for Jake to apply than as an opening for intraracial dialogue and identification, the actual experiencing of a diasporic, masculine community and intimacy. As such, it imagines a third option for communicating the idea of a black transnationality and the political vision of a black global imaginary. In addition to the novel and the romance, we have the act of storytelling itself. As Walter Benjamin observed, "A man listening to a story is in the company of the storyteller; even a man reading one shares this companionship. The reader of a novel, however, is isolated, more so than any other reader."[90] In the act of storytelling, the black nation is imagined through the experience of a community of at least two men—the storyteller Ray, and the listener Jake.

Ultimately, the question at the heart of Ray's romantic tale of global blackness is the viability of nationhood and home for the worldly black male subject. Unlike Jake, who has Harlem and "could pick up love easily on the street,"[91] Ray's intellectual musings on and personal relationship to home, heterosexual couplings, and domesticity throughout *Home to Harlem* ultimately reflect a sharp critique of nationality and black heterosexuality. His images of home rely purely on his memory and re-creation of Haiti. In his dreams he replays the conventional trope of the Caribbean male exile imaginatively re-creating his island home:[92]

> He flung himself across void and water, back home. Home thoughts, if you can make them soft and sweet and misty-beautiful enough, can sometimes snare sleep. There was the quiet, chalky-dusty street and, jutting out over it, the front of the house that he had lived in.[93]

However, Ray's sleepy dream is disturbed by the working-class black railroad men around him:

> Sleep remained cold and distant. Intermittently the cooks broke their snoring with masticating noises of their fat lips, like animals eating. Ray fixed his eyes on the offensive bug-bitten bulk of the chef. These men claimed kinship with him. They were black like him. Man and nature had put them in the same race. He ought to love them and feel them (if they felt anything). He ought to if he had a shred of social morality in him. . . . Race. . . . Why should he have and love a race?[94]

Passages such as these have led to interpretations of Ray as the traditional intellectual both fascinated with and repelled by the masses. While this is true enough, I would argue that this is not simply the cringing of the highbrow intellectual from the people, but a cringing from the national terms in which masculine solidarity and racial peoplehood is being understood and constructed during this period. This cringing from "social morality"—a phrase McKay will use again in Ray's voice in *Banjo*—comes not from a racial self-hatred and antiblack nationalism per se, but from the concomitant and linked critique of the gendered terms of historical nationalism, a critique emerging from the recognition of the connections between masculine desires for sovereignty and home on one hand and imperialism and race war on the other.

In Ray's musings we find an emergent antinational discourse that contemplates the possibilities non-nationhood might provide for black male subjects desiring to be in community with each other, on different terms. As Ray continues:

> Races and nations were things like skunks, whose smells poisoned the air of life. Yet civilized mankind reposed its faith and future in their ancient, silted channels. Great races and big nations! There must be something mighty inspiriting in being the citizen of a great strong nation. . . .
>
> Ray felt that as he was conscious of being black and impotent, so, correspondingly, each marine down in Hayti must be conscious of being white and powerful. What a unique feeling of confidence about life the typical white youth of his age must have![95]

Like Garvey, Ray recognized "the white [man's] prowess in the law of monopoly," the connections between turn of the century notions of manhood and ideas of racial dominance.[96] However, unlike Garvey, Ray does not hope that this racial fiction "will be an inspiration to some black man or woman to some black boy or girl to go through the world accomplishing something grand and great as the white man is now doing." Rather, as Ray's musings continue, the principle of nationhood and the status of citizenship become evermore corrupted and deformed by their historical inheritance of the racial legacies of colonialism and white European imperialism:

> Knowing that his skin-color was a passport to glory, making him one with ten thousands like himself. All perfect Occidentals and investors in that grand business called civilization. The grand business in whose pits sweated and snored, like the cooks, all the black and brown hybrids and mongrels, simple and earth-loving animals, without aspirations toward national unity and racial arrogance.[97]

Given the context of imperialism, and the brown backs upon whom the imperialist nation-state was being built, a notion of masculinity based on citizenship actually becomes for Ray a thing to be scorned:

> To be the white citizen of a nation that can say bold, challenging things like a strong man. Something very different from the keen ecstatic joy a man feels in the romance of being black. [Nation-hood.] Something the black man could never feel nor quite understand.[98]

While Garvey constructed a masculinist imperial history to shore up the black male subject's right to citizenship in the new imperial national order, McKay denounces the nationalist fiction completely, framing racial diaspora, "the keen ecstatic joy a man feels in the romance of being black," as an alternative form of black masculinity antithetical to nationalism, "something the black man could never feel nor quite understand." Crucial to Ray's thinking is his sense that nationalism is also antithetical to blackness. It is not so much blackness itself but the narrative of black diasporan unity that Ray is using to counter European nationalism. Ray frames blackness as fundamentally diasporic, as itself a strategic essentialism necessary for imagining other forms of black collective organization that could counter the powerful myth of nationhood.

In the multifunctional character Ray, McKay also embodies his own search for a literary form and language, one flexible enough to articulate this sense of the diaspora, his own masculine global imaginary. The historical context of war and revolution—"the total evil that the one had wrought . . . the ultimate splendor of the other"—both inform and obstruct Ray's "dream . . . of writing words some day. Weaving words to make a romance."[99] Ray sees corrupting imperial realities behind the nationalist ideal, "the perfectly-organized national rages, the ineffectual patching of broken, and hectic rebuilding of shattered, things."[100] In addition, "he had perception enough to realize that he had lived over the end of an era . . . [and] his spiritual masters had not crossed with him into the new":

> Even as the last scion of a famous line prances out this day and dies and is set aside with his ancestors in their cold-whited sepulcher, so had his masters marched with flags and banners flying all their wonderful, trenchant, critical, satirical, mind-sharpening, pity-evoking, constructive ideas of ul-

timate social righteousness, into the vast international cemetery of this century.[101]

But unlike Garvey, who planted in that cemetery his own troublesome words, the fiction and romance of a black empire that made him infamous, on the question of a language of black statehood Ray is confused, without a plan for the race, without a vision of the future: "Thank God and Uncle Sam that the old dreams were shattered. Nevertheless, he still felt more than ever the utter blinding nakedness and violent coloring of life. But what of it? Could he create out of the fertile reality around him?"[102] This dilemma, which "seized and worried him from every angle," pushes Ray "toward the sheer precipice of imagination": "It was awful. He was afraid. For thought was a terrible tiger clawing at his small portion of gray substance, throttling, tearing, and tormenting him with pitiless ferocity. Oh, a thousand ideas of life were shrieking at him in a wild orgy of mockery! . . . He was in the middle of a world suspended in space."[103] Ray's torture of articulation, his pain in attempting to imagine the national, the racial, and the transnational together in "a world suspended in space" is informed by his historical moment. Ray is struggling to imagine models of black freedom in the context of empire, war, and revolution. He struggles to create from the vocabularies of statehood that imperial official nationalisms have provided him: "Dreams of patterns of words achieving form. What would he ever do with the words he had acquired? Were they adequate to tell the thoughts he felt, describe the impressions that reached him vividly? What were men making of words now?"[104]

As the figure for the writer in McKay's fiction, Ray lays bare the contradictions McKay and many of the black male intellectuals of this period were dealing with as they tried to imagine a new world at the beginning of the twentieth century. Ray's struggle to write reflects his difficulty in expressing something completely new and outside of the racial and national terms of identity as currently set by the imperial order. As themselves men without nations, black subjects defied all the recognized categories. Ray's sensitivity to the various ideological and philosophical pressures tugging at the world prevents him from finding an easy imaginative resolution in the safety of Harlem and domestic romance: "Jake was as happy as a kid. He would be frisking if he could. But Ray was not happy. The sudden upset of affairs in his home country had landed him into the quivering heart of a naked world whose reality was hitherto unimaginable."[105] Ray's quest is to discover how a more picaresque vision of blackness fits into the new national order. Could he create a new sense of nationality from the community of black men around him, a romance of blackness about the Jakes "nosing through life" like "handsome hounds"? Was there something in blackness, "elements that the grand carnage swept over and touched not?"[106]

Undergirding all of this is Ray's desire to reframe his own masculinity and the terms of his identification with, feelings for, and love of other black men. In Ray, McKay expresses a highly sophisticated understanding of the degrees to which the nation-state structures and organizes narratives of racial citizenship through the discourse of heterosexual domesticity. As Ray imaginatively returns to Haiti to try to imagine the peace that could be achieved for the black male subject in finding home in the Caribbean nation, he moves through a series of dreams whose trajectory ultimately take him away from conventional images of home. Instead, he finds an alternative space of sexual license and blackness, a utopian romance with both Ethiopianist and Orientalist overtones.

Referencing the following passage, Brent Edwards has argued that in *Home to Harlem* Ray holds onto a sense of "nationalist privilege" which he then forsakes for the life of the "vagabond" in *Banjo*:[107]

> [Ray] remembered when little Hayti was floundering uncontrolled, how proud he was to be the son of a free nation . . . some day Uncle Sam might let go of his island and he would escape from the clutches of that magnificent monster of civilization and retire behind the natural defenses of his island, where the steam roller of progress could not reach him. Escape he would. He had faith. He had hope.[108]

But we see the signs and understand more fully the sources of the character Ray's transnational inclinations if we interpret Ray's further reflections on home in *Home to Harlem*. For despite the longing for Haiti expressed in the passage above, Ray is ultimately pulled *away* from national identification and *back* to not just race but the men lying around him, by recalling his own sympathies, affinities, and desires to be in solidarity with his African American, working-class comrades, this underworld of "waiters, cooks, chauffeurs, sailors, porters, guides, ushers, hod-carriers, factory hands."[109] As he laments: "But, oh, what would become of that great mass of black swine, hunted and

cornered by slavering white canaille! Sleep! oh, sleep! Down Thought!"[110]
Here Ray's dream of home is brought up short by his realization that an escape
from American civilization into the dream of a free Caribbean nationhood is a
false escape from an imperialism of the mind that still has a firm hold on
masses of colonized black people across the world and structures globally the
boundaries of home and national identity. In a sense, his is a false freedom if
black nationhood and black masculinity are not conceived in the crucible of an
international diasporan consciousness.

This is the dilemma of the black, transnational, male intellectual: How
does one find home in the context of worldwide imperialism, where ultimately
no man is free if all are not free? No one has the racial passport to glory if
blackness is still an illegal racial category across the globe. Seeking respite
from this torturous reality, Ray takes a few hits of street drugs Jake had
acquired at one of their stops in the city and dreams his version of an Ethiopianist racial fantasy of utopia:

> Immediately he was back home again [in Haiti]. . . . and he was a gay
> humming-bird, fluttering and darting his long needle beak into the heart
> of a bell-flower. [Then] [s]uddenly he changed into an owl flying by
> day. . . . Now he was a young shining chief in a marble palace; slim, naked
> negresses dancing for his pleasure; courtiers reclining on cushions soft like
> passionate kisses; gleaming-skinned black boys bearing goblets of wine
> and obedient eunuchs waiting in the offing. . . .
>
> And the world was a blue paradise. . . . Woods and streams were blue,
> and men and women and animals, and beautiful to see and love. And he
> was a blue bird in flight and a blue lizard in love. . . . Taboos and terrors
> and penalties were transformed into new pagan delights, orgies of Orient-
> blue carnival, of rare flowers and red fruits, cherubs and seraphs and
> fetishes and phalli and all the most-high gods.[111]

The Afro-Orientalism of this passage, features of which we will also see later
in McKay's work, provides the author with a language in which to imagine an
alternative space for and performance of black masculinity.[112] Here the black
male subject flies away from even his Caribbean nation-home to a multicultural premodern dreamscape in which he can actualize in himself the figure
of the black, male, sovereign self. Here in this palace we see a smorgasbord of
at least four forms and performances of sexuality, but the black male intellec-

tual is also freed from sexual and physical restraints, simultaneously "blue bird" and "blue lizard," "in flight . . . and . . . in love," he uses the primitivist language of "taboos," "fetishes," and "phalli" to access an alternative way of imagining his own sexuality outside of a traditional, national, domestic sphere.

When Ray leaves the novel for a journey that, fictionally, will culminate in Marseilles in *Banjo*, he expresses scorn for the New Negro Jake's choice to stay at home in Harlem, ever in search of happy domesticity:

> Harlem nigger strutting his stuff . . . harlem niggers! How often he had listened to those phrases, like jets of saliva, spewing from the lips of his work pals. They pursued, scared, and haunted him. He was afraid that some day the urge of the flesh and the mind's hankering after the pattern of respectable comfort might chase his high dreams out of him and deflate him to the contented animal that was a Harlem nigger strutting his stuff.[113]

Ray is wary of a notion of black masculine identity—"the contented animal that was a Harlem nigger strutting his stuff"—too easily located in a domesticity that could forever imprison his migratory inclinations.

Part I of *Home to Harlem* should be read as McKay's picaresque establishment of Harlem as one type of home, one form of imagining blackness and nation-ness and one way of imagining black male and female identity within the nation. In part II he troubles the question, identifying the struggle to write home and define its different locations as a painful process of disarticulating and deconstructing the vocabulary of nationhood and black domesticity in favor of a romantic language of a free black masculinity in diaspora. Part III attempts to provide closure by returning to the domesticated plot of the national romance. As we follow Jake back to Harlem, we see McKay attempting to envision a new type of home for the migratory black ethnic subject within the American nation-state. Two songs, one a Southern ballad, the other a West Indian folk song, sung at the moment of Ray and Jake's mutual departure, epitomize the paths chosen by each, respectively:

> Empty is you' room,
> Empty is you' room,
> Empty is you' room,
> But you find one in the sea.

Back home in Dixie is a brown gal there,
Back home in Dixie is a brown gal there,
Back home in Dixie is a brown gal there,
Back home in Dixie I was bawn in.[114]

Jake's path eventually places him as a refugee citizen and fugitive within the United States. While he still seeks home, his quest is now informed by a transnational perspective that arms him against the traps of Harlem, the race war, and a safe internal immersion in blackness. While he still finds home domestically in his romance with his brown girl Felice, it is a black love that also comes out from the underworld and blatantly challenges the racial ideologies of the American nation itself. Black love is presented as a counter to whiteness and imperialism, the moving shadow narrative of white America's bourgeois, heterosexual love story.

### BLACK LOVE IN AMERICA

In Jake and Felice's first scene outdoors after they reunite, the two lovers take a walk in a white neighborhood described as "The Block Beautiful": "With its charming green lawns and quaint white-fronted houses, it preserved the most Arcadian atmosphere in all New York."[115] In describing the scene McKay uses the imagery of trench warfare to picture a black Harlem slowly invading white territory in the nation. Unlike Du Bois's image of the black church as a symbol for black progress in Harlem, now in McKay's account it is a white church that figures prominently:

> They had walked down Madison Avenue, turned on One Hundred and Thirtieth Street, passing the solid gray-grim mass of the whites' Presbyterian church. . . . The whites had not evacuated that block yet. The black invasion was threatening it from One Hundred and Thirty-First Street, from Fifth Avenue, even from behind in One Hundred and Twenty-Ninth Street. . . . The Presbyterian church frowned on the corner like a fortress against the invasion. The Block Beautiful was worth a struggle. . . . loud-laughing-and-acting black swains and their sweethearts had started in using the block for their after-noon promenade. That was the limit: the desecrating of that atmosphere by black love in the very shadow of the gray, gaunt Protestant church.[116]

Jake and Felice's black love gives this romance of home a happy ending, but one which is also clearly troubled in McKay's overall narrative schema. The language McKay uses to describe Jake's move toward stability and security as opposed to his more picaresque existence in part I reflects these tensions. While Jake's earlier lifestyle in Harlem is described as "transient rhythms that touch and pass you, unrememberable, and rhythms unforgettable," Jake's final choice rests on a naive desire for closure that to the narrator and Ray has dangerous, delusional, rhythms: "His thought was not touched by the faintest fear of a blood battle. His mind was a circle containing the girl and himself only, making a thousand plans of the joys they would create together. She was a prize to hold. . . . *Imperial rhythms* whose vivid splendor blinds your sight."[117] Jake risks losing the lessons he has learned about the intertwining of sexuality and race war in the safe refuge of a blinding love. But his eyes are opened at the last minute before the novel ends, when the world of nationhood and racial warfare once again intrudes.

While Jake was away, unbeknownst to either man his close friend Zeddy had taken up with Felice. Once Zeddy discovers that Felice is leaving him for Jake, he attacks Jake. Once again, Jake is reminded of the violence associated with love and the inescapable terms in which one finds home in the domesticated romance. Embodied in womanhood, the search for nationhood is inextricably linked to the struggle over territory, rights, and claims: "miserable cock-fights, beastly, tigerish, bloody. . . . Why should love create terror?"[118] Behind Jake's lament is his desire for home and love to represent not race war—a warring between racial camps that occurs over the bodies of women— but rather the ideal of multiracial cooperation in the building of democratic and racially inclusive communities. Instead, the racial violence present within the American state corrupts even the solidarity necessary between black subjects and, by extension, within multinational black communities. It is less the physical attack that disturbs Jake than Zeddy's violation of the principle of black male solidarity in the face of the oppressive American state: "Zeddy looked Jake steadily in the face and said: 'You kain kill me nigger, ef you wanta. You come gunning at me, but you didn't go gunning after the Germans. Nosah! You was scared and runned away from the army.'" Zeddy's betrayal cuts Jake to the quick: "Jake looked bewildered, sick. He was hurt now to his heart and he was dumb."[119] While America has now once again become his, like Ray Jake cannot imagine a home without pain and terror.

Jake resolves to seek his solution in travel but Felice reminds him of his right to nationality and to citizenship, his domestic entitlements: "What you wanta go knocking around them foreign countries again for like swallow come and swallow go from year to year and nevah settling down no place? This heah is you' country, daddy." The couple effect an uncertain compromise: "Now it was Felice's turn. 'You ain't telling me a thing, daddy. I'll be slack with you and desert with you. . . . Jest le's beat it away from Harlem, daddy. This heah country is good and big enough for us to git lost in.'"[120] Lost in the nation these deserters reframe citizenship as exile. The nation-state becomes not the refuge of home but the home of refugees.

The reality of the nation-state as the enemy of black love and the black citizen prevents *Home to Harlem* from being an irresistible romance of the nation. For while the plot does bring the "adventurous hero," Jake, "back to earth and back home,"[121] he cannot afford to give up his mobility, precisely because he needs it for his survival. Jake and Felice's status as a national couple resists the domestication or bourgeoisification of their romance that would turn their quest for freedom into simply a quest for stable love. By traveling through the landscape of the nation now as part of a couple as opposed to simply the solitary hero, Jake takes the romance of blackness, his felicity, with him as refuge in a fugitive existence on the run from the state.

*Home to Harlem* would prove to be the closest McKay would get to articulating in his fiction any national affiliation or relationship to America. McKay could have written his version of the domesticated national romance, a romance of blackness uniting the African American soldier citizen Jake with America. The West Indian character, however, disrupts the novel in three ways: he reinserts the shadow of United States imperialism belying the nation-state's myth of democracy; he offers an alternative, internationalist romance, replete with thrilling stories and revolutionary inventions of black nationhood and black sexual identity; and finally, in telling his tale, Ray reaches across the black Atlantic to connect with his imagined brother. As such the character Ray serves a particular mediating function in McKay's fiction, similar to what Homi K. Bhabha has described as "a chiasmatic 'figure' of cultural difference whereby the antinationalist, ambivalent nation-state becomes the crossroads to a new transnational culture."[122] It is precisely in Marseilles that Ray would briefly find that new and imagined transnational racial home, among Banjo and his crew of traveling seamen and musicians, the subjects of the next chapter.

In 1882 when Ernest Renan first asked "What is a nation?" he was inquiring into precisely the nature of forms of cultural belonging and collective identification in modernity.[123] He recounted a number of possible responses, including the idea of a nation as an imperial dynasty "representing an earlier conquest . . . forgotten by the mass of the people." This was the vision of black nationhood that Garvey spectacularized and put in motion in his vision of the Negro world as an African empire. Renan also described nations as potentially representing "a community of interest [creating] a powerful bond between men." This has often been a primary way of characterizing the political solidarity that constituted the Pan-Africanist movement of the late nineteenth century and early twentieth.[124]

But still, Renan argued, nationalism consisted of more than the political representation of group rights and common interests: "Community of interest brings about trade agreements, but *nationality has a sentimental side to it*, it is both soul and body at once."[125] The sentimental side of imagined communities, what Renan would also describe as "the desire to live together," was precisely what McKay hoped to find and then express in *Home to Harlem*.[126] Harlem, the Negro metropolis, represented modern black subjects' desires for their own self-determination and their willingness to be in partnership with other modern racial subjects, across lines of color, gender, language, and culture, in the imagining and building of a national community. McKay imagined the modern black and colonial world as a multiethnic and racially diverse community within the United States, expressing the desire to live together in solidarity with each other and with their white neighbors. The end of McKay's belief in the liberal ideals of the nation as an expansive imagined community are captured in the final image of his love story of a fugitive black love on the run. In McKay's Harlem, Black Belt of the metropolis, the rows and blocks of houses served only as temporary way stations in the worldly New Negro's quest for acceptance within the city, the national community, and by extension, the state.

CHAPTER 6

# "Nationality Doubtful" and *Banjo*'s
# Crew in Marseilles

*Marseilles*—the yellow-studded maw of a seal with salt water running out between
the teeth. When this gullet opens to catch the black and brown proletarian bodies
thrown to it by ship's companies according to their timetables, it exhales a stink
of oil, urine and printer's ink.

—WALTER BENJAMIN[1]

IN 1922, just before McKay was to leave for Russia he received an unexpected
visitor. As he awkwardly described, "A woman walked in to whom I had been
married seven years before."[2] McKay was in no way committed to maintaining
the marriage: "There were consequences of the moment that I could not face.
I desired to be footloose, and felt impelled to start going again."[3] The woman
was a fellow Jamaican McKay had married in 1916 when he first arrived in
Harlem. One of the consequences of that marriage was his daughter, Ruth
Hope McKay. In his autobiography, he describes this unexpected reminder of
conjugal obligation as one of the catalysts for his trip to Russia: "Go and see,
was the command. Escape from the pit of sex and poverty, from domestic
death, from the cul-de-sac of self-pity, from the hot, syncopated fascination of
Harlem, from the suffocating ghetto of color consciousness. Go, better than
stand still, keep going."[4] This passage reveals some of McKay's own ultimate
decisions about heterosexual domesticity. When McKay first settled in Harlem he had attempted to live the bourgeois life; he married, had a child, and
tried to operate a West Indian restaurant. His strong reaction to the reappearance of his wife is a final renunciation of that lifestyle—he had become
"undomesticated in the blood." The imperative to "go and see" meant leaving

the domestic context, literally and figuratively: "Domestic death" would have signified both his marriage and the end to his travels abroad.[5]

The domestic heterosexual relationship is an essential source of the family of the nation, as Doris Sommer has described: "Part of the conjugal romance's national project, perhaps the main part, is to produce legitimate citizens, literally to engender civilization."[6] This was precisely the consequence of marriage McKay was not prepared to face. Uninterested in the romance of engendering the black nation, the story *Banjo* is built on the abandonment of the only significant female character, Latnah, a woman of mysterious hybridity, as Banjo's friend Malty describes her: "[Latnah was] a li'l woman bumming like us on the beach. I don't know whether she is Arabian or Persian or Indian. She knows all landwidges."[7] As the novel develops Latnah and the main male character Banjo become lovers, even at times sharing a residence. However, at the conclusion of the novel when Ray comments, "It would have been a fine thing if we could have taken Latnah along, eh?" Banjo responds, "Don't get soft ovah any one wimmens, pardner. Tha's you' big weakness. A woman is a conjunction. . . . And theah's things we can git away with all the time and she just kain't. Come on, pardner. Wese got enough between us to beat it a long ways from here."[8]

Why is Latnah's absence necessary to the resolution of the black transnational romance? Why is she forfeited in the masculine quest for racial freedom? While critics of McKay's work have certainly asked these and related questions none have tried to answer them through a queer reading of the novel's constructions of a global black masculinity.[9] If within the confines of McKay's own sense of the national romance women were the obstacles to different forms of identification and community between men, *Banjo* essentially asks, what kinds of communities can and do black men create after their desire for home with the woman of color is gone. In *Home to Harlem* women come to embody the race war itself as it shapes, through the struggle for home and territory, domestic relationships between multinational and multiracial groups of men. Unable to see women as agents in transforming this narrative, in *Banjo* McKay's male protagonists choose to move on without them, as if the only way to reimagine a more worldly black masculinity is as detached from their own investments in women as the site for home.

A queer reading of McKay's second novel allows us to gender the more affective dimensions of constructing belonging in a black international community. The story of black male transnationality *Banjo* provides is very much a gendered story of the formation of alternative male desires. In a sense, McKay tried to answer in his early-twentieth-century novel the question raised by David Eng in the realm of contemporary theory: "What new forms of community could emerge from a diasporic and queer challenge to the linking of home and the nation-state?"[10] The argument here is not that Ray, or any of the primary male characters in Banjo's crew in Marseilles, are themselves experiencing homosexual desires. Rather, Ray's disregard for the heterosexual norms that shape both community and male sexuality in Harlem and the crews' enactment of alternative ways of engaging each other, as men in community, result in the queering of heterosexual assumptions about the formation of a transnational African American masculinity.

To release the traveling black male subject from the domesticity of both the narrative of nation and the heterosexual marriage contract, McKay would ultimately rely not on new models of the state, but on new ways of representing masculine intimacy uncorrupted by male conflicts over women. In *Banjo*, then, McKay's figuring of black masculine subjectivity as "nationality doubtful" also becomes (hetero) sexually doubtful, as the novel asserts a different vision of black masculinity and the construction of male communities, if not explicitly a vision of black male homosexuality.

While the treatment of women of color in McKay's transnational fiction is often misogynistic, as Walter Benjamin has described, "nothing that has ever happened should be regarded as lost for history."[11] In *Banjo: The Story without a Plot*, McKay does succeed in telling an alternative, lost story of global modernity, one that places modern black male subjects in the new world order in a different way. In this chapter I examine *Banjo* more closely as McKay's successful attempt to write a transnational story of the race, one informed by his own travels and experience. That the novel is limited by the male exclusivity that characterizes the alternative, mobile, free community figured in McKay's motley and transnational black "crew" is read here not simply in terms of critique, but as a case study for grounding discussions of black diasporic identity formation in gendered contexts and sexual discourses. In *Race Men* Hazel Carby has called for "more feminist work that interrogates sexual ideologies for their racial specificity."[12] This analysis of McKay's novel seeks to

interrogate *Banjo*'s transnational racial ideologies also for their sexual specificity, acknowledging subaltern masculinity, and not just blackness, as itself a
globalized racial category.

*BANJO'S* PRECURSORS: "THE LITTLE SHEIK" AND
*ROMANCE IN MARSEILLES*

If in *Banjo* McKay would imagine the worldly New Negro male outside of
the confines of the U.S. state, what of the woman of color? Needless to say, the
price of the black male's international mobility is the abandonment of the
woman of color as a figure for the imprisonment of black masculinity in
heterosexualized notions of domesticity and nationhood. Latnah's fate in the
black transnational romance resembles that of a similar female character of
uncertain origin who appears in a brief fairy tale McKay published in *Gingertown* in 1932. *Gingertown*, a collection of short stories about black life written
at the same time as *Home to Harlem* and *Banjo*, includes McKay's own internationalist fairy tale, a tale similar to the brief vignettes on "dark princesses"
Du Bois included in *Darkwater* and then developed in his own black transnational novel. In "The Little Sheik" McKay's main protagonist is "one of
those independent U.S.A. girls a little difficult of placing," another female
character of vague and potentially hybrid racial origin, "[who] had impulsively
deserted her friends and started out alone on a trail with an objective of
sunlight and warmth." McKay's "U.S.A. girl" seeks her "place in the sun."
Like Jake in *Home to Harlem*, she "[wakes] up one morning to find herself
almost miraculously" at home, "in the fortress town of the little sheik."[13]

This little sheik's environs are as sumptuous as those of any black emperor,
and his fortress city is the home of the international: "What a place it was! As
if the God of glorious variety had assembled there all the colors of humanity to
mingle and mix and glow together. The young miss felt that she would lose
herself among such people and ways."[14] In McKay's tale this solitary heroine
wishes to lose herself in a magical and symbolic landscape of romantic internationalism: "barbaric medieval life . . . more vivid and deep-rooted in the
earth than the life of her own great world." However, McKay's little fable of
utopia abruptly shifts tone when the hybrid heroine suddenly discovers that
the fortress town is not meant for the likes of her. As she travels the town's
internationalist landscape with her guide and companion, the little sheik, "her

romantic thoughts were disturbed by the inmates boldly winking." While at first she thinks these winks are directed at her, she soon realizes that, on the contrary, they were directed at "her pretty sheik, a little wickedly, if not unnaturally." This homoerotic disruption of the heterosexual romantic allegory forces the female transnational traveler in McKay's tale to a disturbing realization: "That was the only thing that tempered her joy in this new-found mass of humanity; externally it seemed that women had no active part in it."[15]

For McKay, women such as Latnah and the heroine of "The Little Sheik" embodied the hybrid internationalism of the black transnational journey without ever being able to participate in it themselves. As with Latnah, so too with the American heroine: "So she stepped out of the scene." "But," as McKay continued, "the little sheik remained, and the story, which was put in verse and song." The black transnational male's story provides an alternative vision of global modernity, one in which the little sheiks of McKay's black transnational world play a starring role. As he ends his fairy tale: "You may meet [the little sheik] in any of the towns of that region, for he is an itinerant type, just as piquant as ever before. . . . [He] can show you some stuff in a free, unguided fashion . . . and if you are interested enough to get him in the mood he may give you the low-down of *the true story of the little sheik*."[16]

McKay's unpublished novel, *Romance in Marseilles*, continued the story of these male itinerant types and included a vignette concerning a homosexual love affair between two men in Marseilles.[17] As Wayne Cooper describes, in this novel "McKay frankly and sympathetically discussed for the first time the plight of homosexuals in Western society. In a fully developed substory inserted into the novel almost as an aside, McKay devoted an entire chapter to portraying the homosexual underworld of the docks."[18] Brent Edwards confirms, "In this book (centered on the story of the Nigerian who was the base of the Taloufa character in *Banjo*), there is an entire chapter devoted to a homosexual couple."[19] What is interesting in this novel about "savage loving" is the degree to which three itinerant, marginal communities—African colonials, traveling seamen, and homosexuals—are connected to each other through the liminal space of the docks in Marseilles. While never as explicit as in this unpublished novel, in *Banjo's* Marseilles the "low-down of the true story" of the traveling crew is as shaped by the masculine disavowal of conjugal desires as what we find explicitly articulated in *Home to Harlem* through Ray and renounced by the male homosexual characters in *Romance in Marseilles*.

Yet, if McKay's short story in *Gingertown*, "The Little Sheik," briefly but suggestively reveals the homoerotics central to McKay's narrative of black transnationalism, it also repeats a feature evident in other novels: his use of Orientalist language and metaphors as a figure for the utopian world of black internationalism. In this regard, the internationalist fairy tale provides some insight into the role Russia played in his global imaginary, for McKay's Afro-Orientalism finds its roots much in his perception of Russia and the spectacle of Bolshevik internationalism he was able to observe directly in 1922. McKay's referent for the international was often Orientalist, hearkening back to his first identification with and experience of the Russian revolutionary state as an *Arabian Nights* dream. As we set out to follow Ray and Banjo's fictional journey to the international black community in Marseilles, it is useful to trace the impact of McKay's own trip to Russia as it preceded and shaped the internationalism of his own writing amid his perambulations throughout Europe and Northern Africa.

"THE MAGIC PILGRIMAGE": AFRO-ORIENTALISM, RUSSIA, AND MCKAY'S EARLY INTERNATIONALISM

In part IV of his autobiography, "The Magic Pilgrimage," McKay described how his "senses were stirred by the semi-Oriental splendor and movement of Moscow even before my intellect was touched by the forces of the revolution." As he continued to describe: "It was all like a miracle, all that Byzantine conglomeration of form and color, shedding down its radiance upon the proletarian masses. It was like an *Arabian Nights* dream transforming the bleak white face of an Arctic waste."[20] McKay's hope was that black proletarian faces could be an equal aspect of that magical revolutionary moment, a hope powerfully captured in one image from his trip, as McKay described:

> Whenever I appeared in the street I was greeted by all of the people with enthusiasm [and] a spontaneous upsurging of folk feeling. . . . Never in my life did I feel prouder of being an African, a black. . . . I was a black ikon in the flesh . . . the first Negro to arrive in Russia since the revolution.[21]

In these everyday spectacles of blackness at the heart of the Bolshevik revolution, McKay employed a similar kind of visual politics as Garvey, a politics he commended Garvey for in his essay "Soviet Russia and the Negro": "American Negroes are not as yet deeply permeated with the mass movement spirit and so fail to realize the importance of organized propaganda. It was Marcus Garvey's greatest contribution to the Negro movement; his pioneer work in that field."[22]

Allowing his own body to be used by the Communists, McKay participated in the Bolsheviks' attempts to racialize their own global imaginary, McKay's black masculinity standing as a metonymic figure for the colonial world. As the first African to make it to Russia, McKay became the figure for an internationalist blackness: "a symbol . . . of the great American Negro group—kin to the unhappy black slaves of European Imperialism in Africa— that the workers of Soviet Russia, rejoicing in their freedom, were greeting through me."[23]

While the promise of this dream of black Bolshevism was itself never realized, McKay's pilgrimage to Russia would lead him further on the path toward articulating in his art new forms of black international movement. As other scholars have described, in Russia McKay attended the Fourth International Congress for the Communist International in November 1922.[24] An important discussion would take place at that convention, a debate over the status of "the Negro question," a debate in which McKay would play an active and leading role. McKay left for Russia in 1922 already somewhat disillusioned with the possibilities for black organization and revolution in the United States, evidenced by the debacle of the alliance of the African Blood Brotherhood and the Universal Negro Improvement Association. He was even more skeptical when he observed the American Communist Party delegates pronouncing to the convention that "in five years we will have the American revolution." As McKay put it, he chafed at their "false pictures" and "tall rhetoric":

> The Russians from these speeches pictured the workers of America as denied the right to organize and the rights of free assembly and free speech, as denied representation in Congress . . . the American situation as they understood it, was similar to that of Russia under the Czarist regime just before the revolution.[25]

When asked to speak, McKay found himself unable to create similar revolutionary fictions: "Truly, I could not speak such lies. I knew the American workers in 1922 were generally better off than at the beginning of the World War in 1914 . . . Leavenworth was not Siberia. And by no stretch of the imagination could the United States be compared to Great Russia."[26] Yet these limited comments in his autobiography regarding his role at the convention were surprising in light of his own active participation in the discussions around the Negro question throughout the event. For it was Claude McKay who, at this convention, would first challenge the Comintern to think about and include black subjects in their revolutionary narrative.

When McKay had first joined the editorial staff of the radical magazine *The Liberator* in 1921, he had stated that he hoped to "further a solution of the Negro problem in the revolution."[27] His membership in the African Blood Brotherhood further evidenced his interest in the project of black revolution.[28] At the Fourth Congress he got his chance to speak as "one of the spokesmen of Negro radicalism in America."[29] In an essay written for the *Crisis* in 1923, "Soviet Russia and the Negro," McKay gave his own interpretation of the consequences of black participation in the war:

> The World War has fundamentally altered the status of Negroes in Europe. It brought thousands of them from America and the British and French colonies to participate in the struggle against the Central Powers. Since then serious clashes have come about in England between the blacks that later settled down in the seaport towns and the natives.[30]

In identifying these black (and primarily male) communities remaining throughout Europe after the war, McKay brought to the Comintern's attention a particular phenomenon—enclaves of black ex-soldiers and seamen, scattered throughout the European metropoles, unattached to either the European states or any nationally defined black state elsewhere. McKay's hope was precisely that these communities of black migrants could be organized not around nationalism, but into the revolutionary class movement of the Communist International.

McKay spoke from this position at the Comintern, expressing also his concern that, in the United States in particular, "The American capitalists are setting out to mobilize the entire black race of America for the purpose of fighting organized labor." It was in his comments regarding this race war organized by world capital that McKay began to sound a much more urgent note, at times using the alarmist language that he had criticized the American

Communist Party's delegates for using: "The situation in America today . . . is much uglier and more terrible than was the condition of the peasants and Jews of Russia under the Tzar."[31] As he also described in his autobiography, "I said I thought the only place where illegal and secret radical propaganda was necessary was among the Negroes of the South."[32] As McKay's comments on the Negro question made clear, it was not so much that he thought the American communists were lying about conditions in the United States; rather, they were, almost willfully, looking for revolution in all the wrong places: "the Socialists and Communists of America . . . are not willing to face the Negro question."[33] McKay critiqued American communists for their inability to see the central role that race war—and race discourse more generally with its roots in colonialism—has played in the development of the capitalist mode of production.

No one would deny the historical accuracy of McKay's pessimism regarding the possibilities for an American revolution by 1922. However, the caesura in his account of the American delegates' false internationalism lay in his evasion of his own active presence at the congress in pushing for their understanding of the Negro question. As Wayne Cooper has summarized:

> In *A Long Way from Home* his account of his participation in the proceedings of the congress . . . was misleading. . . . He failed to acknowledge frankly that he spoke as *both* a black Communist and a black writer who desperately wanted the Comintern to understand the position and potential of blacks within the international Communist movement . . . he had, in fact, come to Moscow primed to attack American Communists for their reluctance to deal with the race problem.[34]

McKay came to Russia to participate in and observe the international romance of revolution created by the Bolsheviks after a year of organizing activity in New York that had ended with few actual political results.[35] In Russia he would find his own political abilities and imagination as an organizer tested by the magnitude of the task of creating a real international revolutionary movement. As he would lament in his autobiography:

> How, then, could I stand before the gigantic achievement of the Russian revolution and lie? What right had I to tell these people who had gone through a long death struggle to conquer their country for themselves,

that the American revolution was also in travail? What could I presume to tell them?[36]

Instead, McKay would turn to the imaginative skills he possessed as a writer to envision the grand task of creating a truly multiracial world order. When a young Communist at the convention responded to McKay's defeatism by demanding that he "do [his] part to help make the revolution" McKay responded: "Tell the young comrade that I am a poet."[37] After 1922, McKay pulled back from the real-life romance of revolutionary statehood represented by Russia to explore *in literary form* the possibilities of community for black and colonial subjects. As he would also tell his Russian audience:

> I told them that it was a great honor for me to be there to behold the triumph of their great revolution. I told them that I felt very insignificant and dumb before that wonderful thing. I said that I had come to Russia to learn something, to see with my own eyes and try to write a little of what I had seen.[38]

One of the most significant aftereffects of McKay's trip to Russia was his experimentation with prose and the novel. As he wrote in his autobiography sixteen years later, "I came out of Russia with my head on my shoulders and my pen in my pocket and determined to write at all costs. . . . And in ten years I wrote five books and many poems."[39] He would produce over the course of the next ten years some of the more enduring images and narratives of the black transnational in the midst of modernity. He attributed his clarity to the "tremendous reception" he received in Russia, which "was a great inspiration and urge to write more. I often felt in Russia that I was honored as a poet altogether out of proportion to my actual performance. And thus I was fired with the desire to accomplish the utmost."[40]

After leaving Russia McKay spent the ten prolific years between 1923 and 1933 in exile in Europe, on "The Cynical Continent" as he named part 5 of his autobiography. In Paris he would "mix in among the cosmopolitan expatriates," the "lost generation" of American modernists, "lured to Europe because life was riper, culture mellower, and artistic things considered of higher worth than in America."[41] In Europe McKay found "confusion—all the ferment and torment and turmoil, the hesitation and hate and alarm, the sexual inquietude and the incertitude of this age, and the psychic and romantic groping for a way out."[42] McKay, however, was not plagued in the same ways by the modernist angst over American "civilization and its discontents."[43] He vigorously argued for the vitality and freedom of American culture and national identity, a vitality specific to a nation with all the raw material for multiracial democracy in the making. McKay's narrator in *Banjo* would compare America's "unclassical rhythms" with "the veritable romance of Europe" and find the latter wanting:

> It was America that was for him the living, hot-breathing land of ro-
> mance. Its mighty business palaces, vast *depots* receiving and discharging
> hurrying hordes of humanity . . . the raucous vaudeville mob-shouting of a
> newly-arrived nation of white throats, the clamor and clash of races and
> the grim-grubbing position of his race among them—all was a great fever
> in his brain, a rhythm of a pattern with the time-beat of his life, a burning,
> throbbing romance in his blood.[44]

This was the messy, noisy, colorful story of modernity that McKay set out to explore and narrate upon leaving Russia. If, as Malcolm Cowley described, the lost generation arrived in Europe "deracinated," uprooted and exiled from a sense of their own cultural soil and traditions, McKay's urge to write, "the urge that had sent me traveling abroad," was the opposite.[45] While they were seeking national cultural traditions in Europe to which they could more right-fully belong, a cultural home to settle the disruptions produced by war and revolution, McKay was seeking to understand the forces that had uprooted the New World Negro in the first place. As he put it, "Color-consciousness was the fundamental of my restlessness."[46] In his fictional record of his travels, he articulated the strategies the New World Negro would use to keep himself afloat and in motion in a war-torn, racially divided world.

A STORY WITHOUT A PLOT:
JAZZING AND BLACK NATIONALITY IN *BANJO*

The structure of *Banjo* is analogous to that of *Home to Harlem*: the novel has three parts, the first introducing the African American character Banjo, the second introducing Ray, the Caribbean character, and the third representing the move toward closure. However, *Banjo* is a more truly transnational text in form and content than either *Home to Harlem* or McKay's later novel, *Banana Bottom*. As much about the Caribbean and North America as any other of

McKay's fictions, the novel represents McKay's attempt to explore internationalism as an alternative source for black identity. It also represents his effort to imagine an alternative site of home for the black male subject migrating within and moving across transnational boundaries.

For all intents and purposes, *Home to Harlem* and *Banjo* should be read as two halves of the same novel, two episodes in the same story. Both were written between 1923 and 1925 while McKay was living an expatriate life in Morocco and France, and both were published within a year of each other. The novels are linked explicitly in form with the reappearance of the picaresque and in content with the reappearance of the Caribbean character Ray and briefly, toward the end of *Banjo*, Jake, the primary African American character from *Home to Harlem*.

Like *Home to Harlem*, *Banjo* also begins with another African American character, Lincoln Agrippa Daily, otherwise known as Banjo due to his banjo playing throughout the streets and bars of "the Ditch," a marginal area in the French seaport town of Marseilles. Banjo's crew originates from the peripheral, unemployed communities that edge liminal spaces such as seaports. For them, "bumming" is an active way of life rather than a function of circumstance. Banjo's crew is a motley one, including Malty Avis, a West Indian migrant seaman; Ginger, recently imprisoned for vagabondage; the Senegalese Dengel; and Bugsy. The crew forms an unusual ethnic formation of sorts, composed of migrating black subjects who claim vagabondage and criminality as a way of life:

> They were all on the beach, and there were many others beside them—white men, brown men, black men, Finns, Poles, Italians, Slavs, Maltese, Indians, Negroids, African Negroes, West Indian Negroes—deportees from America for violation of the United States immigration laws—afraid and ashamed to go back to their own lands, all dumped down in the great Provencal port, bumming.[47]

In *The Practice of Diaspora* Brent Edwards argues for an understanding of the vagabondage of McKay's crew as a form of black internationalism, but one that specifically "would appear to mark a shift in McKay's political focus away from the proletariat, traditionally conceived, and toward such cosmopolitan, fleeting communities of men." As Edwards continues,

The book's fascination with Marseilles's transient denizens points less to an interest in the expansion and unionizing of the port city's industrial maritime base than to the margins of that development. Though some of them serve on ships to get to Marseilles, the black boys of *Banjo* are not even the short-term ship workers, the stokers and mess help, who are at the bottom rung of the labor pool. Every now and then, they find day work as dockers and loaders. But this is hardly steady employment. . . . Banjo, Ray, Bugsy, and Taloufa are men who would rather beg for food from sympathetic black crews on Mediterranean coal freighters than work under the racist capitalism that is the only available mode of labor relations.[48]

Edwards then uses this observation to argue for an understanding of the crew within Marx's definition of the *Lumpenproletariat*, further explaining why McKay may have felt the need to move away from a strictly Bolshevik narrative of internationalism.

My argument here differs slightly, for what Edwards's account fails to capture is the degree to which the masculine identities of the men in Banjo's crew are still shaped and defined by the maritime world on whose periphery they seem to wander. The novel's opening line establishes the importance of this context, as Banjo is introduced in the following manner: "Heaving along from side to side, like a sailor on the unsteady deck of a ship, Lincoln Agrippa Daily, familiarly known as Banjo, patrolled the magnificent length of the great breakwater of Marseilles, a banjo in his hand."[49] In this first chapter entitled "The Ditch," Banjo's crew is also introduced with their prior identities as black mariners front and foremost:

Malty's working life began as a small sailor boy on fishing-boats in the Caribbean. When he became a big boy he was taken by a cargo boat on his first real voyage to New Orleans. From there he had started in as a real seaman and had never returned home.

Sitting on Malty's right, the chestnut-skinned fellow . . . Ginger . . . held the long-term record of existence on the beach. He had lost his seaman's papers. He had been in prison for vagabondage and served with a writ of expulsion. But he had destroyed the writ and swiped the papers of another seaman.[50]

"The Ditch" establishes the importance of the transatlantic maritime context Linebaugh, Rediker, and Bolster have identified for shaping the international way in which these black men construct themselves as men. As Nassy Brown has also argued in her approach to the "anthropology of diaspora": "As the very basis of local identity, the seafaring tradition is implicated in the gendered construction of travel. . . . It is *precisely* because seafaring is so staunchly male that it forms such a fertile object of inquiry."[51] Nassy Brown's argument brings us to two linked realizations. Diaspora is a site for the production of both *gendered* and *racial* identities. As such, seafaring as a male space can still also be a foundational site for the creation of alternative masculine forms of diasporic black community.

The structure and themes of *Banjo* bear some similarity to more canonical works by American modernists written during the same period. One sees reproduced here the fragmentation of identity and peoples which resulted from World War I and the sense of despair about the meaning and future of modernity. However, in an almost explicit juxtaposition McKay makes it clear that the response of the black transnationals to the upheavals of their time is different from that of the white expatriates in Marseilles or the American modernists more generally:

> Most of the whites, especially the blond ones of the northern countries, seemed to have gone down hopelessly under the strength of hard liquor, as if nothing mattered for them now but that. They were stinking-dirty, and lousy, without any apparent desire to clean themselves. With the black boys it was different. It was as if they were just taking a holiday.[52]

This sense of black exile as offering latitude and freedom is embodied in the character Banjo himself. Like the subtitle of the novel, Banjo's personal history is a story of intranational migrations without a plot:

> Banjo was a great vagabond of lowly life. He was a child of the Cotton Belt, but he had wandered all over America. His life was a dream of vagabondage that he was perpetually pursuing and realizing in odd ways, always incomplete but never unsatisfactory. He had worked at all the easily picked jobs—longshoreman, porter, factory worker, farm hand, seaman.[53]

Having started early at the vagabond life, Banjo continues in this vein as a soldier during World War I:

He was in Canada when the Great War began and he enlisted in the Canadian army. . . . From there he crossed to the States, where he worked at several jobs. Seized by the old restlessness for a sea change while he was working in an industrial plant, he hit upon the unique plan of getting himself deported.[54]

Banjo, grounded in the specific context of wartime America and a world consumed with nationalist ideologies, makes the bold and unimaginable step of giving up his nationality. On one hand, he makes himself vulnerable to the official state; on the other, he increases his own migratory flexibility. Restless for a sea change, Banjo's renunciation of his American citizenship also subverts the state's power over the seas themselves.

Though Linebaugh and Rediker's insights on the nature of hydrarchy have their historical bearing in the maritime world of the seventeenth century, their observation that the ship became "an engine of capitalism" and a "zone of freedom" or setting of resistance still applies to Banjo's own early twentieth-century sense that, in the life of the seafarer, he might find an alternative mode of being than that available in the modern nation-state. In Linebaugh and Rediker's narrative, the communities created in the seventeenth century by pirates and buccaneers represent one of these potential, alternative, modes of being, as they describe:

> The early shapers of the [buccaneer] tradition were those whom one English official in the Caribbean called the "outcasts of all nations"—the convicts, prostitutes, debtors, vagabonds, escaped slaves and indentured servants, religious radicals, and political prisoners. . . . These workers drifted to uninhabited islands, where they formed maroon communities. Their autonomous settlements were multiracial in nature.[55]

According to Linebaugh and Rediker, pirate ships in particular attempted to turn the world of the maritime state "upside down."[56] Among other things, they kept supplies to feed starving mutinous sailors and soldiers and maintained a "carnivalesque quality . . . the eating, drinking, fiddling, dancing, and merriment . . . inimical to good discipline at sea."[57]

Banjo's decision to renounce his nationality can be seen as following in the tradition of these outcasts of all nations, and the community of itinerant men created in Marseilles in the postwar period bears a striking similarity to seventeenth-century buccaneer communities. In both instances, the transatlantic world produces and organizes wealth, political power, and state forms of empire and capital, while simultaneously creating spaces for resistant identities, communities, and cultural forms. If, as Linebaugh and Rediker describe, ships were at one and the same time, "the first place where working people from . . . different continents communicated" and the place where "all the contradictions of social antagonism were concentrated,"[58] then the port of Marseilles in the early-twentieth-century world of *Banjo* could well be seen as a site of similarly doubled meanings. Merely one stop in the maritime travels of modern industrial empire and capital, Marseilles was also a potential site for these motley crews of men to ground the forms of social organization experienced on board ship or at sea in the less respectable spaces of colonies, seaport towns, and cosmopolitan urban centers.

Banjo's denationalization has little to do with his alienation or horror from his experiences during World War I. Denationalization is a personal choice for him, one in which he uses the laws of the state to facilitate his own free movement. Banjo's bold move confounds and amuses American immigration officials, who also recognize it as a new and inventive form of resistance within the context of a new, nationally organized maritime world:

> Banjo was a personality among the immigration officers. They liked his presence, his voice, his language of rich Aframericanisms. They admired, too, the way he had chosen to go off wandering again. (It was nothing less than a deliberate joke to them, for Banjo could never convince any American, especially a Southern-knowing one, that he was not Aframerican.) It was singular enough to stir their imagination, so long insensible to the old ways of ship desertion and stowing away.[59]

The charm of the fiction itself, the story Banjo is telling by wandering from his nationality, captures the imagination of the officers rather than their belief in its accuracy. Banjo imagines and enacts new possibilities for black masculine identity formation, and it is his courage and ingenuity that are appreciated by the immigration officials. In freely choosing vagabondage as an identity, Banjo attempts to obtain the utopian transnational ideal, his own passport to glory free of nationality.

Banjo's move is an expensive one because American nationality is much in demand on the transnational market. Speaking as a colonial subject, even Ray the West Indian underestimates the benefits blacks reap from an American passport, literally and figuratively. American national identity can be sold and exchanged as valuable currency on the global market:

> An American seaman (white or black) on the beach is always treated with a subtle difference by his beach fellows. He has a higher value than the rest. His passport is worth a good price and is eagerly sought for by passport fabricators. And he has the assurance that, when he gets tired of beaching, his consulate will help him back to the fabulous land of wealth and opportunity.[60]

Nationality and identity here become denaturalized and politicized; different nationalities carry with them varying cultural, political, and even economic values. It is the symbolic and literal value of the American black in a transnational context that makes *Banjo*, for one thing, as much an American story, a story of imperial American nationhood and nationality, as a transnational one.

These denationalized black subjects are not the fluid, multiple-identity protagonists of postmodernism. They are men grounded in an Atlantic history; as Ginger says at one point, "There ain't a jack man of us that ain't got a history to him as good as any that evah was printed."[61] But their history is a verbal story, whose record lies in an oral and aural culture submerged beneath the national print cultures of the twentieth-century Western imperial world. *Banjo* is an imaginative social document of early-twentieth-century transnational black communities, forming in the interstices of nationalist imperial centers. These are the postwar black communities McKay described to the Russian communists, black ex-soldiers left behind in Europe after the war. The challenge for the black writer, as the character Ray will also articulate throughout the novel, is how to create "art out of [this] fertile reality."[62]

Gilroy has pointed out that one of the central exchanges occurring in these transnational spaces was one of not just black bodies but also of black culture.[63] As Brent Edwards also movingly describes, "*Banjo* is above all else a book about a boy who wants to start a band."[64] Banjo's banjo is an important artistic site for the expression of this new black global imaginary and alternative masculine reality. As Banjo describes for the reader, spreading his art across the globe from Hamburg to Genoa and back, his instrument, the banjo, has come to represent it all, home, self, and nation: "Banjo caressed his instrument. 'I nevah part with this, buddy. It is moh than a gal, moh than a pal; it's mahself.'"[65] This sense of mobility, exchangeable identities, vagabondage, and music is figured actively throughout the novel as a form of "jazzing," a specifically black way of being in and expressing the condition of marronage in the world of the early twentieth century. Jazz is Banjo's art, encompassing multiple, early-twentieth-century black musical genres, including folk ballads, blues songs, and vaudeville tunes, but jazzing is also an underground lifestyle that acts as an alternative to white modernity. Jazzing signifies on white modernity with a critique and embodies black health and vitality.

Banjo's "orchestry" is itself one figure for a self-determined jazzing nation of black international men. The orchestry is Banjo's dream, his romance of blackness: "Oh, Banjo's skin was itching to make some romantic thing. . . . And one afternoon he walked straight into a dream—a cargo boat with a crew of four music-making colored boys, with banjo, ukelele, mandolin, guitar, and horn."[66] One member of the crew in particular, the West African character Taloufa, stands out as an important figure for adding a sensual element to the crew's instrumentals, and a sexualization of their rough and ready performances in the streets and taverns of the Ditch. Taloufa is described as one who "loved all music with a lilt, and especially music that was heady with sensuousness."[67] That sensuousness seeps into McKay's descriptions of Taloufa's music making:

> Taloufa had a voluptuous voice, richly colored like the sound of water lapping against a bank. . . . When Taloufa sang . . . his eyes grew bigger and whiter in his charmingly carnal countenance, the sound came from his mouth like a caressing, appealing command and reminded one of a beautiful, rearing young filly of the pasture that a trainer is breaking in.[68]

It is Taloufa's song that inspires one of the band's greatest performances in the novel:

> Taloufa had taught them a rollicking West African song, whose music was altogether more insinuating. . . . So Goosey played the solo. And when Banjo, Taloufa, and Malty took up the refrain, Bugsy, stepping with Dengel, led the boys dancing. Bugsy was wiry and long-handed. Dengel, wiry, long-handed, and long-legged. And they made a striking pair as abruptly Dengel turned his back on Bugsy and started round the room in a

bird-hopping step, nodding his head and working his hands held against his sides, fists doubled, as if he were holding a guard. Bugsy and all the boys imitated him, forming a unique ring, doing the same simple thing, startlingly fresh in that atmosphere, with clacking of heels on the floor.

It was, perhaps, the nearest that Banjo, quite unconscious of it, ever came to an aesthetic realization of his orchestra.[69]

From two men coupling, Bugsy and Dengel, to a man dancing freely with the others following his lead, Banjo and his crew perform a free and unspirited expression of black masculinity, "startlingly fresh in that atmosphere" yet, in a sense, made possible by Marseille's liminality as a border space between land and sea, as a seaport connecting the imperial metropole to the colonies. As they dance, the crew and the audience of males described as watching them are oblivious of and indifferent to the women who surround them. Soon, however, "A troop of girls filed in from the boxes. . . . They broke in among the boys and began dancing with them in their loud self-conscious way." This female invasion of a brief but utopian male moment and space inevitably introduces into the narrative violence and conflict between men and, ultimately, one man's death.

Banjo's ability to tell his story through music is the same project Ray is attempting to accomplish through words. But this project also looks different from the one Ray had imagined in *Home to Harlem*. Banjo is an organic intellectual, leading the black diaspora through music and performance. Banjo's is also a particularly African American story:

> The banjo is preeminently the musical instrument of the American Negro. The sharp, noisy notes of the banjo belong to the American Negro's loud music of life—an affirmation of his hardy existence in the midst of the biggest, the most tumultuous civilization of modern life.
>
> Sing, Banjo! Play, Banjo! Here I is, Big Boss, keeping step, sure step, right long with you in some sort a ways.[70]

Banjo's modernism is one that is in step with and shadowing that of white America. His art is the communication of diaspora through mass cultural exchange and popular performance. Banjo's homeless crew is a microcosm of the world of displaced colonial subjects and migrants, but also a world of color creating new performances of blackness on the global circuit. While Garvey lamented the popular black performers' representation as an object of ridicule, saying, "We are 280 millions of homeless people, with no country and no flag. In America they make a joke of it that every nation has a flag but the coon. You will find that in mimicry and song,"[71] Banjo takes up his banjo and turns black homelessness into a virtue. He makes his own displacement the cause for celebration and the source of expression: "The American darky is the performing fool of the world today. He's demanded everywhere. If I c'd only git some a these heah panhandling fellas together, we'll show them some real nigger music."[72]

Part I of *Banjo* emphasizes the lifestyle of Banjo and his crew and sets up the resistant nature of forms of black masculinity performed outside the boundaries of accepted national narratives. In this section McKay also demonstrates how the challenge of this tortured articulation of race, nation, and ethnicity can be expressed by a different romance of blackness than the one Ray has at his disposal in words. This is what Ray discovers when he realizes "there's nothing in the world so interesting to me as Banjo and his orchestra."[73] In categorizing the novel as a picaresque many scholars also take this to mean that it follows no specific trajectory, merely following the drifting movements of these characters as they travel, without a plot, throughout the story. However, the novel's division into three parts does articulate a clear structure. In part II of the novel McKay uses the character Ray to provide an even broader geopolitical context to Banjo's jazzing. In so doing McKay reveals a fugitive black transnational male community living in the shadows of war, revolution, and empire, their movements and identities shaped and constrained by broader geopolitical realities. For McKay it was not enough then to simply identify these alternative forms of traveling black male communities. He also sought in *Banjo* to reveal the ways in which black masculine mobility and freedom were penalized by the larger maritime reach of imperial state forms.

## "OFFICIAL FISTS": THE WORLD'S STORY AND THE BLACK MALE SUBJECT

In part II of the novel the character Ray arrives in Marseilles, intending to gather material for another chapter in a book recounting his travels throughout the modern world. Ray arrives in the French seaport consumed by the pressing desire to write, to articulate his experiences: "He had struck the town in one of those violent periods of agitation when he had worked himself up to the pitch of feeling that if he could not give vent to his thoughts he would break up into a thousand articulate bits."[74] Ray needs a plot that will put the "articulate bits" of himself, of his story, and that of other black transnational men like himself together. This story of the black male's experience of the postwar world is a valuable one, as Ray describes later in the novel:

> You see Goosey, a good story, in spite of those who tell it and those who hear it, is like good ore that you might find in any soil—Europe, Asia, Africa, America. The world wants the ore and gets it by a thousand men scrambling and fighting, digging and dying for it. The world gets its story the same way.[75]

Europe fought for her story during World War I and emerged from the decline of her empires, after Versailles, with the new master-narrative of the national state. The story Ray seeks to tell is one that could capture instead the diasporic romance of blackness, a romance of his race with or without national statehood.

The first thing Ray notices in Marseilles is its difference from Harlem as a space of blackness. Du Bois's image of Harlem, one in which black citizens have paved over America's white streets and built beautiful black homes as a testament to their own potential as property-owning members of the national community, reappears in *Banjo* when Jake from *Home to Harlem* briefly joins the crew toward the end of the novel. Jake brings this description of changing developments in the new black metropolis:

> The Block Beautiful had gone black and brown. One Hundred and Twenty-fifth Street was besieged and bravely holding out for business' sake, but the invaders, armed with nothing but loud laughter, had swept around it and beyond. And higher up, the race line of demarcation, Eight Avenue, had been pushed way back . . . and other pale avenues were vividly touched with color. The Negro realtors had done marvels.[76]

In Marseilles we leave this domestic picture of the nation as a suburban neighborhood, literally advancing the race within the city, and return to McKay's image of the modern American and European nation-states as "vast *depots* receiving and discharging hurrying hordes of humanity." In Marseilles the racial internationalism of global commerce, the link between the new national states and the older colonial economic networks, is laid bare.

Upon Ray's arrival in Marseilles he is met by "picturesque proletarians from far waters whose names were warm with romance: the Caribbean, the Gulf of Guinea, the Persian Gulf, the Bay of Bengal, the China Seas, the Indian Archipelago." As Ray recounts the transnational movement of migrant labor across the globe from colony to metropole, from periphery to core, he maps a transnational trade circuit that has a definite pattern and direction: "Rice from India, rubber from the Congo, tea from China, brown sugar from Cuba, bananas from Guinea, lumber from the Soudan, coffee from Brazil, skins from the Argentine, palm-oil from Nigeria, pimento from Jamaica, wool from Australia."[77] His tracing of the commercial routes of mercantile imperialism serves as an ironic indictment of the unidirectional movement of wealth from colony to metropole that runs parallel to modern colonialism. This is a global story that undercuts any and all romantic narratives of blacks' upward mobility within the nation. Ray's indictment becomes more explicit as his narrative continues:

> Barrels, bags, boxes, bearing from land to land the primitive garner of man's hands. Sweat-dripping bodies of black men naked under the equatorial sun. . . . Brown men half-clothed, with baskets on their backs, bending low down to the ancient tilled fields under the tropical sun. Eternal creatures of the warm soil, digging, plucking for the Occident world its exotic nourishment of life, under the whip, under the terror.[78]

In a paragraph set off from the rest of the text, almost a digression, Ray lays bare the seedy racial underside of the postwar romance of internationalism created at Versailles:

> There was a barbarous international romance in the ways of Marseilles that was vividly significant of the great modern movement of life. Small, with a population apparently too great for it, Europe's best back door, discharging and receiving its traffic to the Orient and Africa, favorite port of seamen on French leave, infested with the ratty beings of the Mediterranean countries, overrun with guides, cocottes, procurers, repelling and attracting in its white-fanged vileness under its picturesqueness, the town seemed to proclaim to the world that the grandest thing about modern life was that it was bawdy.[79]

In Ray's romance, modernity and civilization are still inextricably linked with terror "under the whip." It is a reality that undergirds the "great modern movement" of migrants and capital across the globe. If in the seventeenth century, "hydrarchy was attacked because of the danger it posed to the increasingly valuable slave trade with Africa,"[80] in Marseilles the dream of the suburb and the bawdy world of the Ditch are inextricably attached to international commerce. As Ray describes one particular French suburb, during a rare instance in the novel in which the reader is given a view of the world outside of the Ditch:

> The suburban route was melancholy. . . . Now there was nothing but dead and rotting leaves everywhere and some withered blackberries.
>
> The chauffeur's place was like any of the common suburban lots owned by the great army of the lower middle class of modern cities. . . . What made the chauffeur so unbearably ugly to him now was that he was trafficking obscenely to scramble out of the proletarian world into that solid respectable life, whence he could look down on the Ditch and all such places with the mean, evil, and cynical eyes of a respectable person.[81]

Marseilles, the Ditch, is the French nation's backyard, a colonial backyard that on one hand marginalizes the periphery but on the other provides them access to the core, in the form of both human and commercial traffic from "the Orient and Africa." Favored spot of the European tourist, it also represents the underworld of the Third World in full display, in both its offensive and consumable aspects. Undergirded by imperial whiteness, this international cemetery of the twentieth century represents all that is bawdy and, ultimately, uncivilized about modern Western culture.

In Ray's narrative of the black subject's experience of modern colonialism and imperialism, Marseilles is a different kind of symbolic home for the dislocated black migrants produced by European colonialism and war. It resembles the multiracial chaotic communities on board the ships of empire and global commerce: "In no other port had he ever seen congregated such a picturesque variety of Negroes. . . . It was as if every country of the world where Negroes lived had sent representatives drifting in to Marseilles."[82] This international convention of Negroes are not Garvey's empire builders but drifters, whose racial philosophy has no plot, no "rudder," "literature," or "doctrine," except that of vagabondage. Their bawdiness signifies black vitality, the health epitomized by Banjo and his crew, a fun-loving group of male vagabonds who somehow together form a new kind of alternative community despite their national differences. So Banjo can say at one point, to stall a fight about ethnic differences within the group, "You and me and Ginger and Malty am just like we come from the same home town."[83] Race and nation are ultimately resolved as noncategories, as easily slipped into and slipped out of as Banjo's initial deportation scam: "You got to show me that there's any more to it [nationality] than there is to naturalization, that you and me and Malty is," says Ginger.[84]

As Ray stays on with the crew in Marseilles, his observations as a black participant-observer of the early-twentieth-century Western world crystallize. Setting the novel in the immediate postwar period, McKay is able to articulate through Ray the fissures in Europe's peacetime efforts to use nationalism to secure peace and disguise imperial rivalries:

> The panic in the air had reached even Marseilles, the most international place in the country. Up till yesterday these very journals had been doping the unthinking literate mob with pages of peace talk. Today they were feeding the same hordes with war. . . . Ray grinned . . . he was grinning at the civilized world of nations, all keeping their tiger's claws sharp and strong under the thin cloak of international amity and awaiting the first favorable opportunity to spring. During his passage through Europe it had been an illuminating experience for him to come in contact with the mind of the average white man. A few words would usually take him to the center of a guarded, ancient treasure of national hates.[85]

For Ray it is precisely his blackness, that is, his denationalized and therefore somewhat independent status, that affords him his unique position as a participant-observer of modernity:

> [Ray] was not unaware that his position as a black boy looking on the civilized scene was a unique one. He was having a good grinning time of it. Italians against French, French against Anglo-Saxons, English against Germans, the great *Daily Mail* shrieking like a mad virago. . . . Oh it was a great civilization indeed, too entertaining for any savage ever to have the feeling of boredom.[86]

In his travels Ray's aversion to nationalism and domestication had been a central aspect of his masculinity and identity: "He had enjoyed his role of a wandering black without patriotic or family ties. He loved to pose as this or that without really being any definite thing at all."[87] What this critical perspective on nationality affords him is precisely a fresh lens on the political and ideological workings of empire. His antinationalism is the result of both his denationalized status and his perpetual wanderings:

> The sentiment of patriotism was not one of Ray's possessions, perhaps because he was a child of deracinated ancestry. To him it was a poisonous seed that had, of course, been planted in his child's mind, but happily, not having any traditional soil to nourish it, it had died out with other weeds of the curricula of education in the light of mature thought.
>
> It seemed a most unnatural thing to him for a man to love a nation—a swarming hive of human beings bartering, competing, exploiting, lying, cheating, battling, suppressing, and killing among themselves; possessing, too, the faculty to organize their villainous rivalries into a monstrous system for plundering weaker peoples.[88]

Ultimately, the result of Ray's travels and observations is his ability to envision black transnationalism as an alternative, his ability to find his own narrative of a wandering black masculinity: "The vagabond lover of life finds individuals and things to love in many places and not in any one nation. Man loves places and no one place, for the earth, like a beautiful wanton, puts on a new dress to fascinate him wherever he may go."[89] As he asserts elsewhere,

> It was no superior condescension, no feeling of race solidarity or Back-to-Africa demonstration—no patriotic effort whatsoever—that made Ray love the drifters. He loved it with the poetical enthusiasm of the vagabond black that he himself was. . . . [The] most precious souvenirs of it were the joyful friendships that he had made among his pals.[90]

McKay would have given us a good story by any black transnational's standards if *Banjo* had ended with the conclusion of the novel's second part. But *Banjo* refuses the reader a satisfying sense of romantic closure. McKay was well aware, based on his own travels and experiences, that black transnational identity offers the migrating black male subject a tenuous freedom at best. Hence, the crew's breaking up at the end of part II of the novel heralds the reappearance of the imperial state in the narrative of black transnationalism. By the end of part III, we are left with an ambiguous picture of the vagaries and vulnerabilities of the black male transnational in the context of international imperialism.

McKay provides a larger historical context to the more immediate change which precipitates the group's hard times, Banjo's departure. As the narrator says, "A psychological turn sometimes foreshadows a material change, or *vice versa*, even in obscure isolated cases, the boys felt that something was happening and realized that it was becoming very difficult for them to gain their unmoral bohemian subsistence as before."[91] McKay then proceeds to describe a *world* sea change, reflecting the cracking down on radical formations and modern forms of hydrarchy generally throughout Europe and the maritime world. This sea change begins in part II in the chapter entitled "White Terror," with the simultaneous arrival in Marseilles of an "American squadron, an American freighter and two large English ships, one from South Africa and another from India."[92] The crew's interactions with these ships' white sailors invoke the lessons they learned as black soldiers during World War I. As Banjo describes:

> When I enlisted in the army during the war . . . mah best buddy said I was a fool nigger. He said the white man would nevah ketch him toting his gun unless it was to rid the wul' of all the crackers, and I done told him back that the hullabaloo was to make the wul' safe foh democracy and there wouldn't be no crackers when the war was "ovah and ended," as was done said by President Wilson, as crackers didn't belong in democracy. But mah buddy said to me I had a screw loose, for President Wilson wasn't moh'n a cracker. And mah buddy was sure right. For according to my eyesight, and Ise one sure-seeing nigger, the wul' safe foh democracy is a wul' safe foh crackerism.[93]

White seamen, as "the traveling representatives of American culture" are not true transnational travelers. Instead, "the white American sailor . . . sees everything, but he learns nothing" because he wears the blinders of nationalism: "He carries abroad with him everything that should be left back home."[94] The reign of white terror is felt by the crew in the increased removal of black mariners, the archetypal figures for the black transnational, from the ships coming into Marseilles:

> Some of [the Crew] had an imperfect common-sense knowledge of some of the things that were taking place in the important centers of the world

and that those things were threatening to destroy their way of life. . . . Great Britain's black boys, for example. They observed that colored crews on British ships west of Suez were . . . being replaced by white crews. The beach boys felt the change.[95]

This sea change disturbs even Ray's desire for narrative closure:

[Ray] had wanted very much to leave taking intact the rough, joyous, free picture of the beach boys' life in the regimented rhythm of the Ditch. . . . But life is so artistically uncompromising, it does not care a rap about putting a hard fist through a splendid plan and destroying our dearest artifice.[96]

The real nature of the "hard fist" becomes even more clear in the chapter entitled "Official Fists," a chapter dominated by the beach boys' official interactions with imperial authorities such as the police and the immigration officers. One of their crew, Bugsy, dies. Banjo and Goosey are threatened with repatriation. Banjo and Malty are prevented from boarding one of their regular ships to panhandle: "The officer said to the white seaman: 'Don't let any of them niggers on here.'"[97] As the boys step back onto the dock they are accosted by the police, "taken to the police station on the Quai du Lazaret and given a merciless beating. Each of them was taken separately into a room by the policemen, knocked down and kicked. Then they were turned loose."[98] Ray himself, "when passing two policemen in the street leading to his hotel (one leaning against the door of a house and the other standing carelessly on the pavement)," is beaten and arrested.[99] When Ray inquires as to the reason for his arrest and harsh treatment he is told, "that the policemen had made a mistake, owing to the fact that all the Negroes in Marseilles were criminals."[100] As Ray confirms afterward, "to me the policeman's fist was just a perfect expression of the official attitude toward Negroes."[101]

The official attitude toward Negroes is more fully revealed in the story of the character Taloufa. Taloufa, a West African member of the crew's circle who had recently decided to return to Britain, is spotted in the Ditch. When the boys find Taloufa he tells them that he was refused entrance into Great Britain. He shows Ray a slip of paper with his name and fingerprint which reads:

The above-named is permitted to land at this port on condition that he proceeds to London in charge of an official of the Shipping Federation, obtains document of identity at the Home Office, and visa (if required), and leaves the United Kingdom at the earliest opportunity.

(Signed) . . . . . . . . . . . . . . . . . . . . . . . . . . . . .

Immigration Officer.

As the story continues, "When Taloufa arrived in England, the authorities would not permit him to land, but wanted him to go home direct to West Africa."[102] Taloufa's story demonstrates blacks' exclusion from narratives of official nationalism in Europe. The Home Office does not protect black subjects, citizens, and colonials; it polices them. The political relevance and cultural power of Garvey's Black Star Line becomes clear in this context, where imperial official nationalism can so explicitly prevent the communication and travel of black subjects across the diaspora and hence destroy the foundation for black transnational communities and formations such as that of the crew. This form of white terror is the primary subject of discussion across the diaspora:

> Colored subjects were not wanted in Britain. This was the chief topic of serious talk among colored seamen in all the ports. Black and brown men being sent back to West Africa, East Africa, the Arabian coast, and India, showed one another their papers. . . . The majority of the papers were distinguished by the official phrase: Nationality Doubtful. . . . They were agreed that the British authorities were using every device to get all the colored seamen out of Britain and keep them out, so that white men should have their jobs.[103]

Ray's belief in the hypocritical plot of official nationalism and the penalization of the black male subject within the national narrative is confirmed:

> The happenings of the past few weeks from the beating up of the beach boys by the police to the story of Taloufa's experiences were, to Ray, all of a piece. A clear and eloquent exhibition of the universal attitude, which, though the method varied, was little different anywhere.
>
> When the police inspector said to Ray that the strong arm of the law was against Negroes because they were criminals, . . . what he unconsciously meant was that the police were strong-armed against the happy irresponsibility of the Negro in the face of civilization.
>
> For civilization had gone out among these native, earthly people, had

despoiled them of their primitive soil, had uprooted, enchained, trans-
ported, and transformed them to labor under its laws, and yet lacked the
spirit to tolerate them within its walls.[104]

The flip side of denationalization as freedom was the criminalization and
penalization of the black male subject, now somehow defined as outside the
bounds of citizenship within the nation-state.[105] The national-imperial order,
which had denationalized blacks in the first place, was now criminalizing
them and preventing them from claiming legitimate citizenship. Banjo's only
ace in the hole, in McKay's final image of the black transnational, is to keep
on moving.

*Banjo* as a novel has partly escaped categorization because it is difficult to
know where to place it. It fits within no national literary tradition and follows
no conventional formula. Due to its setting in Marseilles this "Story without a
Plot," as the subtitle tells us, seems to have little to do with the themes evident
in either African American literature or the literature of the Anglophone
Caribbean. Yet, considering McKay's preoccupation with questions of literary
form, *Banjo's* subtitle is not accidental. Why is this novel a story without a
plot? If narratives of nationhood are also narratives of the self, fictions of
identity, a story without a plot gives writer and reader a certain latitude in
writing and imagining the self. It also frees writer and reader from imagining
that self within the limited confines of the nation, as African American,
African, and Caribbean characters move through a metropolitan, rather than
a colonial landscape.

However, *Banjo* also claims to be a story without a plot because it explicitly
articulates the worldly black male subject's renunciation of the heterosexual
narrative of domesticity and nationhood. McKay's *Banjo* envisions a different
form of family and community for the black male and hence a different notion
of home and nation. In the novel, nationality doubtful could stand also as a
figure for sexuality doubtful, as McKay's crew of black boys locate their desires
for home in their own musical itinerant community rather than in heterosexual romances. Marseilles thus becomes the setting for a new, masculine romance of the race, one in which black men are free to desire and free to move.

If we focus on Banjo and the crew's "vagabond internationalism"[106] simply within the context of industrial capitalism, reading their lifestyle through Marxian lenses and world systems theories of race and class, we miss their equally important location in a black transatlantic context that has always been tenuously defined in relationship to the theoretical critique of capital. Vagabondage alone does not capture the specifically male space of black seafaring that scholars such as Jeffrey Bolster have already identified and that this book seeks to elaborate in the context of McKay's fiction. Black seafaring under a number of different official and unofficial conditions, from the African fishermen of the Mediterranean to the stowaway travels of runaway slaves, has always been a space for creating specific alternative transnational versions of black masculinity operating in transatlantic space. Black seamen represent, throughout Atlantic history, identity formations and gendered communities that embody and manifest both residual and emergent structures of feeling, alongside and adjacent to the dominant capitalist mode of production.

Banjo and his crew are intimately connected to and literally live and feed off of the maritime Atlantic—even when they themselves are beached or grounded. When they feed on the leftovers from ships they are also not marginal to those spaces for, at least in the initial stages of the novel, these are ships that, despite the crew's vagabondage, they also delight in having "the full run of."[107] As most of Banjo's crew leave Marseilles for a future that we are led to understand will continue to be one of trying to maintain their own agency and free movement within the framework of the greater mobility afforded them by employment within the maritime industry, the final image of the crew that we get at the close of the novel is the following:

> It was indeed in every way a cargo of good luck that the boys were han-
> dling. They were no longer "on the beach." A wealthy shipowner from the
> Caribbean basin, profiting by the exchange rate, had bought a boat, which
> he was overhauling to take back to the West Indies. And the boys were on
> the boat.
>
> It was a formidable polyglot outfit. The officers represented five Euro-
> pean nations. The crew were supposed to be Caribbean. Malty was chosen
> to find and recommend the men. He got his gang in first. . . .

Malty also took West African boys, a "colored" South African, a reed-like Somali lad, and another Aframerican. . . . They were all going "on the fly" and none of them was thinking of staying with the boat after the trip.[108]

Because their masculinity is so profoundly shaped by the more specifically gendered context of black seafaring, I would argue that their placement within the capitalist mode of production needs to be more layered, moving beyond the category of the *Lumpenproletariat* in which Marx, or even Fanon rereading Marx, might have placed them.

Where I believe the narrative of vagabondage is more relevant, then, is in terms of how McKay defines these men's sexuality. Precisely what vagabondage allows them is freedom from domesticity and a form of black masculinity grounded in heterosexuality and tied to the national narrative. By focusing in his definition of vagabondage on the industrial sphere of employment, Brent Edwards and others miss the degree to which what is actually freed for the crew is not their dependence on ships and seafaring as a way of life, but rather, their dependence on women and the nation as the final source of home and employment.

To return to a quote from the text, Ray describes the black transnational male's longings as that of "the vagabond lover of life [who] finds individuals and things to love in many places and not in any one nation." Here Ray employs what at first appear to be heterosexual metaphors in his description: "Man loves places and no one place, for the earth, like a beautiful wanton, puts on a new dress to fascinate him wherever he may go." The diasporic territories traversed are imaged once again as the woman of color, a planetary female being whose territorial nationalities become merely the dresses she wears to seduce the unattached worldly black male traveler. But since we know that the woman of color is typically incidental to the communities and couplings Ray finds himself drawn to, what is important here is the "wanton" nature of Ray's own desire to find homes unbounded by domesticity. When he elsewhere pits the worldly New Negro's irresponsibility against civilization and morality, the latter terms reference the more bourgeois social dimensions of national life, the private spheres of family and intimacy and the public forms of social affiliation and belonging.

Ray makes clear the links between the private sphere of family life and the public life of the nation in his disgust for the chauffeur, his suburbia-seeking friend:

> That chauffeur will marry with a clear conscience . . . become a respectable *père de famille*—a good taxpayer and supporter of a strong national government, with a firm colonial policy, while you and I will always be the same lost black vagabonds, because we don't know what this civilization is all about.[109]

Once again, heterosexual domesticity undergirds citizenship and nationality, and it is this form of civilization that Ray asserts is not an aspect of the modern New Negro male's transnationality. In the liminal space of the black transnational, somewhere between home and vagabondage, nation and internationalist revolution, the wandering black male subject re-creates himself as inhabiting an alternative mode of masculine being, one that is also governed by different expressions of his sexuality.

Ray's reflections on sexual relations in the Ditch are telling in this regard:

> He felt that there was something fundamentally cruel about sex which, being alien to his nature, was somehow incomprehensible, and that the more civilized humanity became the more cruel was sex. It really seemed sometimes as if there were a war joined between civilization and sex.[110]

Here in Ray's voice, McKay refigures the race war on the terrain of sexuality as a battle not between the sexes but between different conceptions of desire and sexuality, with the black subject's masculinity caught in-between:

> And it also seemed to him that Negroes under civilization were helplessly caught between the two forces. There was an idea current among the whites that the blacks were over-sexed. . . . But from his experience and close observation. . . . what he inferred was that white people had developed sex complexes that Negroes had not. . . . And maybe that vastly big difference of attitude was a fundamental, unconscious cause of the antagonism between white and black brought together by civilization.[111]

In *Banjo* and within the context of the Ditch, sexual relations between men and women have a different meaning than in *Home to Harlem*. As we are introduced to Banjo in the first chapter, so too are we introduced to his sexual philosophy and activities. As he describes relations with "the first playmate of his dream port," it is clear that Banjo feels no inclination to romanticize a love connection that was primarily a commercial encounter. Unlike Jake, Banjo also makes clear early on that domesticity and safety is not what this picaresque hero is looking for. Hence, when Malty, a member of his crew, gets jealous that Banjo and Latnah have become lovers, the typical male conflict over a woman quickly dissipates into something much more tender between the two men themselves: "All the boys crowded to the door and flowed out into the alley, to watch. The antagonists sparred. Malty hiccoughed ominously, swayed forward, and, falling into Banjo's arms, they both went down heavily, in a helpless embrace, on the paving-stones."[112]

In defiance of the race war as it plays itself out on the body of women, Latnah does not cause a permanent rift between the two men, and later on in the novel Banjo quite happily accepts Latnah's liaison with Ray, without any expression of masculine possessiveness. Latnah too, in turn, is represented as having no desire for monogamy; when Banjo disappears for days on end, "Latnah was not fretful about his absence. He would come again when he wanted to, just as casually as when they had first met. She had no jealous feeling of possession about him." Latnah's willingness to respect Banjo's "insistence on freedom of desire for himself" hinges on her not being black or American. "She was Oriental," McKay tells us, and her foreignness, represented here literally in Orientalist terms, reflects McKay's own tendencies to stereotype, racially and sexually, hybrid international female subjects, thereby releasing the black male from the traps and trappings and the loyalties and affiliations of a pure, black, racial home.[113]

Banjo's heterosexual vagabondage is only one instance in which we can find a critique of normative heterosexuality in the proletarian, colonialist space of the Ditch. To eliminate any room for doubt concerning the novels' sexual politics, McKay reintroduces the character Jake as a vehicle for rewriting the national romance of his previous novel. Outside of the nation, black masculinity and mobility get reframed within the context of the traveling, transnational lifestyle and philosophy of the black mariner. One day (aptly enough), "The boys went into the Seamen's Bar and there was *Home to Harlem* Jake drinking with a seaman pal at the bar. He and Ray embraced and kissed."[114] McKay makes a meta-narrative intervention here, inserting *Home to Harlem* as text into *Banjo*'s story without a plot. No attempt is made at verisimilitude or at hiding McKay's desire for the two novels to speak to each other. As Jake and

Ray's exchange continues, the terms of their relations of intimacy as men and the boundaries of male heterosexuality within the nation are expanded, revealing even further the stakes of this intertextual discussion. Black masculinity is reimagined in an international, globalized, transnational context, a redefinition that begins with Jake and Ray's fraternal kiss.

McKay chooses to underscore this embrace as representing a moment in which black men are able to freely admit to their desire for each other, their longing to be in each other's company. As Jake exclaims immediately following the kiss, and Ray responds:

> "The first time I evah French-kiss a he, chappie, but Ise so tearing mad and glad and crazy to meet you this-away again."
> "That's all right, Jake, he-men and all. Stay long enough in any country and you'll get on to the ways and find them natural."[115]

Literally the men are discussing kissing each other in a European style specific to the French national context, yet we know from a story such as "The Little Sheik" that when McKay refers to what is or is not natural behavior between men, he is quite consciously referencing sexuality. It is no stretch to read a homoerotic subtext in the double entendre in this interaction between Jake and Ray. The idea that Jake's presence in this new country of black transnational males in Marseilles is also taking him away from the narrative of bourgeois heterosexuality and domesticity already constructed in Harlem is made explicit only a few lines later:

> Jake told Ray of his picking up Felice again and their leaving Harlem for Chicago. After two years there they had a baby boy. And then they decided to get married. Two years of married life passed and he could no longer stick to Chicago, so he returned to Harlem. But he soon found that it was not just a change of place that was worrying him.
> "I soon finds out," he said, "that it was no joymaking business for a fellah like you' same old Jake, chappie, to go to work reg'lar ehvery day and come home ehvery night to the same ole pillow. Not to say that Felice hadn't kep' it freshen' up and sweet-smelling all along. . . . But it was too much home stuff, chappie. . . . I just stahted up one day and got me a broad."[116]

Jake leaves Harlem, the nation, and Felice, not for the life of the vagabond but for the life of the seaman, where he can reconfigure his masculinity, his wanderlust, differently outside of the confines of the nation that he can within it, "And now it's bettah. I don't feel like running away from Felice no moh. Whenevah I get home Ise always happy to be with her and feel that Ise doing mah duty by [my son]."[117]

In 1918 Claude McKay was briefly arrested in Pittsburgh for not having his immigration papers or his registration card, and he would be continually interrogated throughout his travels in Europe, so much so that he would assert playfully at one point, "While scrupulously complying with official regulations regarding passports, identity cards and visas, etc., in all my traveling in strange places, I have always relied on my own personality as the best passport."[118] McKay's distinction was to perceive his own statelessness and the worldly wanderings of other black colonial male subjects like himself not just as their exile from national narratives and state forms, but also as an opening to new sites for the creation of alternative black masculinities and subjectivities. Modernist conceptions of exile, even those foregrounded in postcolonial literature and criticism, are different from the conceptions formed by McKay and other traveling New World Negroes on the black transnational circuit. The language of the latter is McKay's language in *Banjo*, and he was able to use that language to shape his own sense of self. As Ray, the traveling West Indian writer, would say of Banjo and his crew at the end of the novel:

> He admired the black boy's unconscious artistic capacity for eliminating the rotten-dead stock words . . . and replacing them with startling new ones. There were no dots and dashes in their conversation . . . no act or fact of life for which they could not find a simple passable word. He gained from them finer nuances of the necromancy of language and the wisdom that any word may be right and magical in its proper setting.[119]

Ray's experience of the crew's oral culture, their music, and their stories opens up a new world. He finds among this motley crew the language and the words he so desperately sought to describe a modern black identity. This is the language Ray ultimately tries to draw on in telling his own story, a language of male desire for alternative visions of black intimacy and community.

In the context of European and North American imperialism, the public culture of print is not always the most useful or accessible mechanism for affirming blackness or constructing alternative modes of being. In his periodization of the rise of the novel and the decline of the art of storytelling, Walter

Benjamin described and lamented a process emerging from the aftermath of World War I, one which sets a final context for McKay's own search for literary form. Benjamin asks: "Was it not noticeable at the end of the war that men returned from the battlefield grown silent—not richer, but poorer in communicable experience? What ten years later was poured out in the flood of war books was anything but experience that goes from mouth to mouth."[120] In what we might call McKay's war books, *Home to Harlem* and *Banjo*, it is precisely this ability to exchange experiences that characters such as Ray and Jake, Banjo and Taloufa, are trying to identify in these transnational black communities and to help re-engender. In a world in which newly imagined national communities have no way of envisioning forms of belonging inclusive of black and colonial subjects, McKay's fear is Benjamin's, that in the world of isolated and alienated black subjects, "the gift for listening is lost and the community of listeners disappears."[121] Not surprisingly then, storytelling is valued in *Banjo* precisely when it looks more like a form of jazzing, the expressive musical culture created by Banjo and his crew in Marseilles.

When challenged as a writer Ray reveals the fundamentally communal desires and values embodied in his writing, the context in which his practice of diaspora makes sense:

> if I am writing a story—well, it's like all of us in this place here, black and brown and white, and I telling a story for the love of it. Some of you will listen, and some won't. If I am a real story-teller, I won't worry about the differences in complexion of those who listen and those who don't, I'll just identify myself with those who are really listening and tell my story.[122]

For Ray, community is enacted in the act of telling and listening to a story, not by official categories of race and nationality. When Ray euphemistically declares "I'm not a reporter for the Negro press," he stresses neither his role as a race man interested in re-presenting a respectable, bourgeois blackface to a white American audience, nor as the print journalist intent on imagining strictly national forms of black community. Ray's only interest lies in the telling of a good story in the world: "I am writing for people who can stand a real story no matter where it comes from."[123]

In a conversation McKay had in Morocco in the summer of 1927, one year before *Home to Harlem* was published, a native messenger from the British consulate asked McKay if he was an American. McKay replied, "I said I was born in the West Indies and lived in the United States and that I was an American, even though I was a British subject, but I preferred to think of myself as an internationalist." McKay traced in his response the paths and identities he had accumulated over the course of his travels, but his tongue-in-cheek statement that followed also underscored the transnational geopolitical forces shaping his sense of his own nationality. As he continued his self-description: "The *cahoush* said he didn't understand what was an internationalist. I laughed and said that an internationalist was a bad nationalist."[124]

McKay's internationalism went far beyond Russia as did he, and while he was never officially penalized for his travels, he did record in his narratives the geopolitics shaping the travels of his fellow colonial male subjects. *Banjo* reveals the ways in which empire polices the practice of alternative forms of mobility and sexuality, the black male's "freedom in flight" and "freedom to love" outside the paradigms and narratives of the nation-state.

Paul Robeson in *Song of Freedom* (1936). Courtesy of the Douris Corporation (www.classicmovies.com).

# CHAPTER 7

# C. L. R. James and the Fugitive Slave
## in *American Civilization*

If self-interest alone prevails with nations and their masters, there is another power. Nature speaks in louder tones than philosophy or self-interest. Already are there established two colonies of fugitive negroes, whom treaties and power protect from assault. Those lightnings announce the thunder. A courageous chief only is wanted.

—ABBÉ RAYNAL[1]

IN 1936, TWO years after Claude McKay returned to the United States, the already prominent Caribbean intellectual C. L. R. James wrote and produced a play about Toussaint L'Ouverture, the nineteenth-century leader of the Haitian Revolution. This play, originally titled *Toussaint L'Ouverture*, was performed in London in 1936 at the Westminster Theatre, with Paul Robeson playing the lead role.[2] James drew the material for this play from his research for *The Black Jacobins*, his groundbreaking history of the Haitian revolution. *The Black Jacobins* was another romance of the race, to use Ray's term from McKay's novel, a revolutionary narrative of black empire and the search for a Negro state. The story Ray tells Jake when they first meet, the one that produces Jake's transnational epiphany, was an almost prophetic summary of the history James would write ten years after the publication of McKay's novel.

McKay's emphases also mirrored many of the main points of James's historical argument. Like McKay, James situated the slave revolution in Haiti within the history and the democratic ideals of the French Revolution. James also compared the slave revolution with the struggle for American independence. The Haitian Revolution was an important founding narrative in black transnational discourse. It was an exalted romance of the race that had the power of history behind it, the power of "ideas so big that they had lifted up ignorant people, even black, to the stature of gods."[3] The Haitian Revolution provided black intellectuals with a way to write black slaves into revolutionary history.

Given that James was already writing a history of the Haitian revolution, however, it is interesting that he also chose to write a version of this story as a play. At one point James argued that certain historical ideas required particular literary forms: "Each historic rebel, rebels against something very specific and it takes a specific literary form, precisely because of its specific social character."[4] This chapter begins by arguing that James's play was written specifically to explore the tensions of black state formation. While James's history provided the details of how the black Jacobins entered the revolutionary narratives of the nineteenth century, it was the dramatic form of the play that allowed James to isolate out in all its purity the question of what happens to the slave state, *after freedom*. As with Garvey, the figure of the black sovereign Toussaint L'Ouverture becomes in James's hands not just a figure for a revolutionary masculinity but the representative leader playing out the tensions and the possibilities inherent within the race, for leadership and self-government.[5]

James and McKay shared more than just an interest in the Haitian Revolution itself. They both placed at the center of their narratives the revolution's black leaders, Toussaint L'Ouverture and Jean-Jacques Dessalines. Both black masculinity and black globality were central terms in James's attempt to portray the Haitian leaders dramatically. We find evidence for this in James's own writings on Paul Robeson, the African American actor he chose to play the lead role. Reflecting back on his sense of Robeson's fame and strengths in an essay he wrote in 1970, James described the actor's presence in the most masculine and physical of terms: "There was his magnificent self. He was some six feet six inches in height and built in proportion, but he always had the silhouette and litheness of a great athlete. He was obviously immensely strong, strong enough to deal with two or three men at a time. Even in ordinary speech you were aware of his magnificent voice. He was . . . a man of unusual intelligence."[6] Robeson's physical and intellectual presence only added to his magnetic appeal to audiences across the black world and other colonial worlds of color. As James would also describe in a personal correspondence with Anna Grimshaw for a potential autobiographical chapter entitled

"Robeson and Me," "wherever Paul Robeson went he could get five thousand people, wherever—he went to Asia, to India—wherever. And the American government has seen to it that no black man will ever have that popularity."[7] In "Paul Robeson: Black Star," James specifically described the role Robeson played in choosing one of Toussaint's most dramatic speeches in the play: "Paul was reading his part in the scene and suddenly his voice opened up and the transition from his usual quiet undertone to the tremendous roar of which he was capable was something to hear. . . . When he reached 'Those lightnings announce the thunder. A courageous chief only is wanted,' he stopped. . . . 'James,' he said, 'I don't want to go any further. I think it should stop here.'"[8]

C. L. R. James's interest in Toussaint L'Ouverture as a historical character reflected his belief in the importance of the great "personality in history."[9] James argued that great personalities and historical figures were not just unique individuals but rather that they were also constituted by the social ideas of their time: "Each great character is rooted in his own age . . . that is what makes the characters 'original.'"[10] Furthermore, as James would say in describing the tragic hero of drama, great historical characters emerged from the collision of differing visions of society:

> All the great tragedies deal with [the] . . . question of the confrontation of two ideas of society and they deal with it according to the innermost essence of the drama—the two societies confront one another within the mind of a single person.[11]

In *The Black Jacobins* James used the tragic figure of Toussaint L'Ouverture to dramatize precisely this type of historical moment—the slaves' confrontation with European imperial power and their transformation of the colony into a society of freed slaves.

Accounts of the drama of black revolution in Haiti had been circulating throughout the revolutionary Atlantic from the moment of the black state's inception, appearing in classics of Western literature such as Wordsworth's sonnet "To Toussaint L'Ouverture" and, as Susan Buck-Morss has argued, shaping key texts in continental philosophy.[12] Throughout the African diaspora the Haitian Revolution provided a paradigmatic tale of black freedom and the creation of alternative New World black societies. In her broader exploration of forms and expressions of black masculinity compatible with the nation-state Hazel Carby has argued:

In the 1930s a number of male intellectuals, both black and white, created historical discourses of black manhood in the service of a revolutionary politics. . . . The figure of Toussaint L'Ouverture emerged in this period as a popular model for creating contemporary images of a revolutionary black male consciousness. The revolution in Haiti, frequently linked to rebellions by those enslaved in North America, was used as the historical landscape in which the possibilities for black male autonomy, self-government, and patriarchal black nationhood could be enacted. The work of C. L. R. James is particularly important in this context.[13]

As Carby continues to describe, James's work was key in his exploration of a central dilemma for the construction of a revolutionary masculine consciousness—how to articulate the relationship between the sovereign leader and the black masses? Carby argues that "James sought to develop a theory of a direct, unmediated relation between the heroic male figure and the people. . . . [an] ideal of the black male hero as one inspiring as well as expressing the social passions of the people."[14] It was in James's fiction that the gendered politics and the ideologies of masculinity shaping such a desire revealed themselves, for in the writing of a novel such as *Minty Alley*, Carby argues, "The world of the working class is imagined overwhelmingly through the figures of women. . . . The class divisions of James's fictional world are gendered: the masses are feminized; the point of view of the intellectual/middle-class protagonist is masculine."[15] Carby concludes, "When James abandoned fiction to write about revolutionary politics and revolutionary heroes, he also gave up trying to write about women."[16]

Within the context of the Caribbean revolutionary narrative, Belinda Edmondson also confirms Carby's account of the politics of gender in James's work on revolution. Edmondson points to the centrality of revolutionary masculinity in Caribbean discourse, also specifically referencing James: "His emphasis on one central, masterful personality in an otherwise Marxist account of revolution makes sense only if we understand it to be a particularly West Indian, particularly middle-class and male version of revolutionary discourse."[17] Edmondson goes on to demonstrate the specifically gendered politics of fiction and writing within the Caribbean landscape: "Toussaint's recasting as a Jamesian author-figure of the revolution is useful to us as a metaphor for the privileged relationship of the author to revolutionary engagement in

Caribbean narrative: that is, [male] authors 'author' revolution through fiction." Here Edmondson's observations parallel Carby's insight that James "sees Toussaint not only as a fearless warrior and stern but loving father to his people, but as a man with the ability to bear and realize the revolution; James grants to the black male hero the organs of female reproduction."[18]

As was also evident in McKay's fictions, black internationalist and revolutionary masculinities have the capacity to engender and birth new black social formations and communities. Here, black masculinity is as much *reproductive* as productive in the global context of world capitalism and imperialism. And, as we saw in McKay's account, this powerful masculine ability does not extend across gender lines: "But while the heroic male figure can appropriate the reproductive power of the female body to bring forth an act of rebellion, feminization alone can only mark the abject."[19] Edmondson argues that a source for this gendered structure in black male revolutionary fiction is the pressing masculinist need to take on the responsibility of rewriting history:

> From another angle, however, this desire to fictionalize Caribbean history is arguably a desire to *rewrite* the ending of the Caribbean historical script. . . . Since violent conquest is in its turn associated with the rites of manhood, the reclamation of history has come to signify the "reclamation"—or the constitution, to be more precise—of Caribbean masculinity in much of Caribbean discourse.[20]

As Carby described in the specific instance of James's fiction, Edmondson elaborates the price of this need in terms of Caribbean fiction as a whole: "The desire of the novel of revolution to liberate the Caribbean space by remaking it, literally and figuratively, in the image of Caribbean man is tied to its corresponding impulse to 'erase' the symbolic body of the black woman. As a symbol of the slave past, the black woman represents a double threat."[21] This chapter builds on Carby's and Edmondson's gender analyses of James's work, by foregrounding the specific category of the state. Here I argue that revolution and masculinity are also integrally linked in black transnational discourse, a discourse less directly tied to either Caribbean nationalist claims to previous colonial island territories or African American citizenship claims to territory within the American nation as a whole. Because of that distinction, the state emerges in black transnational discourse as an even more strongly desired entity, precisely because it contains the power to embody a diasporic, transnational, racial body politic not easily defined in territorial terms. In James's work on the Haitian Revolution, as in the work of other black male transnational intellectuals, the state is embodied metonymically in the figure of the black male sovereign, a black emperor able to represent the masses *globally*, and not just nationally, on the world stage of early-twentieth-century geopolitics.

I would also argue that James used the specific literary form of drama to foreground the question of the black state in a way that was not available to him when he wrote his early fiction. In the play *The Black Jacobins*, the differing visions of society that confronted one another in a character such as Toussaint L'Ouverture went beyond the dialectic between the imperial masters and their slaves and the subsequent dialectic between the black leader and the masses. The play actually dramatized conflicting *black* visions of the possible nature and future of the Haitian state.

For the black Jacobins in San Domingo at the beginning of the nineteenth century, the modern black nation-state was at its very moment of political birth. As Eugene Genovese has argued, what distinguished the Haitian Revolution from other slave rebellions throughout the Americas was precisely that it was not just a revolt against slavery but also a revolutionary struggle for the slaves' political independence—their access to state forms.[22] Most other slave revolts, led by maroons, resulted in "colonies of fugitive negroes, whom treaties and power protect[ed] from assault."[23] These revolts created fugitive maroon outposts that still existed within the political boundaries of the colony. The Haitian Revolution marked a truly revolutionary turning point precisely because it took as its central mission the creation of an independent black state.

James's use of drama to explore contradictory visions of black statehood had an obvious contemporary relevance for black audiences in the late 1930s and 1940s. This was the moment, during and between the wars, when blacks in the Caribbean, America, Europe, and Africa were wrestling with the possibilities for their own political freedom in the context of modern debates on national self-determination and colonial self-government. In a series of essays James wrote on theater in the 1940s and 1950s, he argued that the popular audience was actually central to the drama precisely because drama was essentially a performance of the history of the nation. James used as his example the dramatic audiences of the classical era. He asked:

What were the circumstances under which [the works of classical Greek drama] were produced? The great drama of Aeschylus, Sophocles and Euripedes was first and foremost a popular drama. The whole Athenian nation, or rather the whole city-state was there, from the highest officials down to those slaves who were allowed to come. . . . The power [of these plays] came from the Athenian democracy. When democracy declined the great Athenian drama declined with it.[24]

The classics showed that art and politics were intimately connected in the social life of a nation. The popular audience, as spectators of the nation's history, also had a certain set of expectations that the good drama had to fulfill.[25] The play had to question and then ultimately resolve the issue of the security of the state. As James put it, "An audience would follow the fortunes of Cassius, Brutus, Mark Antony and the rest; but it would never lose sight of the fact that the play had to settle the problem of the government of Rome."[26]

In the 1930s the story of the Haitian Revolution mattered precisely because it gave black audiences and playwrights the chance to explore the possibilities and limits of black statehood. What was *The Black Jacobins* about? The play consisted entirely of a series of conversations between Toussaint and his officers on the appropriate nature of the future Haitian state. The scenes of the play are set in rooms devoted to the discussion of government, the Haitian and French leaders' military headquarters and offices. Many options for San Domingo's political future are presented to Toussaint as governor: a colony under Spanish rule, a monarchy with British support, a republic such as America, a dominion of France. The play consists of the leaders' debates over these options, debates that raise a series of important questions about the nature of black identity.

What are the political inclinations and desires of the black masses? How do they fit into the modern world order? Are they by nature African or European, and if the latter, are they really French? Are they Old World or New World, African, European, or something completely different? This chapter begins by exploring how James used the dramatic form to explore and resolve these questions in his dramatic reenactment of *The Black Jacobins*. This chapter then turns to James's writings on the Negro question and American Civilization during his first stay in the United States between 1938 and 1956. Here I argue that when James turned away from the globally imagined black state to study the place of the modern black subject within the nation and his or her possibilities for freedom, he also chose to rewrite history but not in the form of a revolutionary narrative of the quest for statehood. Rather, in his focus on the flight of the African American fugitive slave, whose movements can never hope to be realized in the form of an independent black state within the United States, James suggested an alternative conception of revolutionary movement which also eliminated a role for the black leader.

Here the fugitive slaves, as a more loosely defined figure for the black masses in gendered terms, move as a group on their own initiative and self-direction, achieving in their journeys an unmediated impact on the state itself and its representative leaders. As a metaphor for the people, the fugitive slave articulates a much more complex and contradictory relationship to nationhood and statehood, the domestic sphere, than that articulated in the vision of a revolutionary masculine leader. To the degree that the figure of the fugitive slave forced C. L. R. James to theorize the place of the domestic or local within the global, this chapter ends by suggesting that we can find in James's later work the beginnings of a critique of the gendered politics of black transnationalism and pathways toward envisioning an equal role and place for the woman of color in a black masculine global imaginary.

## THE DREAM OF AN IMPOSSIBLE FRATERNITY

Until you cut yourself off from all symbols of colonialism and slavery . . . and be truly independent, you will remain just an old man with a dream of an impossible fraternity.

*The Black Jacobins*[27]

Four leaders of the Haitian revolution—Toussaint, Dessalines, Christophe, and Möise—provide the main action of the plot of *The Black Jacobins*, but their activities and decisions are observed and commented on by their counterpart in the play, the foot soldiers of the revolution. A revealing exchange between two of these black soldiers, Marat and Orleans, first articulates the play's guiding dilemma. After the revolution, the San Domingo slaves have little sense of their place in a fraternal community of French citizens.[28] As Orleans says, "Everybody says Liberty-Equality-Fraternity. All right, Liberty is when you kill the master; Equality, he's dead and can't beat you again; and Fraternity. *(He pauses.)* What is that Fraternity?" (1.2). This is the opening question of the play. After the San Domingo slaves have achieved "Liberty and Equality"—the slogans of the French revolution—in the colony, what is the exact nature of their political relationship to France, the metropole? "What is that Fraternity" that comes after freedom? "Everybody talks about it but nobody says what it is."

If the meaning of fraternity is already the central issue for the black soldiers after the revolution, the catalyst that sparks a similar question among their leaders is the announcement in the second scene of act one of the French abolition of slavery. Before Toussaint hears of abolition he insists that the revolution does not necessarily extend to the slaves in the colony the fraternal kiss of French citizenship. When he hears the slaves singing the anthem of the French Revolution he objects, saying, "We are Africans, and Africans believe in a King. We are slaves and we believe in liberty and equality. But we are not republicans" (1.2). By claiming liberty and equality but omitting the third term, fraternity, Toussaint inadvertently answers the question that Marat and Orleans debated earlier. He rejects European notions of citizenship in the imperial French republic in favor of a return to older Ethiopianist visions of African monarchy.

Toussaint frames this royalist return—"We are Africans and Africans believe in a King"—as the expression of an inherent African political nature. But when he says "We are not republicans," he is also rejecting the imperial fallacy at the heart of the colonial mentality, the myth that the black colonial shares in the rights and privileges of citizenship in the metropole. Toussaint resists precisely because he suspects that even black slaves freed by revolution will never be included as full citizens of France. They may do better by staying within the protected structure of a new colonial relationship with Spain.

When France herself acknowledges the slaves' freedom by abolishing slavery, however, the terms of the debate shift. In this second scene in act one, the moment when abolition is announced sets the stage for the action to come and bears quoting at some length:

> (The lights in the small room go off and once more the main area is illuminated. Toussaint stands as he was before, opposite to Dessalines and the ragged soldiers. Into the middle of them rushes a young soldier, Lieutenant Möise. He waves a copy of the periodical Le Moniteur over his head. He shouts to the soldiers.)

MÖISE: News, citizens! News!

*(Möise has not seen Toussaint and his attention is drawn to him by the concentration on Toussaint of Dessalines and the other soldier. Möise therefore turns towards Toussaint. His enthusiasm is momentarily checked by Toussaint's glance.)*

TOUSSAINT: Well, Lieutenant Möise, what is this new title by which you are addressing us? Since when have we become citizens? Only members of the French republic are citizens.

MÖISE: General, we are citizens. I have news. General, let me tell you the news.

*(Toussaint seems unwilling to make the concession, but Möise is so enthusiastic and is appealing so strongly that Toussaint partly relents.)*

TOUSSAINT: All right, Lieutenant Möise, tell us this news of yours.

*(One of two soldiers join the crowd behind Dessalines, and Möise dramatically takes the centre of the stage. He waves the paper in his hands and speaks rhetorically.)*

MÖISE: We are citizens, sailors from the ship tell me. They give me a paper and it is here in the paper.

TOUSSAINT: What, Lieutenant, is in the paper?

MÖISE: Former slaves from San Domingo, Bellay *(Looking up)*, black man *(Reads again)*, go to France, to the Chamber of Deputies to represent San Domingo. President of Chamber welcome him and give him Fraternal kiss. President of French Chamber give black slave from San Domingo fraternal kiss. French sailor tell me. And I read it in the paper here. In *Le Moniteur*, the official paper. Slavery in every colony, abolished! (1.2)

News of the fraternal kiss, the kiss of official, imperial nationalism, travels on the high seas on the same Atlantic route on which black seamen were carrying the story of black revolution and self-government to other black freedmen and slaves throughout the diaspora. Over a century later, black captains of Garvey's Black Star Line would also travel these sea routes, helping to put in motion his twentieth-century spectacle of a modern black nationality. As they carried one message, sailors on American and British imperial fleets in Europe would be informing their black counterparts in Marseilles that this same dream of black citizenship was over. McKay's official label for stateless black subjects, "nationality doubtful," marks an end to the black colonial's romance with imperial nationalism that was first consummated when the island republic of Haiti dared to place itself at the center of imperial world narratives. In Haiti at the turn of the nineteenth century, the colonial world of slavery is poised to enter the modern world of the Western empires.

The real tension of *The Black Jacobins* begins with Möise's announcement, for the abolition of slavery in France opens up the question of the nature of black political identity in a new world. What type of citizens can emancipated black slaves be? Ideological questions become political and strategic ones as Toussaint attempts to define and then secure the meaning of the emancipated slaves' freedom in a world that is still dominated by the Western imperial powers. As governor of San Domingo, Toussaint is vulnerable to a number of temptations on this front. The emancipated San Domingo slaves could join the fraternal community of French citizens, but the Spanish, the Americans, and the British introduce other options. The Spanish offer the San Domingo slaves a new colonial status within their own empire. The British suggest that they owe allegiance to no one and should establish their own independent monarchy. And the Americans provide the model of an independent democratic republic.

Despite his initial ambivalence toward French nationalism, Toussaint is immediately clear that the fact that the black Jacobins are no longer slaves means the Spanish offer is no longer acceptable. He must break the promise of a new colonial relationship with Spain. In act one, scene two, as the Spanish delegate is about to be arrested by Toussaint's soldiers, he objects loudly with the words Toussaint had used before: "But you are Africans and Africans believe in a King." Toussaint responds, "We were slaves and slaves believe in freedom. . . . Marquis, you suffer from the delusion that an African is a special breed of animal different from the rest of the human species. Different he is but only when he is brought across the Atlantic and dumped in the Antilles" (1.2).

In the dramatic monologue that follows, one of the play's more profound passages, James points to the fundamental changes to African personality wrought by European colonialism and the transatlantic passage. In the act of disruption produced from the slave trade and colonialism, African identity has itself undergone fundamental shifts in the New World. As the slaves traveled beyond the borders of Africa they traveled beyond the boundaries of old ways of thinking. Fixed categories of black identity—"Africans believe in a king"— no longer hold. As James would say elsewhere, "The African who made the Middle Passage and came to live in the West Indies was an entirely new historical and social category. He was not an African, he was a West Indian black who was a slave."[29] Modern conditions now require modern solutions; modern times call for modern responses. The search for freedom and self-determination becomes the new world slaves' highest priority:

> TOUSSAINT: . . . Look at these people, General. Some of them under-stand only one French word—*Liberté. (Möise is now gesturing to the crowd of men, who are eagerly listening.)* They will join anything, or leave anything, for *Liberté.* (1.2)

The slaves' revolutionary desire for freedom overrides all nationalist ideologies—fraternity will take the form required to ensure that freedom.

Toussaint's position on the nature of black political freedom will sharpen as the play continues, but it is his officers who come to stand as different visions of a future Haitian society and the state that will govern it. Toussaint's primary foil in this regard is Jean-Jacques Dessalines, who articulates his own position in the third scene of act one. If, in act one, scene two, James presents the ideal of French citizenship for the San Domingo slaves, in act one, scene three, he lays out its opposing vision—independent black statehood. This time the British imperialists serve as the catalyst.

The British General, recognizing "the consolidation of black power in a black state," argues that Toussaint should secure that state with a monarchy: "We in England have proved beyond the shadow of a doubt that such stability can only be established by a monarchy" (1.3). Toussaint's officers are left alone to debate the English General's proposal, and it is at this point that Dessalines emerges as the voice for full autonomy and independence:

> DESSALINES: . . . I know the slaves. We are an African people. We like a king. We would like to know that the island belongs to us. Toussaint will be as good a king as anybody. I think we ought to take it. (1.3)

In this scene Dessalines presents a vision that is new in its call for the slaves' independence, but old in its dependence on the ancient African belief in monarchy. Christophe, in his support of Dessalines, underscores the new: "Dessalines means what the Englishman is offering us. To establish San

Domingo as an independent island free of France, with its own king and its own government" (1.3). But he also points out that this is a contested vision with "strong arguments for and strong arguments against." Yet the officers continue to do their best to convince Toussaint of a fraternity built on the slaves' autonomy:

> CHRISTOPHE: . . . The British Government would support a black state. We would have a king and he suggested that you, Governor, should be the first king.
> DESSALINES: The King of England would welcome you, Toussaint, as his brother. (1.3)

The abolition of slavery presents the thesis of black freedom, the possibility that the emancipated slaves can participate in European fraternity as citizens of the French republic. Dessalines presents the antithesis of this vision, San Domingo's separate and autonomous existence as a black monarchy. The play now poses a fundamental question—what vision of black statehood will Toussaint choose to lead?[30]

If James's perspective in the play mirrored that of Dessalines, *The Black Jacobins* would be a much less complex performance of black nationhood. As it is, given James's belief that at the "end" of a play "there must . . . be fundamental solutions," it is no surprise that Dessalines' perspective is triumphant at the play's conclusion.[31] What distinguished James from many of the other black transnational intellectuals before him, however, were his arguments explicitly against national self-determination. These arguments developed throughout James's career and ultimately shaped his support of West Indian federation in the late 1950s and early 1960s.

We see the precursor to James's arguments against national self-determination here in his black transnational drama. This is also what distinguishes the cultural politics of *The Black Jacobins* from other black empire dramas like it. For at the moment Toussaint is faced with the choice between fraternity with the French state and the creation of an independent black state, he stands precisely in that liminal space I have termed the black transnational, the space between the nationalist desire for independence and the internationalist desire for a movement based on terms other than national self-determination.

Toussaint ultimately refuses the British General's proposal of monarchy and chooses to leave San Domingo under French colonial rule, saying "It is the French Government . . . which has freed the slaves of San Domingo. . . . A French colony we are and a French colony we will remain, unless France attempts to restore slavery" (1.3). Toussaint tries to negotiate with France for a limited form of self-government that would follow the model of the American republic and create a constitution still based on the principle that "We do not seek independence. We are not ready for it. France will be elder brother, guide and mentor" (2.2). The French, however, soon reveal their unwillingness to play this elder fraternal role. It is at this point, as Toussaint struggles with French resistance to an even limited autonomy in San Domingo, that the audience gets a clearer sense of Toussaint's perspective on black independence.

Toussaint's exchange with the French Colonel Vincent in the second scene of act two reveals three things. First, Toussaint realizes that even after freedom, the ex-slave would still be regarded and treated more like a criminal than a citizen. Toussaint, and San Domingo along with him, would never be more to France than a colony of maroons:

> TOUSSAINT: . . . I am a General, I am Commander-in-Chief and Governor of San Domingo, but if I make any serious mistakes all that can go—tomorrow. I will be a hunted fugitive and it will be because I am black and an ex-slave. (2.2)

Here Toussaint confirms that a vision of fraternity that is premised on the black colonial male's equal inclusion in the French republic as citizen will always be denied due to his race and the condition under which he was integrated into Western civilization in the first place, slavery:

> VINCENT: This is something entirely new. America has become independent but America is a big country and. . . .
> TOUSSAINT: You mean that Americans were free men and not slaves. They were white and not black. (2.2)

In recognizing his own always-fugitive relationship to a Western ideal of republican citizenship built, however, on the racial doctrines of imperialism and colonialism, Toussaint then describes for Colonel Vincent his third realization:

> TOUSSAINT: In San Domingo we are an outpost of freed slaves. All around us in the Caribbean black men are slaves. Even in the indepen-

dent United States, black men are slaves. In South America black men are slaves. Now I have sent millions of Africans to the United States.... But it is not to build a fortune for myself so that if anything goes wrong I can escape and live like a rich man. No, Vincent. If this Constitution functions satisfactorily, I intend to take one thousand soldiers, go to Africa and free hundreds of thousands in the black slave trade there and bring them here, to be free and French. (2.2)

Rather than a vision of black nationhood, James ascribes to Toussaint the vision of scattered black male communities, outposts of freed and slave communities, connected through the transnational movement for black freedom. This vision looks elsewhere for fraternity, to the other colonies of fugitive negroes scattered throughout the colonial world. Since San Domingo is too small to ever be anything but a maroon nation, James focuses on Toussaint's proposal that the freed slaves use France's *political* resources, the formal extension of the rights of citizenship to black colonial subjects, to mobilize for the real freedom of the diaspora as a whole. Toussaint looks outward and struggles to make citizenship and fraternity in the Western world politically meaningful for men throughout the entire African diaspora.

Toussaint's transnational vision of black freedom and his proposal for a constitution are ridiculed by Napoleon Bonaparte in act two, scene three. One can almost see the specters of Marcus Garvey and the Emperor Jones hovering behind Bonaparte's description of Toussaint and his officers: "Commanding Officer? Those blacks with epaulettes on their shoulders? They are soldiers of a carnival" (2.3). As Bonaparte mobilizes for colonial warfare, Toussaint's closest and most trusted allies begin to scatter around him. Dessalines in one quarter calls for autonomy and monarchist rule; Möise in another invokes the model of bourgeois democracy, "a Declaration of Independence, like the United States" (2.4). Revolts across the island are "imperilling the state" (2.4). And the policies Toussaint tries to implement are seen by his own leaders as naive and futile dreams. As Möise says when he is brought before Toussaint on the charge of treason: "Until you cut yourself off from all symbols of colonialism and slavery . . . and be truly independent, you will remain just an old man with a dream of impossible fraternity" (2.4).

As the second act ends and the third act begins, Dessalines assumes the leadership of the island and the play.[32] In the first scene of act three, as

Dessalines plots Toussaint's capture by General Leclerc, it is clear that Toussaint's dream of impossible fraternity, a dream that included a larger struggle for the freedom of black slaves across the diaspora, holds him hostage and prevents him from acting decisively when the fight for full independence is the black Jacobins' only remaining option. When Dessalines assumes the leadership of the island the play reaches that end point where, "There must, therefore, be fundamental solutions."[33] By act three, scene two, also the final scene in the play, Dessalines provides stability, ending James's transnational drama with the establishment of an independent black government in San Domingo:

> DESSALINES: And now I have to tell you all something. I have been waiting for this moment and now the moment has come. I am going to be the Emperor of Haiti. Emperor, not King. They offered Toussaint to be King and he didn't take it. But nobody is going to offer me anything. I, Dessalines, am going to be the Emperor of Haiti. Napoleon wants to be Emperor of France. I will be Emperor of Haiti. (3.2)

Dessalines's final vision of empire does not include any of the forms of government imagined for San Domingo throughout the play—colony, monarchy, dominion, republic, nation-state. Rather, through Dessalines, James finally resolves the question of the black state with a trope that is familiar in black transnational discourse: the trope of the black empire. Why does the black empire appear at the end of *The Black Jacobins*?

The dream of a black empire is a necessary fiction for the maintenance of an internationalist vision of black freedom embodied in the autonomous black state. As a fiction it is part of a fundamentally modern black global imaginary, not dependent on ancient African beliefs in monarchy, but rather on the ex-slaves' experience of imperial power in the New World. For Dessalines, the distinction between emperor and king is the dream of imperial power, the Garveyite fantasy of meeting the modern European empires on their own global terms.

*The Black Jacobins* is ultimately about what the dream of independent black statehood enables and limits in terms of the scope of a transnational vision of black freedom. The dream of a black empire provides the necessary dramatic resolution for the emancipated slaves' fugitive existence, marooned in a world of imperial power. A black imperial state that could somehow marshal its own diasporic resources is an incredibly powerful and important utopian vision, empowering in the context of European imperial and colonial oppression. Hence, Dessalines is not a vilified character in James's play; his triumph at the end is a real one, with little sense of irony on James's part.

This final culminating vision of the black state, however, is a frozen "final tableau," one that rigidifies the movement for black freedom in imperial state forms (3.2). As the freed slaves reappear at the end of the play shouting "Dessalines! Emperor! Haiti!" the only event dimming the play's triumphant conclusion is the news from offstage of Toussaint's death (3.2). Toussaint's ghost haunts this final frozen tableau—his absence is the source of the play's tragedy. For while Toussaint represented for James, as the heroic black sovereign and liberator, a new transnational masculine conception of black subjects as fugitives who find freedom in the West in their fraternity with each other, his heroic stance is a threat to the independent black state he has chosen to create and maintain. Toussaint's ultimately antinationalist vision must be sacrificed for the sake of national unity, and what ultimately holds the black state together is the more common heroic figure of the black emperor, Dessalines.

The dream of black sovereignty holds within it the hope of the black subject's integration into a family of man in which the black male could achieve some form of true fraternity with his white male fellow citizens in the nation and with fellow nation-states throughout the world. The unfortunate legacy of colonialism for a black nationalist politics is the disruption of this seemingly universal dream of integration in the nation (whose universality is ultimately bounded by race and gender) by the realities of race war. This was then the question James would take up, as he turned to the history of slavery in the United States as a means of evaluating the place of the modern, urban black subject within the space of the American nation.

THE "NEGRO QUESTION":
INTEGRATION AND THE FUGITIVE SLAVES

In act one, scene two of *The Black Jacobins*, the soldier Marat complains that "everybody talks about [fraternity] but nobody says what it is." In 1991 Immanuel Wallerstein asked the same question, "What does the slogan, 'liberty, equality, fraternity' really mean?"[34] Liberty and equality are aspects of freedom that, in their respective realms of politics and economics, are relatively easy to define. Wallerstein argued that they are also somewhat inseparable, "Liberty-equality is a single concept" because it is impossible to imagine

> how one can be "free" if there is inequality, since those who have more always have options that are not available to those who have less. . . . [and, similarly] how there can be equality without liberty since, in the absence of liberty, some have more political power than others, and hence it follows that there is inequality.[35]

Fraternity, however, remains a separate, distinct, and somewhat murkier concept. Fraternity implies freedom in the realms of society and culture, community in an ideal sense, the belief that all men are equal and have a universal claim to the rights, privileges, and benefits of the civilizational project. For the left, fraternity has also meant man's total integration with the world around him. For C. L. R. James, this realm of civilization was inseparable from politics. In his study of American civilization during his years in the United States, James would focus on the degree to which America, too, had succeeded in creating a fraternal community for its citizens. For James, the success of the American civilizational project rested on the treatment of the American Negro.

One year after the production of *The Black Jacobins* in England, C. L. R. James came to the United States on a speaking tour for the Socialist Worker's Party, his topic being "The Negro People and World Imperialism." As Scott McLemee says in his introduction to James's writings on the "Negro question" during the 1940s, suddenly in 1939 "something strange happened"—James decided to stay in the United States, as a fugitive, an outlaw, from mainstream American society.[36] Because of his politics and his illegal immigrant status, James went underground while he was in the United States, becoming involved in a number of Trotskyist factions, black radical groups, and white intellectual circles. He lived on the fringes, "on the border between Harlem and the white community": "I usually lived somewhere in between where blacks and whites were living, so that my visitors would not be particularly noticeable, either to my neighbors or to the police."[37] In a sense then James lived on the domestic color line, that line of demarcation between black and white America that also marked the extent and limits of African American integration into American national society. As such, he was well placed to comment on the status of the Negro's integration, a lively debate among white and black American intellectuals in the 1940s.

The key to James's contribution to a discourse on the Negro question was his Marxist revision of the concept of integration. The concept appears often in James's American writings during the 1940s, linking the work he was doing in England, imagining black statehood in a modern world context, with the work he was doing on the Negro question in the United States. By integration James meant a human being truly at one with the modern world in which he lived, or as he would say in *American Civilization*, "man as an integral human being, a full and complete individuality."[38] James took his conception of integration one step further, however: the source of man's modern discontent was his alienation from the state.

American civilization was important to James precisely because, aside from the Greek city-states of old, the American republic was the only other political model that he felt had tried to maintain a more integrated notion of citizenship. The innovation of the American revolutionaries was that they took the political slogans of the French Revolution—liberty, equality, fraternity—and enshrined them in the Declaration of Independence as new social ideals. As James described, "Liberty, freedom, pursuit of happiness, free individuality had an actuality and meaning in America which they had nowhere else. The Europeans wrote and theorized about freedom in superb writings. Americans lived it."[39]

In James's assessment, however, the Americans were revising from a previous classical model:

> The founders of the American nation knew quite well what was the difference between a democracy and a republic. Classical scholars as many of them were, they discussed and agreed that a democracy in America was impossible. By democracy they meant the democracy of Athens. They . . . believed that this was possible only in the small city-state, one city. For a large country, it could not work.[40]

The classical model stood for James as the truest approximation of a real social and political democracy. In the Greek city-state each citizen was fully integrated into the politics of the state: "A man was supposed to take part in *everything*."[41] As James argued about the Greek drama, in the city-state "*everything* is political."[42] Though this gave an immense amount of power to a state that was fully integrated into all aspects of the nation's social and cultural life, the fact that this state was accessible to the individual citizen also meant that integration went both ways: "The new democracy had no bureaucracy, it had no organized priesthood, every citizen took part in the government, took part in debates, voted, served on the various assemblies. . . . The state was all-powerful, controlling everything, but *he* [the individual citizen] was the state."[43] James continued:

> Integration was the source of the miraculous outpouring of creative genius which distinguished the Greeks. . . . in the world as [the Greek citizen] knew it, every man (who was not a slave) felt that the state, composed of free assemblies of free citizens, was the embodiment of the city-state and that his personal individuality could only be expressed through it.[44]

The individual citizen gained access to the life of the nation through his direct and unmediated relationship with the state. This vision of the state was the ideal haunting James's play. Modern man's quest was the same as that of the black Jacobin (who was no longer a slave): "a new sense of belonging," "community," "'My' country," that went far beyond the notion of "democracy as voting, etc."[45]

By invoking the Greek city-state as the modern ideal, James made a radical departure from modern twentieth-century conceptions of political freedom. If this sense of profound integration was "the great need of modern man," then "under those circumstances the state is not a state at all, in the modern sense of the word."[46] National self-determination would not address the modern crisis if the national state could not produce the fully integrated citizen. By raising the problem of integration to the level of modern man's relationship to the state as a whole, James then also raised to a new philosophical level the question of the Negro's integration into the American nation-state.

Integration of course had a much more specific meaning in the context of American and African American history and civil rights discourse. Debates over the possibilities for African Americans' integration into American society as full citizens were a defining feature of black political thought during the 1930s and 1940s. Perhaps the most scathing dismissal of the black intellectual's preoccupation with integration came from Harold Cruse in his controversial work *The Crisis of the Negro Intellectual*. Cruse's reflections came from his own experiences in Harlem during the 1940s and his sense of the chaos of ideological currents expressed by black literary and cultural movements during this period. As he described it:

> Harlem in 1940 was just beginning to emerge from the depths of the Great Depression and it seethed with the currents of many conflicting beliefs and ideologies. It was the year in which Richard Wright reached the high point of his literary fame, with *Native Son*. . . . Everything in Harlem seemed to be in a state of flux.[47]

Cruse set out to clarify this confusion by identifying its central dialectic as that between "integrationism" and "separatism." He located the origin of this dialectic in the mid–nineteenth century, in the moment of slavery and the Civil War:

> It is important to note that just prior to the Civil War there was conflict among Negroes over what would be the best course of action for the soon-to-be emancipated slaves. Should they return to Africa or emigrate to Latin America; or should they remain and struggle for racial equality in the United States?[48]

For Cruse these represented two basic paths to African American freedom—flight to Africa and the dream of an independent state, or political and social integration within America. Though the historical situation of the American slaves was different from that of the black Jacobins, Cruse's question here mirrored Toussaint's central dilemma in James's play. Would the emancipated slaves' political freedom come from independent statehood—the political ideal also represented in the dream of a return to Africa—or with the extension of the full rights of French citizenship to the now-freed slaves of San Domingo—Toussaint's impossible dream of the slave's full integration into Western civilization?

In the 1940s James approached these debates over integration from a much different context. The problem of the Negro was a problem for world civilization as a whole. For James, integration was much more than a political or social strategy; it meant nothing less than the alleviation of the modern subject's intense alienation. This ideal then had its own valences for the modern black subject in the United States.

As James studied American civilization it became clear to him that the integration of the Negro into the nation's social life was no longer by the 1940s an intellectual choice, but rather, an economic reality. As he traveled among black communities in the northern and southern states, James observed that America's impending social crisis came not simply as the result of the Negroe's increased exclusion from American society but rather "with the development of the American economy . . . with his increasing *integration* into produc- tion."[49] While intellectuals debated whether the Negro should strive for eco- nomic nationalism, James observed his already existing imbrication within the American capitalist economy. In true Marxist fashion, James argued that the necessities of capitalist production—the integration of all national subjects into the productive process—had generated a cultural and social contradiction. As the American Negro was increasingly integrated into America's economic structures, that activity became "more and more a social process" that then intensified the Negro's consciousness of "his *exclusion* from democratic privi- leges as a separate social group in the community." While the integration of the Negro into American capitalism ran in one direction, his integration into the social life of the nation and the political life of the state ran in the other.

For James, this contradictory reality was a function of the Negro's histori- cally racialized position within the American slave economy:

> Between 1830 and 1860 the Southern planters cultivated the theory of Negro inferiority . . . being driven to do this by the increasing divergences between the developing bourgeois democracy in the United States and the needs of the slave economy. To conquer the formidable threat of white and Negro unity . . . the Southern plantocracy elevated race consciousness to the position of a principle. The whole country was injected with this idea. Thus, side by side with his increasing *integration* into production which becomes more and more a social process, the Negro becomes more than ever conscious of his *exclusion* from democratic privileges as a separate social group in the community. *This dual movement is the key to the Marxist analysis of the Negro question in the U. S. A.*[50]

James provided a Marxist revision of the concept of integration so central to African American politics and culture. American nationalism, the American national consciousness, was built on a twofold ideology. On one hand, it advocated full integration—life, liberty, and the pursuit of happiness—as a political and social ideal. On the other hand, this great American ideal was embodied in a national state that had introduced racial doctrines to preserve itself against the crisis generated by slavery. The Civil War and slavery produced different imperatives than life, liberty, and the pursuit of happiness. The conservation of the national state became the highest priority: "By 1901, an end had been reached. For half a century the United States has sought by legislation and institutions and the propagation of ideals to create . . . a new democracy. . . . The result is democracy by state or as its enemies call it 'statism.' "[51] "Democracy by state" produced a "conspiracy of silence"[52] in the American body politic that limited the free rein of democratic practice. But the real point here was the centrality of race, colonialism, and slavery as the context in which capitalism and democracy developed in the United States.

Throughout the joined histories of colonialism and modernity, the capitalist mode of production has functioned globally as a powerful, integrative force, one that also destroys social relations as it integrates new communities and economies.[53] Race, by which I mean the racial ideologies and racial logic that shaped European discourses of civilization and Enlightenment, has often been the tool by which capitalism destroys and justifies the destruction of civilizations, societies that represent alternatives to the capitalist mode of production. For these alternative societies, which may represent alternative modes of production, coeval modalities of being, and different ways of viewing the world, their destruction is necessary for their availability to capital as markets, providers of labor, and even alienated cultural consumers. What C. L. R. James understood was that, throughout history, these societies have not been mute—they too have a structural reaction which includes the compulsion to preserve their societies, their epistemologies, and cultures, in performance, oral forms, and narratives. This reaction has also taken on the shape of the enemy it is fighting, the integrative force it is resisting. In the Negro struggle for freedom, race consciousness is both the result of integration, which comes with racial hierarchies since integration itself does not necessarily imply integration *as equals*, and a response to integration, which then offers visions of a different global future. To say that race has been the shadow of empire and forms of global integration since the days of colonization is also to mean that racial formations and ideologies have been the limit and the threat to imperial global designs and political forms.

For the African American then, integration meant a contradictory movement rather than simply the movement upward. The higher the Negro went socially, culturally, and economically, the more aware he became of his political exclusion from the democratic privileges of being an American. Slavery was the defining moment, when racial ideologies used to justify the economic mode of production had political consequences that undermined the possibilities for true fraternity for the African American. As Toussaint described it to the French Colonel Vincent: "Americans were free men and not slaves. They were white and not black. . . . I will be a hunted fugitive and it will be because I am black and an ex-slave."[54]

James's theoretical insights led him in a different direction than Harold Cruse.[55] Integrationism and separatism were not two opposing intellectual strains in black American culture but rather two elements of the same process: "To the degree that the Negroes are more integrated into industry and unions their consciousness of racial oppression and their resentment against it become heavier, not less."[56] By this James meant two things. First, the Negro's racialization was the product of his integration into the American slave economy, not his separate and separatist response to political exclusion. Second, since his racialization would be only further and further exacerbated by his increased integration into production, "The history of the Negro in the U. S. is a history of his increasing race consciousness, a constantly increasing desire to vindicate his past and the achievements and qualifications of the Negro race as a race."[57] All black racialist and nationalist ideologies were generated out of this context and became, in their own way, part of the process of the Negro's Americanization.

James's ultimate insight on the Negro question was that the desire for a black nation within a nation, black self-determination, was itself not a move for segregation, independence, or autonomy, but rather a push for the Negro's full integration in the American state. It reflected the desire on the part of the American Negro to redefine his relationship to American nationalism: "Whereas in Europe the national movements have usually aimed at a separation from the oppressing power in the United States the race consciousness and chauvinism of the Negro represent fundamentally a consolidation of his forces for the purposes of integration into American society."[58] For James, the desire for self-determination and race freedom were not the search for the consolidation of black nationhood in a separate and independent black state, but rather the desire for black citizenship in the American nation-state. By extension, nationality was not an essential identity of social groups struggling for power in America but, rather, the site of the struggle over the meaning of fraternity itself. The Negro's desire for integration was "a powerful psychological and philosophical urge" for a direct relationship with the national state: "This need of the individual for universality, for a sense of integration so powerful among all modern oppressed classes, is the key to vast areas of social and political jungles of today."[59] Nationality and integration, then, were also about the Negro's desire to be a part of a world community of free, modern subjects.

James's perspective on integration then shaped his critical analysis of the politics of black self-determination.[60] As he put it, "Self-determination for the American Negro is (1) economically reactionary and (2) politically false because no Negroes . . . want it."[61] James argued that ideologies of separatism in the race movement in America, be they radical or conservative, were not reflective of the desires of the black masses. This was a significant deviation on James's part, given that self-determination had been the banner call for black transnationals and black nationalists throughout the first decades of the twentieth century. James had a profoundly dialectical understanding of the relationship between black self-determination and the process of integration. He did not abandon the idea of self-determination completely; he simply saw it as a principle around which to organize movement, rather than as an end in and of itself. It was this insight that also led to his profound understanding of the real impact of the Garvey movement.

James was much clearer than many of his contemporaries on the meaning of Garveyism for the migrating black masses, a black proletariat now seeking political liberty and economic equality in America's northern cities. Garvey's followers during the first three decades of the twentieth century were also the sharecroppers and tenant farmers James would live with and organize in the South in the 1940s. While the North may have represented freedom from severe oppression, these black migrants were also facing the same question that occupied the black Jacobins of James's play—What fraternity was going to be possible in the North with their fellow white American citizens, after freedom? Would the state protect that fraternity, embodied as Du Bois envisioned it in black homes secured in a nation of millions?

James's experiences organizing in the South confirmed his belief that blacks could expect no protection, as citizens, from the American government. As he observed, "If Negroes depend on the government, they are going to be dragged from trolleys, and beaten up; they and their wives and children will be shot down by rioters and police; and their homes will be wrecked and burned."[62] In a sense, then, black citizens in America were stateless, despite their common nationality with white Americans. Their fugitive migrations to the North, during and after slavery, represented a real search for a political home in a nation state in which they held, at best, a secondary status and little protection.

If the integration of the Negro meant his confidence that he could enter onto the stage of history as an equal with the white man who was once his master, then he needed a vision of political and cultural freedom that was his own. Though a mythic vision on the one hand, the dream of an independent African state also provided a concrete vision of real political independence. Like the black Jacobins, once again, it was the confidence that the vision of the independent black state represented, one that could meet the imperialists on their own terms, that inspired Garvey's followers.

Garvey's vision was particularly powerful among the black working poor, the group of American blacks not at all able to imagine themselves participating in Du Bois's suburban vision of America. In one of his discussions with Trotsky about the Negro question James identified why his black contemporaries were so unable to look beyond the surface and see the real power of Garveyism. He directly referenced an essay by Walter White on Marcus Garvey in Locke's anthology of the New Negro, quoting directly from White's description of Garvey's attitude toward mulattos: "In *The New Negro* by Alain Locke there is a reference to the fact that Garvey preached an exclusively black doctrine of race—only Negroes who were black were truly Negroes. This statement is of the first importance."[63] What White saw as the "paradox of color" and the dangerous flaw of Garveyism—its use of racial doctrines to exacerbate divisions between the different classes in the African American community—James recognized as the source of its appeal. Garvey's racial doctrines also held within them a developing class consciousness among the lowest migrant stratas of African American society:

> In America today, there are caste divisions among the blacks themselves and these are based on color. . . . The blacks, the poorest, the most oppressed. . . . It was on this stratum that Garvey built his movement; . . . they had just emigrated and were still coming in hundreds of thousands

from the South, a proletarian and sub-proletarian mass getting better wages for the first time and rising to the possibilities that even the limited freedom of the North allowed them.[64]

The vision of a self-determined African empire gave Garvey's UNIA the ability to reach so deeply into the black working and poor populations of America, precisely because it offered the black masses a vision of global freedom, different than the impossible domestic vision of upward mobility promoted by the black middle-class elites. As James would put it:

> the great response to . . . Freedom in Africa . . . seems to point to the fact that self-determination, i.e. a black state in the South would awaken a response among these masses, as bitterly as it is opposed by all the intellectuals and more literate among the Negroes.[65]

Garvey's pure black was the migrating black proletariat, whose investment in the idea of a black state, either in the south or in Africa, represented "nothing tangible but the promotion of a new society."[66] This was what was important to James about Garveyism, not his dream of empire with its lack of a real political program. For James, the black masses' attraction to Garvey's ideologies of liberation reflected not so much a real desire to separate from mainstream American society but, rather, the desire on their part to transform American society so that their integration within the state could be possible. Garvey the black emperor, with his Black Star Line to Africa, was there to embody a form of leadership for both visions. As James would put it: "The Negro masses felt the stir of the period, and it was that which made Garvey."[67]

Garvey's followers were also fulfilling a historical dynamic that had first been established during the Civil War. Like Cruse, James argued that the Civil War was the crucial moment in the African American struggle for freedom and fraternity. James, however, highlighted the role of the *fugitive* slaves during the Civil War, presenting an alternative to the two paths Cruse laid out for the slaves—flight to a separate African state, or stasis within the American state. In his essay "Negroes in the Civil War: Their Role in the Second American Revolution," James focused on the period between 1830 and 1865 and the runaway slaves' movement North on the underground railroad.[68] Though he described in detail the impact of the Nat Turner revolt on the organization of the Negroes and the terror of the white South, it was not the slave revolt that ultimately stood out for James as the source of the slaves' revolutionary inclinations. Rather, "the Negroes, discouraged by the failures of the revolts between 1800 and 1831, began to take another road to freedom. Slowly but steadily grew that flight out of the South which lasted for thirty years and injected the struggle against slavery into the North itself."[69]

In identifying the flight for freedom as the main motivating factor for the slaves' mobilization and migration, James paralleled the historical argument of Eugene Genovese: "The great body of escaping slaves, of course, had no political aims in mind. For years rebellious slaves had formed bands of maroons, living a free life in inaccessible spots."[70] James saw the movement of the American slaves as following in the tradition of the maroons: "Now they sought freedom in civilization and they set forth on that heroic journey of many hundreds of miles, forced to travel mainly by night, through forest and across rivers, often with nothing to guide them but the North Star and the fact that moss grows only on the north side of trees."[71] But the fact that this movement sought "freedom in civilization" is crucial—the American slaves were fleeing into the nation rather than away from it, toward "integration" rather than separation. Despite their lack of a truly revolutionary program—the creation of a new state—this intranational migration of fugitive slaves had an incredible disruptive impact on the existing nation-state itself:

> When the news of the 1848 revolution in France reached Washington, the capital, from the White House to the crowds in the streets, broke out into illuminations and uproarious celebration. Three nights afterward, 78 slaves, taking this enthusiasm for liberty literally, boarded a ship that was waiting for them and tried to escape down the Potomac . . . The patience of the South and of the Northern bourgeoisie was becoming exhausted. Two years later, the ruling classes, South and North, tried one more compromise. One of the elements of this compromise was a strong Anti-Fugitive Slave Law.[72]

Whereas Cruse saw the pre–Civil War discourse of the slaves as part of this binary between integration and separation, James argued that the slaves' flight was itself a desire to participate in the American discourse of freedom. James's further insight was that the slaves' desire for integration exposed the contradictions of America's racial nationalism. By fleeing into the nation the fugitive slaves were challenging the conception of the state as a whole.

The response of the state to the slaves' fugitive actions was further confirmation of the revolutionary significance of their flight. The fugitive slave laws were precisely the attempt to keep the nation-state's borders intact, to keep the slaves, both geographically and structurally, in their economic and political place as noncitizens in American society. But "the escaping slaves continued to come" and in doing so they shook the foundations of American national unity: "Long before the basic forces of the nation moved into action for the inevitable showdown . . . [the] revolting slaves had plowed up the land and made the nation irrevocably conscious of the great issues at stake."[73] By becoming fugitives the slaves irrevocably altered the national dynamic.

For James, the most dramatic phenomenon in the history of Negro revolt in America was not the attempt or desire to secure independence but, rather, this fugitive migration to the North:

> Between 1830 and 1860, sixty to a hundred thousand slaves came to the North. When they could find no welcome or resting place in the North, some of them went on to Canada. But they never ceased to come. With the Civil War they came in tens and then in hundreds of thousands.[74]

This movement alone was radical. The escaping slaves refused to stay circumscribed within the political and economic borders of the nation, the Black Belt, that, in one sense, the black nationalists and the Communists of the 1920s wanted to send them back to. For James the importance of the Black Belt was not its existence as a separate, autonomous ground for freedom but rather that it was the space that could not contain the runaway slaves. In their act of leaving they released revolutionary forces into the American nation as a whole. In the context of American nationalism, their most militant action was to become fugitives rather than revolutionaries for independence.

The movement of the runaway slaves North is the first act that creates the conditions for black revolutionary activity in the North from the 1920s through the 1940s. The slaves' choice of flight is of course the same path north that will be traveled by figures such as Jake and Felice later in McKay's *Home to Harlem*. Focusing simply on the slaves' movement as revolutionary in and of itself, James eliminated the need for a sovereign black male leader, thereby reopening a space for exploring the structural location of black men *and* black women in the urban north of the United States. In his attempt to map the possibilities for the integration of the modern black subject in the new postwar

American nation, James returned in *American Civilization* to the site of urban modernity and to the domestic space of the home. In his writing we see the traces of a modern, alienated, masculine African American subject, whose only recourse within the nation is to travel with an eye constantly looking beyond America's borders to the larger black world. However, at the end of his outline for the work *American Civilization*, James articulated a vision of revolution that would place the conditions and experiences of black women at the center. In so doing, he offered a tentative direction for black male intellectuals across the diaspora to travel in the further development of new frameworks for a transnational black masculinity.

BLACK PEOPLE IN THE URBAN AREAS OF THE UNITED STATES

At the close of an essay written in 1970 entitled "Black People in the Urban Areas of the United States," James boldly asserted:

> I believe that if black people in American cities watch what is happening to them, observe also what is taking place among the white people and familiarize themselves with the situation in European countries where great numbers of people from the underdeveloped areas are filling important positions in the workforce, they will find that there is a unified experience and a unified conception of future development which puts them, the urban blacks of the United States, in the very forefront of those who are thinking and working out the kind of life they wish to live in the future.[75]

Here James described a dynamic occurring in the late twentieth century within the urban centers of the industrialized nations of Europe and America, the reappearance of empire's colonialist past and capitalist future in the new global communities and worlds of color now located in the metropolitan cities themselves. As James began the essay saying, "The title [is not] a mere geographical or demographic statement. . . . It is, in reality, a statement in profound importance in America today. . . . for thinking in terms of the whole city means that you are automatically thinking in terms of the state and from the state you find yourself facing the whole nation."[76]

For James it was people of color in urban centers and workplaces who would be the agents of social change for new visions of the future. Their desire for domestic integration within the nation would spur them to social movement, and social movement was inevitably tied to global economic forces and global political alliances: "Here we must go further and place the situation within the context of an international perspective. It is from America's urban blacks that many people all over the world have historically gained a consciousness of the problems that black people suffer and their attempts to overcome them."[77]

James's observations about the centrality of urban America in the 1970s can be connected to his discussions of African American history from the 1940s and 1950s during his first stay in the United States. At the end of *American Civilization*, his grand historical sketch for an even lengthier tome he planned to write on United States politics and culture, James entitled his most preliminary chapter on the contemporary United States, "Negroes, Women and the Intellectuals." "Under the heading of Negroes," he continued to describe, "we deal with what is another major problem in the modern world—the problem of minorities."[78] In the section on "The Negroes in the United States," James reiterated the dynamic of integration that he had laid out in previous writings:

> We touch upon certain aspects which illuminate the fundamental relation between this minority question and the basic social structure and development of the nation as a whole. . . . The Negroes struggle against segregation and separation. But every effort that they make results in minor adjustments and greater segregation and separation.[79]

Taking black struggles over housing as merely one example, James briefly laid bare the diminishing mobility afforded by the American suburban dream of space in the nation: "Negro pressure for living space, for freedom, does not result in their being admitted freely to live where they wish; it results in the pressure being carefully directed towards certain specific areas, 'now thrown open to colored,' and an increase in segregation."[80] Freedom to move, freedom to love, freedom to live—all aspects of his earlier understanding of freedom in civilization—were now circumscribed by and within domestic space. This was a condition that had a bearing on broader questions of the nature of citizenship within the nation as a whole. James concluded, "Negroes taken as a whole . . . are selected here because they are symptomatic of the nation as a whole. . . . The Negroes are Americans and in them, in their combined segregation and integration, can be seen indications of the national crisis,

strains, capabilities, needs and hopes, as in no other section of the population."[81] Black subjects were not the only population alienated by the tensions
and contradictions of American nationality; they were simply the subjects
who revealed those tensions most clearly.

In his discussion of the contemporary American Negro of the 1940s and
1950s, James discussed black subjectivity in the aggregate in ways similar to his
discussion of the fugitive slave as a historical figure for the racial collective.
However, in his attempt to give the Negro at mid-century an individual voice
and consciousness, James returned to powerful tropes of a revolutionary masculinity. In James's hands, the moment the subaltern seek to speak, they are
represented by men. James turned to black male writers such as Richard
Wright and Chester Himes, arguing "The Negro writer represents the extreme peak of *American* revolt against the intolerable psychological burdens
placed upon individuals in every part of the modern world."[82]

In a talk given in 1940 titled "A Fireside Chat on the War by Native Son,"
James invoked another important fugitive in African American literary history, Richard Wright's Bigger Thomas.[83] James's choice to portray himself to
black workers in the voice of this native son reflected the two dialectical
features of African American nationality. James spoke as a native on one
hand—the modern New Negro of the Americas who had traveled far from the
Africa of old—but as a fugitive on the other—the displaced, stateless, criminalized black drifter of doubtful nationality. Marking this dichotomy, James
then attempted to give the global racial collective imprisoned within the
nation a revolutionary voice.[84]

Speaking as Bigger Thomas, James dramatized his own belief that the
native son represented the articulation of an emerging consciousness among
black Americans, centered in the mindset of the fugitive and the outlaw. Bigger
Thomas was Jake Brown gone astray, a Jake who, by killing his Felice and his
chances at black love, makes his criminality literal and forsakes his chance at the
domestic romance. In his review of *Native Son* that same year, James quoted
Wright saying, "Black Bigger did the things he did because American capitalist
society has made an outcast of the black man."[85] For James, Bigger was not just
one unique social type. He was reflective of an emerging collective consciousness: "He is not traveling up a by-path. He is on the main road, only further on
than the rest of his people."[86] By the 1940s, Bigger Thomas's fugitive actions
and travels are an expression of hopelessness among American Negroes but also

an expression of their increasing militancy: "Only where he acted against isolated persons, they will act against organized society."[87]

James's ultimate insight on the Negro question was that a Bigger Thomas represented not the destruction of the dream of integration but, rather, its fulfillment. The American Negro, like McKay's Jake Brown, was not interested in renouncing the domestic romance and separating from the nation-state. Rather, his flight revealed his fundamental desire for domestic integration with that state. In the black domestic romance of the 1940s, however, the only way he would achieve integration as a fugitive ex-slave would be to destroy the state that made his integration impossible. Now, when Harlem's Jake Brown traveled into the white neighborhoods and houses of the Beautiful Block, he ended up like Bigger Thomas: "Trapped on the roof, he counts his bullets, and leaves the last one for himself. It is pride in himself, as a free man with a hardly-bought freedom. He will not capitulate to those white men—it is revolutionary pride."[88]

Bigger Thomas's revolutionary pride had its much more celebrated ancestry in the proud figure of the fugitive slave leader and liberator, the great personality Toussaint L'Ouverture. L'Ouverture's impossible dream of black fraternity was an example of revolutionary black global desires that exceeded the borders of the national political imagination. As James would eloquently describe:

> Firm as was his grasp of reality, old Toussaint looked beyond San Domingo with a boldness of imagination. . . . While loaded with the cares of government, he cherished a project of sailing to Africa with arms, ammunition and a thousand of his best soldiers . . . and making millions of blacks "free and French." . . . What spirit was it that moved him? . . . In him born a slave and a leader of slaves, the concrete realization of liberty, equality and fraternity was the womb of ideas and the springs of power, which overflowed their narrow environment and embraced the whole of the world.[89]

This passage in particular confirms for Hazel Carby that "ideologies of masculinity, whether conscious or unconscious" were shaping James's understanding of black revolutionary consciousness.[90] In James's construction, this masculine global consciousness traces a trajectory from Toussaint L'Ouverture to his twentieth-century descendant, Bigger Thomas.

But James also mobilizes a slightly different figure for the racial and national collective than that of the revolutionary male, in his essay at the end of *American Civilization* and later writings. Asserting at the beginning of the chapter that he has selected as his focus three "elements, Negroes, women and intellectuals," James explains that it is these three groups in particular who will best enable him to "try to get a little closer to the actual and intimate lives of the population."[91] James focuses on the bourgeois female subject's own relationship to discourses of citizenship and fraternity as another way of getting at the nature of domestic confinement writ large. As Carby identified in her interpretation of class and gender politics in *Minty Alley*, James makes another connection in this essay between the working class and the female subject, describing her "bitterness and sense of frustration [as] the direct counterpart of the sense of hopelessness and frustration felt by the masses of workers in modern industrial production."[92]

The key difference here is that "woman" is no longer a symbolic means to embody the people in an individual form but, rather, women function as a social class in and of themselves, placed in their own relationship to capital and the state rather than simply as metaphors for the industrial working class. In turn, domesticity itself becomes a sphere that is organized by and integrated within the capitalist mode of production:

> These interminable blocks of apartments are not related to the needs of the people who live in them. They are related to certain necessities of the economy. . . . The circumstances of work, of transport, of home and life, are determined. . . . [Before] Life was a heroic adventure for anyone who wanted to act. For the modern individual it is a deadly routine. And for the woman . . . *the responsibility of making something tolerable and interesting out of this formidable apparatus of mechanized routine living devolves by social tradition and practise upon her.*[93]

Here James suggests that the values of freedom in civilization—the freedom to love, the freedom to move, the freedom to live—are not achievable in the realm of the individual historical personality, as that personality has been represented in characters in literature and in certain brands of national discourse focused on individual agency. As he puts it, "equality is not an individual need or the subjective passion of a few intense or rebellious people."[94] As he also adds, "In all these books the individual is somehow made responsible by his or her own individual efforts to make adjustments to dislocations and antagonisms whose whole roots are in forces totally beyond their individual powers."[95] In James's real-life terms, the love story of national romance offers nothing more than another map of women's own social oppression by bourgeois domesticity and boundedness within ideologies of home: "Into this structure, with every square inch mapped, the woman is thrown with a man and given the impossible task of overcoming the handicaps inherent in the whole structure."[96]

Instead, for James identity transformations are generated out of collective acts of resistance, and for women, the truly revolutionary act and narrative would involve the transformation of the domestic sphere itself: "A revolution in individual relationships as great as the revolution pointed at in the labor process."[97] As James envisioned this new utopia within the domestic sphere:

> Men and women will be equal when from the very start, cooking, washing, and other household duties, child care, personal adornment, games, sports, etc., are taught to children by a world which makes no distinction at all between the sexes. The age of chivalry must go. . . . Only when men . . . can turn their hands to every single social and domestic necessity in the home and not feel it a disruption of their personality pattern to do so, will there be any possibility of equality. . . .
>
> Now it is obvious that what is envisioned here is a revolution indeed.[98]

Among black male transnational intellectuals, James is to be commended for subjecting himself and his own masculinity to such a harsh and radical feminist critique and reorganization. He would also add that the benefits of such a vision of black masculinity far outweighed the costs: "And no modern man who observes society at all objectively could deny that on such a basis, if universally admitted and not so much admitted as practiced, man as a social being has everything to gain and nothing at all to lose."[99] In this brief sketch James revealed the universalist gendered underpinnings of his own earlier discussions of man's integration within the nation. In a much later essay written in 1981, "Three Black Women Writers: Toni Morrison, Alice Walker, Ntozake Shange," James would also suggest that only the black woman writer, freed by force from masculinist identifications with the liberatory nation-state and extricated by choice from her responsibilities for the affective dimensions of nationhood, would truly be able to articulate the alienation of the woman of color within the domestic, not in heroic individualist terms but as part of the larger social collective:

> Marx pointed out many years ago that women were more exploited than the proletariat. . . . Now women are beginning to say: "Who and what are we? We don't know. Hitherto we have always tried to fit ourselves into what men and what masculine society required. Now we are going to break through that." These three women have begun to write about Black women's daily lives.[100]

In his autobiography *Here I Stand*, Paul Robeson movingly linked the modern, worldly New Negro male's right to travel within and without the nation with the legacy of the fugitive slave in American history: "From the very beginning of Negro history in our land, Negroes have asserted their right to freedom of movement. [For] tens of thousands of Negro slaves, like my own father . . . the concept of *travel* has been inseparably linked in the minds of our people with the concept of *freedom*."[101] From the 1930s through the 1950s, the insurgency of black male mobility in the United States was revealed by how often black male intellectuals were penalized for it. By 1960, Du Bois and Robeson had had their passports revoked, Marcus Garvey and C. L. R. James had been criminalized as Caribbean radicals and deported from the United States, and other prominent African American male intellectuals such as James Baldwin and Richard Wright had fled the country for exile in Paris.

However, James's insight at the end of *American Civilization* has also been borne out in the gender politics of postcolonial nation-states. The truly revolutionary black transnational narrative necessitates a recognition on the part of male intellectuals of the race war's impact on gender and sexual relations and the need for a transformation of the domestic sphere privately and publicly conceived. This is the revolutionary truth that women of color, globally, have always understood. From the moment questions of freedom and national sovereignty were constituted in the limited terms of the heroic revolutionary narrative and the national romance, the dream of fraternity was doomed to be a reality for only one half of the race. The role of making the black male subject feel at home in the state, "the responsibility of making something tolerable and interesting" out of national civilization, would be too great a burden for any individual woman or female collective to bear.

# CHAPTER 8

# America Is One Island Only:
# The Caribbean and American Studies

If one were to choose a single word to encapsulate Caribbean history, that word would
have to be "geopolitics" . . . the relationship between geography and international relations.
The most important part of Caribbean geography has been the sea . . . and what the history
of archipelagic areas teaches us is that even the mightiest of naval powers cannot totally
dominate each and every square mile of sea and island.

—ANTHONY P. MAINGOT[1]

AT THE END OF Herman Melville's 1851 classic *Moby-Dick*, the character
Ishmael tells us that he alone has survived to tell a story. His account of the
failure of the American republic, allegorized in the sea story of a New England sea captain, a ship, and a great white whale, provided an exemplary text
for C. L. R. James to develop ideas he raised at the conclusion of *American
Civilization*. Of Ishmael, the American intellectual, James would ask, what
are the conditions that produced his isolation and alienation and is he, as a
particular masculine personification of the United States, implicated in the
republic's downfall? James's description of American intellectuals broadly at
mid-century in "Negroes, Women and the Intellectuals" would find their
perfect personality in history in the character of Ishmael: "So the majority of
the intellectuals drifted along, knocking from pillar to post and finding themselves in the strangest places."[2]

But what James also found on Melville's *Pequod* was *multiple* masculine
personalities in global history. In Ahab, Ishmael, and the crew, he saw modern
dictator, intellectual, and a complex, multinational proletariat; but he also saw,
in the three harpooners—Queequeg, "a South Sea cannibal"; Tashtego, "a
Gay-Head Indian from Massachusetts"; and Daggoo, "a gigantic Negro from

the coast of Africa"—Bederman's "masculine modern-day savage."[3] These three were colonial men who, though now integrated (metaphorically) into modernity as citizens of modern states and laborers under modern capital, also represented and embodied the traces of their own colonial island histories *and* empire's circumpacific and circumatlantic travels. If, for James, the crew of the *Pequod* represented a counternarrative to industrial modernity and the New World islander's place within it, the colonial savages, Queequeg, Tashtego, and Daggoo, represented residual colonial histories and emergent modes of global masculinity, traveling into the future alongside imperial capital's new national ships of state.

This chapter closes *Black Empire* first by analyzing James's account of the relationship between Ishmael and the harpooners, Queequeg in particular. In his analysis of an explicit homoerotics between these two male characters, James envisioned new forms of social relations between what we might call today the First World and the Third World subject. Here I reread James's rereading of Melville as a discussion of the possible relationship of the isolated U.S. American intellectual, citizen in the modern nation-state, to the colonial American world of empire and its island subjects.[4] I then continue to read James's reading of *Moby-Dick* against the grain as a specific political state-ment about American transnationalism. In *Mariners, Renegades and Cast-aways* James described the future of the United States as an internationalist nation and the role of the New World black working-class subject within that future. Finally, the chapter closes by focusing on James's hopes for West Indian federation, seeing in his discussion a Caribbean desire to offer a dif-ferent model of American democracy than that embodied in the North Amer-ican nation-state.


THE HARPOONERS AS MASCULINE FIGURES
FOR NEW HUMAN RELATIONS

The key to understanding the importance of the harpooners in James's re-reading of Melville's novel lies in James's portrayal of Ishmael as the American intellectual. As we are first introduced to Ishmael, both in the novel and in James's retelling of it, the character is a well-educated teacher whose desire to be a seaman reflects his need to be one of and with the people. On James's *Pequod* Ishmael is the figure for "life on land," "civilization" as a "narrow, cramped, limited existence."[5] James adds, "Thus shut out from the world outside, he cannot get out of himself"—another way of saying that Ishmael, shut in the nation, has subsequently withdrawn into himself. James then continues, "The only truly civilized person he can find in New Bedford and Nantucket is a cannibal savage, the harpooner, Queequeg, and the story of their relations is, like all great literature, not only literature but history."[6]

Here James uses history, his-story, to invoke the human story. Queequeg and Ishmael's romance is symbolic of neither the national nor the especially revolutionary. Rather, James intimates, in their relationship lies a different kind of global story about human civilization. When Ishmael first sees Queequeg he sees an unbounded masculinity, what Geoffrey Sanborn has also described as a conception of "savage masculinity" as without limits, in the colonial discourse shaping Melville's account:

> It identifies the savage as a man in the process of becoming civilized, and it enables the civilized man to see in the savage an image of his own limitless energies at a stage in which they are absolutely liberated from any restraining feminine influence. In [this] masculinist fantasy, vengeful cannibalism represents a declaration of independence from the feminized social sphere.[7]

James's quotations from Melville show the former's own impressions of these colonial savages as he observes them through the eyes of Ishmael, the civilized intellectual. First James points to their uniqueness in Melville's narrative: "Now it is true that harpooners of savage origin were not unknown in the whale fishery at the time, but it is certainly most unusual to find each of the three harpooners of Ahab's ship a savage, and each a representative of a primitive race."[8] He then comments, often, on the special qualities among the other men, the officers and the crew of the *Pequod*: "They are all men of magnificent physique, dazzling skill and striking personality."[9] He quotes Melville describing them as exhibiting on board ship an almost "frantic democracy,"[10] and sees them as representing the utmost in "personal splendor as men."[11] Also, the cannibal savage Queequeg is the *Pequod*'s most skilled mariner, as James interprets the text:

> As soon as they get off the land into the boat from New Bedford to Nantucket, Queequeg shows himself what he will later turn out to be, not

only brave and ready to risk his life, but a master of his seaman's craft. To his splendid physique, unconquered spirit and spontaneous generosity, this child of Nature has added mastery of one of the most important and authoritative positions in a great modern industry.[12]

Along with "Queequeg's untamed and undefeated appearance" James also highlights in Queequeg's masculine personality "an equally distinctive calm and self-reliance."[13] James inserts, "Where could one find men like this? The men Ishmael knew were pent up in lath and plaster, tied to counters, nailed to benches, clinched to desks."[14]

As James continues to quote from and read Melville's description of Queequeg through Ishmael's eyes, we see something powerful passing between these two different men. As James quotes Ishmael's first impressions of the "cannibal savage": "Through all his unearthly tatooings, I thought I saw the traces of a simple, honest heart; and in his large, deep eyes, fiery black and bold, there seemed tokens of a spirit that would dare a thousand devils. . . . He looked like a man who had never cringed and never had had a creditor."[15] James quotes from Ishmael's description of Queequeg again:

He made no advances whatever; appeared to have no desire to enlarge the circle of his acquaintants. All this struck me as mighty singular; yet, upon second thoughts, there was something almost sublime in it. Here was a man some twenty thousand miles from home, by the way of Cape Horn, that is—which was the only way he could get there—thrown among people as strange to him as though he were in the planet Jupiter; and yet he seemed entirely at his ease; preserving the utmost serenity; content with his own companionship; always equal to himself.[16]

In James's choice of this passage lies an assertion that will become even more explicit as his political thoughts on the possible future Caribbean state develop. This is the assertion that the colonial subject, the colonial state, even when integrated into the modern, industrial world economy, keep itself at a distance and retain some aspects of self-governance and self-sufficiency, very much like Queequeg, "always equal to himself."

Ishmael, in stark contrast, is a man in a perpetual state of desire. Fundamentally, "He does not feel at home in the world and he is constantly aware of this."[17] In James's analysis Ishmael is the American citizen who, as an intellectual, has grown disillusioned with the promise of the American dream. In James's words, "Ishmaels, we say, live in every city block . . . the man of good family and education . . . he sees his fellow men as ridden with his own sense of homelessness and despair."[18] Ishmael sees what lies under the skin of America's Beautiful Blocks, expressed in James's reading in the symbolism of the whiteness of the whale:

> For Ishmael who believes in nothing and therefore constantly analyzes all that he sees to find something, everything in the world is appearance, something superficial, put on. He examines it and below is nothing but bare, dead, white blankness. Whatever is beautiful is only deception, a color added to this dead unending whiteness, as a whore puts paint on her face to cover the rottenness inside.[19]

Here the painted and wanton nation-state holds no attraction to the intellectual citizen, disenchanted with the trappings of modern nationality. Instead Ishmael, the figure for modern civilization, is the intellectual without hope, whose skills at being thoughtful about his own nationality have degenerated into despair and inaction. In that state he becomes susceptible to two types of longings—the first, a longing for interpellation by the monomaniacal state. This need shapes Ishmael's passive participation in the obsessive missions of leaders such as Captain Ahab with his quest for the white whale.

But Ishmael also feels a second desire for alternative communities and forms of social belonging:

> With terror in his soul, Ishmael follows Ahab, as the guilt-ridden intellectual of today, often with the same terror, finds some refuge in the idea of the one-party totalitarian state. . . . But if Ishmael, the intellectual, is so strongly attracted to the man of action, equally strong on him is the attraction of the crew. That in fact is what makes him modern. He must decide.[20]

The crew offers Ishmael a different notion of democracy and community than that offered by Ahab, the figure for the national state. James figures that second form of desire, for a different idea of community and individual subjectivity within community, also as a masculinity shaped by homoerotic desire. As he states, "Ishmael begins by clinging to the powerful Queequeg and, in typical modern fashion, his relationship with him on land has all the marks of homosexuality."[21] On board the *Pequod*, under the strenuously masculine direction of Ahab's imperial authority, Ishmael's struggles to achieve an intimacy with the crew are recaptured by James in his paraphrasing of the famous passage on homosexual desire in Melville's novel: "One day when [Ishmael and Queequeg] are squeezing spermacetti, all their hands in the soft fluffy mixture together, he experiences a sensation of comradeship and fraternity such as he had never felt before, and he wishes they could all squeeze sperm forever."[22]

Ishmael finds fraternity and imagined community not on land in the nation, but in the sensuous, strenuous labor and intimacy of physical working conditions he shares with colonial subjects at sea. As the figure for the American intellectual, the challenge he faces is to literally step outside of the domestic sphere of the United States and enter into a hands-on working dialogue with colonial intellectuals of color. These are subjects who, like the harpooners who "are not primitive savages [but] the most skillful seamen and the most generous and magnificent human beings on board," are masters of the ways of American empire as they impact both populations at home and at sea.[23]

In Ishmael's and Queequeg's relationship James saw "the search for a new basis of community," a search submerged within and overshadowed by the monomaniacal imperatives of the national state.[24] His reading was foreshadowed in the closing pages of *American Civilization* itself, for it was there that James first suggested that one could find in Melville's narrative an alternative vision of American masculinity:

> Melville relates a homosexual episode at the beginning of *Moby Dick* with an ease and lack of self-consciousness which is amazing in a writer of that period writing for his public. . . . The American male has had a passion for human relationships, social and personal, general and intimate, and it is this which above all constitutes the high civilization of the United States. . . . Under these developing social circumstances there has been a powerful impulse to intimate friendships with men but hedged around by a safeguard of stern prohibition against this intimacy becoming perversion.[25]

This too, for James, had classic antecedents, as did many of his most idealistic hopes for modern civilization and nationality: "The highly cultivated Greeks of that age sought adequate companionship in two ways, homosexuality and a peculiar group of women [who] broke openly with the restrictions upon their sex and gave up all advantages of a protected domesticity."[26]

In "Negroes, Women and the Intellectuals," James admitted to a certain awkwardness in writing "*around* the sexual relation" and "in regard to homosexuality." He continued, "By the time this sketch is developed into a finished book, I shall be more in a position to decide what to write, how far to go, and whether to write on it at all."[27] James was never able to develop his sketch into a full-length monograph, but his promise to attempt to reimagine all of human social relations through the lens of gender and sexuality, is fulfilled in his brief but suggestive studies of the figure of the colonial savage on Melville's *Pequod*. What he *could* assert in *American Civilization* was his sense that his discussions of American political, economic, and intellectual history in earlier chapters, was integrally connected to his study in his concluding chapter of "the most intimate private lives and personal relations of the American people."[28] In his discussions of Caribbean political life throughout the 1950s and early 1960s, James would more fully develop his insights into possibilities for imagining alternative, self-sufficient, social relations, in the realm of Caribbean political geography.

If transatlantic history over the centuries has been shaped by the movements of empire and capital, then that history also includes the multiple communities uprooted and set in motion by those same forces, communities powerfully embodied in Melville's three harpooners. Unlike the mythic Calibans of Caribbean revolutionary history, these three savages embody the opposite of the forceful masculinity of the revolutionary black liberator. As the least empowered members of Ahab's crew they are far from sovereign; they are also submissive and often passive in the face of Ahab's monomaniacal rage. Yet, as the crew is pit against the embodiment of the dictatorial state, these savages are contrasted with Ishmael, the Yankee intellectual: "As against the educated individual in his isolation and inward tortures, [Melville] dramatized the basic qualities of the crew in the three harpooners."[29] Together, James would argue, "The harpooners and the crew are the ordinary people of the whole world."[30]

In his "story of Herman Melville and the world we live in," James used the relationship between the crew and Ahab to comment on the relationship of small islanders to larger state structures and economic forces. But in the relationship between Ishmael the American intellectual and the three harpooners, James also evaluated the possibilities for freedom in modern nationality and the place of the colonized within national histories. Ishmael alone remains to tell the story because he is the quintessential and ideal modern subject within the nation, equipped with the intellect to understand the past and foresee the future but blind to the dangers of the immediate present. His longing for a relationship with the colonial subject reflects his desire to revisit and revise the imperial and national past and to imagine a different global future.

## THE STORY OF HERMAN MELVILLE AND THE WORLD WE LIVE IN

As James's final significant work written during his first stay in America, published in the 1950s in the context of the Cold War, *Mariners, Renegades and Castaways* has often been read as his attempt to use Melville's literary classic to interpret the state of America at the middle of the twentieth century. The text has become a classic in the study of American culture, a status partly achieved due to Donald Pease's introduction to the 2001 reprint edition. Here Pease argues for the text's centrality to a "new Americanist" understanding of American studies, one "capable of bringing about transnational and international relations of a kind then excluded from the field of American Studies [that] turns this work from the historical past toward a future that has emerged within our present." As Pease continued, "The book's republication might enable a transition from American Studies to Transnational American Studies."[31]

James's use of Melville's ship, the *Pequod*, as a metaphor for United States imperialism in the nineteenth century was revealing. In the image of the American ship of state James would identify a United States empire built as much on deterritorialized maritime international trade as on the conquest of national territory. But I would argue that James was also trying to make a specific political statement about America's transnationalism in his present and heading into our future. James was describing the future of America as a new kind of transnational empire and as a central player in the international economic world system emerging in the years following Henry Luce's identification of an American Century in 1941.[32] The world we live in, as James saw it at the middle of the twentieth century was one in which the European economic empires were slowly but surely being dominated by the international economic and political force of the United States.

In his historical writings on the United States in *American Civilization*, James argued that the initial creation of the American republic was "one of the great events in international and political history . . . the organization of a new state on lines hitherto unknown in the history of the world."[33] This promise of a "new democracy" remained for James a crucial symbolic aspect of the meaning of America. Yet in *American Civilization* he also argued that in tandem with America's political model of republican nationalism ran an enterprising, outernational economic spirit of mercantile capitalism. The American republic as a political formation did not necessarily capture all that was significant about American state formation and national consciousness in its totality. For James, Melville's *Pequod* and the ship's captain and crew embodied the mercantile capitalism of a nineteenth-century American empire. As he would say of the world Melville created on the *Pequod*:

> Melville, as every truly great writer, sees history in terms of men. These Nantucketers were heroic men. And they did heroic deeds. Whalers have explored unknown seas and archipelagoes. . . . The whaling vessels rounded Cape Horn and established international commerce. They gave impetus to the liberation of Peru, Chile and Bolivia from the yoke of Spain. . . . That was America.[34]

For James, the New England whaling ship was the perfect metaphor for an American national state built on an international economy, an enterprising American spirit that feverishly moved beyond the borders of the nation-state to the empire of the sea. As James quoted Melville:

> These naked Nantucketers, these sea hermits, issuing from their ant-hill in the sea, [have] overrun and conquered the watery world like so many Alexanders; parceling out among them the Atlantic, Pacific, and Indian Oceans. . . . Let America add Mexico to Texas, and pile Cuba upon Canada; let the English overswarm all India, and hang out their blazing banner from the sun; two thirds of this terraqueous globe are the Nantucketer's. For the sea is his; he owns it, as Emperors own Empires.[35]

In a metaphor resonant with our contemporary globalized world, of capital moving freely across international state borders, James was arguing that the seas themselves had become the new terrain of empire and that from its inception the American republic had evinced a form of imperialism.

James then articulated a complex (and at times overly idealized) relationship between the enterprising nature and free movement of a nineteenth-century American empire and the rigid racial structures that developed domestically with the evolution of the United States as a nation-state. Early in *Mariners* James laid out his critique of the modern nation-state as an international political formation after World War I:

> The political organization of Modern Europe has been based upon the creation and consolidation of national states. And the national state, every single national state, had and still has a racial doctrine. This doctrine is that the national race, the national stock, the national blood, is superior to all other national races, national stocks, and national bloods. This doctrine was sometimes stated, often hidden, but it was and is there, and over the last twenty years has grown stronger in every country in the world.[36]

There was no debate for James that the nation-state itself, as a political institution and idea, had failed at achieving its core political goal—the ideal of universal democracy. In *Mariners* James argued that the reasons for this were rooted not in theory but in history. The terms in which the nation-state was conceived held the roots of its own collapse. In the 1940s, James was living and writing in an America in the aftermath of World War II, a war in which Hitler had even more explicitly attempted to realize the fascistic elements of racial nationalism. James saw the horrors of twentieth century race war as the "natural but necessary conclusion" to fundamental racial contradictions built into national states. As he would describe, "The Nazis fastened onto this [theory of the superiority of the national race] and discarding all half-truths, decided to carry it to its logical conclusions."[37]

Like Randolph Bourne in 1918 and like Melville before him, James saw in America's diverse nationalities a new internationalism that had the potential to produce a state created along different lines than those of Europe. James's use of a passage from Melville's novel *Redburn* as one of his opening epigrams to *Mariners* illustrated his shared belief that:

> There is something in the contemplation of the mode in which America has been settled, that, in a noble breast, should forever distinguish the

prejudices of national dislikes. . . . Settled by the people of all nations, all nations may claim her for their own. . . . We are not a nation, so much as a world.[38]

It is too simple to say that an American state built along these internationalist lines would exclude nationalist ideologies. Even a transnational America would need a discourse of the nation, a way of understanding the nation that could build a sense of peoplehood among the imagined national community. Rather, the promise of a transnational American state was that it could escape the racial doctrines that gave nationalism its dangerous edge. The promise of America was that it would achieve a true multinationalism and thus an authentic nonracialism—"the European who scoffs at an American, calls his own brother *Raca*, and stands in danger of the judgment."[39]

While Randolph Bourne predicted the national prejudices at the core of the conflict in Europe during World War I, he elided the racial doctrines at the core of nationalism itself. Transnational or not, an America that retained core racial ideologies would place itself on the same path toward destruction. James's conclusion was that America, as of 1851, had firmly placed itself upon that path. The American national state undermined its own ideals when it used racial doctrines to justify slavery.[40]

The whalers who had been a part of America's mercantile imperial enterprise were distinguished from the imperialist nation herself in that they were removed from colonialism and the slave economy: "[Colonial slavery's] dominant economic structure is not the free individual, expressing himself fully in industry or in adventure on the seas seeking trade." Slavery produced instead a classed and racialized society: "Since cotton has become an important element of world production, the dominant economic pattern is that of aristocratic plantation-owner and Negro slave."[41] If the movement of the slave trade disrupted African institutions and their concomitant conceptions of black identity, the institution of the slave plantation also disrupted the movement of a free and industrious American capitalism built on trade on the high seas. If the Africans were now slaves, the seafarers were now their masters: "A wealthier class of men who had made money in shipping (the fishing business had been almost entirely theirs); and were now engaged in cotton manufacture."[42]

Remembering the Atlantic genealogy Captain Dean traced in his own sea story, the rich, mutual, and cooperative working relationship embodied in the friendship and partnership of his ancestors, the Scottish Captain Slocum and the native African Said Kafu, these were the kinds of inter-racial and multi-racial intimacies deformed by the master and slave relationship imposed structurally by slavery and capitalism. Similarly, on the *Pequod*, Ahab's position as master of the American ship of state alienates him from his crew, the mariners, renegades, and castaways of James's title. As James puts it, "Compare Ahab's Guinea-Coast slavery of solitary command and these three savages."[43] Captain Ahab's form of national leadership, his direction of the metaphoric United States ship of state, produces an authoritarianism that is necessary in order to preserve the slave society of the *Pequod* and prevent dissent and mutiny.

James finds in *Moby-Dick* Melville's similar disgust with a racialized white nationalism: "The color white . . . is a color of terror . . . whenever he sees whiteness, it is a symbol of his spiritual isolation, his loneliness, his revulsion against the world."[44] The white whale Moby Dick then becomes the metaphor for the racial arrogance and national prejudices at the heart of American capitalism, the embodiment of the racial doctrines eating at the heart of a now distorted American democracy. In *Mariners, Renegades and Castaways* James used his literary analysis of Melville's classic to sum up his observations of the decline of American civilization. He would make similar observations in a more theoretical and historical form in his notes on *American Civilization*.

However, the ultimate context for James's reading of Melville's *Pequod* can be found in his later writings on Caribbean federation, as they reveal his clear sense that the United States's ship of state at mid-century was assuming a role in the world greater than her European contemporaries and different from the empires that had gone immediately before her. When James turned his critical gaze to the sovereign and independent nation-states of Europe, he saw not the ordered national world of imperial myth, the world mapped at Versailles over thirty years earlier. Instead he saw a world in which the European economic empires were slowly but surely being dominated and undermined by the international economic force of the United States. By 1945, as the Age of Empire gave way to the American Century, Europe was already being swept up by globalizing forces emanating from the United States: "These formerly proud and powerful states are now continuously dependent on all sorts of aid, economic, financial, military from the United States," James described.[45] As the European empires had to rely increasingly on external forces to bolster their economies, this then had its effects on the independence of their political institutions:

> Politically it is the same. These powers came into existence and were able to thrive on imperialist exploitation because they established the national, independent state [devoted] exclusively to the national interest, independent of all other states. . . . Today that independence is gone. . . . The European imperialist states, which formerly conducted their own affairs and the affairs of their vast empires, today as far as foreign policy is concerned, are not more than satellites of the United States.[46]

As the European empires became more and more integrated into a global political economy dominated by the United States, their sovereignty diminished and the goals of foreign relations changed: "Nearly every great war between the European powers has been fought over the colonial question. . . . Today that is finished. The only war, the only serious war that we face is the war for world domination, not for colonial territory."[47] Instead of an imperialism based on colonialism, territorial conquest, and racial nationalism, James saw an imperialism based on global expansion and the control of the world economic system—a new vision of empire, grounded in United States hegemony and military might.[48]

Tracing the vision of the United States laid out in *Mariners* to James's writings on the Caribbean in the late 1950s and early 1960s, one can see a trajectory that locates hope for the future not in a redeemed North American state but in the subaltern American community of workers on the *Pequod* whose presence poses a challenge to that new state of empire. James saw in the 1940s and 1950s the beginning of two new political and economic processes, decolonization and globalization, that would drastically change world society in the second half of the century. James saw the future in the present, the emergent aspects of what we now commonly call a transnational world, a postmodern world of globalized national economies, United States dominance, and an increasingly integrated European core.

James argued that the European empires were turning to federation as a response to these pressures, creating institutions such as Benelux and the European Common Market "to unify their production on a continental scale." Federation was providing Europe with an ability to strengthen their struggling, dependent economies through integration: "The road out is *continental-*

*ization* . . . of the various economies. Europe must become one unit."[49] Continentalization as an idea, provided a way for nation-states, competing in a new world order dominated by the United States, to place themselves in a geographical position to participate as more equal players in the global economy.

Fernand Braudel, Etienne Balibar, and Immanuel Wallerstein have all argued that the national state was only one of multiple forms that the capitalist world economy could have, and has, taken to organize itself politically:

> In the history of capitalism, *state forms other than the national have emerged* and have for a time competed with it, before finally being repressed or instrumentalized: the form of empire and most importantly, that of the transnational politico-commercial complex, centered on one or more cities.[50]

James had a similar historical insight. As he would say in *Modern Politics*:

> If you study the history of capitalism you will see that it began with rather small units. These units steadily increased. (There was a certain amount of capitalism in Ancient Greece. . . . [A]nd it was the capitalistic elements that caused the progressive developments in the City-States of Ancient Greece.) We watched capitalistic elements in the City-States of the Middle Ages, the immense comparative wealth that they produced; also the destruction that they caused in the civilization of the time.[51]

For James, the nation-state was simply the political form that took hold because it was the one that proved the best in facilitating capitalism's success: "The national states are essentially the states which were created and helped to create capitalism in the form that we know it today."[52]

If, as Saskia Sassen has described, cities offer a potential alternative geography of our contemporary globalized world, James's abilities to read the future in the present also led to his focus on cities to create a vision of a new world order beyond nationalism and the nation-state.[53] However, James returned to the ancient world for his models of future political utopia. In his dream of West Indian federation James chose to look back to the ancient past and use the Greek city-state as a metaphor and a model to imagine a new type of political universe taking shape in the Caribbean. This form of modern politics, as he would title one of his essay collections on politics in the Caribbean, was one that was guided, geographically, by the shape of the island archipelago. And the Caribbean itself was an important region in the modern world precisely because it was producing a mobile, migrant proletariat, moving between the islands but also back and forth between the islands and the United States. Again, it was in Melville's highly resonant literary text that James chose to inscribe onto the *Pequod*'s crew these islander's most exalted ideals.[54]

## THE CARIBBEAN IS NOW AN AMERICAN SEA

When James said in 1962, "The Caribbean is now an American sea," he pointed to the late-twentieth-century articulation of a much older historical dynamic.[55] From the beginning of the twentieth century, when Garvey first observed the segregated conditions of black Caribbean workers employed by the United States in the construction of the Panama Canal or when Briggs reported on the military force of the United States in the invasion of Haiti, American racial and national doctrine has shaped the development of Caribbean identity. If Melville's American Nantucketers owned the sea "as Emperors own Empires," then the Caribbean Sea lay at the heart of that empire. If, as James paraphrased Melville, "in 1851, while white American officers provided the brains, not one of two of the thousands of men in the fishery, in the army, in the navy and the engineering forces employed in the construction of American canals and railroads were Americans," then black men from the Caribbean were among the first islanders employed in the American imperial enterprise.[56]

The American *Pequod* had always encompassed the people of the Caribbean colonial world. In the *Pequod* James saw the signs of a new transnational economic order dominated by the United States, but he also saw in its multiracial and multinational crew the other side of contemporary transnationalism and globalization, the mass movements of Third World and First World immigrant workers across multiple national borders throughout the Americas, Europe, Africa, and Asia. In James's reimagining of the community created by the crew on Melville's *Pequod*, we see a deterritorialized, diasporic, world that has traveled in the wake of the ships of empire throughout modernity. That world, as James would reconstruct it in his imaginative rewriting of Melville's story, was a world of island men who, like the motley crews on board ships, had been forced to live with difference: "They came from all over the world, were islanders from places like the Azores and the Shetland Islands."[57]

In 1960 James's fellow Caribbean, George Lamming, would also link the United States and the Caribbean with the following powerful image: "America is very much with us now; from Puerto Rico right down to Trinidad. But America is one island only; and we are used to living with many islands."[58] According to Lamming, what the Caribbean could teach the United States was precisely how to live with colonial difference:

> From the very beginning we were part of the island of China, and the island of Africa and the island of India. . . . [And] there is every reason why America should be in our midst. A large chunk of Africa, that is also a part of us, has always been the conscience of America. And America can learn, by her presence in the Caribbean, how we have lived with that dilemma.[59]

Seen from the perspective of the Caribbean, the United States is a world turned upside down, simply one island among many in the Caribbean archipelago of the New World, all struggling to find ways to transform their rich and painful colonial legacies. As James would quote Césaire at the end of his 1962 appendix to the history *The Black Jacobins*:

> but the work of man is only just beginning
> and it remains to man to conquer all
> the violence entrenched in the recesses
> of his passion
> and no race possesses the monopoly of beauty,
> of intelligence, of force, and there
> is a place for all at the rendezvous
> of victory.[60]

Ultimately, in *Mariners* James called for a federated solidarity between the workers on the various ships of state and empire, a federation that would cross national lines and connect New World Negroes working in the core states and in the island peripheries, like the multiracial societies created by black seamen and immigrant workers of color. The seeds of James's vision for the New World lay in his observations of the *Pequod*'s crew. While a central focus of *Mariners* was James's analysis of Ahab's monomaniacism he also asked: "How did [Melville] in 1851 see the ordinary people whom these monsters bind in chains, exploit, corrupt, and ultimately ruin?"[61] In other words, how were ordinary people responding to an American state and world society, gone mad with a national arrogance founded on racial exploitation?

For James the answer to this question lay in an important passage in which he describes the *Pequod*'s crew:

> The crew gives the final proof that Melville is constructing a strictly logical pattern. They are a pack of ragamuffins picked up at random from all parts of the earth. . . . Nearly all on Ahab's ship were islanders, and in fact, nearly all the nations of the globe had each its representative. *Isolatoes*, Melville called them, not acknowledging the common continent of men, but each *Isolato* living on a separate continent of his own.[62]

Here, at first the crew seems to depict an entity similar to Randolph Bourne's dream of a transnational American state that could embody and represent the world. James highlights the crew's resemblance to Anacharsis Clootz's eighteenth-century vision of a Universal Republic:

> Anacharsis Clootz was a Prussian nobleman who embraced the French Revolution of 1789. . . . [H]e was an ardent advocate of the Universal Republic. . . . He gathered together representatives of all the nationalities he could find in Paris, including silent and bewildered Ishmaelites and Chaldeans, and pleaded for the inclusion of all in the brotherhood of nations.[63]

In James's reading Melville's genius was to recognize the ultimate impossibility of that dream, a dream of internationally cooperative national states also represented by the League of Nations: "But whereas Clootz thought of uniting all men in a Universal Republic, based on liberty, equality, fraternity, brotherhood, human rights, etc., Melville in 1851, had not the faintest trace of these windy abstractions from the beginning of *Moby Dick* to the end."[64]

These visions of a Universal Republic did not account for the tensions that arose from national states and an international world order built on the tenets of territoriality and racial superiority. The development of nationalism in the modern world would work to keep men isolated and divided from each other, "each *Isolato* living on a separate continent of his own." For nationalism, isolationism *was* the other side of independence—the national state created the isolatoes of the modern world. These isolated, alienated subjects, citizens without community, would not find spiritual and political integration in the ideal of a Universal Republic.

Instead, federation is the term James cites most often when describing the crew's moments of unity on the *Pequod*: "Yet now, federated along one keel, what a set these Isolatoes were!"[65] Federation is not the same as revolution, however, for it does not change the crew's willingness to go along with Ahab's mission. As James continues to describe, "Melville took great pains to show that revolt was no answer to the question he asked."[66] James, paraphrasing Melville, cites a story in the novel of another revolt, in which the mutineers escape their ship and return to land. James himself concludes, however, "That's all. Everything goes back to just where it was before. That is exactly what would have happened in 1851 if there had been a revolt on the *Pequod*. We would have been left in the end exactly where we had been in the beginning."[67] This particular comment also sheds light on James's dismissal of black revolt in Melville's *Benito Cereno*. There the story of Babo's, the colonial savage, failed revolutionary bid for freedom could only serve as propaganda while not changing world society in a revolutionary way.

In James's analysis neither the *Pequod* nor the crew had any hope of escaping the racial state: "When the *Pequod* set out so bravely and boldly, it carried in its heart, in the captain's cabin, the monomaniac Ahab, as genuine a part of that society."[68] These isolatoes were not a group of men cut off from their own histories, transcending either the strengths or weaknesses of their own national and racial pasts. As James would further describe:

> The *Pequod* is taking a voyage that humanity has periodically to take into the open sea, into the unknown, because of the problems posed to it by life on the safe sheltered land. The *Pequod* set out on that voyage. But, as always on these journeys, mankind finds reflected in the water only the image of what it has brought with it.[69]

James goes to great pains to show that Melville's crew of ragamuffins are not free-floating—they carry their nationality with them as they board the drifting *Pequod*. Their national differences are constitutive in the society they create among themselves on the ship.

Melville's mariners, renegades, and castaways are not a hybrid crew whose origins are unidentifiable and therefore insignificant in meaning and influence. On the contrary, they all originate from some place—"nearly all the

nations of the globe had each its representative"—and are inherently distinct—
"not acknowledging the common continent of men, but each isolato living on
a separate continent of his own." James's insight is that the crews' distinct
nationalities will always mitigate against the ideal of a Universal Republic.
Their challenge, then, is not to transcend their national differences to imagine
a world without race but, rather, because they are forced together despite their
differences, to imagine a multiracial and multinational world.

This American proletariat could make new connections with each other in
a cooperative fraternity found and constructed through their common work:

> The chief thing about Melville's crew is that they work. They are not
> suffering workers, nor revolutionary workers, nor people who must be
> organized. . . . What matters to them primarily, as it does to all workers,
> and in fact to all people, is the work they do every day, so many hours a day,
> nearly every day in the year.[70]

Federation does not assure "these candidates for the Universal Republic"
integration within the utopian vision of a free and inclusive world state.
Instead, the only thing that binds the *Pequod's* crew together is that "they work
together on a whaling-ship. They are a world federation of modern industrial
workers. They owe allegiance to no nationality. . . . They owe no allegiance to
anybody or anything except the work they have to do and the relations with
one another on which that work depends."[71] What James is imagining here is
a New World proletariat united not simply around the idea of one shared
nationality but on the basis of their own raced position within the economic
world system represented by the *Pequod*. If the American captains of empire
lead the ship of the world, it is the workers of the New World who drive that
ship and give it motion. As their nationalities are constituted by their relationship to their colonial masters, their *transnationalities* are constituted by their
relationships *with each other* and the work they do together. Federation is the
solution James sees for a New World proletariat struggling to find moments of
unity in a world in which internationalist consciousness is increasingly fractured by racial nationalism.

While Caribbean and American black subjects share a common history of
New World slavery, their struggles for liberty, equality, and fraternity over the
course of the nineteenth and twentieth centuries have also varied greatly,
based on a central structural distinction in their national histories. As a ter-

ritorial majority black colonial subjects in the Caribbean have historically been able to choose nationhood as their political route to freedom. For African Americans, on the other hand, the black nation within the nation was never a real and viable political option. Instead, as a national minority, African Americans have struggled to assert their rights to full citizenship as members of a national community within the United States.

This is a particularly thorny contradiction if one is trying to identify and theorize something like a black transnational formation. As Immanuel Wallerstein has described, the New World "dialectics of black freedom" actually consists of two separate dialectics.[72] One is situated within an international framework—individual Caribbean nation-states fighting for their own cultural, economic, and political diversity by breaking away from a hegemonic European world system. The other occurs in a national context—African Americans trying to promote their own group rights by laying claim to the ideals of cultural equality and political and economic uniformity that are the foundation of America's democratic pluralism. How do we imagine transnational alliances between members of a racial group who seem, politically, to be moving in opposite directions?

Black transnational intellectuals such as James understood that what Caribbean and American black subjects also share is a history of working, living, loving, and moving together under the overarching, transatlantic framework of the imperial state, European and American. As Wallerstein has also pointed out in comparing and contrasting the dialectics of African American and Caribbean freedom: "It has been the states which have had the upper hand in both contradictions . . . for one simple reason: they have controlled the most physical force. . . . This has made the state the most powerful cultural force in the modern world and the most schizophrenic."[73] That schizophrenia creates the space for alternative formations, other ways of understanding racial, sexual, and national identity that no hegemonic subject could fully contain. As Hardt and Negri also argue, the schizophrenic nation-state is one that constantly seeks order and integration, most often by means of the wanton's seduction—the domestic entrapments of sentimental nationality on land—but also by means of the sovereign's force if necessary—the monomaniacism of a Captain Ahab at sea. In James's hands, federation would allow the mariners, renegades, and castaways of the New World not to live in an impossible isolated exile from the West, the revolutionary, masculine narrative of colonial independence, but to find in each other the solidarity necessary to survive *in their dependent position* within that world.

Federation then meant a change in attitude. It forced the crew to create new relations with each other that looked beyond their respective European and colonial nationalities. If race and nationalism could not be fully transcended, then it was only in the work the men of the *Pequod* were doing together as they journeyed with Ahab on his monomaniacal quest that they were able to find new ways of imagining community in difference. James's interpretation of Melville's crew as a New World proletariat is important not simply because it expressed his socialist vision of workers' solidarity. More importantly, it represented the turn away from the master-slave dialectic that had so characterized colonial relations. It represented the crew themselves turning away from the dream of the internationalist state imposed from above—the Universal Republic of Enlightenment theory and ideology—and turning to new networks of solidarity created among themselves as they work. The crew's turn away from their masters marked a subaltern class consciousness based on new affiliations: "For him now the crew embodies some type of social order. Their association at work gives them interests, ideas and attitudes that separate them entirely from the rest of society."[74] This is precisely the community Ishmael, the American intellectual, yearns to be part of. And this community relies on no leader to enact its own liberation.

In James's interpretation of the islanders of the *Pequod* we see the real historical shadow of the Caribbean. Caribbean islanders joined the crew of Melville's America—"An Anacharsis Clootz deputation from all the isles of the seas"—believing if not in the Great American Dream, then at least in the hope that they too had a part to play in the modern, integrated, world of nation-states. What was only metaphor here—the crew cutting themselves off from empire to imagine new forms of social and political identification— James would try to realize in real political terms in his proposal for a new geographic understanding of economic and political relationships in the Caribbean, postindependence. While America as one island had tried and failed to create multiracial democracy, the Caribbean would bring its own special conditions to bear on the question of nationalism, with different if not greater results. Anna Grimshaw has stated: "For James, federation became the collective symbol of the search for a new conception of nationhood appropriate to the world of the late twentieth century."[75] George Lamming, a different kind of American intellectual, would describe this even more lyrically in a 1960 essay he entitled, "Ishmael at Home": "For Africa like the Caribbean is now very much at sea, and even though we—like them—may not be able to tell which port we shall harbour in, we would like the chance to reverse Prospero's magic with the waves."[76] Federation was the means by which Queequeg's, Tashtego's, and Daggoo's island descendants could chart a different course for democracy in the New World.

THE "CONTINENTALIZATION" OF THE ISLANDS

James's writings on the Caribbean in the late 1950s and his earlier work during the 1940s on the Negro struggle in the United States form a necessary whole in understanding his thinking about modern black political freedom and the future of world civilization. James's notion of federation offered a different way of conceiving of the black transnational struggle, one that ultimately saw the ideal of fraternity, the desire to live together, not in terms of the independent black state but rather as a network or chain of dependent islands that were fundamentally stateless.

James laid out his conception of the struggle for national independence in the Caribbean in a series of speeches he gave throughout the West Indies in the late 1950s and early 1960s. One was a set of speeches he gave between 1958 and 1959, both arguing in favor of West Indian federation and subsequently evaluating its failure. He also gave a longer series of lectures in which he contextualized for Caribbean people his sense of their unique role in world political history. These later speeches were collected in 1960 in a monograph entitled *Modern Politics*.

Anticolonial struggles often center around the relationship between the ex-slave and the imperial master, the colony and the metropolitan state. Hence in James's play, Möise argued that the only way to break the colonial mentality was to hold up full autonomy and independence as the ultimate goal: "Until you cut yourself off from all symbols of colonialism and slavery . . . and be truly independent, you will remain just an old man with a dream of impossible fraternity."[77] James's contribution to black transnational discourse was precisely that he argued the opposite. In James's opinion, "Freedom from colonialism is not merely legal independence, the right to run up a national flag and to compose and to sing a national anthem. It is necessary also to break down the economic colonial system."[78] To break down the economic colonial system meant the exact opposite of Dessalines's vision—not a new independence but new relations of dependence between the islands in the West Indian Federation:

> The West Indies for three hundred years has had its centre—intellectual, financial and economic—in London, so that the lines of communication ran from Port of Spain to London, from Kingston to London, from Georgetown to London and from Bridgetown to London—the economic, financial and intellectual lines ran to London. Now federation demanded that the lines of communication should run from island to island, not from island to the control body in Britain.[79]

Here James was basically asking Caribbean people to focus on two new things: controlling the movement of their own economies but also, in so doing, creating new identifications between members of the British Commonwealth islands that could replace the primary colonial relations of master and slave, black and white, colonizer and colonized.

The process of breaking up the Old Colonial System required a remapping of colonial relations: "That is what the Federation needed—to break this connection and substitute another connection."[80] Imperialism created "economic, financial and intellectual" connections between the European nation-states and the marginalized, subnational units of the colonial world. James argued that "to break up the Old Colonial System" the Caribbean islands had to break away from the European state and devote their energies to strengthening their own regional, peripheral economic relations. In a black transnational, as opposed to a colonial or postcolonial world, the primary "lines of communication" had to run from island to island, island-city to island-city, rather than to "the control body in Britain."[81]

What this would mean in practice was that the islands would replace their colonial connections with the metropolitan states, not with the independent black state, but with an island-state system that could facilitate movement along economic, financial, and intellectual lines that ran between the islands rather than to one central state. In James's opinion, this was precisely the virtue of the Greek city-states, what had moved them forward so quickly on the path of civilization: forms of culture, the practice of a democratic politics, and actual fellow citizens could travel easily between the states, crossing city-state lines:

> the Greek City-States moved so far and so fast, and that is my hope for the development of the West Indies too. Those states were so small that everybody had a grasp of what was going on. Nobody was backward; nobody was remote; nobody was far in the country; and people in the West Indies are even closer because we have methods of transport that bring us very rapidly together.[82]

The Greek city-state offered James a utopian model of political freedom because it was a network made up of political units much closer in size to the physical realities of the Caribbean. Federation could turn the size of the islands, a potential weakness, into a strength, creating a new national community built not on territory but on the free movement of people, resources, and ideas between territories. This, for James, was also the key to the good life: life, liberty, and the pursuit of happiness.

In his proposal for a Constituent assembly made up of "all parties in the West Indies" that would "take part in the formation of the Constitution and the establishment of the new state," subject to ratification by the people, James modeled the Greek notion of direct democracy and citizenship, where "every citizen took part in the government, took part in debates, voted, served on the various assemblies. . . . The state was all-powerful, controlling everything, but *he* [the individual citizen] was the state."[83] This, for James, was the true challenge of West Indian national independence, for he did believe that the two were connected.[84] More so than legal independence, the real question for the Caribbean was whether the islands could meet the challenge of creating a new vision of society, one in which the individual citizen would feel himself to be in fraternity with the Caribbean state:

> When the British flag goes down and the national flag goes up and there will be no more cruisers and soldiers to come, and all authority depends upon what is native and rests upon the attitude of the people, then these islands are going to test for themselves how far it is possible for them to achieve the democracy which has evaded so many other territories.[85]

The question was whether the West Indian nation could give the black colonial a different way of imagining the national community and, consequently, the state itself.

In her conception of the global city Sassen focused primarily on the movements of capital. In 1952 James was already studying the other side of transnationalism, the movements of people—the mariners, renegades, and castaways of the modern and postmodern world. James's conception of West Indian federation only enhanced what he already saw to be true—the need to form new ways of representing and protecting such a mobile and vulnerable proletariat.

The success of federation as a metaphor for black freedom, if not as a political reality, can be seen in the way the idea still haunts Caribbean geopolitics and Caribbeans' pan-ethnic, regionally informed sense of themselves in the world. The collapse of the West Indian Federation in 1962 also ended the hopes of a generation of intellectuals of Caribbean origin who had believed in federation as a way of changing the direction and definition of democracy in the Americas. In an interview as recent as 1992, Stuart Hall described the failure of West Indian federation as the primary reason for his own decision to stay in Britain, and he had this to say about what that political movement in the Caribbean had meant to him and his cohort:

> Up until 1954, I was saturated in West Indian expatriate politics. Most of my friends were expatriates, and went back to play a role in Jamaica, Trinidad, Barbados, Guyana. We were passionate about the colonial question. . . . With the emerging postcolonial independence, we dreamt of a Caribbean federation, merging these countries into a larger entity. If that had happened, I would have gone back to the Caribbean . . . and tried to play a role there. That dream was over at the moment in the 1950s when I decided to stay.[86]

The dream of federation gave Caribbean intellectuals hope, a hope to counteract their despair with the failures of the nation-state.[87] Contemporary Caribbean intellectuals express skepticism about the degree to which ideas of regional integration today can offer any true refuge from the larger integrative forces of global capital and globalization. As Paget Henry has observed:

> In spite of its many restructurings, the production of Caribbean labor as a cheap commodity has remained the item of exchange by which Western

capitalism has defined the peripheral role of the region. It is this highly exploitable labor power . . . that continues to . . . determine the specific places we occupy in the ever-more global production networks of Western capitalism.[88]

One could argue that existing regional organizations are mostly in the service of better facilitating the Caribbean's ability to turn hybrid, mobile subjects into labor—placing the New World proletariat on the wave of globalization, with no ability to stem the current.[89]

However, if we believe that Caribbean history is inextricable from international relations, as Anthony P. Maingot argues, then the following is also true: "The Caribbean . . . has long experienced dynamic tension between the enunciation of hegemonic principles, the incapacity to enforce them, and the reality of economic and political pluralism." Maingot continues, "In [the twentieth] century the United States has had an advantage in establishing the rules of the game; it has not, however, been able to monopolize them."[90] This is also the principle James's three harpooners of Melville's novel represent, the calm but unbending refusal of the colonial subject to refrain from enacting new forms of social relations. It is in this sense that Caribbean and transnational male intellectuals, in turning away from the language of statehood and empire and toward alternative, submerged, social formations throughout diasporic geography and history, found different worlds of color in America herself, an America broadly defined to include the archipelago and the continent, the peoples on the mainlands and the islanders at sea.

C. L. R. James had his own Leninist conception of where black and colonial subjects fit within the central contradictions of world capitalism. In "The Revolutionary Answer to the Negro Problem in the United States" he would quote Lenin twice, saying:

> Let me repeat it please. Small groups, nations, nationalities, themselves powerless against imperialism, nevertheless can act as one of the ferments, one of the bacilli which will bring on to the scene the real fundamental force against capitalism—the socialist proletariat.[91]

But the socialist proletariat, the masculine social agents James predicted, were already succumbing to racial and social stratifications integral to the constitutions of new twentieth-century European and American nations. Hence as he read Melville, so too must we read even James's *Mariners, Renegades and Castaways* against the grain, to rediscover those small groups that can act as ferments—Caribbean islanders, colonial savages, women of color, multinational and multiracial intellectual communities—working together across state and disciplinary lines to reveal the new problems facing modern nationalities at the turn of a new century.

CONCLUSION

# Dark Waters: Shadow Narratives of U.S. Imperialism

I move through a Black land
where the future
glows eternal and green
but where the symbols for now
are bloody and unrelenting

—AUDRE LORDE, "CONCLUSION"[1]

OBSERVING THE NEW mobility of people, money, and ideas across the globe, one commentator in the *New York Times Book Review* of 30 September 2002 envisioned "all of mankind in the same boat on the unsettled seas of a new millennium," subject to "the physical laws of markets and democracy that have provided this vessel with buoyancy, while largely ignoring the struggle going on over who controls the rudder and compass."[2] The review, not coincidentally, was of Michael Mandelbaum's account of the centrality of World War I and the discussions at Versailles in establishing the terms of political discussion in the twentieth century. Strikingly, of course, nowhere in this or any other contemporary account of the geopolitical aftermath of World War I is race specifically mobilized as a category for analyzing the attitude toward colonial populations and territories in the postwar discussions.[3] No one travels, as Du Bois did, through the worlds of color within and without the United States that constituted colonial space at the turn of the twentieth century.

Tyler's review serves as a useful parallel here in closing for his use of the image of the ship of state, now to represent the movements of the world at large. In this portrayal of a world on the unsettled seas of a new millennium, we see the very questions of mobility versus sovereignty explored here but

269

operating on an even broader terrain. Picture us all, colonial worlds of color and metropolitan states, on a level playing field in the larger global imaginary, plagued in equal ways by current discussions of the crisis of the nation-state under the pressures and forces of multinational capital.

More recent events in the years immediately following Tyler's review demonstrated that we are naive in thinking our world is shaped simply by a dichotomy between free movement and statehood. Rather, different subjects and states experience the rights afforded by way of those conditions differently. Also, certain states today are gaining powers to redefine their sovereignty in multiple ways and claiming through military force new ways of penalizing the racial and ethnic other, both within and without domestic national borders. As Roshan Muhammed Salih described Guantanamo Bay, Cuba, in November 2003, "More than 600 foreign nationals have been detained without charge or access to lawyers and family members in the U.S. naval base since November of 2001. The U.S. has refused to recognise them as prisoners of war, or allow their status to be determined by a tribunal as required under the Geneva Conventions."[4] As Salih explains further, "The Guantanamo prisoners are in legal limbo. . . . [Defined by the United States] as 'enemy combatants' . . . they are outside the normal legal framework and can be held indefinitely without trial or access to lawyers."

For the prisoners at Guantanamo Bay, as scholars Amy Kaplan, Judith Butler, and Ruth Wilson Gilmore described in their addresses to the 2003 American Studies Association conference in Hartford, as incoherent as empire may feel, their one certainty is that of their own perpetual imprisonment by the sovereign powers of the U.S. state.[5] And this remains true even if the latter resists being defined solely according to that global role.[6] The landscape where dynamics of American empire are often at their clearest, where national sovereignty and the rights of citizens fall sway to the power of racial categories and the state reveals itself as the face of empire, has often been the island itself.

In 1988 James Clifford proposed that "We are all Caribbeans now in our urban archipelagos. . . . Perhaps there's no return for anyone to a native land."[7] While a powerful metaphor in Caribbean and American discourse, the claim to an equally displaced and migratory status does not reflect the material, transnational fact that racial subjects have always been located differentially in urban and archipelagic spaces. In a sense, the metaphor breaks down by race, to the degree that race often determines *how* we inhabit the metaphoric space

of the Caribbean, as metropolitan or colonial subjects. The metaphor is therefore less useful if it erases specifically black diasporic histories and if it allows
us to say we are all Caribbean without interrogating our own location in
relationship to empire and the national state.

For Caribbean American intellectuals such as C. L. R. James and Audre
Lorde, such a metaphor proved to be a luxury. James would learn, at the end of
his first sojourn in America, that as much as the archipelago can be the site for
new imaginings of home, it can also reveal itself as the gulag archipelago of the
nation-state.[8] Like Marcus Garvey before him, James did not leave the United
States in 1953 by choice but, rather, was deported because of his illegal status
and because his political writings and activities were seen as subversive in an
atmosphere increasingly determined by the Cold War. Like Garvey's autobiographical essays in prison, *Mariners* became James's method for protesting
his treatment by American officials.[9] Today James's account is especially pre-
scient if we place his insights on the meaning of Ellis Island for United States
democracy and internationalism in the context of the state's current role and
presence in Guantanamo Bay.

There is, however, one important difference: located on the island of
Cuba, Guantanamo Bay is not within the United States's territorial national
borders. Yet, scholars argue, the United States has found new ways to apply its
sovereignty outside of its own national geography and territory. What contemporary accounts fail to mention, is that this too is not a new occurrence in
Caribbean archipelagic space. Thirty years after James's account of his own
penalization, Audre Lorde would witness and record similar events as part of
the aftermath of the United States's invasion of the island of Grenada. Her
report reveals surprising homologies between United States interventionist
policy in the Caribbean in the early 1980s and the world we are living in today
at the beginning of the twenty-first century.

## THE ISLAND AS PENAL COLONY

While on Ellis Island, James used the same metaphor of Melville's *Pequod* to
encapsulate the multinational and multiracial society now detained by the
U.S. state.[10] Ellis Island was the distortion of the island ideal. On the world of
Ellis Island, James, the isolated Caribbean islander, lived as a castaway decidedly excluded from any imagining of national community: "What matters is

that I am not an American citizen, and just as I was about to write, I was arrested by the United States government and sent to Ellis Island to be deported." On the island James was abused, neglected, and insulted while he was severely ill in a series of events he described as important enough to write about because they reflected the real limits of the "attitude to aliens in the United States" and the state's role in regards to transnational subjects. For James it was specifically the state's presence on Ellis Island that was at issue, as he would say somewhat ironically, "I expect if I had been on a desert island after some shipwreck, I would have managed much better." Like the crew of the wrecked *Sea Venture*, James was treated as a fugitive from the claims and subjections of the state and interpellated as criminal: "The guards at night either sat just outside the door or actually in my room. I had committed no crime. . . . Yet this penal régime was imposed upon me . . . this imposition which I have always associated with homicidal criminals and dangerous lunatics." On the island, James argued, he was outside the boundaries of civilization, not because of his own savage nature but because of the "inhuman and barbarous" treatment of the American state officials.[11]

James drew a number of conclusions from his stay on Ellis Island that cast a different perspective on America's ability to fulfill the dream of being a transnational nation and the domestic implications of its increased global role today. First, James argued, "national arrogance" is at the heart of the "policy-making echelons" of the United States Department of Immigration, an arrogance demonstrated in their belief that "an alien is not a human being." In a comment directed at the American citizenry themselves, James argued that his quarrel with the American state was precisely that they contradicted their own ideals. American immigration law, the instrument of the state, was created ideally to advocate for and protect the immigrant: "Such a procedure could have originated only in a country where the traditional role of . . . civil liberties, are such as to have created for the alien every possible opportunity to make as good a case for himself as possible." In a rhetorical move reminiscent of Briggs's dialogues with Woodrow Wilson, James gave the American government the benefit of the doubt that their internationalist ideals were sincere:

> The only interpretation of such a procedure is that it was intended to break down barriers and not to set them up, to declare to the alien, and to American citizens, and to the whole world that the United States took

upon itself the responsibility of seeing that as far as possible he was treated as a potential citizen.[12]

James asserted his faith that United States policy on immigrants reflected a real belief in inclusive citizenship and therefore a true cosmopolitanism. In this ideal transnational America, a multiracial conception of citizenship was a thing to be nurtured and protected by the state. Yet instead, James's experiences on Ellis Island revealed an American internationalism based on the old imperialist values. By treating the alien as a criminal, the United States government was turning American nationality into a piece of property: "set[ting] itself up in opposition to an alien as if the two of them are a pair of gangsters contending over some piece of territory."[13] Citizenship becomes, once again, a piece of colonial property for imperial masters to conquer, redistribute, and reclaim at will. The result is "complete chaos," and America as embodied by Ellis Island becomes a prison for its citizens as much as its aliens.

For James, the dangerous consequences of America's position on the alien question was best expressed by one judge's learned opinion, "We may be on a slope which leads down to aboriginal slavery." James's strongest indictment of the American state was that, by its very actions, it was turning citizenship itself into a new form of slavery—citizenship as the very absence of free movement. For James, the descendant of the fugitive slave, this was too high a price to pay for the "American passport to freedom": "Never shall I submit myself to any inquisition and grovel in the dirt, as the price for bail or for assistance or for citizenship, or for anything at all."[14]

In his "Natural But Necessary Conclusion" James argued with American civilization by rhetorically taking at face value the idea that the internationalism of American society was true. In terms of its population, America *was* a globalized nation, "entangled as no modern nation has ever been in ever-growing relations with the vast masses of the world."[15] The question was, was the state an equally globalist and internationalist state? Could the American government really nourish and protect the multinationalism already present within its own borders, a multinationalism represented on Ellis Island itself? On Ellis Island, James would describe a community of penalized mariners reminiscent of Banjo's crew in Marseilles: "The whole of the world is represented on Ellis Island. Many sailors . . . Germans, Italians, Latvians, Swedes, Filipinos, Malays, Chinese, Hindus, Pakistanis, West Indians, Englishmen,

Australians, Danes, Yugoslavs, Greeks, Canadians, representatives of every Latin-American country."[16] One man in particular stood out, a fellow Caribbean islander:

> A young Latin American sailor. His ship was in harbor in Santo Domingo which is ruled by Trujillo, a byword . . . for tyranny and savage brutality. A man he knew came to him and told him he had hidden in his house two men wanted by the government. Their lives were at stake. Could he help to stow them on board his ship? . . . I wish [defenders of democracy] could have seen the simplicity and naturalness with which this young sailor said that he agreed. He risked his life as easily and spontaneously as Tashtego or Daggoo.[17]

Some of these seamen on Ellis Island were the freedom fighters of the second half of the twentieth century, the men of nationality doubtful, the refugees from and victims of myriad, tyrannical regimes across the globe. Like the maroons on the islands and the fugitive slaves on the runaway railroads, they had scores of stories to tell: "At any moment, a man in the same ward in the infirmary can tell you of events . . . barbarities would pass from hand to hand, and evoke astonishing tales of corroboration. It is from these sailors that . . . I picked up, sometimes at second-hand, sometimes confused, sometimes contradictory but always authentic views."[18] James's hope was that what could be new about America's internationalism was its willingness to grant citizenship freely to the alien and despised of other nations, those already defined as criminal by America's less democratic neighbors. James would conclude:

> This is my final impression. The meanest mariners, renegades and castaways of Melville's day were objectively a new world . . . looking for federation. . . . The crowning irony of the little cross-section of the whole world that is Ellis Island [is that] while the United States Department of Justice is grimly pursuing a venomous anti-alien policy . . . the despised aliens, however fiercely nationalistic, are profoundly conscious of themselves as citizens of the world.[19]

Throughout the twentieth century, America's ability to fulfill James's dream was hampered by its own activities abroad in ways that reverberated back upon the domestic community. This was the special insight Audre Lorde brought to bear on American democracy and internationalism at the end of the twentieth century, as she too met and listened to the stories of Caribbean freedom fighters and refugees from empire. James ascribed agency to women of color in transforming their roles within the domestic sphere. Audre Lorde demonstrated the special contribution of the Caribbean American female intellectual as she traveled outside of domestic space to enter the colonial world of the Caribbean isle and record anew the story of empire for a new millennium.

## AUDRE LORDE, CARRIACOU WOMAN

In her opening note to "Grenada Revisited: An Interim Report," the closing piece in Lorde's signature essay collection, *Sister Outsider*, she describes the urgency she felt to include this final entry: "I spent a week in Grenada in late December, 1983, barely two months after the U.S. invasion of the Black Caribbean island my parents left some sixty years earlier. It was my second visit in five years. This is an interim essay, a report written as the rest of *Sister Outsider* was already being typeset."[20] Lorde's report was written for an American audience and as such plays a particular role in the study of United States empire and the study of American culture. As Amy Kaplan has described in other accounts, Lorde's essay can be seen as offering "an inventory of counter-evidence, from which one can plot shadow narratives of [America's] imperial histories."[21]

Like many other black transnational intellectuals before her, when Lorde first visited Grenada she "came seeking home." On her first visit in 1978, three years before James recognized that black women and black women writers might represent their own "social movement in the United States,"[22] Lorde found in the Caribbean a female world she would describe in her biomythography as that of the Carriacou woman.[23] As she traced her own matriarchal genealogy, Lorde followed the historical archipelagic journeys of her female ancestors as they "set forth on inter-island schooners" from "Carriacou, spice island off the coast" to "Grenville town, Grenada" and back again.[24] As they navigated the island seas, these women formed mobile female communities, the very communities of women of color left behind by their seafaring transnational male counterparts:

Here Aunt Anni lived among the other women who saw their men off on the sailing vessels, then tended the goats and groundnuts, planted grain and poured rum upon the earth to strengthen the corn's growing, built their women's houses . . . wove their lives and the lives of their children together. Women who survived the absence of their sea-faring men easily, because they came to love each other, past the men's returning.[25]

In *Zami: A New Spelling of My Name*, Lorde renamed herself as the inheritor of this female transnational, interisland legacy: "*Zami. A Carriacou name for women who work together as friends and lovers.*"[26]

On the Caribbean islands Lorde identified communities of mobile Caribbean women creating alternative lifestyles and forms of intimacy in the absence of men. In between this and her next visit in 1983, the women on these islands had experienced revolution and occupation. On 13 March 1979 they saw the "bloodless coup of the New Jewel Movement which ushered in the People's Revolutionary Government (PRG) of Grenada under Prime Minister Maurice Bishop."[27] Lorde's second visit occurs three months after "the invasion of Grenada by the United States on October 25, 1983" and, as she laments,

> The second time I came to Grenada I came in mourning and fear that this land which I was learning had been savaged, invaded, its people maneuvered into saying thank you to their invaders. I knew the lies and distortions of secrecy surrounding the invasion . . . the rationalizations which collapse under the weight of facts; the facts that are readily available, even now, from the back pages of the *New York Times*.[28]

In her study of the migration narrative Farah Jasmine Griffin identified a particular literary persona often adopted by black women writers of the twentieth century to express their mobility and the alienation of the black subject moving through an urban, modern world. In migration narratives by Gwendolyn Brooks and Ann Petry, Griffin argues that "the omniscient narrators of these texts play the role of journalists, streetwise reporters who detach themselves and present the readers with a case for consideration and action."[29] Here Griffin builds on the figure of the stranger she finds "in the work of the German-Jewish sociologist Georg Simmel," "a figure whose membership within a group involves being at once outside and within its boundaries."

Griffin also argues that the stranger is a "cosmopolitan figure" like all "foreigners [who are] driven by persecution to wander in search of a new home. . . . Within the context of the African-American community, the stranger is that figure who possesses no connections to the community."[30]

Lorde, the sister outsider, exemplifies this category of the stranger, to the degree that she sits in an uneasy and ambiguous national relationship to Caribbean and African American culture. A second generation Caribbean American, not born in the Caribbean yet raised in an ethnic Caribbean household, one would expect Lorde's writings to demonstrate the detachment and sense of alienation in exile that shapes the racial immigrant's double-consciousness. Yet Lorde's work has been characterized by its strong and impassioned language of activism and political commitment as she strenuously sought to engage with and speak for women of color at home and abroad. Lorde also consistently interrogated her own location within and relationship to multiple narratives of identity including her own race, gender, sexuality, and nationality.

This imperative characterizes her report on Grenada, for though she too adopts the stance of the conscientious reporter she also rigorously attempted to place herself, *as an American citizen*, in relationship to United States imperial actions and the life of the Carriacou woman:

> I came to Grenada the second time six weeks after the invasion, wanting to know she was still alive, wanting to examine what my legitimate position as a concerned Grenadian-american was toward the military invasion of this tiny Black nation, by the mighty U.S. I looked around me, talked with Grenadians on the street. . . . Grenada is their country. I am only a relative. I must listen long and hard and ponder the implications of what I have heard, or be guilty of the same quick arrogance of the U.S. government.[31]

In this sense Lorde differs strikingly from Griffin's estranged African American migrants to the north. As the engaged American citizen *and* Caribbean American transmigrant, with complicated attachments to multiple homes, Lorde assumes the literary persona of the outsider-reporter to create a different effect—a critical detachment from her United States home *as* empire.[32]

Lorde sees in Grenada what James saw on Ellis Island, the American state's violation of the meaning of citizenship and nationality, self-government, self-possession, the individual's right to sovereignty. If for James in 1962 the Caribbean could still be envisioned as a male space on a revolutionary trajectory embodied by leaders such as Toussaint L'Ouverture and Fidel Castro, after the failed Grenadian revolution the Caribbean is now an invaded isle, and the masculine Caribbean subject is imprisoned in his own home by the forces of an empire abroad.

In "Grenada Revisited" Lorde wrote not a migration narrative but a shadow narrative of empire, a contemporary version of the essay genre Briggs first inaugurated in his critique of the United States invasion of Haiti, but also a literary descendant of Du Bois's attempt to create a new "field of inquiry, of likening and contrasting each land and its far-off shadow."[33] The shadow narrative is premised on the engaged listening of an American citizenry and national community, receptive to reevaluating the terms of their own national belonging from the context of international geopolitics. Lorde is on a fact-finding mission for the American public, the American intellectual as intrepid reporter, with an unstinting willingness to name and record the contradictions of empire and democracy. Citing propagandistic newspaper accounts that counter Caribbean realities, Lorde asserts: "Nineteen eighty-four is upon us, and doublethink has come home to scramble our brains and blanket our protest."[34]

Rereading Lorde's account of the Grenada invasion and the media reports surrounding it from the vantage point of today, one is amazed at the degree to which the small Caribbean island of Grenada was the staging ground for wartime initiatives that now characterize the United States's foreign interventions in the "war on terrorism." To mention a few, Lorde argues that in 1983, "For the first time in an american war, the american press was kept out until the stage could be set. This extends by precedent the meaning of military censorship in this country."[35] Like the *Sea Venture* that once shipwrecked in the Caribbean and led to a mutiny, an American *Ocean Venture* traveled the waters of the Caribbean in the 1980s, training its officers and crew on ways to manage dissent in the alternative, marooned, political communities of the Caribbean in the late twentieth century:

> Beginning in 1981, the United States rehearsed the invasion of Grenada openly. It practiced the war game *Ocean Venture* in which it bombed the Puerto Rican island of Vieques, calling it "Amber of the Amberdines" (Grenada of the Grenadines). In this grisly make-believe, a situation is

supposed to occur where americans are held hostage. As we know, this was the first excuse used to justify the invasion of Grenada.[36]

Close to the turn of a new millennium, what were once colonial ventures are now war games where citizens and foreigners are held hostage by imperial fictions. The first image of Grenadian men in the essay, the contemporary descendants of seafaring black islanders, the leaders of "the country that mounted the first Black english-speaking People's Revolution in this hemisphere,"[37] is one of a globally imagined black masculinity now imprisoned:

> P.S.Y.O.P.S., the psychological operations unit of the U.S. occupation forces—a new development heard from in combat here for the first time— was quick to plaster [the island] with posters of Bernard Coard and General Hudson Austin, stripped naked and blindfolded, holding them up to ridicule and scorn. . . . Months later, these men are still being held incommunicado in Richmond Hill prison, St. Georges, by "security forces," non-Grenadian. They have not been charged nor brought to trial as of this writing, nor have the forty-odd other Grenadians still detained with them.[38]

For Lorde, the complicated relationships between home and empire, race and domesticity, identity and nation, clearly necessitate black transnational linkages between Caribbeans and African Americans. In a passage that echoes with the underlying message of Eugene O'Neill's drama of black empire at the beginning of the twentieth century, Lorde declaims:

> In addition to being a demonstration to the Caribbean community of what will happen to any country that dares to assume responsibility for its own destiny, the invasion of Grenada also serves as a naked warning to thirty million African-americans. Watch your step. We did it to them down there and we will not hesitate to do it to you. Internment camps. Interrogation booths. Isolation cells hastily built by U.S. occupation forces. Blindfolded stripped prisoners. House-to-house searches for phantom Cubans. Neighbors pressured to inform against each other. No strange gods before us.[39]

Now, twenty years later, we find ourselves back in the Caribbean in Guantanamo Bay. Reading Lorde's report one realizes that in the shadows of empire there really are "no new ideas."[40] Key elements of war we see now were rehearsed twenty years earlier in a Caribbean landscape that throughout the twentieth century increasingly became the stage for the United States's war games and imperial military experiments.

What kind of space is Guantanamo Bay, Cuba? How does it relate to other outposts of empire, the fugitive colonies of the 1920s and 1930s, like Marseilles, France, and the Harlem Black Belt? Does the twentieth century mark not just the dominance of the newly independent nationalist state but the suppression of emergent efforts at black sovereignty in the world we live in and the repression of insurgent attempts to imagine alternative forms of multiracial, multinational social community? Lorde returned to Grenada six weeks after the invasion to interrogate her own location and to see how the Carriacou women had survived. Through her eyes we see the woman of color left behind on island shores resolute and not silent: "Grenadians are a warm and resilient people (I hear my mother's voice: 'Island women make good wives. Whatever happens, they've seen worse'), and they have survived colonizations before."[41] From the windows of her own oppression, by both nationalisms and internationalisms, the Caribbean woman of color may have the clearest eye on the United States's role in the world at large. The Carriacou woman asks us to consider, what are the ways in which we understand our own desires for national affiliation and community, and can these be fulfilled without the interpellations of the state? What does it mean to imagine black love and its related terms, black femininity and masculinity throughout the diaspora, without the securities of home, nation, and heterosexuality?

For New World and U.S. American intellectuals, Audre Lorde provides one of the clearest models of an Ishmael at home, an intellectual who had the courage in a state of emergency to leave her own racial and national context and travel through dark waters to learn from the people living in the fugitive colonies outside the nation and the penalized ghettos within. There are "no new ideas waiting in the wings to save us as women, as human," she asserted, no innocent revolutionary histories, no pure national romances, to replace the masculine global imaginary of the twentieth century for a new millennium. For the black feminist imaginary of a twenty-first century, nothing but retracing the records of the woman of color's journey through imperialist and black nationalist histories—the female fugitive slave's sea voyage narrative, emerging from the residues of colonial and transatlantic history:

I dreamed there was a record album called *Black Women*. The front of the album was a baroque painting depicting a galleon on rough seas. . . . Inset was the portrait of a large light-skinned woman—in a white turban and plain white bodice: dressed as a slave. This woman was also at the helm of the galleon and was identified in fine writing as the first black navigator. The painting, the writing continued, had been taken from a manuscript entitled *Emergam*, Munich, 1663. The dream continued—the manuscript had been proved a fake. We argued about the false and the real . . . (*Emergam* is the first-person future of the latin verb *emergere*: to rise up, emerge, free oneself.)                                —Michelle Cliff[42]

# NOTES

1. Briggs, "Program of the A. B. B.," 1249. All citations from *The Crusader* magazine are taken from a collection that includes most issues, republished as a three-volume set with the final volume in the series encompassing volumes 3–5 of the magazine. The collection was published by Garland in 1987 with an introduction by Robert A. Hill cited separately here. All page numbers used throughout in discussing individual issues or articles in *The Crusader*, including the page numbers of the introduction, refer to the Garland multivolume set.

2. See R. Hill, "Racial and Radical," xlii.

3. The metaphor of the ship of state is itself not uncommon in American political discourse (see C. Miller, *Ship of State*).

4. In *Imagined Communities*, Anderson coins the term "official nationalism" to describe a "willed merger of nation and dynastic empire" that was consolidated after World War I (86). Similarly, in *The Age of Extremes*, Hobsbawm observes that Woodrow Wilson's proposal at the end of the war to set up a League of Nations was one concrete attempt to establish a worldwide political institution that could manage the crises resulting from the decline of empire and the development of the modern nation-state after the war (35). Following the lead of both Anderson and Hobsbawm, throughout this book I refer to the principles of national self-determination that emerged from the Treaty of Versailles as an imperial form of internationalism, grounded in official nationalisms throughout Europe and the Americas

that promoted the sovereign nation-state as the ideal political form for modernity. Also see Wallerstein's work for a more specific discussion of the political alternatives represented in the debates between Woodrow Wilson and V. I. Lenin regarding the new world order put in place after World War 1 (see *Geopolitics and Geoculture*, 2, 10, 141–42; and *After Liberalism*, 108–16, 238–39).

5. Simpson, *North of Jamaica*, 48.

6. Kelley makes this point in his discussion of black American and Caribbean communists during the same period in *Race Rebels*, 105.

7. See Kelley's *Hammer and Hoe* and Robinson's *Black Marxism* for just two highly influential sources on the black radical tradition. More recent historical accounts of black intellectuals' engagement with Russian internationalism in particular, such as Baldwin's study *Beyond the Color Line and the Iron Curtain* and Winston James' *Holding Aloft the Banner of Ethiopia*, also add to this discussion, but Edwards' approach of identifying patterns between individual figures and texts and using close readings to frame a more encompassing theoretical argument about black internationalism as a social, cultural, and intellectual formation most closely resembles my own approach here.

8. Edwards, *The Practice of Diaspora*, 10.

9. See also Edwards, "The Uses of Diaspora."

10. Edwards, *The Practice of Diaspora*, 5.

11. Ibid., 14–15.

12. Ibid., 11.

13. In the 1960s and 1970s, a first surge of scholarly interest in Garvey, beyond that of his contemporaries from the 1920s and 1930s, came with the publication of Cronon's *Black Moses* and A. Garvey's *Garvey and Garveyism*. In the debates surrounding the success and significance of Garvey's movement throughout the 1960s and 1970s, Vincent's *Black Power and the Garvey Movement* and Martin's *Race First* were key texts for broadening the focus on Garvey's nationalism to the Pan-African context of the 1920s. By the time of the publication in 1974 of Clarke's edited collection, *Marcus Garvey and the Vision of Africa*, the editor could say "To call the movement [Marcus Garvey] brought into being a 'back-to-Africa movement' is to narrow its meaning" (3). In *The World of Marcus Garvey* Stein brought a more class-based structural analysis to bear on Garvey's movement, arguing for more attention to intraracial class relations, reinforced by broader race relations within the context of wars, the Depression, and world politics. In a different vein, Watkins-Owens has introduced ethnicity on one hand and American nativism on the other as more specific lenses through which to analyze both Garvey's political formation as a Caribbean immigrant in the United States and the sources of his ultimate failure (*Blood Relations*). Stein and Watkins-Owens's critiques have been followed most recently by the study of the patriarchal character of the movement and its leadership in Ula Taylor's biography, *The Veiled Garvey*. Here Taylor takes a nuanced feminist approach, highlighting both the movement's gender and sexual politics

but also the role of women members and leaders in contesting those constraints (see, for example, 43–45).

14. Both Cooper (*Claude McKay: Rebel Sojourner in the Harlem Renaissance*) and Tillery (*Claude McKay: A Black Poet's Struggle for Identity*) offered key accounts of McKay's life and work, focused on both his poetry and writing in relationship to the Harlem Renaissance and his engagement with the Communist International. But Winston James has argued more recently that we should prioritize McKay's Caribbean context and synthesize it with his American radicalism in the highly influential *Holding Aloft the Banner of Ethiopia* and a biography of McKay's early years, *A Fierce Hatred of Injustice*. There has been a strong tradition in Caribbean literature of writing on McKay's novel *Banana Bottom*, a literature Edmondson reviews in her definitive reading of the novel within the framework of a gendered analysis in *Making Men*. Three recent works read McKay in terms of themes also relevant to this study: Hathaway's *Caribbean Waves*, which focuses on issues of displacement as they appear in McKay's narratives; Edwards's *The Practice of Diaspora*, which offers a reading of *Banjo* that focuses on the novel's relationship to Francophone black and diasporic literatures; and Baldwin's study *Beyond the Color Line and the Iron Curtain*, which focuses on McKay's engagement with Russian internationalism. While discussions in those three works share certain themes with the approach to McKay and his novels provided here, their readings occur without the specific context of empire and its relationship to questions of masculinity and sexuality that are *Black Empire's* focus.

15. In *Caribbean Waves*, Hathaway focuses on McKay's rendering of the mulatto woman more broadly and West Indian women specifically, arguing that "some of the author's most powerful biases converge" in his depictions of these categories of women (61). Hathaway attributes this demonization of women to widespread conceptions of women's sexuality during this period as "representing a pervasive threat to male authority" (62). In contrast, Hathaway sees the female character in *Banjo* as achieving a kind of equal status with the male characters in the context of a more international society, in contrast to "his negative association of women with urban America in *Home to Harlem*" (73). Edwards, too, in *The Practice of Diaspora*, sees Latnah as representing McKay's "uneven approach": "A cogent feminist critique is combined with a problematic insistence about the 'nature' of woman" (209). In chapters 5 and 6 I also explore and compare McKay's constructions of women in these two novels, but my focus on the framing context of empire and heterosexual domesticity leads me to a slightly different reading of the ultimate positioning of these female characters in relationship to men by the end of each novel.

16. The literary and academic revival of C. L. R. James has been a news topic in the press since the mid-nineties (see, for example, Berman, "The Romantic Revolutionary," and Eakin, "Embracing the Wisdom of a Castaway"). This phenomenon was prompted by an outburst of new scholarship following James's death in 1989 and Buhle's biography of the year before (*C. L. R. James: The Artist as Revolutionary*). Buhle's earlier edited collection,

*C. L. R. James: His Life and Work*, was striking in the breadth and range of scholars represented who have been drawn to James as an intellectual presence over the course of the twentieth century. That interdisciplinary range would continue to characterize biographical scholarship on James, from Worcester's political biography (*C. L. R. James: A Political Biography*) to Nielsen's more literary study, *C. L. R. James: A Critical Introduction*. For a second political study of James see also Bogues's *Caliban's Freedom*. Much of this renewed popular and academic interest was also made possible by Grimshaw's comprehensive edited collections of much of James's writings and her insightful contextual analyses that accompanied them (*The C. L. R. James Reader*; *American Civilization*, edited and introduced by Grimshaw and Hart and including an afterword by Robert A. Hill; and *Special Delivery*). For more edited collections specifically placing James's work within the Marxist intellectual tradition, see McLemee and Le Blanc, *C. L. R. James and Revolutionary Marxism*; and Glaberman, *Marxism for Our Times*. McLemee's *C. L. R. James on the 'Negro Question,'* a collection of James's newspaper columns and essays from his early years in the United States, is a key text for positioning James's black radicalism specifically in relationship to African American history, culture, and literary tradition. Finally, also see Cudjoe and Cain, *C. L. R. James: His Intellectual Legacies*, for a collection of essays that reviewed James's career overall as he moved throughout multiple geographic territories.

17. Buhle and Henry collaborated on an essay collection that located James and his work specifically in the Caribbean context in *C. L. R. James's Caribbean*. Also see Farred, *Rethinking C. L. R. James*, a collection seeking to demonstrate James's centrality to "current debates around the issues of postcoloniality and popular culture." For more of Henry's important contributions to re-situating James's radicalism within a Caribbean historical and philosophical context, see *Caliban's Reason*. Most recently, in *C. L. R. James and Creolization*, King argues that James's work across these different fields and spaces can and must be read as a coherent whole. Defining creolization as a process by which European, African, Amerindian, Asian, and American cultures are amalgamated to form new hybrid identities and cultures, King uses this process to understand James's work and life, demonstrating how throughout his career and writing, James articulated a discourse with a consistent methodology. King's reading of James's work in relationship to issues of hybridity and creolization is insightful. My work attempts to place that discourse within the broader rubric of empire, understanding empire as those geopolitical forces that, throughout centuries of colonization and imperialism, have used the Caribbean as the stage for producing hybrid discourses and constraining Creole subjects.

18. See Pease's work for a review of James's influence within American Studies in his introduction to the reprinting of *Mariners, Renegades and Castaways* and the essay "C. L. R. James, *Moby Dick* and the Emergence of Transnational Americas Studies." Also see Pease, "National Narratives, Postnational Narration."

19. See Carby, *Race Men*, 113–34, and Edmondson, *Making Men*, 105–7.

20. King's recent work is impressive in this regard for being the first to attempt a theoretical synthesis of James's oeuvre.

21. Hardt and Negri, *Empire*.

22. Ibid., xii.

23. In the broadest of sweeps, necessarily brief and therefore incomplete, the scholarship on European imperialism can be divided into roughly two strands, historical and discursive. The first is reviewed and represented in Hobsbawm's *The Age of Empire, 1875–1914*. Hobsbawm, writing in a twentieth-century tradition that begins with Hobson's 1902 study *Imperialism*, describes the late nineteenth and early twentieth centuries as an imperial age rife with contradictions yet crucial to the shaping of our modern world. Hobson's text, cited in early scholarship as the principal English work on imperialism, was also an important starting point for Lenin's 1916 pamphlet *Imperialism* (reprinted with an introduction by Lewis and Malone that places Lenin's text in dialogue with contemporary discussions of globalization). From a different political perspective, one might also place in this tradition Niall Ferguson's *Empire*, a text interesting for my purposes because it offers British imperialism as a model for the United States's contemporary reemergence as a world power also resembling an empire.

24. See Said, *Orientalism* and *Culture and Imperialism*.

25. For more of an account of the critical intervention Said made as "simultaneously extraordinarily enabling and theoretically problematic," see Young, *Postcolonialism*, 383.

26. This turn was initiated by Kaplan and Pease in their influential collection, *Cultures of United States Imperialism*. An intervention in the field of American studies, their work also laid the groundwork for the emerging notion that the United States performs a different kind of imperialism than heretofore (but see Kaplan's introductory discussion of the problem of American exceptionalism even in discussions of the United States empire).

27. Hardt and Negri, *Empire*, xii, xiv.

28. Pierson, *The Modern State*, 14. Pierson includes sovereignty as one of nine characteristics of modern states, which also include monopoly (control of the means of violence); territoriality; constitutionality; impersonal power; the public bureaucracy; authority and legitimacy; citizenship; and taxation. See also Hardt and Negri, *Empire*, 93.

29. Pierson on territoriality: "Modern states [are] geographic or geo-political entities. States occupy [a] . . . clearly-defined physical space over which they characteristically claim sole legitimate authority" (*The Modern State*, 12). Appadurai's essay, "Sovereignty without Territoriality," is key for placing these questions of sovereignty and territoriality within an emerging discourse on "postnational cartographies," a discourse scholars such as Pease have also utilized in defining a postnational American studies. Appadurai's sovereignty without territoriality posits Caribbean and African diasporic populations as engaged in creating forms of political community that have a "tendency to use the territorial imaginary of the nation-state to grasp and mobilize the large-scale and dispersed populations of the contem-

porary world into transnational ethnic formations" (55). In *Black Empire* I ask that we consider alternative expressions of black transnationality in which *race* stands as the figure for a *global* (rather than a national) imaginary, specifically constituted out of an abandonment of the quest for territorially based state forms.

30. Pierson, *The Modern State*, 40.

31. Hardt and Negri, *Empire*, xii.

32. Amy Kaplan, *The Anarchy of Empire in the Making of U.S. Culture*, 13–14. Kaplan also argues here that the two tendencies, Empire and imperialism, "are not as distinct as Hardt and Negri contend, but that both are at work in varied configurations throughout the history of U.S. imperialism" (15).

33. Throughout I shall use empire with a small "e" to capture a discursive array that includes both "imperialism" and "Empire" as described above.

34. Carr has recently taken a similarly diasporic comparative approach to studying New World politics in terms of colonial geography and history, situating both Caribbean and African American narratives in relation to both the discourses of and the scholarship on nationalism (see *Black Nationalism in the New World*).

35. In *Colonial Desire* Young identifies two discursive meanings and histories for the term "hybridity." In the more familiar usage of the twentieth century, "hybrid" often designates cultural phenomena that are "carnivalesque" and "creolized" or that demonstrate a "radical heterogeneity" (25). Alternatively, Young traces a nineteenth-century genealogy in which the term refers to physiological phenomenon, discussions of species and racial mixing that essentially reveal how "theories of race were thus also covert theories of desire" (9). My account here is indebted to Young's integration of questions of sexuality and desire into his discussions of race, nation, and cultural identity. However, *Black Empire* argues precisely that these should not be seen as two separate discourses of hybridity, nor should we be shocked that in one lies the prehistory of the other. Rather, one quite naturally leads to and provides a genealogy of the other. Imperial racial discourses from the nineteenth century, both concerning and constituted by questions of racial hybridity, are the terrain in which twentieth-century diasporic cultures and subjects are racially and discursively constrained and then able to generate their own alternative discursive offspring. "Hybridity" then becomes specifically a discourse with a genealogy in empire, with different manifestations at different moments of empire, in different subjects' hands. An additional suggestion here is that, despite Young's cogent point that "whichever model of hybridity may be employed . . . hybridity as a cultural description will always carry with it an implicit politics of heterosexuality" (25). As we shall see in the work of James and McKay, this sexual politics can still generate rebellious meanings and constructions of masculinity which, precisely in engagement with and in defiance of a heterosexual politics, create more homosocial desires for community and more homoerotic forms of national longing.

36. Gilroy, *Against Race*, 95, 56–57, 62–65.

37. Hardt and Negri also acknowledge the important role of the colony as a shaping

counterforce in empire's construction and enactment of sovereignty: "Modern sovereignty is a European concept in the sense that it developed primarily in Europe in coordination with the evolution of modernity itself. . . . Although modern sovereignty emanated from Europe, however, it was born and developed in large part through Europe's relationship with its outside, and particularly through its colonial project and the resistance of the colonized" (*Empire*, 70).

38. See Mignolo, "Globalization, Civilization Processes, and the Relocation of Languages and Cultures," for more on colonial, "barbarian" border thinking and *Local Histories/Global Designs* for his description of the colonial intellectual as an "other thinking" (67).

39. Mignolo, "Globalization, Civilization Processes, and the Relocation of Languages and Cultures," 34, 45, 51.

40. Mignolo, *Local Histories/Global Designs*, 39.

41. In this instance, the discourses of a black empire deviate from and sit in a space between those of a black Atlantic formation which Gilroy describes in the following terms: "The modes of belonging articulated through appeals to the power of sovereign territory and the bonds of rooted, exclusive national cultures, are contrasted with the different translocal solidarities that have been constituted by diaspora dispersal and estrangement" (*Against Race*, 8); here Gilroy restates and reworks his influential argument on the meaning of the term diaspora in a black context in *The Black Atlantic*.

42. Lloyd, *Ireland after History*, 27. Also see Lloyd and Lowe, *The Politics of Culture in the Shadow of Capital*.

43. For an excellent review of and debate on the meaning, history, use, genealogy, and politics of the term diaspora in contemporary black studies, see Patterson and Kelley, "Unfinished Migrations: Reflections on the African Diaspora and the Making of the Modern World." This discussion, prompted by an essay by Patterson and Kelley and including responses by scholars Brent Hayes Edwards, Cheryl Johnson-Odim, Agustín Laó-Montes, and Michael West, with further articles on both the West African context and the potential for Afro-Indian alliances by Hakim Adi and Vijay Prashad, respectively, is much too rich to be glossed effectively here. In brief, the essays and commentaries address questions of gender, geography, and language in our definitions of a black diaspora and also posit the difference it might make to think of black *globality* as a framework broader than that of the *diaspora*, with the latter's focus on racial dispersion and descent as primary and originary terms. Furthermore, both the debate and each essay's concomitant footnotes provide an excellent introduction to, review of, and engagement with the work of some of the field's most prominent scholars (figures such as Carole Boyce Davies, Locksley Edmondson, Brenda Gayle Plummer, Paul Gilroy, Michael Hanchard, Winston James) and reference to exciting forthcoming work such as Bair's eagerly anticipated *Freedom Is Never A Final Act*.

44. This analysis certainly builds on and is indebted to the insights of scholars who have approached him from those directions, recognizing their centrality to our cumulative knowledge about Marcus Garvey's project.

45. Work by feminist scholars and scholars of sexuality in deconstructing languages of empire and nation in their correlation with gendered discourses of colonial desire has been key. See McClintock (*Imperial Leather*), Kim Hall (*Things of Darkness*), Young (*Colonial Desire*), and Kaplan and Grewal (*Scattered Hegemonies*). *Black Empire* explores similar questions, of both imperial desires and the colonial subject's desire and search for national forms, but in the specific context of World War I when geopolitical events shaped black male intellectuals' gendered constructions of the racial diaspora in tropes of male sovereignty and female hybridity.

46. See Anderson's *Imagined Communities*, on one hand, where the notion of the nation as an imagined community depends on its bounded nature geographically (30) and Gilroy, on the other, for whom diaspora entails an imagination of community that extends beyond national boundaries (*The Black Atlantic, Against Race*), what he has also termed elsewhere an "outernational" consciousness and critique (see '*There Ain't No Black in the Union Jack*', 190–91).

47. This governmental or structural feature of modern empires, pointed to in the scholarship of various figures and essential to the argument of this book, situates empire primarily as a state form with jurisdiction beyond the geographic borders of the nation, extending into the colonial world. Lloyd, for example, sees "the mid nineteenth century emergence of the British state as governing power" as "definitive" in connecting "the function of the modern state" intimately with colonialism (*Ireland After History*, 7). Pierson defines modern empires as precisely the "external domain of already-established nation-states" (*The Modern State*, 12). Hardt and Negri also define imperialism as "really an extension of the sovereignty of the European nation-states beyond their own boundaries" (*Empire*, xii). They too acknowledge the splitting of empire's construction and enactment of sovereignty into separate domestic and colonial realms: "Modern sovereignty emerged, then, as the concept of European reaction and European domination both within and outside its borders. They are two coextensive and complementary faces of one development: rule within Europe and European rule over the world" (70).

48. Hence David Lloyd's sense of the colony and colonial space as offering an "interface between the state and the popular forms of the colonized . . . a labile space in which each undergoes transformation" (*Ireland after History*, 45).

49. Gilroy makes a similar distinction in describing the difference shaping Martin Delany's notions of racial homeland as "fatherland" versus Robert Campbell's designation of Africa as the "*mother*land." As Gilroy states: "Delany's primary concern was not with Africa as such but rather with the forms of citizenship and belonging that arose from the (re)generation of modern nationality in the form of an autonomous, black nation state" (*The Black Atlantic*, 23).

50. Boyce Davies, *Black Women, Writing and Identity*.

51. Ibid., 113, 96, 113, 88.

52. Griffin, "*Who Set You Flowin'?*"

53. Ibid., 7.

54. See Carby's *Race Men* and Edmondson's *Making Men*, respectively. For Caribbean uses of the term New World Negro, see, for example, Walcott's representation of Caribbean masculinity in his essay "What the Twilight Says."

55. For further examples of Carby's work, important for recovering and analyzing black female political agency and migratory subjectivities, see *Reconstructing Womanhood* and her influential essay, "It Jus Be's Dat Way Sometime: The Sexual Politics of Women's Blues," reprinted in *Cultures in Babylon*. In addition to Boyce Davies's influential *Black Women, Writing, and Identity*, see a series of important edited collections including Boyce Davies and Fido, *Out of the Kumbla*; Boyce Davies and Ogundipe-Leslie, *Moving Beyond Boundaries*; and Boyce Davies, Okpewho, and Mazrui, *The African Diaspora*. Also see Patterson and Kelley, "Unfinished Migrations," for a further review of work noting and challenging "how the masculinist metaphors of diaspora and nationalism lend themselves to genealogical and historical reconstructions that leave women out" (29).

56. Nassy Brown, "Black Liverpool, Black America, and the Gendering of Diasporic Space," 301. Also see Nassy Brown, "Enslaving History."

57. Du Bois, *The Souls of Black Folk*, 54.

58. Lamming as quoted in C. L. R. James, "From Toussaint L'Ouverture to Fidel Castro," in Grimshaw, *The C. L. R. James Reader*, 311.

59. For an account that frames my discussion of the romance of heterosexuality and the politics of heterosexual domesticity, see anthropologist Liisa Malkki's discussions of the metaphor of the family of man in internationalist geopolitical discourses. In "National Geographic" and in "Citizens of Humanity," Malkki argues that internationalism itself, as a political ideology, should also be viewed as a transnational cultural form and that "Both the national and the international . . . are aspects of an overarching 'national order of things'" ("Citizens of Humanity," 41–42). Here Malkki draws from Balibar's influential essay "The Nation Form: History and Ideology" (in Balibar and Wallerstein, *Race, Nation, Class*) to argue that "the international order itself serves to reproduce, naturalize, legitimate, and even generate 'the nation form' all over the world" ("Citizens of Humanity," 42). Malkki's argument here overlaps with my own observations about the World War I moment, but Malkki is specifically interested in the use of the metaphor of the family to represent the system of nation-states put in place after World War I. As she describes, "many forms of idealized, ritualized internationalism celebrate . . . an egalitarian brotherhood or sisterhood of nations . . . but one can hardly miss the continual metaphoric slide from harmonious egalitarianism to steeply hierarchical family and gender metaphors. The *Family* of Nations has senior and junior members, parents and children, just as it has masculine and feminine members" (51). This was precisely the ritual underpinnings of the League of Nations's version of internationalism that would shape black writer Claude McKay's relationship to heterosexual domesticity immediately after the war. (Also see Malkki's discussion of the refugee and the national order of things in the context of post–World War II discussions in

"Refugees and Exile.") Latin Americanist Sommer's work on the national romance is also central to my readings of heterosexual domesticity in McKay's novels in chapters 5 and 6 (see *Foundational Fictions* and "Irresistable Romance").

60. I argue here that in the 1940s, C. L. R. James was beginning to understand the emerging postcolonial world through a transnational framework, centered precisely on the *erosion* of the independence of the nation-state, rather than the postcolonial and neocolonial framework of the late 1960s through the 1980s, centered on the level of independence of new states in the colonial world.

61. See Hardt and Negri (*Empire*, 4, 172–79) for more on the special role of President Woodrow Wilson, the League of Nations, and the United States constitution for creating different languages of empire that constructed a new international order and pointed the way toward a more global order (understanding "international" here as a space in which the politics and competing claims of nations still play a directive role and "global" as the move to an entirely different world order in which the sovereignty of the nation-state has been superseded).

62. See Niall Ferguson's *Empire* and various pieces in the popular press, such as Ignatieff's "The American Empire (Get Used to It.)," with the following question as its subheading: "The Burden: With a military of unrivaled might, the United States rules a new kind of empire. Will this cost America its soul—or save it?" (22).

63. In two works reviewed in the *New York Times Book Review*, Mandelbaum's *The Ideas That Conquered the World* and MacMillan's *Paris 1919*, the authors give accounts of Woodrow Wilson's politics that attempt to make United States discourses of internationalism from the early twentieth century relevant again for our contemporary era of globalization and United States global dominance. While agreeing with one reviewer's assertion that "the Treaty of Versailles is the best starting place for anyone who wants to understand the modern world," I disagree with both reviewers in their lack of an assessment of the authors' avoidance of issues related to racial and colonial self-determination during this period (see Tyler, "The World Cries Uncle," and Judt, "We'll Always Have Paris").

64. Lamming, *The Pleasures of Exile*, 118.

65. The Prospero/Caliban dialectic from Shakespeare's *The Tempest* has been a defining trope in Caribbean New World literature and a key theme in postcolonial literature and criticism. See Lamming's *The Pleasures of Exile* (95–150), Fernández Retamar's *Caliban and Other Essays*, and Césaire's *A Tempest* for Anglophone, Latin American, and Francophone uses of the Caliban trope, respectively. Also see Saldívar, *The Dialectics of Our America*, for an overall summary of "The School of Caliban" in Caribbean discourse and literary criticism (123–48). In *Black Empire* the terms "Caribbean" and "West Indian" are used interchangeably to describe the region and its peoples, with the latter having slightly more applicability as a specific designation for matters concerning the English-speaking islands, also the primary focus here. Unlike Lamming, however, I do not agree that one can "switch from

island to island without changing the meaning." Language and cultural differences among the islands and continental areas of the Caribbean impact their differing approaches to and perspectives on questions of both state and identity formation. For an integrated approach to the region that also attempts to stay attentive to the local in interesting ways, see Kurlansky's *A Continent of Islands*.

66. Glissant, *Caribbean Discourse*, and Benítez-Rojo, *The Repeating Island*.

67. See Clifford, *The Predicament of Culture*, 173. Also see Caren Kaplan's deconstruction of Clifford's notion of "cosmopolitan hybridity" contained in her general critique of the concept of travel as an assertion of Eurocentric, modernist, and masculinist paradigms in *Questions of Travel*, 127. Colonial hybridity, as opposed to cosmopolitan hybridity, contextualizes the travels of both colonial and metropolitan subjects within modernity as also reconfiguring the journeys of the colonized and the colonizer, over time and across space, within and against the framework of empire. For one such use of the term "colonial hybridity," also see Lloyd, *Ireland after History*, 46.

68. In *Nations Unbound*, Basch, Glick Schiller, and Szanton Blanc use the term "transnational" to describe a new type of immigrant who retains physical, emotional, and political connections to both their nation of origin and their nation of settlement (7). In so doing they also argue for a view of their work as providing a structural analysis that differs from the discourse of contemporary transnational cultural studies. They assert: "Scholars of transnational culture speak in the vocabulary of postmodernism and make reference to hybridity, hyperspace, displacement, disjuncture, decentering, and diaspora . . . [and] 'creolization'" (27). Though "productive of a new imagery," the authors claim "much of this discourse on transnationalism has remained evocative rather than analytical" (28) and argue in contrast: "We think that the current period, in which the construct of the deterritorialized nation-state is being forcefully articulated, can best be conceived as the moment of a new nationalism" (30). Approaching questions of statehood and belonging from the perspective, one could say, of the migrant as opposed to that of the state, the authors arrive at conclusions parallel to those of scholars such as Hardt and Negri in their discussions of sovereignty. However, in *Black Empire* I argue that these two levels of analysis—the structural and the cultural discursive—are not at all mutually exclusive, and I see the Caribbean island colonies as precisely the stage where discussions that link the two can be historicized and made material in terms of geographic and geopolitical context. Caribbean hybridity finds its origins in coloniality, in a colonial state and structure created from hybridized imperial claims to sovereignty in the region. The desire for and enactment of multiple forms of national belonging have always been essential components of the hybrid political identities and histories of the Caribbean, even before twentieth-century mass transnational migrations out of colonial and national spaces.

69. Linebaugh and Rediker, *The Many-Headed Hydra*.

70. See chapter 4 for more on Sale's discussion of rebellious masculinity as a trope in

nineteenth-century United States revolutionary discourse in *The Slumbering Volcano*. Also see eighteenth-century scholar Aravamudan's coinage of the term "tropicalization" to describe resistant discourses offered by and about colonial subjects in tropical spaces during the long eighteenth century. As he describes, "I would like to propose the term tropicopolitan as a name for the colonized subject who exists both as fictive construct of colonial tropology *and* actual resident of tropical space, object of representation *and* agent of resistance" (*Tropicopolitans*, 4). Of course the most common Caribbean alternative history here is that of Haiti, but again, even that island's revolutionary history can be read both within national and across transatlantic borders. In the late eighteenth and nineteenth centuries Haiti served as both an example of territorial independence from slavery and as a source of inspiration for a broader community of traveling black subjects. Many black sailors unable to be a part of the dream were inspired by it anyway to believe in alternative forms of black freedom. See Bolster, *Black Jacks*, 131–57.

71. In a talk given at a conference in Essex, Peter Hulme quoted White's employment of the term "tropic" from *Tropics of Discourse* to connote both the ideological work of language and tropes in the colonial enterprise, and the geographical space of the Caribbean itself (Hulme, "Hurricanes in the Caribbees: The Constitution of the Discourse of English Colonialism").

72. For example, in their preface Hardt and Negri call for a "geography [of] alternative powers, the new cartography [that] is still waiting to be written—or really, it is being written today through the resistances, struggles, and desires of the multitude" (*Empire*, xvi). Here they fail to engage *blackness*, and the Caribbean and colonial worlds more explicitly, as the stage in which the resistance of the multitudes to Empire and imperialism has been performed, both in everyday acts of resistance and historical waves of marronage and revolution.

73. Du Bois, "Worlds of Color."

74. Du Bois, "Worlds of Color," 385.

75. Ibid., 388, 393–94, 388–89.

76. Ibid., 401.

77. Briggs, "Program of the A.B.B.," 1251.

78. Hobsbawm, *The Age of Extremes*, 22–23.

79. Anderson, *Imagined Communities*, 86.

80. Hobsbawm, *The Age of Extremes*, 55–56.

81. Ibid., 35.

82. Anderson, *Imagined Communities*, 113.

83. Hobsbawm, *The Age of Extremes*, 31.

84. Du Bois, "Worlds of Color," 401–2.

85. Marcus Garvey, "Speech at Royal Albert Hall" (1928), reprinted in Clarke, *Marcus Garvey and the Vision of Africa*, 285.

86. Benítez-Rojo, *The Repeating Island*, 2.

87. C. L. R. James, "From Toussaint L'Ouverture to Fidel Castro," in Grimshaw, *The*

*C. L. R. James Reader*, 296–314. The essay was written in 1962 but originally appeared, along with a revised preface, in the 1963 revised edition of James's *The Black Jacobins*.

88. Ibid., 296, 298, 296.

89. James's language should be more familiar to us today as one used to distinguish diasporic movements, languages, and cultures from those of nation-states (see Gilroy, *Against Race*, 128). For some this form of oppositional movement is postmodern and repetitive instead of one that follows a modernist logic of progression to a revolutionary, culminating finale (see Benítez-Rojo, *The Repeating Island*). For others, these types of movements form random and uncoordinated "local cultures of resistance" in opposition to the grand movements and totalizing narratives of international forces such as globalization, imperialism, and world capitalism (see Lloyd and Lowe, introduction to *The Politics of Culture in the Shadow of Capital*). But for James, not only was "the inherent movement [in the Caribbean] clear and strong," it also had a local and a global orientation.

90. Knight, *The Caribbean*, xiv. Here Knight argues that the ideal of statehood as a way of uniting scattered black communities has shaped the political journey of the Caribbean nations. As he describes, "Creating an independent state was one way to begin the process of harmonizing the various sentiments and attitudes that must eventually be synthesized into a national sentiment" (310). But, he also concludes, "the confidence that these goals—state, nationalism, identity—would provide the panacea for the good life is waning" (308).

91. Edmondson, *Making Men*, 107.

92. Ibid., 10.

93. There are clearly Caribbean women writers and intellectuals addressing these issues of empire, coloniality, national independence, statehood, and federation in the period this book covers, between World War I and Trinidadian and Jamaican national independence (most notably, see Taylor's biography of Amy Jacques Garvey, *The Veiled Garvey*, and Paravisini-Gebert's biography of Phyllis Shand Allfrey (*Phyllis Shand Allfrey*). But the terms of debate, the focus on the male sovereign and his concomitant hybrid partner, is a discourse shaped by masculine concerns, linking racial freedom and national independence with state sovereignty specifically. That some women writers also incorporate these tropes in their narratives only further reinforces my point that the tropes and the discourse are gendered, as much as are the writers.

94. In terms of the broader focus on issues of black female travel and mobility, the work of scholars such as Boyce Davies, Farah Jasmine Griffin, Hazel Carby, Cheryl Fish, and Heather Hathaway are central (also see Griffin and Fish, *A Stranger in the Village*).

95. Du Bois, "Worlds of Color," 411.

96. Ibid.

97. Ibid., 413.

98. Knight, *The Caribbean*, 308.

99. Hardt and Negri on the multitude's critical location within empire: "We should be done once and for all with the search for an outside, a standpoint that imagines a purity for

our politics. It is better both theoretically and practically to enter the terrain of Empire and confront its homogenizing and heterogenizing flows in all their complexity, grounding our analysis in the power of the global multitude" (*Empire*, 46).

100. Labat as quoted in Knight, *The Caribbean*, 307.


I THE NEW WORLDLY NEGRO

1. Schuyler, *Black Empire*, 336.

2. For the sake of clarity, this assumption governs all citations to the story here as authored by Cyril V. Briggs.

3. Briggs, "The Ray of Fear," 614. This issue was also famous in radical circles for inaugurating the founding of the militant ABB.

4. Nazima is also often spelled "Mazima" in the story.

5. See, for example, Hanchard's observation in "Identity, Meaning and the African-American" that "embedded in the tale of the diaspora is a symbolic revolt against the nation-state, and for this reason the diaspora . . . suggests a transnational dimension to black identity" (40). Also see Gilroy's discussions of diaspora in *The Black Atlantic* (4, 29) and *Against Race* (8, 81–84, 123–25) and Edwards's genealogy of the term in "The Uses of Diaspora" and introductory discussion in *The Practice of Diaspora* (11–15).

6. See Worsley's *The Three Worlds* for both the historicization and deployment of theories of the three worlds in studies of national and economic development. For a contemporary attempt to rewrite the story of human development from a scientific antiracist point of view see, Diamond's *Guns, Germs, and Steel*.

7. "Society as a whole is more and more splitting up into two great hostile camps, into two great classes directly facing each other: bourgeoisie and proletariat." Marx and Engels, *The Communist Manifesto*, 35.

8. Briggs, "The Ray of Fear," 614.

9. Ibid.

10. Jamaica and Trinidad were the first two islands in the Anglophone Caribbean to achieve independence in August 1962. The only other Anglophone island to achieve independence in the 1960s was Barbados in 1966.

11. Hill, "Racial and Radical," xi.

12. For a discussion of expressions of the Great Migration in African American cultural and literary forms see Griffin's work in "*Who Set You Flowin'?*"; for a discussion of the "inter-ethnic" black community created in Harlem in the years preceding the Depression due to the influx of West Indian immigrants, see Watkins-Owens's *Blood Relations*.

13. Allen, "The New Negro," 49.

14. Stephens, "Eric Walrond's *Tropic Death* and the Discontents of American Modernity."

15. Gates, "The Trope of a New Negro and the Reconstruction of the Image of the Black," 129.

16. Ibid.

17. John Henry Adams, "The New Negro Man" (1904), quoted in Gates, "The Trope of a New Negro and the Reconstruction of the Image of the Black," 142.

18. Gates, "The Trope of a New Negro and the Reconstruction of the Image of the Black," 139. Hence the significance of the fact that a figure such as Martin R. Delany was commissioned as the first black major in the United States Army.

19. Bederman, *Manliness and Civilization*.

20. Ibid., 4.

21. Also see Carby, *Race Men*.

22. See Carby's discussion in *Race Men* of the presence of Victorian definitions of "gentlemanliness" in DuBois's own writing and self-construction, and her specific critical addition to Bederman's account—that discourses of civilization became yoked in the early twentieth century to discourses of the nation (47).

23. Edmondson, *Making Men*, 6–7. Jamaican American poet Louis Simpson confirmed Edmondson's analysis in his autobiographical account of his own identity formation as a Caribbean male subject (see *North of Jamaica*, 48).

24. Edmondson, *Making Men*, 5.

25. Ibid. This of course meant that, in the Caribbean, the national leader was often well educated and typically from the middle classes, in other words, a member of the colonial intelligentsia. This class identity shaped the gender politics of the actual men who participated in West Indian politics and the masculine tropes they created to imagine political subjectivity.

26. A point Edmondson also notes on page 177 by referencing Bederman's work.

27. In her discussion of nineteenth-century Pan-Africanism before Garvey, Stein points out that "Pan-Africanism was created by an international black elite that included persons from West Africa, the Caribbean, the United States, and occasionally England, the boundaries of the old Atlantic slave trade. They were lawyers, teachers, social workers, journalists, students, civil servants, and churchmen—modern men who made up only a small minority of the black world. . . . They were an elite [who] purveyed new power, new ideas, and new possibilities" (*The World of Marcus Garvey*, 7). Also see Gaines's *Uplifting the Race* for an important discussion of black men's uses of Roosevelt's discourse of "strenuous life masculinity" to construct their own nationalist and internationalist visions of the race (113–14).

28. For more on the African American male's gender construction in a domestic context during the Harlem Renaissance period, see Carby, *Race Men*, 27.

29. Naipaul's famous declaration that Caribbeans were a people without history defined a generation of male scholars and writers in exile such as Louis Simpson, Edward Kamau Brathwaite, George Lamming, and Derek Walcott. See Naipaul's *The Middle Passage*, 29. Also see E. Brathwaite, *Roots*; Lamming, *The Pleasures of Exile*; and Walcott, "What the Twilight Says."

30. As Bolster has identified, this was true for black American seamen even earlier than

their domestic counterparts, American slaves. In *Black Jacks* Bolster tells us that "beginning in 1796, the federal government issued Seamen's Protection Certificates to merchant mariners, defining them as 'citizens' of the United States" (5).

31. There is clear overlap between the trope of the Victorian "gentleman" central in Anglophone Caribbean nationalist discourse and the late-nineteenth-century trope of the New Negro in post–Civil War African American narratives. For example, the heroes in the three black empire narratives discussed in chapter 2 were all clearly represented as college-educated black men. The Victorian ideal of the educated gentleman is clearly a subtext in the image of middle class and elite black male leadership in late-nineteenth-century African American letters. Even the twentieth-century New Negro had these bourgeois elements of the Victorian gentleman, as Carby has described in her re-naming of the trope of the New Negro as the "race man," a dominant figure for black masculine leadership and self-determination in the United States throughout the twentieth century. See Carby, *Race Men*, 20–21. Also see R. Hill, "Making Noise," 181–205), for an account of the blending of the New Negro with the Victorian Caribbean gentleman scholar in Marcus Garvey's early self-construction.

32. Also see Kelley's *Race Rebels* for more of a discussion of the languages of masculinity and revolutionary leadership present in the radical discourse of the New Negro during the late 1920s and 1930s (113–15).

33. Kelley, introduction, 2. James was more invested in the gender and sexual politics of male leadership than Kelley raises here. As I show in chapter 7, James's interests in the masculine leadership of the race led him historically to the fugitive slave, but also to Paul Robeson as the cultural icon of the 1920s who could best represent the race and a modern black subjectivity. Also see discussions of the Jamesian hero and masculinity in Carby's *Race Men* and Edmondson's *Making Men*.

34. Paul Robeson was the African American cultural figure who often best represented and embodied this black, male, working-class internationalism. As such, he appears and reappears throughout my discussions on Marcus Garvey, Claude McKay, and C. L. R. James. In his essay "Paul Robeson," (reprinted in *Spheres of Existence*; page numbers are from the latter) James even went so far as to describe Robeson as having the potential to pick up Garvey's mantle of race leadership: "I was in the United States busily noting all that was going on in politics concerning Black people, and I became certain . . . that if Paul had wanted to he would have built a movement in the United States that would have been the natural successor to the Garvey movement. . . . I can say, and it will be easy to prove, that people were looking to Paul to start such a movement" (262). For discussions of Paul Robeson's complex, layered, and at times contradictory cultural meanings during this period, see Denning's *The Cultural Front*, 115–18, and Carby's *Race Men*, chapter 2.

35. Schuyler, *Black Empire*, 336.

36. Gates, "The Trope of a New Negro and the Reconstruction of the Image of the Black," 132.

37. Ibid., 147.

38. In addition to the works by Allen, Kelley, and James referenced above, see Naison's *Communists in Harlem During the Depression*, 5.

39. Allen, "The New Negro," 53.

40. Ibid.

41. See Denning, who defines cultural fronts as a framework which enables scholars in American Studies to "theorize the relation of culture to politics," to think more broadly about the relationship between actual political movements and the utopian, cultural discourses which may both set the stage for them and exist long after the movements have passed (*The Cultural Front*, xix).

42. Until recently, scholars of Pan-Africanism and Caribbean radicalism in the United States (such as Hill, Kelley, Allen, and James) were primarily the ones to take seriously the radical internationalist cultural politics of the black working class during the 1920s and 1930s. In recent works by a group of Americanists we see the development of a more nuanced and serious approach in American studies to a black cultural and literary politics of radical internationalism that began during this period and extends into the late twentieth century. See Denning's *Cultural Front* but also Smethurst, *The New Red Negro*; Mullen, *Popular Fronts*; and Maxwell, *New Negro, Old Left*. Also see more recently Peterson's *Up From Bondage* and Baldwin's *Beyond the Color Line and the Iron Curtain* for more on shared features in black American and Russian internationalist cultures and discourses. For a recent collection of essays linking race and class radicalism in American culture, see *Left of the Color Line*, edited by Mullen and Smethurst.

43. A number of scholars have described the impact of Caribbean immigrants and their politics on life in Harlem during the early decades of the twentieth century. See Naison's *Communists in Harlem During the Depression* and Watkins-Owens's *Blood Relations* but also Kasinitz's *Caribbean New York*. For a polemical account of the impact of West Indians on African American radical politics, see Cruse, *The Crisis of the Negro Intellectual*. For a comprehensive history of the Caribbean radical tradition in the United States see Winston James's *Holding Aloft the Banner of Ethiopia*.

44. In *Race Against Empire*, her study of black American anticolonialism between 1937 and 1957, Von Eschen charts the later involvement of African Americans during World War II in the fight for African national independence. This study overlaps with hers in its focus on black anticolonialism and the threat it posed to the United States empire in its governmental policies both at home and abroad. However, it differs from hers in that I follow, during an earlier period, the increased interest in the New World, rather than Africa, as the space to locate the black diaspora's desires for statehood and political independence.

45. Garvey scholar Tony Martin has also argued that Garvey's poetry and creative writings published in the pages of the *Negro World* should also be seen as part and parcel of the literary outpouring and consciousness of the Harlem Renaissance. See *Literary Garveyism* and *The Poetical Works of Marcus Garvey*.

46. This phrase first appears as part of *The Crusader's* masthead in February 1920, the same month and year as both the first installment of "The Ray of Fear" and the founding of the ABB ( 597).

47. See Hill, "Racial and Radical," xv.

48. Allen, "The New Negro," 53.

49. Briggs, "The League of Nations."

50. Briggs, "If It Were Only True."

51. Briggs, "What Does Democratic America in Haiti?"

52. Bourne, "Trans-national America" (reprinted in Hansen, *Randolph Bourne, The Radical Will*, 257–58). Bourne's piece was first given as a lecture at Harvard titled "The Jew and Trans-National America" and was first published in *The Menorah Journal* in December 1916. The latter essay can be found in Bourne, *War and the Intellectuals*.

53. Hansen, *Randolph Bourne, The Radical Will*, 255. Emphasis added.

54. Ibid., 258.

55. Bourne's utopian image of a "federated" America of "hyphenates"—"a cosmopolitan federation of national colonies, of foreign cultures"—still has progressive utility today (Hansen, *Randolph Bourne, The Radical Will*, 253, 258). In *Modernity at Large*, Appadurai argues: "For every nation-state that has exported significant numbers of its population to the United States as refugees, tourists, or students, there is now a delocalized *transnation*." He continues: "No existing conception of Americanness can contain this large variety of trans-nations. In this scenario, the hyphenated American might have to be twice hyphenated (Asian-American-Japanese or . . . African-American-Jamaican. . . . Or perhaps the sides of the hyphen will have to be reversed, and we can become a federation of diasporas" (172–73). (Also see Buell's discussion of Appadurai's work in *National Culture and the New Global System*, 215.)

56. Schmitt, *The Concept of the Political*, 55–56.

57. This is one of the central premises of Gilroy's argument in *The Black Atlantic*, that the slave trade created diaspora in the dispersion of Africans to the New World. See also *Against Race*, where Gilroy states: "Slavery, pogroms, indenture, genocide, and other unnameable terrors have all figured in the constitution of diasporas and the reproduction of diaspora consciousness" (123–24). Yet, Gilroy continues: "The nation-state has regularly been presented as the institutional means to terminate diaspora dispersal." Citizenship and nationalism become, for Gilroy, diaspora's unnecessary but historical limit. *Black Empire* then asks, how do diasporic *desires* for both free statehood and free movement get expressed? And as the black intellectuals described here discussed, can the black subject keep moving within the nation? (My questions here are also indebted to the insights of political scientist Michael Hanchard, presented in an unpublished talk to the Institution for Social and Policy Studies, Yale University, 8 May 1997.)

58. Du Bois, *Darkwater*, 146. Du Bois's black transnational perspective still provides a

succinct counterargument to the vision of United States internationalism from 1919 that is being revived at the beginning of the twenty-first century.

## 2 THE WOMAN OF COLOR AND LITERATURE

1. Briggs, "The Ray of Fear," 614.

2. See Gilroy on music and other vernacular forms of performance in *The Black Atlantic* (36, 74–5, 200–1). Here my analysis also benefits from Andrews's preface to Andrews and Gates, *Pioneers of the Black Atlantic*. Andrews provides a framework for rethinking certain authors of slave narratives and their texts as part of a "Black Atlantic community of English-speaking writers, intellectuals, and activists visibly at work in the late eighteenth century, and transnational in their experience and point of view" (vii). Andrews further describes a group of black male eighteenth-century thinkers, including Ottobah Cugoano, John Jea, John Marrant, Olaudah Equiano, and James Albert Okawsaw Gronniosaw. Representing them as "truly men of the world" Andrews asserts, "At home in a fluid and dynamic Atlantic world defined by multiple identifications with Africa, England, and America, the writers . . . cannot be easily categorized as African, African-American, or Afro-British" (viii). Similarly, *Black Empire* seeks to locate male intellectuals such as James, Garvey, McKay and their African American counterparts, men such as Du Bois, Schuyler, and Robeson, as intellectuals who, along with other traveling black subjects such as women and children, inhabit and move through a transatlantic intellectual space and twentieth-century world. As much as the world of the late eighteenth and early nineteenth centuries was shaped by slavery and the slave trade, the world of the late nineteenth and early twentieth centuries was shaped by war, revolution, and the geopolitical development of empire in the form of the modern capitalist nation-state.

3. Hence their emerging centrality in scholarly attempts to theorize such a space of black transnationalism and possibly invent such a canon for the twenty-first century. (See analyses of works by Delany and Du Bois in particular, in recent scholarly works by Carr, Edwards, and Hathaway.)

4. While poet Phyllis Wheatley is often cited as a kind of literary foremother in African American literary canon-formation, from a black transatlantic perspective she also serves as one of many eighteenth-century models of traveling black female subjectivity throughout the Atlantic. More recent feminist scholarship has recovered a variety of important narratives by nineteenth-century black female travelers. Some are included in Griffin's and Fish's *Stranger in the Village*, but see also Ferguson's *Nine Black Women* and Fish's discussion of Nancy Prince in *Black and White Women's Travel Narratives*.

5. Delany, *Blake*; Griggs, *Imperium in Imperio*; Hopkins, *Of One Blood*. *Blake* appeared in serial installments in *The Weekly Anglo-African* magazine between November 1861 and late May 1862. Some chapters have been found in *The Anglo-African Magazine*, January to July

1859. The text cited here is the 1970 republished edition by Beacon Press. Griggs's *Imperium in Imperio* was published by his own press in 1899, a press that catered solely to a black readership. The edition cited here was reissued in 1969 by Arno Press and *The New York Times* as part of the series, "The American Negro: His History and Literature." Hopkins's *Of One Blood* also appeared serially in the *Colored American Magazine* between November 1902 and November 1903. The edition used here is included in the collection *The Magazine Novels of Pauline Hopkins*, published by Oxford University Press in 1988 as part of the Schomburg Library of Nineteenth-Century Black Women Writers series.

6. Each of these narrative strategies bears some relation to events in the nineteenth-century history of United States race relations and must also be read within the broader context of United States foreign policy during this period.

7. See Gilroy, *The Black Atlantic*, 20. Also see Kelley and Lemelle, *Imagining Home*, 68–71, 288; and Sundquist, *To Wake the Nations*, 541. For a more polemical critique of Ethiopianism see Howe's *Afrocentrism*.

8. For an ancient Ethiopian black empire narrative, see Hadas's translation of Heliodorus's *An Ethiopian Romance*. Originally written in the third century, the *Ethiopica* was first translated into French in 1547, Latin in 1551, and finally, translated into English by Thomas Underdowne in 1587. The only modern English version until Hadas's twentieth-century translation was Reverend Rowland Smith's in 1855. In ancient accounts Ethiopia was often used as the name for continental Africa.

9. Delany's *Blake* has been explored as a black Atlantic narrative by Gilroy and as an example of the "politics of representative identity" by Levine (Gilroy, *The Black Atlantic*, 26–29; Levine, *Martin Delany, Frederick Douglass, and the Politics of Representative Identity*, 177–223.) As the narrative's explanatory power in demonstrating relationships between black migration, diaspora, nationalism, and internationalism become clear, it increasingly figures as a key text in contemporary scholarly works (see Carr's discussion of the novel's role in defining an entrepreneurial form of "New World nationalism" in *Black Nationalisms in the New World*, 25–67). I define it as an ur text in the genre of black empire narratives precisely because it contains plots, locations, character types, and a certain relationship to political history that I argue characterized the genre as a whole.

10. Delany, *Blake*, 16.

11. Hill and Rasmussen, afterword, 284. Hill and Rasmussen are the only other scholars who, in their study of African American literature, have also suggested that these black narratives in quest of sovereignty form a subgenre in the canon of black American literature.

12. As Levine describes in his introduction, an idea of "male generational binarism" that appears constitutive to constructions of masculinity in African American thought—"Booker T. Washington versus W. E. B. Du Bois and Malcolm X versus Martin Luther King"—also structures comparative accounts of Delany and Douglass as male leaders of the race (*Martin Delany, Frederick Douglass, and the Politics of Representative Identity*, 5).

13. As analyzed in the works of Boyce Davies, Carby, and Griffin.

14. It would take black feminists such as Angela Davis, for example, to argue that black female domestic work should be seen as proletarian labor, thereby placing women more firmly in the international workers' movement (see *Women, Race, and Class*).

15. See Carby, *Reconstructing Womanhood*, for more on black women as race leaders and writers in the public sphere.

16. For more on gender and sexuality in a national and imperial context see the work of McClintock, Amy Kaplan, Inderpal Grewal, and Caren Kaplan.

17. Gilroy, *The Black Atlantic*, 25.

18. In part I, for example, Delany begins the narrative with an organizer's tour of the south, one that literally maps the perimeters and parameters of a region that could constitute a black nation—the Black Belt of the Southern United States. Part I ends with the more traditional plot of the fugitive slave narrative as Blake guides a slave family to Canada by following the North Star. In part II Blake journeys on the African slaver the *Vulture* to a Portuguese trading post on the coast of Africa. While on this trip he is witness to a near mutiny by African captives on the journey back to the New World. Critics rarely mention this near mutiny by the African captives, and this entire section on the journey to Africa in *Blake* has received little critical attention in the scholarship on the novel. Yet it is a central part of the narrative both in its representation of Blake as a black seaman and in its representation of the black heroism of the African characters. Finally, in the second half of part II we have the culmination of Delany's narrative in the Caribbean, with the creation of Blake's revolutionary organization, the Grand Council of the race in Cuba.

19. Delany's multiple plots in *Blake* have their twentieth-century descendants in novels primarily by African American men. The flight north in Reed's *Flight to Canada* or the tour of the South we get in Johnson's *Oxherding Tale* are more obvious variations on the fugitive slave narrative. However, if we include narratives that extend beyond the borders of the United States, such as the account of an Amistad-style mutiny in Johnson's *Middle Passage*, we start to see elements of the nineteenth-century tradition of black empire narratives focused on the black quest for self-determination and statehood.

20. Delany, *The Condition, Elevation, Emigration, and Destiny of the Colored People of the United States*, 203.

21. Ibid., 203, 51–66.

22. Ibid., 12, 205, 205.

23. See Carby's introduction to *The Magazine Novels of Pauline Hopkins* for more of a discussion of the development and significance of a popular black literature in the second half of the nineteenth century (xxix–xxxiv).

24. Griggs, *Imperium in Imperio*, 62. In Griggs's narrative more so than Delany's, the language of a race war is even more explicit. See Amy Kaplan's discussion of Griggs's text and the black empire he envisioned as the type of black threat pictured in D. W. Griffith's

film *Birth of a Nation*, an adaptation of Thomas Dixon's novel *The Clansman* (*The Anarchy of Empire in the Making of U.S. Culture*, 123–24). Also see Gaines's discussion of Griggs's "rhetorical masculinity" in *Uplifting the Race*, 112–16).

25. In both instances race and miscegenation are at issue. Viola Belgrave, Bernard's wife, kills herself because she realizes that to love a mulatto would lead to the extinction of the race (Griggs, *Imperium in Imperio*, 174). In Belton's domestic situation, the issue of race and blood is inscribed onto the body of Antoinette Piedmont and their child. Accused first of adultery because her son appears to be white, she is allowed a brief reconciliation with Belton at the end of the story as her child "grow[s] darker and darker until he was a shade darker than his father" (256). We see these issues of racial mixture and authenticity again in later black empire narratives, but in the twentieth century these become positive signs for hybridity and a modern, multiracial diaspora.

26. This issue, concerning the nature of the sovereignty of the U.S. state, will remain central in the twentieth-century discourse of black transnationalism. In Griggs's narrative the U.S. state's contradictory policies toward the race are embedded within the Constitution and are expressed in the image of the United States as a sinking ship. In *Imperium in Imperio* Belton uses a simile to make this comparison, saying to Bernard, "You know that there is one serious flaw in the Constitution of the United States, which has already caused a world of trouble [just as] You know that a ship's boilers, engines, rigging, and so forth may be in perfect condition, but a serious leak in her bottom will sink the proudest vessel afloat" (181–82). The leak Belton describes is the tension between federal laws and individual states' rights. As Belton continues, "This flaw or defect in the Constitution of the United States is the relation of the General Government to the individual state," an especially tricky issue for the black citizen who "must therefore fight to keep afloat a flag that can afford him no more protection than could a helpless baby."

27. Hopkins, *Of One Blood*, 574. As with Delany's *Blake*, there are traces of elements from Hopkins's narrative in later twentieth-century African American fiction. Ethiopianist comic books and narratives structure the young black protagonist's search for self in Samuel R. Delany's short story "Atlantis" (in *Atlantis*). Butler's super race of telepaths, for example, in *Mind of My Mind* (1977) and *Wild Seed* (1980) and Johnson's magical Africans in *Middle Passage* all embody elements of fantasy, science fiction, and mysticism that are reminiscent of Hopkins's Ethiopianist and utopian tribe. For an ironic take on the Ethiopianist myth of African kings, see *The Last of the African Kings* by Condé, a Francophone Caribbean writer.

28. Carby, introduction, xiv. As she describes, "This story of origins is used by Hopkins to elaborate the Afro-American literary convention of the search for and the discovery of family, a metaphor for the black diaspora." See Gaines's "Black Americans' Racial Uplift Ideology as 'Civilizing Mission,'" 433–55, for a more critical reading of Hopkins's black imperial discourse. Also see Carr's discussion of Hopkins's creation of a "politicized mulatta culture" and his reading of her novel *Contending Forces* through her trope of the "New Woman," another figure for the woman of color (*Black Nationalism in the New World*, 68–105).

29. Interestingly, in *Of One Blood*, one of the few black empire narratives by a female author, it is the male character Reuel Briggs whose multiracial makeup embodies the diaspora and a world of color. As the narrator comments on his physiognomy, "None of the students . . . knew aught of Reuel Briggs's origin. It was rumored at first that he was of Italian birth, then they 'guessed' he was a Japanese" (Hopkins, *Of One Blood*, 444).

30. Like the nineteenth-century black empire narratives by Delany and Hopkins, Schuyler's stories first appeared serially in the *Pittsburgh Courier* in two parts: as "The Black Internationale: Story of Black Genius Against the World" between 21 November 1936 and 3 July 1937 and as "Black Empire: An Imaginative Story of a Great New Civilization in Modern Africa" between 2 October 1937 and 16 April 1938. Both were reprinted in one collection by Northeastern University Press in 1991, the text cited here.

31. Both works have been analyzed as having a transnational or international focus. Speaking of Du Bois and *Dark Princess*, Sundquist has commented, "Du Bois's importance lies both in the influence of *The Souls of Black Folk*—the founding text of modern African American thought—and in the fact that he made the twentieth-century 'problem of the color line' . . . the point of departure for a diaspora aesthetic. . . . Du Bois was transnational in his intellectual scope, and he must be so studied" (*To Wake the Nations*, 15). Both Gilroy (*The Black Atlantic, Against Race*) and Amy Kaplan (*The Anarchy of Empire in the Making of U.S. Culture*) have answered this call in their recent studies, contributing to a possible rethinking of Du Bois's works, especially *Darkwater* and *Dark Princess*, as two founding texts in a black transnational tradition of African American thought. (See also Edward's discussion of *Dark Princess* in *The Practice of Diaspora*, 233–38.) But, as scholars of Pan-Africanism such as Robert A. Hill have also amply demonstrated, Du Bois was in no way alone in this regard. Even as a transnationalist he should be studied as part of a larger intellectual formation that included both African Americans and West Indians and, therefore, all three fields of American, African American, and Caribbean thought. For more on Schuyler's internationalism, see R. Hill's and Rasmussen's afterword to *Black Empire*. Hill and Rasmussen also identify *Blake* and *Imperio in Imperio* as precursors to Schuyler's narrative, and Du Bois's *Dark Princess* was a novel that Schuyler admired immensely. Also see Hill's further commentary on *Black Empire* in his introduction to a second Schuyler collection entitled *Ethiopian Stories*.

32. Du Bois, *Dark Princess*, xxii.

33. Schuyler, *Black Empire*, 13.

34. Ibid., xi.

35. Ibid., 10.

36. Ibid., 10–11.

37. Ibid., 55.

38. Ibid., 82.

39. As Tate describes in her introduction, *Dark Princess* included sentiments from a pageant Du Bois had created earlier: " 'The Star of Ethiopia,' a spectacle with a cast of 1,200

that dazzled audiences in New York in 1915, Washington in 1916, and Philadelphia and Los Angeles in 1924" (xx–xxi). Du Bois's pageant could be seen as the precursor to the spectacular dramas of black empire that were performed throughout the early twentieth century (see chapter 3).

40. Du Bois, *Dark Princess*, 311.

41. Schuyler, *Black Empire*, 40.

42. Hill and Rasmussen, afterword, 283.

43. Ibid., 279.

44. The quest for literacy has long been identified as a central trope in the migration narratives of African American literature. See Stepto's defining study, *From Behind the Veil*.

45. Schuyler, "The Rise of the Black Internationale," reprinted in *Black Empire*, 328–36.

46. Ibid., 336.

47. For a good literary example of their differences compare their respective 1926 essays, Du Bois's "Criteria of Negro Art" and Schuyler's "The Negro Art Hokum." Both were central pieces in a critical debate on Negro art during the Harlem Renaissance that culminated in a symposium published in *The Crisis* in 1926 entitled "The Negro in Art: How Shall He Be Portrayed?" (For more on this debate see Davis and Peplow, *The New Negro Renaissance*; and Bernard, *Remember Me to Harlem*, xix).

48. Also see Du Bois's *Darkwater* for both his further articulation of a black transnational position and his shorter fairy tale of black empire entitled "The Princess of the Hither Isles."

49. While my use of the metaphor of a black empire to name this early twentieth-century black and transnational imaginary was drawn explicitly from Marcus Garvey's life and work, I view Schuyler's accounts as highly intelligent parodies that also crystallized some of the central tropes of this discourse. His incredibly apt book titles, *Black Empire* and *The Black Internationale*, provide central terms with which we can think through the nature of black internationalism during this period.

50. Schuyler, *Black Empire*, 141.

51. Du Bois, "Worlds of Color," 413–14.


## 3 MARCUS GARVEY, BLACK EMPEROR

1. Anderson, *Imagined Communities*, 118.

2. Edward Steichen, "Paul Robeson as The Emperor Jones," 1933 (International Museum of Photography/George Eastman House, New York).

3. For example, see the image by James Van Der Zee, "Marcus Garvey in Regalia," 1924 (James Van Der Zee, New York) and Robert Hill's interpretation of this famous photograph in "Making Noise."

4. Du Bois, "Back to Africa," 111.

5. R. Hill, "Making Noise," 181.

6. Ibid., 181.

7. Ibid., 184.

8. O'Neill, *The Emperor Jones, Anna Christie, The Hairy Ape*, 8. References to *The Emperor Jones* in the Vintage collection of three plays are cited hereafter by the play's title.

9. *The Emperor Jones* was first performed by the Provincetown Players, an early modern American theater laboratory for new American playwrights to experiment without regard to the commercial value of their productions. The Provincetown Players were crucial for O'Neill's development as the father of modern American drama. *The Emperor Jones* was the second O'Neill play to be produced by the Players, and it was the play that put both playwright and group in the spotlight after O'Neill proved too experimental for Broadway. For more on the Provincetown Players and O'Neill specifically in the development of a modern American theater, see Heller and Rudnick, *1915, The Cultural Moment*, 309–15.

10. O'Neill, *The Emperor Jones*, 3.

11. Ibid.

12. As the presence of the character of the British trader Smithers attests, the West Indies served in the play as a metonymic signifier for the British colonial empire. More specifically, however, the self-determined West Indian nation represented in the play was a direct reference to the independent black Haitian state created after the 1791–1804 slave revolution led by Toussaint L'Ouverture. For a detailed analysis and historicizing of the play's connections to both the Haitian revolution and the 1915 United States invasion of Haiti, see Renda, *Taking Haiti*, esp. 196–212.

13. Also see Renda for an alternative reading of the black Emperor Jones as a figure for the United States empire (*Taking Haiti*, 204–5).

14. O'Neill, *The Emperor Jones*, 41.

15. Ibid., 7.

16. Bederman, *Manliness and Civilization*, 36, 41.

17. Ibid., 167, 231–32. In Bederman's words, "By the 1920s . . . the middle class' fascination with the sexually uncontrolled masculine primitive had given power to new cultural figures like Rudolph Valentino's nostril-flaring, Englishwoman-kidnapping, lustful Arab sheik" (167). This image should be contrasted with the less popular but more compelling image of the black masculine that Robeson represented in a film such as *Jericho* in 1937. In his portrayal of the character Jericho Jackson, an African American who becomes a sheik in Northern Africa, Robeson was able to speak to a number of issues important to a black transnational popular audience, including "resistance to injustice by any means necessary, identification with Africa, and Pan-Arab unity—subjects that would not see celluloid again for many years" (Norton, review of *Jericho*).

18. See Carby, *Race Men*, 50–64.

19. Ibid., 47.

20. Walter White, "The Paradox of Color," 361.

21. O'Neill, *The Emperor Jones*, 34.

22. In *The Black Atlantic* Gilroy suggests that the Black Star Line could be read in this light, also referencing a brief observation made by Linebaugh in an essay entitled "All the Atlantic Mountains Shook" (Gilroy, 13, 226).

23. McClintock, *Imperial Leather*, 352.

24. Ibid., 375, 374–75.

25. Ibid., 375.

26. In a series of essays on black theater in Locke's anthology of *The New Negro*, African American critics used *The Emperor Jones* as proof that the New Negro actor could perform dramatic tragedy. See W. Brathwaite, "The Negro in American Literature"; Gregory, "The Drama of Negro Life"; and Fauset, "The Gift of Laughter."

27. The trope of the black empire and the figure of the black emperor appeared in a number of theatrical productions during the teens through the thirties. Some theatrical examples included Du Bois's own early pageant *Star of Ethiopia* (1913), O'Neill's *Emperor Jones* (1920), William DuBois's [no relation to W. E. B. Du Bois] *Haiti* (1938), the Los Angeles Theatre Project production *Black Empire* (1938), Langston Hughes's *Emperor of Haiti* (1936), and in Britain, C. L. R. James's production *Toussaint L'Ouverture* (1938). The play whose popular cultural reach defined the genre was O'Neill's *The Emperor Jones*, also made into a film in the 1930s. The black actor who defined the figure of the black emperor, a role he played in both O'Neill's *Emperor Jones* and James's *Toussaint L'Ouverture*, was Paul Robeson. Du Bois's *Star of Ethiopia*, DuBois's *Haiti*, and the production *Black Empire* are all described in Fraden, *Blueprints for a Black Federal Theatre*, 65, 170–79; and E. Hill, *The Theatre of Black Americans*, 239. Hill also includes the text of Hughes's play in his collection *Black Heroes*, 1–75, and the text of the 1967 production of James's play, retitled *The Black Jacobins*, in his collection *A Time . . . and a Season*. Finally, see Curtis, *The First Black Actors on the Great White Way*, for another excellent account of early-twentieth-century African American theater.

28. McClintock, *Imperial Leather*, 363–64, 364, 364.

29. Ibid., 364.

30. Garvey, "The British West Indies in the Mirror of Civilization," 77. Also see Robert Hill's interpretation of this essay in "The First England Years and After, 1912–1916," 45.

31. Garvey as quoted in Hill, "The First England Years and After, 1912–1916," 63–64.

32. Garvey, *A Talk with Afro-West Indians*, 83. Again, also see Hill's "The First England Years and After, 1912–1916" for another interpretation of this quote (69). The emphasis added here is mine.

33. For more of Anderson's argument on print culture, the colonial intelligentsia, and the development of colonial nationalisms, see *Imagined Communities*, 63, 67, 71, 81.

34. A. Garvey, "The Early Years of Marcus Garvey," 32.

35. Ibid.

36. Ibid., 32–33.

37. Ibid., 34. This segregated system of pay was a direct result of United States control over the Panama Canal project. See Watkins-Owens, *Blood Relations*, 13–14.

38. Clarke, *Marcus Garvey and the Vision of Africa*, 4.

39. A. Garvey, "The Early Years of Marcus Garvey," 34.

40. Ibid., 34–35.

41. Ibid., 34. Also see Anderson's *Imagined Communities* for more of his discussion of the relationship between dictionaries and the development of both a national language and consciousness (71–72).

42. Anderson, *Imagined Communities*, 114.

43. Ibid.

44. A. Garvey, "The Early Years of Marcus Garvey," 35.

45. Ibid.

46. Hill, "The First England Years and After, 1912–1916," 38.

47. Garvey, articles from the *Pittsburgh Courier*, 35.

48. Ibid.

49. Clarke, *Marcus Garvey and the Vision of Africa*, 7–8.

50. Garvey as quoted in Clarke, *Marcus Garvey and the Vision of Africa*, 8.

51. Ibid.

52. Garvey, *A Talk with Afro-West Indians*, 83.

53. Garvey, "The British West Indies in the Mirror of Civilization," 82.

54. R. Hill, "The First England Years and After, 1912–1916," 47.

55. Garvey, *A Talk with Afro-West Indians*, 84.

56. Garvey, "African Fundamentalism," 21.

57. Ibid., 18.

58. Gilroy, *Against Race*, 231–37, and "Black Fascism."

59. James as quoted in Gilroy, *Against Race*, 231.

60. Gilroy, "Black Fascism," 77.

61. Anderson, *Imagined Communities*, 113.

62. Ibid., 114.

63. Garvey as quoted in Hill, "The First England Years and After, 1912–1916," 40.

64. Garvey, "African Fundamentalism," 10.

65. Ibid., 18.

66. Ibid., 24.

67. Central to Anderson's story of the origin and spread of nationality and nationalism is his argument that the nation was essentially a modular phenomenon, "an invention on which it was impossible to secure a patent. It became available for pirating by widely different, and sometimes unexpected, hands" (*Imagined Communities*, 67). In *Against Race* Gilroy is interested in a similar type of circulation, but in terms of how nationalism has been shaped by Enlightenment racial ideologies. This type of transatlantic circulation between

empire and colony is also described by Linebaugh and Rediker in *The Many-Headed Hydra* and by Roach in *Cities of the Dead*. In their respective discussions of a revolutionary Atlantic, a circumatlantic, and a black Atlantic, Linebaugh, Rediker, Gilroy, and Roach all construct the Atlantic as an oceanic space of cultural and political exchange, a space in which various European political ideals circulated throughout the colonial world "by the circular winds and currents of the Atlantic" (Linebaugh and Rediker, *The Many-Headed Hydra*, 247). However, as Linebaugh and Rediker also add, "what went out in whiteface came back in blackface" as national histories and ideologies seeped into the consciousness of the colonized, the phenomenon that shapes Fanon's renowned work and title, *Black Skin, White Masks*.

68. Gilroy, *Against Race*, 46.

69. Ibid., 67.

70. Hence Gilroy's critiques in *Against Race* of a "planetary commerce in blackness" (13) and "the emphasis on culture as a form of property to be owned rather than lived" (24).

71. Marx, *Capital*, 164.

72. Ibid., 165. My analysis here is indebted to the valuable and original readings of Marx and Fanon afforded by K. Hall in her discussion of blackness as an "object" circulating in seventeenth-century England in *Things of Darkness*, 211–53. Also see McClintock's delineation of various theories of the fetish in *Imperial Leather* (185–95).

73. K. Hall, *Things of Darkness*, 211.

74. Fanon, *Black Skin, White Masks*, 109.

75. Ibid., 112.

76. Andersen, "The Emperor's New Suit."

77. Morse-Lovett, "An Emperor Jones of Finance," quoted in Hill, "Making Noise," 202.

78. Garvey, "African Fundamentalism," 4.

79. Garvey as quoted in Hill, "Making Noise," 199.

80. Hill, "Making Noise," 182–84.

81. Anderson, *Imagined Communities*, 113.

82. Garvey as quoted in Hill, "Making Noise," 199–200.

83. Ibid., 182.

84. Ibid.

85. Garvey as quoted in Du Bois, "Back to Africa," 111.

86. Garvey as quoted in Hill, "Making Noise," 200.

87. Both quoted in Hill, "Making Noise," 200, 183.

88. Garvey, "African Fundamentalism," 23.

89. Elmes, "Garvey and Garveyism," 125.

90. K. Miller, "After Marcus Garvey," 245.

91. Clarke, *Marcus Garvey and the Vision of Africa*, 163. Emphasis added.

92. Worth Tuttle as quoted in Hill, "Making Noise," 193.

93. Garvey, "African Fundamentalism," 11.

94. Ibid., 23.

95. Garvey, articles from the *Pittsburgh Courier*, 101.

96. Garvey, "African Fundamentalism," 5.

97. Elmes, "Garvey and Garveyism," 125.

## 4 THE BLACK STAR LINE

1. Gilroy, *The Black Atlantic*, 4.

2. Nassy Brown, "Black Liverpool, Black America, and the Gendering of Diasporic Space," 300.

3. Ibid., 301.

4. Bolster, *Black Jacks*, 76.

5. Linebaugh and Rediker use the term hydrarchy to "designate two related developments of the late seventeenth-century: the organization of the maritime state from above, and the self-organization of sailors from below" (*The Many-Headed Hydra*, 144).

6. Ibid., 167.

7. Bolster, *Black Jacks*, 75.

8. Ibid., 182. If for Bederman boxing especially validated manly qualities such as personal valor, uncommon courage, and physical prowess then, as Bolster also points out, "Seamen were the first Americans to embrace boxing as a sport" (117) further confirming his sense that ships and seafaring were spaces in which battles over the meaning of masculinity were also being waged by multiple male subjects.

9. Ibid., 188.

10. Originally published in 1929, *Umbala* (Dean and North) was contemporaneous with McKay's two novels, *Home to Harlem* (1928) and *Banjo* (1929), and Du Bois's *Dark Princess* (1929).

11. For other fascinating accounts of traveling black subjects in the nineteenth century, see Parsons's *King Khama, Emperor Joe, and the Great White Queen* and Kennedy's *Black Livingstone*.

12. Bolster, *Black Jacks*, 20, 213, 214.

13. Ibid., 214, 197.

14. See Foulke, *The Sea Voyage Narrative*, for an interesting attempt to carve out a genre of sea literature in which the voyage narrative would play a central role. Of course, as with most literary attempts to define genres, black writers and their contributions are missing from Foulke's account.

15. Dean and North, *Umbala*, 69.

16. Ibid.

17. While Dean never met Garvey, George Shepperson does relate in his introduction to the text two biographical anecdotes that are pertinent here in providing a historical grounding for a genealogy of black empire narratives and sea stories. Shepperson speculates, "Some

of Dean's militancy may have stemmed from the visits to his parents' home in Philadelphia of Major Martin R. Delany." This visit occurred more than a decade after Delany had returned from his expedition to Africa, where he had succeeded in signing a treaty with the ruler of an area in what is now Nigeria for land for a colony of New World black fugitives (ix). While nothing would come of this treaty, Shepperson argues that Delany's political desires for a black state may have been a shaping force for Dean's Ethiopianist dreams in the early years of his boyhood. Then, Shepperson recounts about the latter years of Dean's life, "In 1921 in California, he had friendly meetings with officials of Marcus Garvey's Universal Negro Improvement Association (UNIA); and he spoke warmly of Garvey's attempts to increase the self-respect of peoples of African descent everywhere" (xiv–xv). Shepperson's account provides evidence supporting the idea that Dean's black Atlantic narrative and Garvey's imperial performance functioned as bookends framing Captain Dean's own memoir of his migrations and imperial urges.

18. The *Pedro Gorino*, originally a Dutch ship named the *Stavanger*, provided the first title for Dean's autobiography, published simultaneously in Boston, London, and New York by Houghton Mifflin in 1929.

19. Sale, *The Slumbering Volcano*, 6–7.

20. Douglass, *The Heroic Slave*. Published in 1853, Douglass's tale could be considered another black Atlantic sea story of the late nineteenth century.

21. Sale, *The Slumbering Volcano*, 28.

22. Ibid. Also see Sale, *The Slumbering Volcano*, for a discussion of an African American discourse of masculinity that made appeals to "manliness," such as David Walker's appeal (50, 51).

23. Ibid., 59.

24. Bolster, *Black Jacks*, 2.

25. Ibid.

26. Dean and North, *Umbala*, 256.

27. Mulzac, *A Star to Steer By*. See also a brief biography of Mulzac in Stein, *The World of Marcus Garvey*, 98–100.

28. Mulzac, "Memoirs of a Captain of the Black Star Line," 132–33.

29. Ibid., 138, 135, 135.

30. Hill and Bair, *Marcus Garvey*, liii.

31. Garvey as quoted in Hill and Bair, *Marcus Garvey*, xx.

32. Garvey, articles from the *Pittsburgh Courier*, 36–37.

33. Ibid., 37.

34. Ibid., 53.

35. Ibid., 38.

36. Ibid., 75.

37. Ibid., 38.

38. Ibid.

39. Ibid., 39.

40. Ibid.

41. Ibid., 40.

42. Ibid.

43. Ibid.

44. Ibid., 41–42.

45. As Moore described in his essay "The Critics and Opponents of Marcus Garvey," an addendum was added to the revised UNIA Manifesto of 1920 which included the following objective: "To establish a central nation for the race" (214).

46. Garvey, articles from the *Pittsburgh Courier*, 45.

47. Ibid., 46–47, 51.

48. Ibid., 48–49, 51.

49. See Naison, *Communists in Harlem During the Depression*, 3–30. Also see Draper, *American Communism and Soviet Russia*, 322–26; Vincent, *Black Power and the Garvey Movement*, 74–75; Martin, *Race First* 237–38; and Kelly, *Race Rebels*, 106, 108.

50. While impossible to substantiate Garvey's own boast that the UNIA had a total peak membership of 11 million across the globe, scholars have been able to get more accurate estimates of the number of Garveyites in local branches of the UNIA throughout the United States and the West Indies. For some of these studies see Lewis and Warner-Lewis, *Garvey*.

51. "Digest of Views," *The Crusader* I, 123.

52. Briggs, "Marcus Garvey," 407.

53. Ibid.

54. Ibid.

55. Ibid.

56. Briggs, "The U.N.I.A. Convention," 834.

57. See Levine's *Martin Delany, Frederick Douglass, and the Politics of Representative Identity* and Gaines's *Uplifting the Race* on the role of masculinity in uplift discourse.

58. Briggs, "A Paramount Chief of the Negro Race," 635.

59. Ibid.

60. Ibid., 635–36.

61. Garvey as quoted in Briggs, "A Letter from Marcus Garvey," 663.

62. Briggs, "A Letter from Marcus Garvey," 663.

63. Briggs, "The Universal Negro Improvement Association," 698. Though this piece has no byline, the author writes as the representative of *The Crusader*, undisputedly Briggs's magazine.

64. Briggs, "The U.N.I.A. Convention" and "The African Blood Brotherhood," 729–31.

65. Briggs, "The U.N.I.A. Convention," 729.

66. Briggs, "Program of the A.B.B.," 1251.

67. Briggs, "The U.N.I.A. Convention," 729.

68. Ibid.

69. Briggs, "The U.N.I.A. Convention," 834.

70. Ibid.

71. Ibid., 837.

72. Allen has provided a detailed account of the participants in that meeting and their agenda ("The New Negro"). At this time, partly as a consequence of being identified as the instigators of a riot in Tulsa in June of that year, and partly due to general Communist Party doctrine, the members of the ABB were in the process of deciding to go public. Rose Pastor Stokes stands out in Allen's account as the only significant female leader of the group, conspicuous in the overwhelmingly male and masculinist ABB.

73. McKay's return to the United States in 1921 was evident throughout the pages of Briggs's *Crusader* that year. His poem "Tropical Night" appears in the March issue, his appointment as editor of *The Liberator* is announced in April and May, "Afternoon in Herald Square" appears in June, along with "a review of two very interesting books on Soviet Russia" written by McKay. McKay played a central role in the debate on the merits of taking the ABB to the "surface."

74. Hill, "Racial and Radical," xxxix. As Hill continues to argue, this moment marks Briggs's clarity on the nature of the challenge facing black intellectuals—how to create in one organization real sovereignty, an independent form of statehood for newly self-determined black subjects, while maintaining the internationalism of the black world in a racial movement able to transcend and cross national borders.

75. Briggs, "Program of the ABB," 1249.

76. Moore, "The Critics and Opponents of Marcus Garvey," 224.

77. Vincent as quoted in Moore, "The Critics and Opponents of Marcus Garvey."

78. McKay as quoted in Hill, "Racial and Radical," xlv.

79. Hill, "Racial and Radical," xlvii.

80. C. L. R. James and Richard B. Moore were important architects of the plan for West Indian federation in the 1940s and 1950s. That story is the subject of chapter 8.

81. Moore is one of the few intellectuals to explicitly argue that "Quite similar were the stated programs of the UNIA and the African Blood Brotherhood." Moore, "The Critics and Opponents of Marcus Garvey," 224.

82. Allen describes the differences between black transnational intellectuals during this period in the following terms: "The principal tension among political New Negroes lay along a nationalist/socialist divide in which questions of social identity and of envisioned social structure both played a role" ("The New Negro" 54).


5 CLAUDE MCKAY AND HARLEM

1. Du Bois, "Back to Africa," 117–18.

2. Benjamin, "The Storyteller," in *Illuminations*, 84–85.

3. Chesnutt, *The Conjure Woman*; Toomer, *Cane*.

4. Cooper, *Claude McKay*, 214.

5. Ibid., 228.

6. Ibid., 229.

7. Unsurprisingly, given his ubiquitous presence as the figure for the New Negro of the 1920s and 1930s, Paul Robeson also starred in a screen adaptation of McKay's novel *Banjo*, the 1937 musical *Big Fella*. While the film itself did not do well at the time, scholars continue to describe it as offering Robeson a rare opportunity to "make a racial statement about an ordinary but admirable black man, functioning well in a contemporary, European setting" (Duberman, *Paul Robeson*, 208). Robeson may have liked the part because, unlike *The Emperor Jones*, *Big Fella* was a lighthearted comedy: "He wanted to try his hand at a comic part—as long as it was not some shuffling stereotype" (209). The plot of the film takes a different turn from that of the novel, however, putting the story of transient, black dockworkers in the service of a more sentimental tale of Banjo rescuing and befriending a white child.

8. Benjamin, "The Storyteller," in *Illuminations*, 85.

9. Ibid., 92.

10. McKay as quoted in Cooper, *Claude McKay*, 307.

11. Ibid.

12. In his biography Cooper describes the years between 1923 and 1934 as the expatriate years.

13. This question had preoccupied McKay as early as 1921 when he participated in the African Blood Brotherhood discussion about merging with the Universal Negro Improvement Association. Working as a drama critic for *The Liberator* at the time, McKay had this to say about early performances of O'Neill's black emperor by the actor Charles Gilpin: "'Where do I go from here?' is the question that will trouble Charles Gilpin, after his sensational run in *The Emperor Jones* on Broadway. It is said that the play may be taken to London. . . . But when his London nights are over, he will still have the question where he can go from here" (McKay, "A Black Star," 25). McKay was not impressed with the actor's dramatic success in the role of the black emperor, for as he saw it, once the black actor stepped out of the theater into the nation, there were few places he could go.

14. As described by McKay in *A Long Way from Home*, 306.

15. Ibid.

16. Ibid., 321.

17. Du Bois, "The Browsing Reader," 202. In the screenplay for the 1933 film adaptation of *The Emperor Jones*, Dubose Heyward also represented the New Negro's Harlem by including episodes from Brutus Jones's life prior to his ultimate demise on the island. Specifically, the film traced Jones's trajectory from the rural South to the urban, black, working-class space of Harlem in the 1920s, a black Harlem pictured in ways that mirrored the speakeasies and cabarets, black love and white voyeurism, and Pullman porters and jazz musicians that McKay also described in *Home to Harlem*. This take on Harlem's "under-

world" was not at all representative of the African American critical and artistic community, and it was for this that McKay would receive the greatest criticism from contemporaries such as W. E. B. Du Bois. (*The Emperor Jones*, prod. John Krimsky and Gifford Cochran, dir. by Dudley Murphy, 1933.)

18. McKay as quoted in Cooper, *Claude McKay*, 247.

19. McKay, *A Long Way from Home*, 306.

20. Du Bois, "Back to Africa," 115.

21. Ibid., 118.

22. Ibid.

23. Ibid.

24. Ibid., 118–19.

25. McKay, "A Negro Writer to His Critics."

26. Du Bois, "The Browsing Reader," 202.

27. McKay, "A Negro Writer to His Critics," 133.

28. Ibid., 135.

29. Ibid., 139.

30. Du Bois's essay "Worlds of Color" should be seen as a classic in black transnational literature, offering a shadow narrative to the imperial discourse of the time.

31. McKay, "A Negro Writer to His Critics," 133–34.

32. Ibid., 134.

33. McKay, *A Long Way from Home*, 60.

34. Ibid., 63.

35. Ibid., 61.

36. Ibid., 21.

37. Ibid., 23.

38. Ibid., 63.

39. Briggs, "Loyalty."

40. McKay, *A Long Way from Home*, 153.

41. Ibid., 31.

42. Ibid.

43. Baker, *Modernism and the Harlem Renaissance*, 77.

44. One can find McKay's poem in Locke's anthology, *The New Negro*, but under the title "White Houses," 134. For more on the argument that ensued between Locke and McKay concerning Locke's retitling of the poem see McKay, *A Long Way from Home*, 313–14.

45. McKay, "If We Must Die," 21.

46. McKay, *A Long Way from Home*, 227–28.

47. Ibid., 4, 20, 4.

48. Ibid., 23.

49. Tillery has argued that McKay's shift to the novel was primarily economically motivated, a way of making his creative work pay (*Claude McKay*, 78).

50. McKay, *Banana Bottom*. For more on McKay's attempts to write a Caribbean national romance see Edmondson, *Making Men*, esp. 70–74. Here the Caribbean becomes the most true site of home and domesticity, evidenced in McKay's use of a female protagonist, while still leaving the black men of *Home to Harlem* and *Banjo* moving freely throughout the diaspora. Also see Hathaway's account of gender, home, movement, and internationalism in McKay's fictions in *Caribbean Waves*, 52–85.

51. My interpretation of *Home to Harlem* as a national romance also draws from Anderson's argument that the novel, along with the newspaper, was one of the main forms of print to provide "the technical means for 're-presenting' the *kind* of community that is the nation" (*Imagined Communities*, 24–25). Anderson argues that the novel, as a way of imagining community, required a narrative with a certain sense of chronological time, that followed the movements of an individual hero through a bounded space. The borders of that national space, and the limits it placed on black movement, are key issues in McKay's novels.

52. Sommer, *Foundational Fictions*. While I borrow the term "national romance" from Sommer's account, I am not attempting to insert McKay's narrative into the rich Latin American literary history that Sommer describes. Nor am I arguing that there is a parallel tradition within African American or Anglophone Caribbean literature. Rather, like Edmondson in her borrowing of Sommer's use of the term romance to describe "myths, tropes, and discourses" of the Caribbean (*Caribbean Romances*), I identify in *Home to Harlem* similar romantic themes and tropes as those Sommer describes, precisely to demonstrate that nationalist longings and questions of national belonging were pressing concerns in McKay's fictions.

53. Sommer, "Irresistible Romance," 96. Like McClintock, Sommer builds on Anderson's argument that to write a novel is to imagine the nation. Given Anderson's argument that models of "nation-ness" originated in the Americas, Sommer argues that her historical romances could be seen as "foundational fictions" for narratives of American nationhood more generally.

54. Gilroy has also pointed to the preponderance of love stories, "or more appropriately love and loss stories," in black popular culture in *The Black Atlantic*, 201.

55. Sommer, "Irresistible Romance," 75, 95–96, 95, 96, 90.

56. Anderson, *Imagined Communities*, 30.

57. Since McKay's lead character in *Banana Bottom* is a woman, Bita, who returns to the Caribbean, one immediate conclusion is that he could only imagine the free movement of the black Caribbean woman in a domestic narrative of postcolonial, national independence, rather than in the transnational narrative of freedom of movement abroad.

58. McKay, *Home to Harlem*, 4.

59. Ibid., 7.

60. Ibid., 7–8.

61. Ibid., 8.

62. Ibid., 9.

63. Quotes from *The Emperor Jones* are transcriptions from the film itself. See Hathaway's discussion of McKay's fiction in *Caribbean Waves* for a more thorough account of conceptions "of women's sexuality, and especially urban women's sexuality, as representing a pervasive threat to male authority" in black writing during this period (62).

64. McKay, *Home to Harlem*, 11.

65. Ibid., 15.

66. Sommer, "Irresistible Romance," 96.

67. Baker, *Modernism and the Harlem Renaissance*, 77.

68. McKay, *Home to Harlem*, 23.

69. Ibid., 29.

70. Due in large part to McKay's own discussion of conditions in the southern Black Belt of the United States at the Comintern in 1922, in 1928, the year of *Home to Harlem's* publication, the Fourth Congress of the Comintern formally resolved that the Black Belt be considered an internal nation deserving the right to self-determination.

71. Sommer, "Irresistible Romance," 90.

72. McKay, *Home to Harlem*, 70.

73. Ibid., 35.

74. Ibid., 116.

75. Ibid., 130.

76. See Edward's illuminating account of the issues at stake in the language differences that constitute the black diaspora, his specific focus being French (*The Practice of Diaspora*).

77. McKay, *Home to Harlem*, 131.

78. For an excellent interpretation of McKay's *Home to Harlem* through the lens of ethnicity and black ethnic relations, see Hathaway's *Caribbean Waves*, where she examines the "understudied aspect of difference within racial sameness in the United States" by focusing on the work of McKay and Paule Marshall. Hathaway isolates issues of "displacement and identity that have accompanied migratory experiences" in the case of Caribbean immigrants, arguing that because of the ways "'race' emerges as a dramatic factor affecting the reception and identification of blacks in U.S. society . . . an inquiry into the position of African Caribbean immigrants has significant implications for race, ethnic, and immigration theory" (2–4). This work contributes to Hathaway's discussion of the complexities of Caribbean's racialized *ethnic* formation within the nation by exploring the impact of their own understanding of the *global* dimensions of their multiple nationalities and national allegiances. In other words, *Black Empire* adds to the discussion of black ethnicity in African American literature, a discussion of black *transnationality* as an alternative conception of black racial identity.

79. This is a much more explicit sense of what American self-determination looks like when imposed by white marines than O'Neill's opening reference in *The Emperor Jones*.

80. McKay, *Home to Harlem*, 138.

81. Ibid., 131.

82. Ibid., 132.

83. Ibid.

84. Ibid., 134. Emphasis added. This is the moment the black transnational narrative intervenes in and takes over from the account of black ethnic relations and differences in Harlem provided earlier in the novel (and interpreted by Hathaway).

85. Garvey, "African Fundamentalism," 18.

86. McKay, *Home to Harlem*, 57–8.

87. Anderson, *Imagined Communities*, 143.

88. McKay, *Home to Harlem*, 135.

89. Sommer, "Irresistible Romance," 75.

90. Benjamin, "The Storyteller," in *Illuminations*, 100.

91. McKay, *Home to Harlem*, 152.

92. I say male here because texts by a generation of male Caribbean intellectuals, such as Lamming, Samuel Selvon, Naipaul, Walcott, and Brathwaite, help to set in place this image of the exiled Caribbean intellectual and writer. Since then, a new generation of Caribbean writers, both men and women, based in both the United States and England, have complicated not only the gendered nature of that trope of Caribbean exile, but also the difference diaspora makes as a lens through which to view Caribbean migration. Some of these latter authors include Caryl Phillips, Paule Marshall, Jamaica Kincaid, and Edwidge Danticat. The work of Caribbean female critics such as Carole Boyce Davies, Sylvia Wynter, and Belinda Edmondson has also been central in both pointing toward and shifting this discourse.

93. McKay, *Home to Harlem*, 153.

94. Ibid.

95. Ibid., 153–54.

96. Garvey, "African Fundamentalism," 18. Bederman also argues that it is precisely in this period that a figure such as Theodore Roosevelt began "to exhort the American race to embrace a manly, strenuous imperialism, in the cause of higher civilization" (*Manliness and Civilization*, 184).

97. McKay, *Home to Harlem*, 155.

98. Ibid., 154.

99. Ibid., 226, 225.

100. Ibid., 226.

101. Ibid., 226–27.

102. Ibid., 228–29.

103. Ibid., 156.

104. Ibid., 227.

105. Ibid., 224.

106. Ibid., 228.

107. Edwards, *The Practice of Diaspora*, 205–6.

108. McKay, *Home to Harlem*, 155.

109. Ibid., 224–25.

110. Ibid., 155.

111. Ibid., 158.

112. The term Afro-Orientalism is taken from a talk by Bill V. Mullen entitled "Afro-Orientalism and the 'World Black Revolution,'" Hampshire College, 22 February 2001.

113. McKay, *Home to Harlem*, 264.

114. Ibid., 291–92.

115. Ibid., 301.

116. Ibid., 300–1.

117. Ibid., 311. Emphasis added.

118. Ibid., 328.

119. Ibid., 327.

120. Ibid., 332.

121. Sommer, "Irresistible Romance," 95.

122. Bhabha, *Nation and Narration*, 4.

123. Renan, "What Is a Nation?," 8–22.

124. Ibid., 12.

125. Ibid., 18. Emphasis added.

126. Ibid., 19.


6 *BANJO*'S CREW IN MARSEILLES

1. Walter Benjamin, "Marseilles," in *Reflections*, 129.

2. McKay, *A Long Way from Home*, 149.

3. Ibid., 150.

4. Ibid.

5. Domestic death also signified the racist treatment of black soldier citizens after World War I, treatment that reflected the essential contradiction of their lives in America.

6. Sommer, "Irresistible Romance," 86.

7. McKay, *Banjo*, 10.

8. Ibid., 326.

9. Hathaway, *Caribbean Waves*, 73; Edwards, *The Practice of Diaspora*, 209. These and other scholars have also noted the presence of homosocial and homoerotic resonances in McKay's work. In *Caribbean Waves* Hathaway describes *Home to Harlem* as a "decidedly homosocial novel" (60) and in *The Practice of Diaspora* Edwards notes in a footnote that "One might note a certain homoeroticism in this portrait of black male drifters" in *Banjo* (365 n.47). However none have tackled the centrality of these homoerotic elements to the ways in which we read the transnationalism of *both* novels from the late 1920s. In her analysis of a more contemporary novel, Michelle Cliff's *No Telephone to Heaven*, Belinda Edmond-

son provides a stirring account of both the Caribbean woman of color and the transvestite male character's portrayal of an "international, multi-racial, socially, and sexually diverse band of guerillas" (*Making Men*, 136). Edmondson argues that this group and their concomitant failed attack represent "an ironic replication of the failed revolutionary actions of the male-authored narratives" of Caribbean nationalist history. *Black Empire* reads the portrayal of women of color and diverse sexual subjects in certain forms of black literature not just as signs for the failure of heterosexual, black, nationalist narratives, but also as sites for a new narrative resolution of the struggles of rebellious subjectivities against overarching imperial frameworks, frameworks that would define them as gendered, raced, sexed, and classed in particular ways.

10. Eng, *Racial Castration*, 207.

11. Benjamin, "Theses on the Philosophy of History," in *Reflections*, 254.

12. Carby, *Race Men*, 5.

13. McKay, "The Little Sheik," in *Gingertown*, 260–73.

14. Ibid., 262.

15. Ibid., 267, 265.

16. Ibid., 273.

17. McKay worked on this novel while living in Spain between 1929 and 1930 and, like *Home to Harlem* and *Banjo*, "it dealt with working-class characters in an exotic 'low-life' setting that emphasized the marginality of black existence in Western commercial society" (Cooper, *Claude McKay*, 266). Unlike both of his previous novels, however, this piece, originally entitled *The Jungle and the Bottoms* and then retitled *Savage Loving* before finally assuming its final form, followed a more conventional plot than the picaresque. The novel's main focus was the love affair between an African male, Lafala, and his female lover Zhima. Interestingly, one of McKay's primary problems with the piece was the strength of the "Arab" female character, Zhima: "The Arab girl is growing bigger than I ever dreamed and running away with the book and me," he described to his agent (McKay quoted in Cooper, 267).

18. Cooper, *Claude McKay*, 268.

19. Edwards, *The Practice of Diaspora*, 365.

20. McKay, *A Long Way from Home*, 159.

21. Ibid., 167–68.

22. McKay, "Soviet Russia and the Negro," 96.

23. Ibid., 100. See also Peterson's *Up From Bondage* for a dissection of the "spontaneous upsurging of folk feeling" McKay described experiencing while in Russia.

24. Cooper was the first to recount and analyze McKay's experiences while in Russia, even collecting some of his speeches in *The Passion of Claude McKay*. Two more fuller accounts would be Baldwin's recent *Beyond the Color Line and the Iron Curtain* and Winston James's forthcoming biographical volumes on McKay.

25. McKay, *A Long Way from Home*, 174–75.

26. Ibid., 175.

27. McKay as quoted in Cooper, *Claude McKay*, 163. Here Cooper describes a heated exchange between McKay and Max Eastman, in which this comment is itself a source of contention. See the full exchange reprinted in Cooper, *The Passion of Claude McKay*, 78–90.

28. Cooper argues that McKay was one of the main leaders of Briggs's African Blood Brotherhood (ABB).

29. McKay, "Speech to the Fourth Congress of the Third Communist International, Moscow," 92.

30. McKay, "Soviet Russia and the Negro," 97. This article, reprinted in Cooper's *The Passion of Claude McKay*, appeared first in *Crisis* 27 (December 1923–January 1924).

31. McKay, "Soviet Russia and the Negro," 93.

32. McKay, *A Long Way from Home*, 180.

33. McKay, "Speech to the Fourth Congress of the Third Communist International, Moscow," 93.

34. Cooper, *Claude McKay*, 175.

35. The real heyday of political organizing and activism in Harlem would come in the 1930s, based on the previous work done by activists such as the members of the ABB. See Naison's *Communists in Harlem During the Depression* for more on black activism in New York during this later period.

36. McKay, *A Long Way from Home*, 175.

37. Ibid., 176.

38. Ibid., 175.

39. Ibid., 229.

40. Ibid., 226.

41. Ibid., 243.

42. Ibid., 247.

43. Quoted from Freud's *Civilization and Its Discontents*. See Cowley's discussion of modernist angst among American writers in *Exile's Return*.

44. McKay, *Banjo*, 68–69.

45. Cowley, *Exile's Return*, 8–9, 27; McKay, *A Long Way from Home*, 244.

46. McKay, *A Long Way from Home*, 245.

47. McKay, *Banjo*, 6. Again, for a close reading of McKay's work through the lens of ethnicity, see Hathaway's *Caribbean Waves*.

48. Edwards, *The Practice of Diaspora*, 199–201.

49. McKay, *Banjo*, 3.

50. Ibid., 5.

51. Nassy Brown, "Black Liverpool," 300–301.

52. McKay, *Banjo*, 18.

53. Ibid., 11.

54. Ibid.

55. Linebaugh and Rediker, *The Many-Headed Hydra*, 158.

56. Ibid., 162.

57. Ibid., 164.

58. Ibid., 152.

59. McKay, *Banjo*, 12.

60. Ibid., 19.

61. Ibid., 39.

62. McKay, *Gingertown*, 273.

63. Gilroy, *The Black Atlantic*, esp. the preface and chapter 1, 1–40.

64. Edwards, *The Practice of Diaspora*, 219.

65. McKay, *Banjo*, 6–8.

66. Ibid., 47.

67. Ibid., 102.

68. Ibid., 96.

69. Ibid., 97.

70. Ibid., 49.

71. Garvey, "Speech at Royal Albert Hall," 296.

72. McKay, *Banjo*, 14.

73. Ibid., 92.

74. Ibid., 66.

75. Ibid., 115.

76. Ibid., 293.

77. Ibid., 67.

78. Ibid.

79. Ibid., 69.

80. Linebaugh and Rediker, *The Many-Headed Hydra*, 168.

81. McKay, *Banjo*, 285–88.

82. Ibid., 68.

83. Ibid., 78.

84. Ibid., 80.

85. Ibid., 135.

86. Ibid., 137.

87. Ibid., 136.

88. Ibid., 137.

89. Ibid.

90. Ibid., 203.

91. Ibid., 222.

92. Ibid., 188.

93. Ibid., 195.

94. Ibid.

95. Ibid., 223.

96. Ibid., 248.

97. Ibid., 261.

98. Ibid., 262.

99. Ibid., 264.

100. Ibid., 266.

101. Ibid., 267.

102. Ibid., 311.

103. Ibid., 311–12.

104. Ibid., 313–14.

105. McKay himself learned this during his trip to Morocco, when he was summoned to register at the office of the British Consul. As he said, "I had been passing such a jolly time with no shadow of any trouble. . . . I'd been so absorbed in the picturesque and exotic side of the native life that I was unaware until authority stepped on my sore toe" (*A Long Way from Home*, 301–2). But McKay was one of the luckier ones precisely because, as one compatriot pointed out to him, he was "an American . . . specially protected."

106. Edwards, *The Practice of Diaspora*.

107. McKay, *Banjo*, 61.

108. Ibid., 317.

109. Ibid., 289.

110. Ibid., 252.

111. Ibid., 252–53.

112. Ibid., 37.

113. Ibid., 61.

114. Ibid., 291–92.

115. Ibid., 292.

116. Ibid., 292–93.

117. Interestingly, Felice is impacted in her own way by the spirit of black international-ism sweeping over the era—through the domestic power of the figure of the black emperor himself (only further confirming Garvey's role in bringing the freedoms and possibilities of black transnationalism home to those black subjects unable to travel). As Jake also describes, "In Chicago, Felice had begun reading the *Negro World*, the organ of the Back-to-Africa movement, and when they came back [to Harlem] she was as interested in Liberty Hall as in Sheba Palace. She had even worried Jake to take a share in Black Star Line" (ibid., 294).

118. McKay, *A Long Way from Home*, 301.

119. McKay, *Banjo*, 321.

120. Benjamin, "The Storyteller," in *Illuminations*, 84.

121. Ibid., 91.

122. McKay, *Banjo*, 115.

123. Ibid., 116.

124. McKay, *A Long Way from Home*, 300.


## 7 C. L. R. JAMES AND THE FUGITIVE SLAVE

1. Abbé Raynal, *Philosophical and Political History of the Establishments and Commerce of the Europeans in the Two Indies* (1780), quoted in the 1989 Allison and Busby edition of James's history, *The Black Jacobins*, 25.

2. The play was later revised and retitled in 1967 as *The Black Jacobins*, and it was performed at the University of Ibadan in Nigeria. James did substantial revisions of the play for a sixties audience, including the addition of an epilogue that directly addressed the question facing the newly independent nations of Africa and the Caribbean, namely, the choice between alignment with the capitalist United States or the communist Soviet Union. However, as the reviews and program notes from the 1930s reveal, the general structure and themes of the play remained constant: the debate over the nature of Haiti's independence, the different roles and conceptions of the black leader, and his relationship to the European empires on one hand and the black masses on the other. Few extant copies of James's revisions exist, but an original copy of the play as it was performed in the 1930s is owned by Errol Hill. The text of the play I am using here is collected in *The C. L. R. James Reader* under the title "The Black Jacobins" (Grimshaw, *The C. L. R. James Reader* (hereinafter referred to as Grimshaw), 67–111). This version of the text can also be found in Errol Hill's *A Time . . . and a Season*. A manuscript copy of the 1967 text of the play, with further marginalia, edits, and revisions by James, can be found at the C. L. R. James Institute, 505 West End Avenue, no. 15C, New York, NY 10024.

3. McKay, *Home to Harlem*, 133.

4. James, "Letters to Literary Critics" (1953), in Grimshaw, 232.

5. James would also revisit the story of the black emperor in a slightly more playful form. In the archives of the C. L. R. James Institute one can find "The Story of the African Drums," a three-page children's tale James wrote for his son in 1955, in which the characters "Bad Boo-Boo-Loo" and "Good Boong-Ko" arrive on an island soon after a character named "the Emperor Jones" has established his tyrannical rule. They join in the islanders' drumming which so confuses the Emperor that soon "he fell down exhausted . . . His soldiers ran away, and the Africans came out of the forest and took him prisoner. They took away his guns, and he begged pardon for his crimes against the Republic. So the Republic was restored and the Emperor Jones was put on a boat and told to go find himself somewhere else to live." This was James's succinct and amusing rendition of O'Neill's modernist drama for his own young black transnational audience. (Typescript dated 23 February 1955.) Paul Robeson would also revisit the role of the black emperor in the 1936 film *Song of Freedom*, also his first film in England. Here, both the back to Africa narrative and the performance of

black male sovereignty take on an individual and personal tone. *Song of Freedom* tells the story of a black dockworker named John Zinga, who upon being discovered by a European opera impresario uses his singing as a way to travel to Africa to discover his ancestral roots. Soon he learns that he is a descendent of royalty from the African island of Casanga. Zinga travels to the island with his wife and a black servant, and, after much intrigue and drama, he is recognized as the Africans' rightful king. The film's plot bears striking similarities to nineteenth-century black empire narratives such as Pauline Hopkins's *Of One Blood*. The film also includes Robeson's stirring rendition of the song of freedom that the movie's title heralds. A sense of the stern grandeur of this performance is present in an image from the film included at the beginning of this chapter. The song, aptly enough, was entitled "Black Emperor" (see Norton, review of *Song of Freedom*).

6. James, "Paul Robeson," in *Spheres of Existence*, 256. Carby's analysis of James's construction of a revolutionary masculinity is relevant here, as she describes how aesthetic "body lines" map onto "color lines" in James's portrayals of the black athlete, specifically the Caribbean cricketer, as the embodiment of "colonial manhood" (in *Race Men*, 119).

7. Letter courtesy of Jim Murray from the C. L. R. James Institute.

8. James, "Paul Robeson," in *Spheres of Existence*, 258.

9. James, "Letters to Literary Critics," in Grimshaw, 231. Grimshaw also discusses James's theory of the "personality in history" in her introduction (6).

10. Ibid.

11. James, "Notes on *Hamlet*" (1953) in Grimshaw, 243.

12. William Wordsworth's 1802 poem "To Toussaint L'Ouverture" appears in Aravamudan's discussion of the tropicopolitan power of the Haitian revolution and the figure of Toussaint L'Ouverture in European discourse of the long eighteenth century (*Tropicopolitans*, 310). See also Buck-Morss's essay, "Hegel and Haiti," for a discussion of the Haitian revolution's role in shaping Hegel's philosophical account of the master-slave dialectic.

13. Carby, *Race Men*, 113.

14. Ibid., 116.

15. Ibid., 125. Carby cites the 1971 reprinted edition of James 1936 novel, *Minty Alley*, by New Beacon Books.

16. Carby, *Race Men*, 125.

17. Edmondson, *Making Men*, 106.

18. Carby, *Race Men*, 129.

19. Ibid., 129.

20. Edmondson, *Making Men*, 106.

21. Ibid., 106–7.

22. Genovese, *From Rebellion to Revolution*. James was very much aware of Genovese's argument; he described Genovese's text as, "a book which can hold its own with [the] great historical approximations of Marx and Lenin" (book jacket).

23. Raynal as quoted in James, *The Black Jacobins* (Allison and Busby, 1989), 25.

24. James, "Letters to Literary Critics," in Grimshaw, 221–22.

25. James, "Preface to Criticism" (1955) in Grimshaw, 257.

26. Ibid., 259.

27. James, *The Black Jacobins*, in Grimshaw, 96. All subsequent references to the play will be in the text, identified by act and scene number. The play as it appears in Grimshaw is used throughout.

28. This "fraternity" is of course a male community, a brotherhood of citizens within the national state.

29. James, "The Making of the Caribbean People," in *Spheres of Existence*, 176.

30. James's creation of dramatic tension at this particular moment in the play came from his understanding of the Aristotelian theory of catharsis. For James the cathartic effect worked only at the point at which the audience was engaged with the question of the future of the state. See his 1954 essay "Popular Art and the Cultural Tradition," reprinted in Grimshaw, 252.

31. James, "Preface to Criticism," Grimshaw, 256.

32. There are grounds to question whether the play was originally ordered in three acts. In the manuscript version of the play that has some of James's revision notes for the 1967 production, the text on which he is revising actually has only two acts. In the manuscript version the play breaks for act two at the point at which Dessalines gains control of the plot.

33. James, "Preface to Criticism," in Grimshaw, 256.

34. Wallerstein, *Geopolitics and Geoculture*, 81.

35. Ibid., 81, 82.

36. McLemee, introduction to *C. L. R. James on the 'Negro Question'* (hereinafter referred to as McLemee), xii.

37. James as quoted in McLemee, xxv.

38. James, *American Civilization*, 119.

39. Ibid., 31.

40. Ibid., 152.

41. Ibid., 153.

42. Ibid.

43. Ibid.

44. Ibid., 162.

45. Ibid.

46. Ibid.

47. Cruse, *The Crisis of the Negro Intellectual*, 3.

48. Ibid., 5.

49. James, "The Historical Development of the Negroes in American Society" (1943) reprinted in McLemee, 63.

50. Ibid., 64.

51. James, *American Civilization*, 104.

52. Ibid., 48.

53. See Balibar's preface to *Race, Nation, Class*, where he compellingly argues: "Perhaps we should then invert our interpretation of the Marxist thesis. Instead of representing the capitalist division of labour to ourselves as what founds or institutes human societies as relatively stable 'collectivities,' should we not conceive this as what *destroys* them? . . . If this is so, the history of social formations would be not so much a history of non-commodity communities making the transition to market society," but rather a history of their *"reactions"* to the destruction that threatens (7–8; italics in original).

54. James, *The Black Jacobins*, in Grimshaw, 90.

55. For Cruse, proponents of integration believed in the "Great American Ideal," that all citizens were "full-fledged Americans, without regard to race, creed, or color." Cruse's observation was that "America, which idealizes the rights of the individual above everything else, is in reality, a nation dominated by the social power of groups." This then led him to argue for a black cultural and economic separatism founded on a parallel "Negro ethnic group consciousness," a black "cultural nationalism" within the United States. This "definite strain of thought within the Negro group that encompasses all the ingredients of 'nationality'" offered an opposing vision of the "Negro's" place in American society than "its opposite—the racial integration strain." (*The Crisis of the Negro Intellectual*, 4, 8, 7, 10).

56. James, "The Historical Development of the Negroes in American Society," in McLemee, 68.

57. Ibid., 86.

58. Ibid., 87.

59. James, "From the Master-Slave Dialectic to Revolt in Capitalist Production" (1946), in McLemee, 133.

60. While James understood the impossibility of the domestic narrative of class mobility for the mass of the black population in America, he also strongly objected to the separatist underpinnings of the International's policy on the Southern Black Belt, one that not only saw the Black Belt as an internal colony within the United States, but heralded its future as an independent black state complete with "maps showing the borders of this nation-to-be" (described by McLemee, xix). James would describe self-determination as a "sterile question," and his objection to the policy came precisely from his sense that African Americans' political goal was ultimately not to achieve independence from America but rather the rights of full citizenship.

61. James, "Preliminary Notes on the Negro Question" (1939), in McLemee, 8.

62. James, "The Race Pogroms and the Negro" (1943), in McLemee, 38. James often used his observations to directly criticize Walter White, who by the 1940s had become the national secretary of the NAACP.

63. James, "Notes Following the Discussions" (1939), in McLemee, 14.

64. Ibid., 15.

65. Ibid.

66. Ibid., 16.

67. James, "Marcus Garvey" (1940), in McLemee, 114.

68. James, "Negroes in the Civil War," in McLemee, 99–107. James's thinking here, and his focus on the slave in the American South, also reflected his deep admiration for Du Bois's *Black Reconstruction in America, 1860–1880*, a text whose central concern was the American slaves' attempts for self-determination and self-governance during Reconstruction (see McLemee, xxxii).

69. James, "Negroes in the Civil War," in McLemee, 101.

70. Ibid.

71. Ibid.

72. Ibid., 102–3.

73. Ibid., 103.

74. Ibid., 105.

75. James, "Black People in the Urban Areas of the United States," in Grimshaw, 378.

76. Ibid., 375.

77. Ibid.

78. James, *American Civilization*, 199.

79. Ibid., 207.

80. Ibid.

81. Ibid., 208.

82. Ibid., 211.

83. James, "'My Friends': A Fireside Chat on the War by Native Son" (1940), in McLemee, 17–21.

84. When McKay wrote his poem "If We Must Die" as an expression of the revolutionary consciousness generated from his own fugitive urban existence as a Pullman porter during Red Summer, he too was articulating a historic dynamic. James used McKay's poem as his opening to "A Fireside Chat on the War by Native Son."

85. James, "On *Native Son* by Richard Wright" (1940), in McLemee, 56.

86. Ibid., 57.

87. Ibid.

88. Ibid., 58.

89. James, "The Making of the Caribbean People," in *Spheres of Existence*, 183.

90. Carby, *Race Men*, 120.

91. James, *American Civilization*, 199.

92. Ibid., 215.

93. Ibid., 219. The emphasis is in the original.

94. Ibid., 213.

95. Ibid., 218.

96. Ibid., 219.

97. Ibid., 215.

98. Ibid.

99. Ibid.

100. James, "Three Black Women Writers: Toni Morrison, Alice Walker, Ntozake Shange," in Grimshaw, 411. In the second half of *Making Men*, Edmondson has also argued that Walker, Morrison, and Shange's contemporaries, Caribbean American women writers living and working in the United States during the 1970s and 1980s such as Paule Marshall and Michelle Cliff, have often had to negotiate precisely this masculinist legacy in constructing their own revolutionary racial visions and global female imaginary: "[Their] erasure is 'exhumed' by women writers, who must refigure the meaning of 'revolution' and 'revolutionary' in order to envision anticolonial narrative that does not preclude the meaning of black womanhood" (108).

101. Robeson, *Here I Stand*, 66–67.


8 THE CARIBBEAN AND AMERICAN STUDIES

1. Maingot, "Caribbean International Relations," 259.

2. James, *American Civilization*, 256.

3. James's characterization of Melville's three harpooners can be found in *Mariners, Renegades and Castaways*, 18; Bederman's description of the representation of colonial masculinities during this period is in *Manliness and Civilization*, 42.

4. See Renda's *Taking Haiti* for her coinage of the term "U.S. American" to capture a United States citizen-subject living in a broader "American" hemispheric context. As she describes her rationale, "I use the term . . . to acknowledge that the United States constitutes part but not all of America and to address the problem posed by the word 'American' for students of the Americas" (xvii).

5. James, *Mariners, Renegades and Castaways*, 38.

6. Ibid.

7. See Sanborn's full discussion in *The Sign of the Cannibal*, 51.

8. James, *Mariners, Renegades and Castaways*, 18.

9. Ibid., 18.

10. Ibid., 20.

11. Ibid., 31.

12. Ibid., 40. Interestingly, Bolster has identified the black sailor as a particularly striking figure in Melville's fiction, seeming to represent the utmost in marine masculinity. He quotes from another of Melville's sea voyage narratives, *Billy Budd, A Sailor (An Inside Narrative)*, the following "introduction of a manly black as the archetypal handsome sailor": "In Liverpool, now some half a century ago, I saw under the shadow of the great . . . street-wall of

Prince's Dock . . . a common sailor so intensely black that he must needs have been a native African . . . in his ears were big hoops of gold, and . . . he rollicked along, the center of a company of his shipmates" (*Black Jacks*, 68, 76).

13. James, *Mariners, Renegades and Castaways*, 39.

14. Ibid.

15. Ibid., 38–39.

16. Ibid., 39.

17. Ibid., 40–41.

18. Ibid.

19. Ibid., 42.

20. Ibid.

21. Ibid., 43.

22. Ibid., 44.

23. Ibid., 30.

24. Ibid., 123.

25. James, *American Civilization*, 223–24. Here James, like Benjamin, also marked the significance of World War I in shaping new relations among modern men: "One of the outstanding features of World War I and World War II [was] the development of what has been called 'comradeship' among the men [who, despite] the squalor, the blood, the inhumanity, were recompensed by the consciousness of the relation [of intimacies between men], unknown it seems among modern men in times of peace."

26. Ibid. 221.

27. Ibid., 223.

28. Ibid., 224.

29. James, *Mariners, Renegades and Castaways*, 30.

30. Ibid., 19.

31. Pease, "C. L. R. James's *Mariners, Renegades and Castaways* and the World We Live In," xxx–xxxi. Also see Pease's essays, "C. L. R. James, *Moby-Dick*, and the Emergence of Transnational American Studies" and "National Narratives, Postnational Narration," for his development of the idea of a postnational, transnational American studies.

32. Luce, "The American Century."

33. James, *American Civilization*, 40.

34. James, *Mariners, Renegades and Castaways*, 35.

35. Melville as quoted in James, *Mariners, Renegades and Castaways*, 34–35.

36. James, *Mariners, Renegades and Castaways*, 13.

37. Ibid.

38. Melville as quoted in James, *Mariners, Renegades and Castaways*, 4.

39. Ibid.

40. In Huntington's article "The Clash of Civilizations" and his subsequent book *The*

*Clash of Civilizations and the Remaking of World Order*, we see the racialized language of nationalism repeated in contemporary terms in a notion of world-politics shaped by the belief in different nations' competing cultures and irreconcilable civilizations. See Said's "The Clash of Ignorance" and Sen's "Civilizational Imprisonments" for two strong responses to Huntington's thesis, albeit from different perspectives.

41. James, *American Civilization*, 48.

42. Ibid., 49.

43. James, *Mariners, Renegades and Castaways*, 21.

44. Ibid., 41.

45. See James's essays on federation collected in *At the Rendezvous of Victory*, 85–128 (94). Also see *Modern Politics*, 81–86.

46. James, essays on federation in *At the Rendezvous of Victory*, 91–92.

47. Ibid., 92.

48. Here James's analyses of American civilization and its relationship to both Europe and the global community prefigure some of the key arguments and insights in Hardt's and Negri's recent theorization of the politics of globalization (*Empire*). What James adds to their account is his sense of the Caribbean region and peoples specifically, and the multiracial, multinational subaltern subject more broadly, as resisting and countering the effects of empire in their everyday regeneration and re-creation of alternative ways of imagining community.

49. James, *Modern Politics*, 84.

50. Balibar, "The Nation Form: History and Ideology" in *Race, Nation, Class*, 89. Here Balibar draws from Braudel's *The Perspective of the World*, 97–105, and Wallerstein's *Capitalist Agriculture and the Origin of the European World-Economy in the Sixteenth Century*, 165 et seq.

51. James, *Modern Politics*, 81.

52. Ibid., 82.

53. Sassen, *Cities in a World Economy*, 3. Here Sassen points out that while cities have always been considered "to be part of national urban systems [and] [i]nternational aspects have been considered the preserve of nation-states," in a transnational world of global financial markets and off-shore trading zones, new international relationships emerge between cities themselves. Sassen used the notion of "global cities" to argue that, at the level of "foreign relations," in addition to the relationships between core and periphery nations there was also "the possibility of a systemic dynamic binding these cities" (50). Globalization remaps the borders of nations and communities, creating transnational spaces such as cities within national territories. These global cities represent a new geography of relations that crosscut and intersect state borders.

54. Referencing here the famous Melville passage quoted by James and used in his title; "If, then, to meanest mariners, and renegades and castaways, I shall hereafter ascribe high qualities" (*Mariners, Renegades and Castaways*, 17).

55. James, "From Toussaint L'Ouverture to Fidel Castro," in Grimshaw, *The C. L. R. James Reader*, 308.

56. James, *Mariners, Renegades and Castaways*, 18.

57. Ibid., 18.

58. Lamming, *The Pleasures of Exile*, 154.

59. Ibid. This living with difference within the nation has implications for both a race and a gender politics, for as Crenshaw argued in her essay, "Mapping the Margins": "The problem with identity politics is not that it fails to transcend difference [but] that it frequently conflates or ignores intragroup differences. In the context of violence against women, this elision of difference is problematic . . . when [feminist and antiracist] practices expound identity as 'woman' or 'person of color' as an either/or proposition, they relegate the identity of women of color to a location that resists telling" (94). To the degree that "nationality" also, as the highest order of political identity in the modern nation-state, has been unable to incorporate the identities of woman and person of color together, the modern story of nationality and difference violently erases the woman of color. This occurs in both private and public domestic spheres, legally and culturally, in both imperial and postcolonial nation-states.

60. Aimé Césaire's *Cahier d'un Retour au Pays Natal*, as quoted in James, "From Toussaint L'Ouverture to Fidel Castro," 303.

61. James, *Mariners, Renegades and Castaways*, 17.

62. Ibid., 18.

63. Ibid., 19.

64. Ibid., 20.

65. Ibid., 18.

66. Ibid., 53.

67. Ibid., 54.

68. Ibid., 53.

69. Ibid.

70. Ibid., 22.

71. Ibid., 20.

72. Wallerstein, *Geopolitics and Geoculture*, 192.

73. Ibid., 192–93.

74. James, *Mariners, Renegades and Castaways*, 81.

75. Grimshaw, introduction to *The C. L. R. James Reader*, 19.

76. Lamming, *The Pleasures of Exile*, 155.

77. James, *The Black Jacobins*, in Grimshaw, 96.

78. James, essays on federation in *At the Rendezvous of Victory*, 95.

79. James, "A National Purpose for Caribbean Peoples," in *At the Rendezvous of Victory*, 155.

80. Ibid.

81. Ibid., 155.

82. James, *Modern Politics*, 70.

83. James, *American Civilization*, 153.

84. As James said, "Federation is the means and the only means whereby the West Indies . . . can accomplish the transition from colonialism to national independence, can create the basis of a new nation; and by reorganizing the economic system and the national life give us our place in the modern community of nations" (*At the Rendezvous of Victory*, 90).

85. James's essays on federation in *At the Rendezvous of Victory*, 98.

86. Stuart Hall quoted in an interview with Kuan-Hsing Chen, "The Formation of a Diasporic Intellectual: An Interview with Stuart Hall by Kuan-Hsing Chen" (in Morley and Chen, *Stuart Hall*, 492, 502). Given the impact of the idea of West Indian federation on Hall's own intellectual formation, it is not irrelevant that one of the central insights of black British cultural studies under Hall's stewardship has been precisely the idea that blackness is heterogeneous, federated, and continuously in need of construction. In this interview Hall differentiates his theory of identity from that of "a postmodernist 'nomadic'" saying, "I think cultural identity is not fixed, it's always hybrid. But this is precisely because it comes out of very specific historical formations, out of very specific histories" (502). The argument of this book has been precisely that Caribbean hybridity itself is constituted in and from specific political histories, both imperial and subaltern. I would argue that Hall's work on and insights into ethnicity come out of precisely the black transnational formation that I am describing here, an intellectual formation whose political manifestation culminated in the 1950s in the dream of West Indian federation. (For some of Hall's crucial theorizations of identity and identity politics, see "Minimal Selves"; "Cultural Identity and Diaspora"; "Ethnicity"; and "New Ethnicities.")

87. Also see Thomas's discussion of the New World Group and New Worldism movement in the Caribbean in the 1960s and 1970s ("Caribbean Black Power."). Here Thomas identifies how post-Federation politics in the Caribbean influenced later Black Power movements in the region.

88. Henry, *Caliban's Reason*, 228.

89. For a description of the variety of organizations that currently bear the legacy of the West Indian Federation, the leading one being the Caribbean Community and Common Market (CARICOM), see Maingot, "Caribbean International Relations," 282–83.

90. Ibid., 260.

91. James, "The Revolutionary Answer to the Negro Problem in the United States," in McLemee, *C. L. R. James on the 'Negro Question,'* 142. Not only does James use Lenin's statement in two different essays between 1943 and 1948, "The Historical Development of the Negroes in American Society" (1943) and "The Revolutionary Answer to the Negro Problem in the United States" (1948), but also, in the latter, he quotes it twice. Both essays are reprinted in McLemee's collection.

1. Lorde, *The Collected Poems of Audre Lorde*, 85.

2. Tyler, "The World Cries Uncle," 22.

3. See also Judt's review, "We'll Always Have Paris," of MacMillan's *Paris 1919.*

4. Salih, "German film exposes Guantanamo 'scandal.'" Salih's piece was written before the subsequent scandals in 2004 surrounding the documented abuse of Iraqi prisoners by U.S. soldiers, photographed and reproduced throughout U.S. news media.

5. See Mann's *Incoherent Empire.*

6. As Ignatieff argued in "The American Empire (Get Used To It)," 22. In her presidential address to the American Studies Association later that year, Amy Kaplan argued that "As the United States marshals violent forces around the globe," we are seeing precisely a "shift in public discourse from denying to embracing the idea of empire. Across the political spectrum, politicians, journalists and academics are debating whether the American Empire is in ascendancy or decline, if it is benevolent or self-interested, if a republic can survive as an empire, and what form its global power should take" ("Violent Belongings and the Question of Empire Today"). Also find a full copy of Kaplan's Presidential Address in *American Quarterly.*

7. Clifford, *The Predicament of Culture*, 173.

8. In his afterword to the 1978 edition of *Mariners, Renegades and Castaways*, James would make this connection between his time on Ellis Island, the redemptive trope of the island archipelago, and Solzhenitsyn's text (173).

9. James wrote *Mariners* while imprisoned on Ellis Island and mailed it to "every member of Congress . . . Governors, Mayors of large cities, the Supreme Court, every important official, editor, lawyer, journalist, broadcaster, labor leader, etc." (James, letter to "George," 22 June 1953, Beinecke Library, James Weldon Johnson Collection, Yale University). He ended the book with an autobiographical appendix, "A Natural But Necessary Conclusion," in which he detailed not only his treatment on Ellis Island but also its implications for the future of American international democracy.

10. James, *Mariners, Renegades and Castaways*, 175. As he would put it, "A great part of this book was written while I was being detained by the Department of Immigration. The Island like Melville's *Pequod*, is a miniature of all the nations of the world and all sections of society." James also included a note about language: "The authorities on Ellis Island insist on the word 'detainees' instead of prisoners. After my own experiences and what I have seen, it would be a mockery for me to assist them in still more deceiving the American people. Under that administration the people on the Island are prisoners" (143).

11. Ibid., 125, 137, 138, 140, 140–41.

12. Ibid., 140, 141, 141.

13. Ibid., 142.

14. Ibid., 165, 165.

15. Ibid., 145–46.

16. Ibid., 151.

17. Ibid., 152.

18. Ibid., 153.

19. Ibid., 153–54.

20. Lorde, "Grenada Revisited" in *Sister Outsider*, 176.

21. Kaplan and Pease, *Cultures of U.S. Imperialism*, 94.

22. James, "Three Black Women Writers," in Grimshaw, *The C. L. R. James Reader*, 411.

23. Lorde, *Zami*.

24. Ibid., 13.

25. Ibid., 13–14.

26. Ibid., 255.

27. Lorde, "Grenada Revisited," 177.

28. Ibid., 177.

29. Griffin, *"Who Set You Flowin'?,"* 7.

30. Ibid., 7.

31. Lorde, "Grenada Revisited," 189.

32. See Basch et al. for their description of transmigrants as "Immigrants who develop and maintain multiple relationships—familial, economic, social, organizational, religious, and political—that span [national] borders." (*Nations Unbound*, 7).

33. Du Bois, "Worlds of Color," 386.

34. Lorde, "Grenada Revisited," 184.

35. Ibid., 185.

36. Ibid., 182.

37. Ibid., 189.

38. Ibid., 183.

39. Ibid., 184.

40. Lorde, "Poetry Is Not a Luxury," in *Sister Outsider*, 39.

41. Lorde, "Grenada Revisited," 189.

42. Cliff, *Claiming an Identity They Taught Me to Despise*, 48.

# BIBLIOGRAPHY

Accaria-Zavala, Diane, and Rodolfo Popelnik, eds. *Prospero's Isles: The Presence of the Caribbean in the American Imaginary*. Oxford: Macmillan, 2004.

Allen, Ernest, Jr. "The New Negro: Explorations in Identity and Social Consciousness, 1910–1922." In *1915, The Cultural Moment: The New Politics, the New Woman, the New Psychology, the New Art and the New Theatre in America*. Ed. Adele Heller and Lois Rudnick. New Brunswick, N.J.: Rutgers University Press, 1991.

Anderson, Benedict. *Imagined Communities: Reflections on the Origin and Spread of Nationalism*. Rev. ed. London: Verso, 1991.

Andersen, Hans Christian. "The Emperor's New Suit." 1837. http://HCA.Gilead.org.il/emperor.html.

Andrews, William L., and Henry Louis Gates Jr. *Pioneers of the Black Atlantic, 1772–1815*. Washington: Civitas, 1998.

Appadurai, Arjun. *Modernity at Large: Cultural Dimensions of Globalization*. Minneapolis: University of Minnesota Press, 1996.

——. "Sovereignty without Territoriality: Notes for a Postnational Geography." In *The Geography of Identity*. Ed. Patricia Yaeger. Ann Arbor: University of Michigan Press, 1996.

Aravamudan, Srinivas. *Tropicopolitans: Colonialism and Agency, 1688–1884*. Durham: Duke University Press, 1999.

Bair, Barbara. *Freedom Is Never A Final Act: Women Emerge from the Garvey Movement.* Chapel Hill: University of North Carolina Press, in press.

Baker, Houston A., Jr. *Modernism and the Harlem Renaissance.* Chicago: University of Chicago Press, 1987.

Baldwin, Katherine Anne. *Beyond the Color Line and the Iron Curtain: Reading Encounters between Black and Red, 1922–1963.* Durham: Duke University Press, 2002.

Balibar, Etienne, and Immanuel Wallerstein. *Race, Nation, Class: Ambiguous Identities.* London: Verso, 1991.

Basch, Linda, Nina Glick Schiller, and Cristina Szanton Blanc. *Nations Unbound: Transnational Projects, Postcolonial Predicaments, and Deterritorialized Nation-States.* Langhorne, Pa.: Gordon and Breach, 1994.

Bederman, Gail. *Manliness and Civilization: A Cultural History of Gender and Race in the United States, 1880–1917.* Chicago: University of Chicago Press, 1995.

Benítez-Rojo, Antonio. *The Repeating Island: The Caribbean and the Postmodern Perspective.* Durham: Duke University Press, 1992.

Benjamin, Walter. *Illuminations.* New York: Schocken Books, 1968.

——. *Reflections.* New York: Schocken Books, 1971.

Berman, Paul. "The Romantic Revolutionary." *New Yorker,* 29 July 1996, 68–72.

Bernard, Emily, ed. *Remember Me to Harlem: The Letters of Langston Hughes and Carl Van Vechten, 1925–1964.* New York: Knopf, 2001.

Bhabha, Homi K., ed. *Nation and Narration.* London: Routledge, 1990.

Bogues, Anthony. *Caliban's Freedom: The Early Political Thought of C. L. R. James.* Chicago: Pluto Press, 1997.

Bolster, W. Jeffrey. *Black Jacks: African American Seamen in the Age of Sail.* Cambridge: Harvard University Press, 1997.

Bourne, Randolph S. *War and the Intellectuals: Collected Essays, 1915–1919.* New York: Harper and Row, 1964.

Boyce Davies, Carole. *Black Women, Writing, and Identity: Migrations of the Subject.* New York: Routledge, 1994.

Boyce Davies, Carole, and Elaine Savory Fido, eds. *Out of the Kumbla: Caribbean Women and Literature.* Trenton, N.J.: Africa World Press, 1990.

Boyce Davies, Carole, and Molara Ogundipe-Leslie, eds. *Moving Beyond Boundaries.* New York: New York University Press, 1995.

Boyce Davies, Carole, Isidore Okpewho, and Ali A. Mazrui. *The African Diaspora: African Origins and New World Identities.* Bloomington: Indiana University Press, 1999.

Brathwaite, Edward Kamau. *Roots.* Ann Arbor: University of Michigan Press, 1993.

Brathwaite, William Stanley. "The Negro in American Literature." In *The New Negro.* Ed. Alain Locke. New York: Atheneum, 1992.

Braudel, Fernand. *The Perspective of the World.* Trans. Siân Reynolds. London: Collins, 1984.

Briggs, Cyril V. "The League of Nations." *The Crusader I.* Vol. 1, no. 6. New York: Garland Publishing, 1987, 188.

——. "If It Were Only True." *The Crusader I.* Vol. 1, no. 7. New York: Garland Publishing, 1987, 228.

——. "What Does Democratic America in Haiti?" *The Crusader I.* Vol. 1, no. 10. New York: Garland Publishing, 1987, 329–30.

——. "Marcus Garvey." *The Crusader I.* Vol. 1, no. 12. New York: Garland Publishing, 1987, 406–7.

——. "The Ray of Fear: A Thrilling Story of Love, War, Race Patriotism, Revolutionary Inventions and the Liberation of Africa." *The Crusader II.* Vol. 2, no. 6. New York: Garland Publishing, 1987, 614–16.

——. "A Paramount Chief of the Negro Race." *The Crusader II.* Vol. 2, no. 7. New York: Garland Publishing, 1987, 635–36.

——. "A Letter from Marcus Garvey." *The Crusader II.* Vol. 2, no. 8. New York: Garland Publishing, 1987, 663–64.

——. "The Universal Negro Improvement Association." *The Crusader II.* Vol. 2, no. 9. New York: Garland Publishing, 1987, 698.

——. "The U. N. I. A. Convention." *The Crusader II.* Vol. 2, no. 10. New York: Garland Publishing, 1987, 729.

——. "The African Blood Brotherhood." *The Crusader II.* Vol. 2, no. 10. New York: Garland Publishing, 1987, 731.

——. "Loyalty." *The Crusader II.* Vol. 2, no. 11. New York: Garland Publishing, 1987, 765.

——. "The U. N. I. A. Convention." *The Crusader III.* Vol. 3, no. 1. New York: Garland Publishing, 1987, 834–37.

——. "Program of the A. B. B." *The Crusader III.* Vol. 5, no. 2. New York: Garland Publishing, 1987, 1249–52.

Bryce-Laporte, Roy S., and Delores M. Mortimer. *Caribbean Immigration to the United States.* Smithsonian Institute, RIES Occasional Papers 1. Washington, 1981.

——. *Female Immigrants to the United States: Caribbean, Latin American, and African Experiences.* Smithsonian Institute, RIES Occasional Papers 2. Washington, 1983.

Buck-Morss, Susan. "Hegel and Haiti." *Critical Inquiry* 26 (summer 2000): 821–65.

Buell, Frederick. *National Culture and the New Global System.* Baltimore: Johns Hopkins University Press, 1994.

Buhle, Paul, ed. *C. L. R. James: His Life and Work.* New York: Alison and Busby, 1986.

——. *C. L. R. James: The Artist as Revolutionary.* New York: Verso, 1988.

Buhle, Paul, and Paget Henry, eds. *C. L. R. James's Caribbean.* Durham: Duke University Press, 1992.

Butler, Octavia E. *Mind of My Mind.* New York: Doubleday, 1977.

——. *Wild Seed.* New York: Doubleday, 1980.

Carby, Hazel. *Reconstructing Womanhood: The Emergence of the Afro-American Woman Novelist*. New York: Oxford University Press, 1987.

———. Introduction to *The Magazine Novels of Pauline Hopkins*, by Pauline Hopkins. New York: Oxford University Press, 1988.

———. *Race Men*. Cambridge: Harvard University Press, 1998.

———. *Cultures in Babylon: Black Britain and African America*. New York: Verso, 1999.

Carr, Robert. *Black Nationalism in the New World: Reading the African-American and West Indian Experience*. Durham: Duke University Press, 2002.

Césaire, Aimé. *A Tempest: Based on Shakespeare's The Tempest*. Trans. Richard Miller. New York: Ubu Repertory Theater Publications, 1985.

Chen, Kuan-Hsing and Stuart Hall. Interview. "The Formation of a Diasporic Intellectual." In *Stuart Hall: Critical Dialogues in Cultural Studies*. Ed. David Morley and Kuan-Hsing Chen. London: Routledge, 1996.

Chesnutt, Charles W. *The Conjure Woman*. 1899. Ann Arbor: University of Michigan Press, 1969.

Clarke, John Henrik, ed. *Marcus Garvey and the Vision of Africa*. New York: Vintage Books, 1974.

Cliff, Michelle. *Claiming an Identity They Taught Me to Despise*. Watertown, Mass.: Persephone Press, 1980.

———. *No Telephone to Heaven*. New York: Vintage Books, 1987.

Clifford, James. *The Predicament of Culture: Twentieth-Century Ethnography, Literature, and Art*. Cambridge: Harvard University Press, 1988.

Condé, Maryse. *The Last of the African Kings*. Richard Philcox, trans. Lincoln, NE: University of Nebraska Press, 1997.

Cooper, Wayne F., ed. *The Passion of Claude McKay: Selected Prose and Poetry, 1912–1948*. New York: Schocken Books, 1973.

———. *Claude McKay: Rebel Sojourner in the Harlem Renaissance*. New York: Schocken Books, 1987.

Cowley, Malcolm. *Exile's Return: A Literary Odyssey of the 1920s*. New York: Penguin Books, 1976.

Crenshaw, Kimberlé. "Mapping the Margins: Intersectionality, Identity Politics, and Violence Against Women of Color." In Martha Albertson Fineman and Roxanne Mykitiuk, eds. *The Public Nature of Private Violence: The Discovery of Domestic Abuse*. New York: Routledge, 1994.

Cronon, E. David. *Black Moses: The Story of Marcus Garvey and the Universal Negro Improvement Association*. Madison: University of Wisconsin Press, 1955.

*The Crusader I*. Vol. 1. (1918/1919). New York: Garland Publishing, 1987, 1–432.

*The Crusader II*. Vol. 2. (1919/1920). New York: Garland Publishing, 1987, 433–824.

*The Crusader III*. Vols. 3–6. (1920–22). New York: Garland Publishing, 1987, 825–1395.

Cruse, Harold. *The Crisis of the Negro Intellectual*. New York: Quill, 1984.

Cudjoe, Selwyn R. and William E. Cain, eds. *C. L. R. James: His Intellectual Legacies*. Amherst: University of Massachusetts Press, 1995.

Curtis, Susan, *The First Black Actors on the Great White Way*. Columbia: University of Missouri Press, 1998.

Davis, Angela. *Women, Race, and Class*. New York: Random House, 1981.

Davis, Arthur P., and Michael W. Peplow. *The New Negro Renaissance: An Anthology*. New York: Holt, Rinehart, and Winston, 1975.

Dean, Harry, and Sterling North. *Umbala: The Adventures of a Negro Sea-Captain in Africa and on the Seven Seas in His Attempts to Found an Ethiopian Empire*. 1929. Winchester, Mass.: Pluto Press, 1989.

Delany, Martin. *Blake; or, The Huts of America, a Novel*. Boston: Beacon Press, 1970.

——. *The Condition, Elevation, Emigration, and Destiny of the Colored People of the United States*. Salem, N.H.: Ayer, 1988.

Delany, Samuel R. *Atlantis: Three Tales*. Middletown, Conn.: University Press of New England, 1995.

Denning, Michael. *The Cultural Front: The Laboring of American Culture in the Twentieth Century*. New York: Verso, 1996.

Diamond, Jared. *Guns, Germs, and Steel: The Fates of Human Societies*. New York: Norton, 1997.

Douglass, Frederick. *The Heroic Slave*. In *Autographs for Freedom*. Boston: John P. Jewett, 1853, 174–239. Reprinted in *Frederick Douglass: The Narrative and Selected Writings*. Ed. Michael Meyer. New York: Random House, 1984, 298–348.

Draper, Theodore. *American Communism and Soviet Russia*. New York: Viking Press, 1960.

Du Bois, W. E. B. "Worlds of Color." In *The New Negro*. Ed. Alain Locke. New York: Atheneum, 1992, 383–414. Originally published as "The Negro Mind Reaches Out," *Foreign Affairs* 3, no. 3 (April 1925).

——. "Criteria of Negro Art." *Crisis* 32 (October 1926): 290–97.

——. "The Browsing Reader: 'Home to Harlem.'" *Crisis* 35 (June 1928): 202.

——. *Black Reconstruction in America, 1860–1880*. New York: Harcourt, Brace, 1935.

——. *Darkwater: Voices from Within the Veil*. New York: AMS Press, 1969.

——. *The Souls of Black Folk*. New York: Penguin Books, 1969.

——. "Back to Africa." Reprinted in *Marcus Garvey and the Vision of Africa*. Ed. John Henrik Clarke. New York: Vintage Books, 1974, 105–19.

——. *Dark Princess: A Romance*. Jackson: University Press of Mississippi, 1995.

Duberman, Martin B. *Paul Robeson: A Biography*. New York: Knopf, 1989.

Eakin, Emily. "Embracing the Wisdom of a Castaway." *New York Times* 4 August 2001, A15–A17.

Edmondson, Belinda, ed. *Caribbean Romances: The Politics of Regional Representation*. Charlottesville: University Press of Virginia, 1999.

——. *Making Men: Gender, Literary Authority, and Women's Writing in Caribbean Narrative*. Durham: Duke University Press, 1999.

Edwards, Brent Hayes. "The Uses of Diaspora." *Social Text* 66 (spring 2001): 45–73.

——. *The Practice of Diaspora: Literature, Translation, and the Rise of Black Internationalism*. Cambridge: Harvard University Press, 2003.

Elmes, A. F. "Garvey and Garveyism: An Estimate." 1925. Reprinted in *Marcus Garvey and the Vision of Africa*. Ed. John Henrik Clarke. New York: Vintage Books, 1974, 120–26.

Eng, David L. *Racial Castration: Managing Masculinity in Asian America*. Durham: Duke University Press, 2001.

Fanon, Frantz. *The Wretched of the Earth*. New York: Grove Weidenfeld, 1963.

——. *Black Skin, White Masks*. New York: Grove Weidenfeld, 1967.

Farred, Grant, ed. *Rethinking C. L. R. James*. Cambridge, Mass.: Blackwell, 1996.

Fauset, Jessie. "The Gift of Laughter." In *The New Negro*. Ed. Alain Locke. New York: Atheneum, 1992.

Ferguson, Moira, ed. *Nine Black Women: An Anthology of Nineteenth-Century Writers from the United States, Canada, Bermuda, and the Caribbean*. New York: Routledge, 1998.

Ferguson, Niall. *Empire: The Rise and Demise of the British World Order and the Lessons for Global Power*. New York: Basic Books, 2003.

Fernández Retamar, Roberto. *Caliban and Other Essays*. Trans. Edward Baker. Minneapolis: University of Minnesota Press, 1989.

Fish, Cheryl J. *Black and White Women's Travel Narratives: Antebellum Explorations*. Gainesville: University Press of Florida, 2004.

Foulke, Robert. *The Sea Voyage Narrative*. New York: Twayne Publishers, 1997.

Fraden, Rena. *Blueprints for a Black Federal Theatre, 1935–1939*. Cambridge: Cambridge University Press, 1996.

Freud, Sigmund. *Civilization and Its Discontents*. Trans. James Strachey. New York: Norton, 1961.

Gaines, Kevin. "Black Americans' Racial Uplift Ideology as 'Civilizing Mission.'" In *Cultures of United States Imperialism*. Ed. Amy Kaplan and Donald E. Pease. Durham: Duke University Press, 1993.

——. *Uplifting the Race: Black Leadership, Politics, and Culture in the Twentieth Century*. Chapel Hill: University of North Carolina Press, 1996.

Garvey, Amy Jacques. *Garvey and Garveyism*. New York: Collier Books, 1970.

——. "The Early Years of Marcus Garvey." In *Marcus Garvey and the Vision of Africa*. Ed. John Henrik Clarke. New York: Vintage Books, 1974, 29–27.

Garvey, Marcus. "Speech at Royal Albert Hall." 1928. Reprinted in *Marcus Garvey and the Vision of Africa*. Ed. John Henrik Clarke. New York: Vintage Books, 1974, 284–99.

——. "The British West Indies in the Mirror of Civilization—History Making by Colonial Negroes." 1913. Reprinted in *Marcus Garvey and the Vision of Africa*. Ed. John Henrik Clarke. New York: Vintage Books, 1974, 77–82.

——. *A Talk with Afro-West Indians: The Negro Race and Its Problems*. 1913–14. Reprinted in *Marcus Garvey and the Vision of Africa*. Ed. John Henrik Clarke. New York: Vintage Books, 1974, 83–87.

——. "African Fundamentalism." Reprinted in *Marcus Garvey: Life and Lessons*. Ed. Robert A. Hill and Barbara Bair. Berkeley: University of California Press, 1987, 1–25.

——. Articles from the *Pittsburgh Courier*. 1930. Reprinted in *Marcus Garvey: Life and Lessons*. Ed. Robert A. Hill and Barbara Bair. Berkeley: University of California Press, 1987, 33–114.

Gates, Henry Louis Jr. "The Trope of a New Negro and the Reconstruction of the Image of the Black." *Representations* 24 (fall 1988): 129–55.

Gellner, Ernest. *Nations and Nationalism*. Ithaca: Cornell University Press, 1983.

Genovese, Eugene. *From Rebellion to Revolution: Afro-American Slave Revolts in the Making of the New World*. Baton Rouge: Louisiana State University Press, 1979.

Gilroy, Paul. *'There Ain't No Black in the Union Jack': The Cultural Politics of Race and Nation*. Chicago: University of Chicago Press, 1991.

——. *The Black Atlantic: Modernity and Double Consciousness*. Cambridge: Harvard University Press, 1993.

——. *Against Race: Imagining Political Culture Beyond the Color Line*. Cambridge: Harvard University Press, 2000.

——. "Black Fascism." *Transition* 9, no. 1/2 (81/82): 2000, 70–91.

Glaberman, Martin, ed. *Marxism for Our Times: C. L. R. James on Revolutionary Organization*. Jackson: University Press of Mississippi, 1999.

Glissant, Edouard. *Caribbean Discourse: Selected Essays*. Trans. J. Michael Dash. Charlottesville: University Press of Virginia, 1989.

Gramsci, Antonio. *An Antonio Gramsci Reader: Selected Writings, 1916–1935*. Ed. David Forgacs. New York: Schocken Books, 1988.

Gregory, Montgomery. "The Drama of Negro Life." In *The New Negro*. Ed. Alain Locke. New York: Atheneum, 1992.

Griffin, Farah Jasmine. *"Who Set You Flowin'?": The African-American Migration Narrative*. New York: Oxford University Press, 1995.

Griffin, Farah Jasmine, and Cheryl J. Fish, eds. *A Stranger in the Village: Two Centuries of African-American Travel Writing*. Boston: Beacon Press, 1998.

Griggs, Sutton E. *Imperium in Imperio: A Study of the Negro Race Problem*. 1899. New York: Arno Press, 1969.

Grimshaw, Anna, ed. *The C. L. R. James Reader*. Cambridge, Mass.: Blackwell, 1992.

——. Introduction to *The C. L. R. James Reader*. Cambridge, Mass.: Blackwell, 1992, 1–22.

——, ed. *Special Delivery: The Letters of C. L. R. James to Constance Webb 1939–1948*. Cambridge, Mass.: Blackwell, 1996.

Grimshaw, Anna, and Keith Hart. Introduction to *American Civilization*, by C. L. R. James. Cambridge, Mass.: Blackwell, 1993, 1–25.

Hadas, Moses, trans. *Heliodorus: An Ethiopian Romance*. Philadelphia: University of Pennsylvania Press, 1957.

Hall, Kim F. *Things of Darkness: Economies of Race and Gender in Early Modern England*. Ithaca: Cornell University Press, 1995.

Hall, Stuart. "Minimal Selves." In *The Real Me: Postmodernism and the Question of Identity*. ICA Documents 6. Ed. L. Appignanesi. London, 1988.

——. "Ethnicity: Identity and Difference." *Radical America* 23 (October–December 1989).

——. "New Ethnicities." In *Black Film, British Cinema*. ICA Documents 7. Ed. Kobena Mercer. London, 1989.

——. "Cultural Identity and Diaspora." In *Identity: Community, Culture, Difference*. Ed. Jonathan Rutherford. London: Lawrence and Wishart, 1990.

Hanchard, Michael. "Identity, Meaning and the African-American." *Social Text* 24 (1990): 31–42.

Hansen, Olaf, ed. *Randolph Bourne, The Radical Will: Selected Writings 1911–1918*. Berkeley: University of California Press, 1992.

Hardt, Michael, and Antonio Negri. *Empire*. Cambridge: Harvard University Press, 2000.

Hathaway, Heather. *Caribbean Waves: Relocating Claude McKay and Paule Marshall*. Bloomington: Indiana University Press, 1999.

Heller, Adele, and Lois Rudnick, eds. *1915, The Cultural Moment: The New Politics, the New Woman, the New Psychology, the New Art and the New Theatre in America*. New Brunswick, N.J.: Rutgers University Press, 1991.

Henry, Paget. *Caliban's Reason: Introducing Afro-Caribbean Philosophy*. New York: Routledge, 2000.

Hill, Errol, ed. *A Time . . . and a Season: 8 Caribbean Plays*. Trinidad: University of the West Indies, Extra-Mural Studies, 1976.

——, ed. *The Theatre of Black Americans*. New York: Applause Theatre Book Publishers, 1987.

——, ed. *Black Heroes: Seven Plays*. New York: Applause Theatre Book Publishers, 1989.

——. *The Jamaican Stage, 1655–1900: Profile of a Colonial Theatre*. Amherst: University of Massachusetts Press, 1992.

Hill, Robert A. "The First England Years and After, 1912–1916." In *Marcus Garvey and the Vision of Africa*. Ed. John Henrik Clarke. New York: Vintage Books, 1974.

——. "Racial and Radical: Cyril V. Briggs, *The Crusader* Magazine, and the African Blood Brotherhood, 1918–1922." Introduction to *The Crusader I*. New York: Garland Publishing, 1987, v–lxvi.

——. "Literary Executor's Afterword." In *American Civilization*, by C. L. R. James. Cambridge, Mass.: Blackwell, 1993, 293–366.

——. "Making Noise: Marcus Garvey's *Dada*, August 1922." In *Picturing Us: African American Identity in Photography*. Ed. Deborah Willis. New York: New Press, 1994.

Hill, Robert A., and Barbara Bair, eds. *Marcus Garvey: Life and Lessons*. Berkeley: University of California Press, 1987.

Hill, Robert A., and R. Kent Rasmussen. Afterword to *Black Empire*, by George S. Schuyler. Boston: Northeastern University Press, 1991, 259–310.

Hobsbawm, Eric. *The Age of Empire, 1875–1914*. New York: Pantheon Books, 1987.

———. *The Age of Extremes: A History of the World, 1914–1991*. New York: Vintage Books, 1996.

Hobson, J. A. *Imperialism*. Ann Arbor: University of Michigan Press, 1965.

Hopkins, Pauline E. *Of One Blood; or, The Hidden Self.* In *The Magazine Novels of Pauline Hopkins*. The Schomburg Library of Nineteenth-Century Black Women Writers. Ed. Henry Louis Gates Jr. New York: Oxford University Press, 1988.

Howe, Stephen. *Afrocentrism: Mythical Pasts and Imagined Homes*. New York: Verso, 1998.

Hulme, Peter. "Hurricanes in the Caribbees: The Constitution of the Discourse of English Colonialism." In *1642: Literature and Power in the Seventeenth Century: Proceedings of the Essex Conference on the Sociology of Literature*. Ed. Francis Barker, Jay Bernstein, John Coombes, Peter Hulme, Jennifer Stone, and Jan Stratton. University of Essex, January 1981.

Huntington, Samuel. "The Clash of Civilizations." *Foreign Affairs*, summer 1993.

———. *The Clash of Civilizations and the Remaking of World Order*. New York: Simon and Schuster, 1996.

Ignatieff, Michael. "The American Empire (Get Used to It.)" *New York Times Magazine*, 5 January 2003: 22–27; 50–54.

James, C. L. R. *The Black Jacobins: Toussaint L'Ouverture and the San Domingo Revolution*. 1938. Revised edition with 1962 preface and appendix. New York: Vintage Books/Random House, 1963.

———. "Paul Robeson: Black Star." *Black World*, no. 1, November, 1970.

———. *Minty Alley*. 1936. London: New Beacon Books, 1971.

———. *Modern Politics*. Detroit, MI: Bewick/Ed, 1973.

———. *Spheres of Existence: Selected Writings*. London: Allison and Busby, 1980.

———. *At the Rendezvous of Victory: Selected Writings*. London: Allison and Busby, 1984.

———. *The Black Jacobins: Toussaint L'Ouverture and the San Domingo Revolution*. London: Allison and Busby, 1989.

———. *American Civilization*. Ed. Anna Grimshaw and Keith Hart. Cambridge, Mass.: Blackwell, 1993.

———. *A History of Pan-African Revolt*. 1938. Chicago: C. H. Kerr, 1995.

———. *Mariners, Renegades and Castaways: The Story of Herman Melville and the World We Live In*. Hanover, N.H.: Dartmouth College Press, 2001.

James, Winston. *Holding Aloft the Banner of Ethiopia: Caribbean Radicalism in Early Twentieth-Century America*. New York: Verso, 1998.

——. *A Fierce Hatred of Injustice: Claude McKay's Jamaica and His Poetry of Rebellion*. New York: Verso, 2000.

Jameson, Fredric, and Masao Miyoshi, eds. *The Cultures of Globalization*. Durham: Duke University Press, 1998.

Johnson, Charles. *Oxherding Tale*. Bloomington: Indiana University Press, 1982.

——. *Middle Passage*. New York: Atheneum, 1990.

Judt, Tony. "We'll Always Have Paris." *New York Times Book Review*, 1 December 2002, 10.

Kaplan, Amy. *The Anarchy of Empire in the Making of U.S. Culture*. Cambridge: Harvard University Press, 2002.

——. "Violent Belongings and the Question of Empire Today." ASA 2003 Pocket Program.

——. "Violent Belongings and the Question of Empire Today—Presidential Address to the American Studies Association, October 17, 2003." *American Quarterly* 56, no. 1 (March 2004): 1–18.

Kaplan, Amy, and Donald E. Pease, eds. *Cultures of United States Imperialism*. Durham: Duke University Press, 1993.

Kaplan, Caren. *Questions of Travel: Postmodern Discourses of Displacement*. Durham: Duke University Press, 1996.

Kaplan, Caren, and Inderpal Grewal, eds., *Scattered Hegemonies: Postmodernity and Transnational Feminist Practices*. Minneapolis: University of Minnesota Press, 1994.

Kasinitz, Philip. *Caribbean New York: Black Immigrants and the Politics of Race*. Ithaca: Cornell University Press, 1992.

Kelley, Robin D. G. *Hammer and Hoe: Alabama Communists during the Great Depression*. Chapel Hill: University of North Carolina Press, 1990.

——. *Race Rebels: Culture, Politics, and the Black Working Class*. New York: Free Press, 1994.

——. Introduction to *A History of Pan-African Revolt*, by C. L. R. James. Chicago: C. H. Kerr, 1995, 1–33.

Kelley, Robin D. G., and Sidney J. Lemelle. *Imagining Home: Class, Culture, and Nationalism in the African Diaspora*. New York: Verso, 1994.

Kennedy, Pagan. *Black Livingstone: A True Tale of Adventure in the Nineteenth-Century Congo*. New York: Viking, 2002.

King, Nicole. *C. L. R. James and Creolization: Circles of Influence*. Jackson: University Press of Mississippi, 2001.

Knight, Franklin W. *The Caribbean: The Genesis of a Fragmented Nationalism*. New York: Oxford University Press, 1990.

Knight, Franklin W., and Colin A. Palmer, eds. *The Modern Caribbean*. Chapel Hill: University of North Carolina Press, 1989.

Kurlansky, Mark. *A Continent of Islands: Searching for the Caribbean Destiny*. New York: Addison-Wesley, 1992.

Lamming, George. *The Pleasures of Exile*. New York: Alison and Busby, 1984.

Lenin, V. I. *Imperialism: The Highest Stage of Capitalism*. London: Pluto Press, 1996.

Levine, Robert S. *Martin Delany, Frederick Douglass, and the Politics of Representative Identity*. Chapel Hill: University of North Carolina Press, 1997.

Lewis, Norman, and James Malone. Introduction to *Imperialism: The Highest Stage of Capitalism*, by V. I. Lenin. London: Pluto Press, 1996, ix–lvi.

Lewis, Rupert, and Maureen Warner-Lewis, eds. *Garvey: Africa, Europe, the Americas*. Trenton, N.J.: Africa World Press, 1994.

Linebaugh, Peter. "All the Atlantic Mountains Shook." *Labour/Le Travailleur* 10 (autumn 1982): 87–121.

Linebaugh, Peter, and Marcus Rediker. *The Many-Headed Hydra: Sailors, Slaves, Commoners, and the Hidden History of the Revolutionary Atlantic*. Boston: Beacon Press, 2000.

Lloyd, David. *Ireland after History*. Field Day Essays. University of Notre Dame Press, 1999.

Lloyd, David, and Lisa Lowe, eds. *The Politics of Culture in the Shadow of Capital*. Durham: Duke University Press, 1997.

Locke, Alain, ed. *The New Negro*. New York: Atheneum, 1992.

Lorde, Audre. *Zami: A New Spelling of My Name*. Persephone Press, 1982.

———. "Grenado Revisited: An Interim Report." In *Sister Outsider: Essays and Speeches*. Trumansburg, N.Y.: Crossing Press, 1984, 176–90.

———. *Sister Outsider: Essays and Speeches*. Trumansburg, N.Y.: Crossing Press, 1984.

———. *The Collected Poems of Audre Lorde*. New York: Norton, 1997.

Luce, Henry R. "The American Century." *Life*, February 1984.

Macmillan, Margaret. *Paris 1919: Six Months That Changed the World*. New York: Random House, 2002.

Maingot, Anthony P. "Caribbean International Relations." In *The Modern Caribbean*. Ed. Franklin W. Knight and Colin A. Palmer. Chapel Hill: University of North Carolina Press, 1989.

Malkki, Liisa. "National Geographic: The Rooting of Peoples and the Territorialization of National Identity Among Scholars and Refugees." *Cultural Anthropology* 7, no. 1 (February 1992): 24–43.

———. "Citizens of Humanity: Internationalism and the Imagined Community of Nations." *Diaspora* 3, no. 1 (1994): 41–67.

———. "Refugees and Exile: From 'Refugee Studies' to the National Order of Things." *Annual Review Anthropology* 24 (1995): 495–523.

Mandelbaum, Michael. *The Ideas That Conquered the World: Peace, Democracy, and Free Markets in the Twenty-First Century*. New York: Public Affairs, 2002.

Mann, Michael. *Incoherent Empire*. New York: Verso, 2003.

Martin, Tony. *Race First: The Ideological and Organizational Struggles of Marcus Garvey and the Universal Negro Improvement Association*. Westport: Greenwood Press, 1976.

———. *Literary Garveyism: Garvey, Black Arts, and the Harlem Renaissance*. Dover, Mass.: Majority Press, 1983.

———. *The Poetical Works of Marcus Garvey*. Dover, Mass.: Majority Press, 1983.

Marx, Karl. *Capital: A Critique of Political Economy*. Trans. Ben Fowkes. New York: Vintage Books, 1977.

Marx, Karl, and Frederick Engels. *The Communist Manifesto: A Modern Edition*. 1848. New York: Verso, 1998.

Matthews, Mark D. "Perspective on Marcus Garvey." *Black World*. February 1976.

Maxwell, William J. *New Negro, Old Left: African-American Writing and Communism Between the Wars*. New York: Columbia University Press, 1999.

McClintock, Anne. *Imperial Leather: Race, Gender and Sexuality in the Colonial Contest*. New York: Routledge, 1995.

McKay, Claude. "If We Must Die." *Liberator*, July 1919: 21.

———. "A Black Star." *Liberator*, August 1921: 25.

———. "Soviet Russia and the Negro." *Crisis*, vol. 27 (December 1923–January 1924): 61–65, 114–18.

———. *Banjo: A Story without a Plot*. New York: Harcourt Brace Jovanovich, 1929.

———. *Gingertown*. New York: Harper, 1932.

———. *Banana Bottom*. New York: Harper and Brothers, 1933.

———. *A Long Way from Home*. New York: Harcourt, Brace, 1970.

———. "Speech to the Fourth Congress of the Third Communist International, Moscow." 1923. Reprinted in *The Passion of Claude McKay: Selected Prose and Poetry, 1912–1948*. Ed. Wayne F. Cooper. New York: Schocken Books, 1973, 91–95.

———. "Soviet Russia and the Negro." 1923. Reprinted in *The Passion of Claude McKay: Selected Prose and Poetry, 1912–1948*. Ed. Wayne Cooper. New York: Schocken Books, 1973, 95–106.

———. "A Negro Writer to His Critics." 1932. Reprinted in *The Passion of Claude McKay: Selected Prose and Poetry, 1912–1948*. Ed. Wayne Cooper. New York: Schocken Books, 1973, 132–39.

———. *Home to Harlem*. Boston: Northeastern University Press, 1987.

McLemee, Scott, ed. *C. L. R. James on the 'Negro Question.'* Jackson: University Press of Mississippi, 1996.

———. Introduction to *C. L. R. James on the 'Negro Question.'* Jackson: University Press of Mississippi, 1996, xi–xxxvii.

McLemee, Scott, and Paul Le Blanc, eds. *C. L. R. James and Revolutionary Marxism: Selected Writings of C. L. R. James, 1939–1949*. New Jersey: Humanities Press, 1994.

Mignolo, Walter. "Globalization, Civilization Processes, and the Relocation of Languages and Cultures." In *The Cultures of Globalization*. Ed. Fredric Jameson and Masao Miyoshi. Durham: Duke University Press, 1998.

———. *Local Histories/Global Designs: Coloniality, Subaltern Knowledges, and Border Thinking*. Princeton, N.J.: Princeton University Press, 2000.

Miller, Charles A. *Ship of State: The Nautical Metaphors of Thomas Jefferson, with Numerous*

*Examples by Other Writers from Classical Antiquity to the Present.* Lanham, Md.: University Press of America, 2003.

Miller, Floyd J. Introduction to *Blake: or, The Huts of America, A Novel*, by Martin Delany. Boston: Beacon Press, 1970, xi–xxix.

Miller, Kelly. "After Marcus Garvey: What of the Negro?" 1927. Reprinted in *Marcus Garvey and the Vision of Africa.* Ed. John Henrik Clarke. New York: Vintage Books, 1974.

Moore, Richard B. "The Critics and Opponents of Marcus Garvey." In *Marcus Garvey and the Vision of Africa.* Ed. John Henrik Clarke. New York: Vintage Books, 1974.

Morley, David, and Kuan-Hsing Chen, eds. *Stuart Hall: Critical Dialogues in Cultural Studies.* London: Routledge, 1996.

Morse-Lovett, Robert. "An Emperor Jones of Finance." *New Republic,* July 1923.

Mullen, Bill V. *Popular Fronts: Chicago and African-American Cultural Politics, 1935–46.* Urbana: University of Illinois Press, 1999.

Mullen, Bill V., and James Smethurst, eds. *Left of the Color Line: Race, Radicalism, and Twentieth-Century Literature of the United States.* Chapel Hill: University of North Carolina Press, 2003.

Mulzac, Hugh. *A Star to Steer By.* New York: International Publishers, 1963.

——. "Memoirs of a Captain of the Black Star Line." In *Marcus Garvey and the Vision of Africa.* Ed. John Henrik Clarke. New York: Vintage Books, 1974, 127–38.

Naipaul, V. S. *The Middle Passage; Impressions of Five Societies: British, French and Dutch in the West Indies and South America.* New York: Macmillan, 1963.

Naison, Mark. *Communists in Harlem During the Depression.* New York: Grove Press, 1983.

Nassy Brown, Jacqueline. "Black Liverpool, Black America, and the Gendering of Diasporic Space." *Cultural Anthropology* 13, no. 3 (1998): 291–325.

——. "Enslaving History: Narratives on Local Whiteness in a Black Atlantic Port." *American Ethnologist* 27, no. 2 (2000): 340–70.

Nielsen, Aldon Lynn. *C. L. R. James: A Critical Introduction.* Jackson: University Press of Mississippi, 1997.

Norton, Chris. Review of *Jericho.* The Paul Robeson Centennial Collection. Kino on Video, 1998. *Images.* http://www.imagesjournal.com.

——. Review of *Song of Freedom.* The Paul Robeson Centennial Collection. Kino on Video, 1998. *Images.* http://www.imagesjour nal.com.

O'Neill, Eugene. *The Emperor Jones, Anna Christie, The Hairy Ape.* New York: Vintage International, 1995.

——. *The Long Voyage Home and Other Plays.* New York: Dover Publications, 1995.

Paravasini-Gebert, Lizabeth. *Phyllis Shand Allfrey: A Caribbean Life.* New Brunswick, N.J.: Rutgers University Press, 1996.

Parsons, Neil. *King Khama, Emperor Joe, and the Great White Queen: Victorian Britain Through African Eyes.* Chicago: University of Chicago Press, 1998.

Patterson, Tiffany Ruby, and Robin D. G. Kelley. ""Unfinished Migrations: Reflections on the African Diaspora and the Making of the Modern World."*African Studies Review* 43, no. 1 (April 2000): 1–68.

Pease, Donald. "National Narratives, Postnational Narration." *MFS Modern Fiction Studies* 43, no. 1 (spring 1997): 1–23.

——. "C. L. R. James, *Moby-Dick*, and the Emergence of Transnational American Studies." *Arizona Quarterly* 56, no. 3 (autumn 2000): 93–123.

——. "C. L. R. James's *Mariners, Renegades and Castaways* and the World We Live In." Introduction to *Mariners, Renegades and Castaways: The Story of Herman Melville and the World We Live In*, by C. L. R. James. Hanover, N.H.: Dartmouth College Press, 2001, vii–xxxiii.

Peterson, Dale E. *Up From Bondage: The Literatures of Russian and African American Soul.* Durham: Duke University Press, 2000.

Pierson, Christopher. *The Modern State.* New York: Routledge, 1996.

Reed, Ishmael. *Flight to Canada.* New York: Random House, 1976.

Reid, Ira. *The Negro Immigrant, His Background, Characteristics, and Social Adjustments.* New York: Columbia University Press, 1939.

Renan, Ernest. "What Is a Nation?" 1882. In *Nation and Narration.* Ed. Homi K. Bhabha. London: Routledge, 1990.

Renda, Mary A. *Taking Haiti: Military Occupation and the Culture of U.S. Imperialism, 1915–1940.* Chapel Hill: University of North Carolina Press, 2001.

Roach, Joseph. *Cities of the Dead: Circum-Atlantic Performance.* New York: Columbia University Press, 1996.

Robeson, Paul. *Here I Stand.* Boston: Beacon Press, 1958.

Robinson, Cedric J. *Black Marxism: The Making of the Black Radical Tradition.* London: Biblio Distribution Center, 1983.

Said, Edward. *Orientalism.* New York: Pantheon Books, 1978.

——. "The Mind of Winter, Reflections on Life in Exile." *Harper's Magazine* 269 (September 1984).

——. *Culture and Imperialism.* New York: Knopf, 1993.

——. "The Clash of Ignorance." *The Nation* 4 October 2001.

Saldívar, José David. *The Dialectics of Our America: Genealogy, Cultural Critique, and Literary History.* Durham: Duke University Press, 1991.

Sale, Maggie Montesinos. *The Slumbering Volcano: American Slave Ship Revolts and the Production of Rebellious Masculinity.* Durham: Duke University Press, 1997.

Salih, Roshan Muhammed. "German film exposes Guantanamo 'scandal.'" Aljazeera.net. 4 November 2003.

Sanborn, Geoffrey. *The Sign of the Cannibal: Melville and the Making of a Postcolonial Reader.* Durham: Duke University Press, 1998.

Sassen, Saskia. *Cities in a World Economy.* Thousand Oaks, Calif.: Pine Forge Press, 1994.

Schmitt, Carl. *The Concept of the Political.* 1932. Chicago: The University of Chicago Press, 1996.

Schuyler, George. "The Negro-Art Hokum." *Nation* 122 (June 16, 1926): 662–63.

——. *Black Empire.* Boston: Northeastern University Press, 1991.

——. *Ethiopian Stories.* Boston: Northeastern University Press, 1994.

Sen, Amartya. "Civilizational Imprisonments." *New Republic,* 10 June 2002, 28–33.

Shepperson, George. Introduction to *Umbala: The Adventures of a Negro Sea-Captain in Africa and on the Seven Seas in his Attempts to found an Ethiopian Empire,* by Harry Dean and Sterling North. Winchester, Mass.: Pluto Press, 1989, vii–xxiii.

Simpson, Louis. *North of Jamaica.* New York: Harper and Row, 1972.

Smethurst, James Edward. *The New Red Negro: The Literary Left and African American Poetry, 1930–1946.* New York: Oxford University Press, 1999.

Sommer, Doris. "Irresistible Romance: The Foundational Fictions of Latin America." In *Nation and Narration.* Ed. Homi K. Bhabha. London: Routledge, 1990.

——. *Foundational Fictions: The National Romances of Latin America.* Berkeley: University of California Press, 1991.

Stein, Judith. *The World of Marcus Garvey: Race and Class in Modern Society.* Baton Rouge: Louisiana State University Press, 1986.

Stephens, Michelle. "Eric Walrond's *Tropic Death* and the Discontents of American Modernity." In *Prospero's Isles: The Presence of the Caribbean in the American Imaginary.* Ed. Diane Accaria-Zavala and Rodolfo Popelnik. Oxford: Macmillan, 2004.

Stepto, Robert B. *From Behind the Veil: A Study of Afro-American Narrative.* Urbana: University of Illinois Press, 1979.

Sundquist, Eric J. *To Wake the Nations: Race in the Making of American Literature.* Cambridge: Belknap Press of Harvard University Press, 1993.

Sutton, Constance R., and Elsa Chaney, eds. *Caribbean Life in New York City: Social and Cultural Dimensions.* New York: Center for Migration Studies, 1987.

Tate, Claudia. Introduction to *Dark Princess: A Romance,* by W. E. B. Du Bois. Jackson: University Press of Mississippi, 1995, ix–xxviii.

Taylor, Ula. *The Veiled Garvey: The Life and Times of Amy Jacques Garvey.* Chapel Hill: University of North Carolina Press, 2002.

Thomas, Bert J. "Caribbean Black Power: From Slogan to Practical Politics." *Journal of Black Studies* 22, no. 3 (March 1992): 392–410.

Tillery, Tyrone. *Claude McKay: A Black Poet's Struggle for Identity.* Amherst: University of Massachusetts Press, 1992.

Toomer, Jean. *Cane.* New York: Boni and Liveright, 1923.

Tyler, Patrick E. "The World Cries Uncle." *New York Times Book Review,* 22 September 2002, 22.

Vincent, Theodore G. *Black Power and the Garvey Movement.* Berkeley: Ramparts Press, 1971.

Von Eschen, Penny. *Race Against Empire: Black Americans and Anticolonialism, 1937–1957.* Ithaca, N.Y.: Cornell University Press, 1997.

Walcott, Derek. "What the Twilight Says: An Overture." In *Dream on Monkey Mountain, and Other Plays.* New York: Farrar, Straus and Giroux, 1970.

Wallerstein, Immanuel. *Capitalist Agriculture and the Origin of the European World-Economy in the Sixteenth Century.* London: Academic Press, 1974.

———. *Geopolitics and Geoculture: Essays on the Changing World-System.* Cambridge University Press, 1991.

———. *After Liberalism.* New York: New Press, 1995.

Watkins-Owens, Irma. *Blood Relations: Caribbean Immigrants and the Harlem Community, 1900–1930.* Bloomington: Indiana University Press, 1996.

White, Hayden. *Tropics of Discourse.* Baltimore, 1978.

White, Walter. "The Paradox of Color." In *The New Negro.* Ed. Alain Locke. New York: Atheneum, 1992, 361–68.

Worcester, Kent. *C. L. R. James: A Political Biography.* Albany: State University of New York Press, 1996.

Worsley, Peter. *The Three Worlds: Culture and World Development.* Chicago: University of Chicago Press, 1984.

Young, Robert J. C. *Colonial Desire: Hybridity in Theory, Culture, and Race.* New York: Routledge, 1995.

———. *Postcolonialism: An Historical Introduction.* Malden, Mass.: Blackwell, 2001.

# INDEX

Page numbers in italics refer to illustrations.

Andersen, Hans Christian, 96–97
Anti-Fugitive Slave Law, 232, 233
antislavery movement, 105
archipelago, character of an, 28
authoritarianism, in national leadership, 251

"Back to Africa" (Du Bois), 133–36
Baker, Houston, Jr., 140, 147
Balibar, Etienne, 254, 328n53
*Banana Bottom* (McKay), 130, 142, 177
banjo, role of, 183–84, 185
*Banjo: The Story Without a Plot* (McKay), 130, 132, 142, 168, 177–203
Basch, Linda, 23, 24
Bederman, Gail, 40–41, 78, 103, 242
Benelux, 253
Benítez-Rojo, Antonio, 23
*Benito Cereno* (Melville), 258
Benjamin, Walter, 129, 130, 155, 167, 169, 201–2
Bhabha, Homi K., 82, 164
*Big Fella* (musical), 315n7
bill of rights, at UNIA convention, 115–16
*Billy Budd, A Sailor (An Inside Narrative)* (Melville), 330–31n12
Bishop, Maurice, 276
Black Belt: importance of, 233, as internal nation, 318n70, 328n60
black drama, 75–79, 206–7, 210–11, 308n26. See also *Emperor Jones, The*; Robeson, Paul
black emperor, 325n5; effect of, 99; as embodiment of state fetishism, 83; Garvey's role as, 80, 91, 97, 101. See also *Emperor Jones, The*
black empire: fantasy of, 220, 304n27; narratives of, 59–73, 305n25; in theatrical productions, 308n27; versions of story of, 325–26n5
*Black Empire* (Schuyler), 60, 68; as Ethio-

pianist romance, 70–71; language of race supremacy in, 69–70; woman as pilot in, 71
black female subjectivity, as domestic, 61, 145
black freedom: federation as metaphor for, 265; international narrative of, 114, 218–19; New World "dialectics" of, 260; right to, 20; within exile, 180
black internationalism, 3–5; coloniality and, 47; diasporic sense of black identity in, 48; in literary texts, 48; working class place in, 137
*Black Jacks* (Bolster), 105
*Black Jacobins, The* (James), 28, 205, 210–11, 212–20, 256, 325n2; cultural politics of, 217; plot and structure of, 212–21, 327n32
black liberator, paradigm of, 61, 66
black love, 162–64, 165
black male: postwar experience of, 187; as subject, 186–95; thinkers, in 1700s, 301n2
black male sovereign: charisma of, 14; focus on, 15; Garvey as, 21; as metaphor for state, 13; projection of, on black male body, 18
blackness: heterogeneous, 6; a stage for resistance, 294n72; theory of international, 4; transatlantic conception of, 100
"Black People in the Urban Areas of the United States" (James), 234–40
*Black Power and the Garvey Movement* (Vincent), 124
*Black Reconstruction in America, 1860–1880* (Du Bois), 329n68
*Black Skin, White Masks* (Hall), 95–96
black soldier, bounded horizons of, 144, 320n5
Black Star Line, 22, 106, 214; Briggs's endorsement of, 118; cultural politics of,

109; as financial enterprise, 108; formation of, 111; stock certificate, *xiv*; symbolic power of, 108–9, 110

black state: model of, 84, 92; visions of independent, 210, 216, 230, 231

black subjects: denationalized status of, 85; marginality of in West, 321n17; nationality of, 3; representations of, 7

black transatlantic, labor history of, 105

black transnationalism: as alternative, 20, 191; gendering of discourses on, 19; impact of, 324n117; international imperialism and, 192; liminal space of, 198, 217; revolution and masculinity in, 209–10

*Black Women, Writing and Identity: Migrations of the Subject* (Davies), 16–17

*Blake; or, The Huts of America* (Delany), 59, 60–63, 66–68, 301–2n5, 302n9, 303nn18–19

Bolshevism: as model, 3, 12; role of revolutionary ideology of, 42–43

Bolster, W. Jeffrey, 103, 104, 105, 180, 196

Bonaparte, Napoleon, 218

Bourne, Randolph, 53–54, 250, 251

boxing, 41, 78, 311n8

Boyce Davies, Carole, 16–17, 18

Braudel, Fernand, 254

Briggs, Cyril Valentine, 26, 35, 46; at *Amsterdam News*, 47; Black Internationale and, 50; disillusionment of, 52–53; as editor of *The Crusader*, 1; endorsement of Black Star steamship line by, 118; on expectations of equal treatment, 139; on Garvey's convention, 199–20; intellectual clarity of, 314n74; splits with Garvey, 117–19, 123–24; works by, 35–36, 37–38, 51–53, 57, 61, 119. *See also* "League of Nations, The"; "Paramount Chief of the Negro Race, A"; "Ray of Fear, The"; "What Does Democratic America in Haiti?"

"British West Indies in the Mirror of Civi-

lization, The: History Making by Colonial Negroes" (Garvey), 84, 89–90

Brooks, Gwendolyn, 276

Buck-Morss, Susan, 207

Buhle, Paul, 7

Burroughs, Edgar Rice, 78

Butler, Judith, 270

Caliban, 23, 24

*Cane* (Toomer), 129

capitalist economy: Negro American in, 226; as powerful integrative force, 227; relationship of nation-state to, 254

Carby, Hazel, 7, 17, 18, 66, 78, 169, 207–8, 209, 237, 238

Caribbean: as American sea, 255–62; exile and, 319n92; geopolitics of, 241; historical significance of, 24, 28; as McKay's site of home, 317n50; movement in, 295n89; as region, 292–93n65; as site of heterogeneity and mobility, 23–24; as source of labor, 265–66; state, citizenship in, 264–65

Caribbeans, influence of, on black intellectuals, 23

*Caribbean Waves* (Hathaway), 318n78, 322n47

Caribbean women: alternative lifestyles of, 276; journey of, through imperialist and black nationalist histories, 280–81; writers, 29, 295n93, 330n100

Carricou woman, world of, 275

Castro, Fidel, 29, 278

catharsis, Aristotelian theory of, 327n30

Chesnutt, Charles, 129

Christophe, 212, 216–17

circumatlantic space, 100, 104

cities, international relationships between, 332n53

citizenship: as absence of free movement, 273; desire of blacks for American, 228; as

citizenship (*continued*)
exile, 164; free black movement toward, 64; violation of meaning of, 277–78

city-state, Greek, 223–24; James on, 264; as a metaphor, 254; as modern ideal, 224, 264

civilization, discourses of, 90, 91, 92

Civil War (U.S.), as critical moment for African Americans, 231

Clarke, John Henrik, 99

class: gendered divisions of, in James's fiction, 208; mobility, impossibility of, 328n60; transnationalities of working, 259; warfare, 145

Cliff, Michelle, 281, 330n100

Clifford, James, 23, 24, 270

Clootz, Anacharsis, 257

*C. L. R. James Reader, The*, 325n4, 326n9, 326n11, 327nn24–25, 30; Anna Grimshaw on James, 261; *The Black Jacobins* in, 324n2; "Letters to Literary Critics" in, 206, 209, 210–11; "Notes on Hamlet" in, 207; "Popular Art and the Cultural Tradition" in, 217; "Preface to Criticism" in, 211, 217. *See also* James, C. L. R.

colonial: "mentality," 2–3, 256, 333n59; relations, remapping of, 263; space, theorizing within, 12–13; status, Spanish offer of new, 215; subjects, transnational cultural politics of, 49–50; ventures, transformed as war games, 279–80

coloniality: black internationalism and, 47; empire and, 9; longing for integration in, 16; racial doctrines of, 218–19

colonies, problem of democratic rule in, 25

colony: empire's hybridity and, 12; self-sufficiency of, 244; as site for analysis of empire, 11; versus nation, 11–12

commodity form, fetishistic qualities of, 95–96, 99

commodity spectacle, 81

communication, postcolonial lines of, 263–64

Communist International, Fourth Congress of, 130, 173–76; Negro question at, 174

communists, critique of American, 175

community: alternative ways of imagining, 332n48; basis of, 137, 246; in difference, 261

"Conclusion" (Lorde), 269

*Condition, Elevation, Emigration and Destiny of the Colored People of the United States, The* (Delany), 63–64

conferences, international, 47–48

*Conjure Woman, The* (Chesnutt), 129

consciousness, black: global political, 8, 80, 112; revolutionary, 237

Cooper, Wayne, 171, 175

Cowley, Malcolm, 177

creolization, 286n17

*Crisis of the Negro Intellectual, The* (Cruse), 224–25

*Crusader, The*, magazine, 1, 35, 50, 117, 118, 283n1

Cruse, Harold, 224–25, 228

Cuffee, Paul, 105, 106

Cuffee, Silas, 106

cultural fronts, defined, 299n41

cultural nationalism: black, 328n55; discussions of, 80–81; expressed through visual spectacle, 81

cultural politics, radical international, 299n42

culture, globalization of, 136

*Dark Princess* (Du Bois), 60, 68–69, 70–71

*Darkwater: Voices from Within the Veil* (Du Bois), 55, 170

Dean, Harry, 104–5, 106, 107–8, 312n18

"décalage," defined, 4

decolonization, 253

Delany, Martin R., 59, 60–64; expedition of, to Africa, 311–12n17; works by, 59, 60–64, 66–67, 302n9, 303nn18–19. See also *Blake; or, The Huts of America*; *Condition, Elevation, Emigration and Destiny of the Colored People of the United States, The*

democracy, direct, 264

denationalization, as form of resistance, 182–83

desire: for both home and freedom, 144; different conceptions of, 198–99, 201

Dessalines, Jean-Jacques, 151, 212, 216; as leader, 219–21. See also Haitian Revolution

development, national and economic, 296n6

diaspora: absence of women in narratives of, 18; creation of modern black, 112, 289nn41, 43; as fugitive, multinational black colony, 13, 14; historical limit of, 300n57; movements in, 295n89; nationhood and, 36; as symbolic revolt, 296n5; uses of, 4, 5–6, 289n44

division of labor, capitalist, 328n53

domestic heterosexual relationship, importance of to state, 168

domesticity, heterosexual, politics of, 291–92n59

domestic loyalty, questions of, 143

domestic sphere, revolutionary transformation of, 238, 240

dominance, racial, manhood and, 156–59

Douglass, Frederick, 61, 107

Du Bois, W. E. B., 329n68; on colonial shadow of empire, 33; compared with Schuyler, 72; compares modern Negro and Jews, 30; on Garvey, 75; as leader, 61; loses passport, 24; New Negro movement and, 39; Pan African Congresses and, 47; on postwar color line, 19–20, 24–26; transnational focus of, 305n31; works by,

11–12, 52, 55, 60, 68–69, 70–71, 72–73, 133–36, 170. See also "Back to Africa"; *Black Reconstruction in America, 1860–1880*; *Dark Princess*; *Darkwater: Voices from Within the Veil*; "Worlds of Color"

Eastman, Max, 322n27

economic and political relationships, geographic understanding of, 261

economic system, colonial, breakdown of, 262–63

Edmondson, Belinda, 7, 17–18, 29–30, 41, 86, 208–9

Edwards, Brent Hayes, 3–5, 7, 159, 171, 178–79, 183, 197

Ellis Island, 271–75; description of, 273–74

Elmes, A. F., 101

*Emperor Jones, The* (O'Neil), 74, 307n9; celebration of masculine savagery in, 79; diminishing forms of black masculinity in, 77–78; film, 146, 315n17; Haitian state and, 307n12

empire: American, idea of, 335n6; coloniality and, context of, 9; colony and, transatlantic circulation between, 309–10n67; colony as site for analysis of, 11; defined, 290n47; description of, 13; dominance of as model, 92; language of sovereignty of, 19; state of, 9–22; United States in discussions of, 10. See also black empire; imperialism

*Empire* (Hardt and Negri), 9–10

Eng, David, 169

"epidermalization," 94–95

Ethiopianism, 60, 62, 65–66, 70–71, 92–93, 154, 213

*Ethiopian Romance, An* (Heliodorus), 302n8

ethnicity, 318n78, 322n47, 334n86

European Common Market, 253

exile, Caribbean as space of, 23, 24

family: and nation, links between, 197–98; search for, as metaphor, 66

Fanon, Frantz, vii, 94–96, 197

fascism, black, 93, 100

federation: black, 1–2, 116; Caribbean, 90, 252; European, 253–54; failure of, 117; meaning of, 261–62, 263; as metaphor for black freedom, 265; plan, 123, 124; as solution for New World proletariat, 259

fetishism: black emperor Garvey as embodiment of, 83, 84, 92; in desire for state, 82–84; skin color as, 95–96

fiction, Caribbean, gendered politics of, 208–9

"Fireside Chat on the War by Native Son, A" (James), 236–37

First World War. *See* World War I

*Foreign Affairs* (journal), 25

France, abolition of slavery in, 213–15

fraternity, meaning of, 213, 222, 229

freedom, racial, 218–19; masculine definitions of, 15

free movement: of black Caribbean women, 317n57; emphasis on, 22; "From Toussaint L'Ouverture to Fidel Castro" (James), 28; of New Negro, 71

fugitive slave laws, 64, 105

fugitive slaves: impact of, on state, 212; role of, 231–34

Funchal, as seamen's haven, 108

Gaines, Kevin, 119

Garvey, Amy Jacques, 7, 86–88

Garvey, Marcus, vii; ability of, to mobilize black masses, 99; as black fascist, 93; as black intellectual, 3, 6–9, 19; as black sovereign, 21; Black Star Line and, 125; charismatic appeal of, 76–77; connections with *The Emperor Jones*, 76–77, 101; deportation of, 110, 119, 124, 125, 240; early politic-

ization of, 86–87; early travels of, 84–91; global imaginary of, 81–82; Harlem Renaissance and, 299n45; as head of UNIA, 1; imperial racial geography of, 91–99; influence of World War I on, 110–11; letter of, to secretary of state for the colonies, 85; at *Negro World*, 47; politics of representation of, 97; as printer, 85; as publisher, 87; splits with Briggs, 117–19, 123–24; unique role of, 80; on Versailles Conference, 27; vision of, of political community, 83; working class politics of, 44, 230–31; works by, 84, 89–90, 92. *See also* "British West Indies in the Mirror of Civilization, The"; "Nothing Must Kill the Empire Urge"; *Talk with Afro-West Indians, A*

Garvey movement: real impact of, 229; success of, 284–85n13; visual spectacle in, 75–76

Gates, Henry Louis, Jr., 40, 45–46

gender, politics of: in James's Marxist analysis, 238; living with difference and, 333n591; and Lorde's take on Grenada, 276

Genovese, Eugene, 210, 232

gentleman, Victorian, 40–42, 48–49, 298n31

"gentlemanliness," 17–18, 107

Gilmore, Ruth Wilson, 270

Gilpin, Charles, 315n13

Gilroy, Paul, 12, 13, 58, 62, 83, 93–95, 103, 183

*Gingertown* (McKay), 142, 170

Glick Schiller, Nina, 23, 24

Glissant, Edouard, 23

globalization, 31, 253

governmental options debates, 211

governmental structures, purpose of, 15

Grenada: invasion of, 271, 278; People's Revolutionary Government of, 276, 279;

as staging ground for foreign interventions, 278

"Grenada Revisited: An Interim Report" (Lorde), 275

Griffin, Farah Jasmine, 17, 276, 277

Griggs, Sutton E., 59, 65

Grimshaw, Anna, 206, 261

Guantanamo Bay, 270, 279

Haiti, 149–50, 151; as example, 293–94n70; future of, 210; invasion of, 77, 255; longing for, 159, 160; nature of independence in, 325n2

Haitian Revolution, 205–6; ; importance of, to dramatists, 211; leaders of, 212; as struggle for independence, 210–11. *See also* Dessalines, Jean-Jacques; L'Ouverture, Toussaint

Hall, Kim, 95–96

Hall, Stuart, 265, 334n86

Hardt, Michael, 9–10, 22, 23, 260

Harlem: cabarets in, 147, 148; as home for black fugitives, 146–47, 149, 152–53, 161; image of trench warfare and, 162; multi-ethnic nature of black community in, 49; political organizing and activism in, 322n35; "underworld" of, 315–16n17

Harlem Renaissance, 21, 45; as domestic antithesis to black transnationalism, 134–35, 137; influence of Caribbean on, 46; international ideologies within, 46–47; McKay on, 132–38

Harris, Frank, 138–39

Hathaway, Heather, 7, 317n50, 318n78, 322n47

Henry, Paget, 265

*Here I Stand* (Robeson), 240

*Heroic Slave, The* (Douglass), 107

heterosexuality, explicit critique of, 150

Heyward, Dubose, 315–16n17

Hill, Robert A., 1, 7, 61, 66, 71, 76, 90, 97, 123, 124

Himes, Chester, 236

history: of black nationalist movements, 7; of black radicalism, 7; black transatlantic maritime, 6; hybridity of imperial, 8; revolutionary nature of Caribbean, 28

Hobsbawm, Eric, 20, 27, 283n4

home: as feminist space, 62; racial diaspora as, 154; woman of color as, 13–14, 142, 148

*Home to Harlem* (McKay), 45, 130, 131, 132, 137–38, 142, 144–65, 177–78, 233; in *Banjo*, 199; critique of black heterosexuality in, 155; critique of nationality in, 155; as national romance, 317n51; as proletarian novel, 133; reaction against, 133. *See also* McKay, Claude

homosexuality, 150, 171, 246–47, 320–21n9

Hopkins, Pauline, 59, 65, 66, 325–26n5

housing, black struggles over, 235

hybridity, 8, 288n35, 293n67

"hydrarchy," 104, 181

"hyphenates," 300n55

identity: Caribbean, and American racial doctrine, 255; Harlem as rootedness in racial, 152–53; heterogeneous racial, 153; impact of war and revolution on black, 43; linkage between racial and sexual, 148; models of political and cultural, 42; theory of, 334n86

"If We Must Die" (McKay), 140–41

immigrants, Caribbean, impact of, 299n43

immigrant workers, mass movement of, 255–56

immigration law, American, 272

imperialism: autocracy of modern, 25; culture of, 31; European, 9, 77, 287n3; imagining African, 91, 92; internationalism as, 283n4; *Pequod* as metaphor for, 248, 249;

Locke, Alain, 25, 45, 79, 230

*Long Way From Home, A* (McKay), 130, 175

Lorde, Audre, 269, 271; as Carriacou woman, 274–81; as conscientious reporter, 277; as an Ishmael at home, 280; as second-generation Caribbean American, 277; works of, 269, 275, 276. *See also* "Conclusion"; "Grenada Revisited: An Interim Report"; *Sister Outsider*; *Zami: A New Spelling of My Name*

L'Ouverture, Toussaint, 29, 151, 205, 206, 207, 208, 212, 213, 237, 278; transnational vision of black freedom of, 218–19. *See also* Haitian Revolution

Love, Dr. Robert, 86

*Lumpenproletariat*, 179, 197

Maingot, Anthony P., 241, 266

*Making Men* (Edmondson), 29–30

Mandelbaum, Michael, 269

*Manliness and Civilization* (Bederman), 40–41

*Mariners, Renegades and Castaways* (James), 248–52, 267; American transnationalism in, 242; analysis of *Moby-Dick* in, 252; fate of ordinary people in, 256–57, 258

maritime context, importance of, 179–80, 196

marooned society, 140

maroons, traditions of, 232

Marseilles, port of: description of, 188–89; difference of, from Harlem, 187–88; in early 1900s, 182; liminality of, 185

Marshall, Paule, 330n100

Martin, Tony, 7

Marx, Karl, 95–96, 179, 197

masculine: Caribbean subject, imprisonment of, 278; intimacy, new ways of representing, 169; leadership, 298n33

masculinity: alternative constructions of black, 48, 246, 247–48; black, as reproductive, 209; black, transnational intellectuals' sense of, 43; global black, 6, 168–70; of harpooners in *Moby-Dick*, 242–48; nature of West Indian, 17–18; rebellious, 293n70; revolutionary, 326n6; savage, 78–79, 243–44; shift in American discourse about, 40–41

master and slave relationship, imposition of, 252

McClintock, Anne, 80–81, 82–83

McKay, Claude: alternative black identity in, 21; analyses of, 7–8; arrest of, 201; biographical works about, 285n14; biography of, 129–30; as black intellectual, 3, 6–9, 19; communist internationalism of, 133, 135, 174–76; construction of women by, 285n15; 317n57; in *The Crusader*, 314n73; on *The Emperor Jones*, 315n13; European exile of, 176–77; on Garvey, 173; gendered assumption in novels of, 142; Harlem Renaissance and, 132–38; homoerotic elements in works by, 320–21n9; internationalism of, 44–45, 202–3; at *The Liberator*, 47; marriage of, 167; outsider mentality of, 140; perception of, of Russia, 172–77; as Pullman porter, 329n84; search by, for narrative form, 138–65; switches to prose, 138–39, 176, 316n49; unique position of, as colonial subject, 131; works by, 130, 132, 140–41, 142, 168, 170–72, 173, 174, 175, 177–203. See also *Banana Bottom*; *Banjo: The Story Without a Plot*; *Gingertown*; *Home to Harlem*; "If We Must Die"; "Little Sheik, The"; *Long Way From Home, A*; "Romance in Marseilles"; "Soviet Russia and the Negro"

McKay, Ruth Hope, 167

McLemee, Scott, 222

Melville, Herman, 142, 330–31n12

middle class, growth of black, in northern United States, 133

Mignolo, Walter, 12–13

migration: African-American narrative of, 17, 39, 129; Caribbean, as diaspora, 319n92

Miller, Floyd J., 63

*Minty Alley* (James), 208, 238

mirror of civilization, as metaphor, 91

mixture, racial, issues of, 304n25

mobility: black, within racialized global context, 59, 112; of *Blake* protagonist, 62–63; facilitation of, 20; social, reinterpretation of black, 131; versus sovereignty, 269–70

*Moby-Dick*, 241, 242–48

modern civilization, Ishmael as figure for, 244–45

*Modern Politics* (James), 254, 262

*Modern State, The* (Pierson), 10

Möise, 212, 215

monarchy, ancient African belief in, 213, 216–17

Morocco, 25, 202

Morrison, Toni, 239–40, 330n100

Morse-Lovett, Robert, 97

Moscow, semi-Oriental splendor of, 172

multitude, location of within empire, 295–96n99

Mulzac, Hugh, 108, 109

Muray, Nickolas, 78

music making, McKay's descriptions of, 184–85

Naipaul, V. S., 43, 297n29

Naison, Mark, 46

narrative form, McKay's search for, 138–65

narratives: of black diasporan unity, 157; of black empire, 59–68, 305n25; of black sea voyages, 106–9, 311n14; early African

American, gender roles in, 58; Ethiopianist, 154; internationalist, late 1800s, 57–68; of migration, 276; shadow, 275, 278

Nassy Brown, Jacqueline, 18–19, 103, 105, 180

nation: as imagined community, 165, 290n46; links of, to family, 197–98; racialized ethnic formation within, 318n78; versus colony, 11–12

National Club, 87

national independence, African, 299n44

nationalism: in Africa, 90; critical perspective on, 190–91; geopolitics of black, 20; lack of boundaries of, in black, 100–101; official, 194, 283n4; radicalized language of, 331–32n40; use of, to secure peace, 190

nationality: doubtful, 194; gender and, 333n59; lack of official, 54

national leader, in Caribbean, 297n25

national romance, 142, 143, 317nn51–52

national sentiment, questions of, 143

nationhood: diaspora and, 36; ideal of, 295n90; possibilities for, 64

nation-states: Ahab as figure for, 245, 246, 247; black African, 73; citizenship as right in, 42; as creator of isolates, 257–58; dream of international cooperation among, 257; as the enemy, 164; gender politics of postcolonial, 240; as international norm, 26–27; as masculine, 16; metaphoric role of woman of color in, 16; modern, characteristics of, 287n28; power of postwar model of, 2, 4; schizophrenic, 260; traditional, 10; transnational black rhetoric about, 16; white world of European, 36

*Native Son* (Wright), 225, 236–37

Nazima, Princess, 35. *See also* "Ray of Fear, The"

Negri, Antonio, 9–10, 22, 23, 260

Negro: art, critical debate on, 306n47; inferiority, theory of, 226; official attitude toward, 193–95; ship of state, as metaphor, 1–2, 8, 283n3

"Negroes in the Civil War: Their Role in the Second American Revolution" (James), 231

"Negroes, Women and the Intellectuals" (James), 247

"Negro People and World Imperialism, The" (James), 222

*Negro World*, 47, 76, 112, 117

New Jewel Movement, 276

New Negro, 17, 21; Americanness of, 43–44; artistic use of trope of, 45–46; black nationalism of, 39; Caribbean radicals and, 39–50; defining subjectivity of, 65; ideology of, 40, 89; international mobility of, 71; as modern masculine construct of black subjectivity, 36; self-determined blackness of, 41; sources for primary identifications of, 59; working-class politics of, 44, 45

*New Negro, The* (Locke), 25, 45, 79, 230

New Negro movement, radical period of, 46; tensions within, 314n82

New Worldly Negro, 21, 68–73

New World politics, 288n34

New World slavery, common history of, 259–60

*New York Times Book Review*, 269

*North of Jamaica* (Simpson), 2

"Nothing Must Kill the Empire Urge" (Garvey), 92

Ntozake Shange, 239–40, 330n100

*Of One Blood; or, The Hidden Self* (Hopkins), 59, 60, 65–66, 325–26n5

O'Neill, Eugene, 75, 76, 79, 279

orientalism, 9–10

*Orientalism* (Said), 9

*Our Own* (newspaper), 87

Pan-Africanism, 12, 66, 67, 297n27; anticolonial discourse in, 49; as diasporic movement, 15

Panama Canal, construction of, 255

"Pan-Nationalism," 46

"Paramount Chief of the Negro Race, A" (Briggs), 119

"Paul Robeson: Black Star" (James), 207

Pease, Donald, 248

Petry, Ann, 276

Pierson, Christopher, 10

political democracy, classical model of, 223–24

political identity, class-based models for, 37

political organizing, heyday of, in Harlem, 322n35

postmodern sensibility, Caribbean, 23

*Practice of Diaspora, The* (Edwards), 3–5, 178–79

proletariat: American, 259; socialist, 266

Pullman porters, 45, 329n84

race: consciousness, as response to integration, 227; contradictory U.S. policies about, 304n26; destabilizing power of, 14; "the," gendered as global, 8; relations in 1800s, 302n6; vision of, as transnational, 99; war in America, 37–38, 174–75

*Race Men* (Carby), 169

radical tradition, black, 284n7

Randolph, A. Philip, 45

Rasmussen, R. Kent, 61, 66, 71

"Ray of Fear, The: A Thrilling Story of Love, War, Race Patriotism, Revolutionary Inventions and the Liberation of Africa" (Briggs), 35–36, 37–38, 57, 61

*Redburn* (Melville), 250

Rediker, Marcus, 24, 104, 105, 180, 181, 182
Red Summer, 1919, 140
Renan, Ernest, 165
Renda, Mary, 307nn12–13
representation: argument for real, in global black freedom movement, 122; forms of black, 121–22; Garvey's politics of, 97
revolution: black transnational, 154; novel of, as gendered, 28–30. *See also* Haitian Revolution; Russian Revolution
"Revolutionary Answer to the Negro Problem in the United States, The" (James), 266
Roach, Joseph, 100
Robeson, Paul, *56, 74, 75, 78, 204,* 240, 298n33, 298n34, 307n17, 315n7, 325–26n5; in *The Black Jacobins,* 205; described, 206–7
"Romance in Marseilles" (McKay), 142, 171
romances, historical, as "foundational fictions," 317n53
Roosevelt, Theodore, 78, 319n96; as white supremacist, 40
Russian Revolution: internationalist vision in, 37; as model, 139

Said, Edward, 9
sailors, black, 18, 88, 130; on high seas, 107–8; as *Lumpenproletariat,* 197; number of, 104; self awareness of, 105
sailors, white American, 192–93
Sale, Maggie Montesinos, 107
Salih, Roshan Muhammed, 270
Sanborn, Geoffrey, 243
Sassen, Saskia, 254, 265
Schmitt, Carl, 54
Schuyler, George, 35, 45, 60, 68, 305n30; on black nationalism, 306n49; compared with Dubois, 72; and "The Rise of the Black Internationale," 72

seafaring tradition, in gendered construction of travel, 179–80
Second World War. *See* World War II
self-determination: black, politics of, 41, 229; ideal of, 147; lack of political, 2–3; national, 51, 217; and process of integration, 228, 229
separatism versus integrationism, 225
sexuality: constructions of, 131; doubtful, 195
Shaw, George Bernard, 138
*Sheik, The* (film), 78
ship of state, Negro, 1–2, 8, 109–10, 283n3
Simmel, Georg, 276
Simpson, Louis, 2, 43
*Sister Outsider* (Lorde), 275
slavery, classed and racialized society of, 251
slave ship revolts, 107
social change, urban people of color as agents of, 234–35
Socialist Worker's Party, 222
solidarity, racial, black, 152
Sommer, Doris, 142, 143, 146, 154, 168
*Song of Freedom* (film), *56, 204,* 325–26n5
sovereign, male, gendered and fetishistic power of, 91
sovereignty: defined, 10; imperial language of, 19, 288–89n37; new global form of, 10–11; racial, ideal of, 5; versus mobility, 269–70
"Soviet Russia and the Negro" (McKay), 173, 174
"Star of Ethiopia, The" (pageant), 305–6n39
*Star to Steer By, A* (Mulzac), 108
Stein, Judith, 7, 42
Stokes, Rose Pastor, 314n72
"Storyteller, The" (Benjamin), 129
storytelling, act of, 155, 202
stranger, definition of, 277

superiority, racial, Nazi theory of, 250

Szanton Blanc, Cristina, 23, 24

*Talk with Afro-West Indians, A: The Negro Race and Its Problems* (Garvey), 89

*Tarzan of the Apes* (Burroughs), 78

Taylor, Ula, 7

*Tempest, The* (Shakespeare), 24, 292n65

territoriality, 287–88n29

*Things of Darkness: Economies of Race and Gender in Early Modern England* (Hall), 95–96

"Three Black Women Writers: Toni Morrison, Alice Walker, Ntozake Shange" (James), 239–40, 330n100

Toomer, Jean, 129

"To Toussaint L'Ouverture," 207

transnational America, 53

transnationalism, 94, 292n60, 293n68; appeal of, for black working poor, 82, 93; black, 14, 38, 39; combined with anticolonialism, 71–72; contemporary, 22; masculine vision of, 18

travel: black female subjects and, 295n94, 301n4; geopolitics of, 203; politics of, 21

Trinidad, national independence of, 28, 38, 296n10

"tropicalization," 293–94nn70–71

Trotsky, Leon, 230

Turner, Nat, 231–32

Tuskegee Institute, 89

Tuttle, Worth, 99

Tyler, Patrick E., 269–70

*Umbala* (Dean and North), 105, 106, 107

underground railroad, 231

United States: imperialism of, 52–53, 150; new internationalism of, 250–51; as one island among many, 256, 330n4; state of, in mid-1900s, 248–49

United States Department of Immigration, 272

Universal Negro Improvement Association (UNIA), 1, 44; dual politics of, 88–89; evaluation of future of, 122; federation of, with African Blood Brotherhood, 117–25; 1920 International Convention of, 76, 113–15, 122–23; organization of, 88; peak membership of, 313n50; representativeness of, 121

Universal Republic, 257–58

vagabondage: as form of black internationalism, 178–79; heterosexual, 199–201; sexual, 196–203

Valentino, Rudolph, 78

Versailles, Treaty of, as imperial form of nationalism, 115, 283n4

Versailles Conference, exclusion of non-Europeans from, 27–28

Vesey, Denmark, 105

Vieques, 278

Vincent, Theodore G., 124

visual spectacles, function of, 98–101

Walcott, Derek, and New World Negro, 17, 291n54

Walker, Alice, 239–40, 330n100

Walker, David, 105

Wallerstein, Immanuel, 221–22, 254, 260

Washington, Booker T., 89, 61

Watkins-Owens, Irma, 7

wealth, unidirectional movement of, 188

West Indian federation, failure of, 26, 27, 28, 265

whale: symbolism of, 245; as metaphor for racial arrogance, 252

whaling ship, as metaphor, 249–50

"What Does Democratic America in Haiti?" (Briggs), 52–53

MICHELLE ANN STEPHENS is an assistant professor of English,
American Studies, and African American Studies at Mount Holyoke College.

LIBRARY OF CONGRESS CATALOGING-IN-PUBLICATION DATA

Stephens, Michelle Ann, 1969–
Black empire : the masculine global imaginary of Caribbean intellectuals in the
United States, 1914–1962 / Michelle Ann Stephens.
p. cm. — (New Americanists)
Includes bibliographical references and index.
ISBN 0-8223-3551-4 (acid-free paper) — ISBN 0-8223-3588-3 (pbk. : acid-free paper)
1. African Americans—Intellectual life—20th century. 2. Caribbean Americans—
Intellectual life—20th century. 3. African American intellectuals—Biography.
4. Garvey, Marcus, 1887–1940—Political and social views. 5. McKay, Claude, 1890–
1948—Political and social views. 6. James, C. L. R. (Cyril Lionel Robert), 1901– —
Political and social views. 7. African Americans—Race identity. 8. Masculinity—
Political aspects—United States—History—20th century. 9. African Americans—
Politics and government—20th century. 10. Black nationalism—History—20th
century. I. Title. II. Series.
E185.6.S745 2005
320.54'6'0973—dc22      2005002678